"DEVASTATING . . . THE STORY OF JIM VALVANO AND NORTH CAROLINA STATE IS THE STORY OF BIG-TIME COLLEGE ATHLETICS, IN WHICH MONEY AND WINNING ARE ALL AND VIRTUALLY EVERYTHING ELSE—FROM ACADEMIC STANDARDS TO THE WELL-BEING OF 'STUDENT-ATHELETES'—ARE NOTHING."

—*Washington Post Book World*

"A SCATHING INDICTMENT . . . Peter Golenbock details with the relentlessness of a storm. . . . No amount of breast-beating or tears can becloud that fact." —*Chicago Tribune*

"UNDOUBTEDLY DISTURBING AND READABLE." —*The Dallas Morning News*

"A sobering perspective on college sports . . . a worthwhile read." —*The Virginian Pilot*

"Controversial—caused an uproar at North Carolina State."

—*Memphis Commercial Appeal*

"THE BOOK THAT LOOSED A THOUSAND LIPS." —*Los Angeles Times*

"One day V's (Coach Jim Valvano) going to fall. One by one he's destroying people. . . . It's Tobacco Road down there, boy."

—Teviin Binns, one of the former North Carolina State players who tell their story of the season in basketball hell in this book

PERSONAL FOULS

Peter Golenbock

SIGNET
Published by the Penguin Group
Penguin Books USA Inc., 375 Hudson Street,
New York, New York 10014, U.S.A.
Penguin Books Ltd, 27 Wrights Lane,
London W8 5TZ, England
Penguin Books Australia Ltd, Ringwood,
Victoria, Australia
Penguin Books Canada Ltd, 2801 John Street,
Markham, Ontario, Canada L3R 1B4
Penguin Books (N.Z.) Ltd, 182–190 Wairau Road,
Auckland 10, New Zealand

Penguin Books Ltd, Registered Offices:
Harmondsworth, Middlesex, England

This is an authorized reprint of a hardcover edition published by
Carroll & Graf Publishers, Inc.

First Signet Printing, October, 1990
10 9 8 7 6 5 4 3 2 1

PRINTED IN THE UNITED STATES OF AMERICA

For Alvin "Doggie" Julian, who loved the game until the day he died, for Herm Alswanger, who loved his players, and for all those players who dreamed of the pros but who ended up doing something else.

Introduction

The corruption of our young has become the national pastime across America. As we head into the 1990s, the old-fashioned values are more and more being turned upside down. Education used to be revered, and sports used to be fun, and as a kid, my memory is that money was for baseball cards, the movies, and root beer floats, not for drugs.

Too many kids today don't admire the right people. Used to be, the cop on the beat and the teacher in the classroom were the role models. Now, it seems, it's anyone driving a red Porsche with a wad of dough in his pocket—regardless of how the gains are gotten.

Crack dealers are looked up to by ghetto kids, while white-collar kids talk about their desire to emulate city slickers like Ivan Boesky and Wall Street's cheats, the inside traders. They want to be winners, too. Rules are for suckers. No one can resist the smell of money.

I suppose it shouldn't be surprising to find that corruption of values exists in the world of sports, even collegiate amateur sports, that bastion of hypocrisy. As an example of where everyone's priorities lay, recently two sports agents, Norby Walters and Lloyd Bloom, were convicted of racketeering and mail fraud for paying money to college kids to be their agents—while the athletes were still in college.

An objective observer might ask why a kid, no matter what his age, shouldn't have a professional doing the negotiating for him. Why shouldn't a high school kid have an agent to get the best deal from the colleges, for instance? But the NCAA outlaws agents prior to graduation, in no small part because agents tend to try to convince talented players to go pro early, depriving the colleges of the talent of the athletes and the kids of an education. It's the way agents make a living.

What was interesting was that the two agents were accused of defrauding not the athletes but the colleges. The colleges were crying foul because they lost the services of those players when they were declared ineligible.

These two agents were found guilty and surely will be punished for their crimes against college sports. During the testimony at the trial, it was clear that few of the athletes made more than a token attempt to study and that no one was remotely expecting them to graduate. Where was the lawsuit against the colleges for neglect of their duties?

The larger question brought by the Walters-Bloom case, however, still remains. Does anyone care about the most heinous crime against the kids: the corruption of values engendered by the whole system?

Is there something wrong with bringing to a college kids who aren't students and have no interest in being students? Is there something wrong with kids taking courses like Leisure Alternatives or being handed A's without having to take the course or taking special music classes designed just to get athletes through? Is there something wrong with a basketball program in which precious few of the so-called student-athletes ever graduate and the administration works hard to cover the fact by using phony statistics and doubletalk?

In a nutshell, what *Personal Fouls* is about is the corruption of values and broken dreams. It is an inside look at the underbelly of college athletics strictly from the players' perspective. It involves recruiting and how athletes are handled, manipulated, used, and finally spit out and discarded when their usefulness has expired. It is not about bending rules so much as it is about disillusioning our youth.

The fight to publish *Personal Fouls*—against those who wish it never to see the light of day—is also related to the current battle by coaches to maintain the status quo in college sports.

Last winter, when the NCAA sought to do something about athletes who are unfit students when they enter college an outcry arose from certain coaches. Proposition

42 would have prevented high school graduates with less than a C average and less than a 700 on the SATs from getting an athletic scholarship. We have been barraged with arguments from coaches such as John Thompson of Georgetown and John Cheney of Temple, arguing that Proposition 42 discriminates against young basketball players, especially blacks, because they will have a tougher time getting into college.

Advocates for the new rule say that something is needed to force youngsters to study, and that if third-graders know in advance what they have to do in order to be Michael Jordan—study—they will do it.

Apparently neither parents nor high school rules have been able to change the emphasis for so many of these kids from practicing their dribbling to concentrating on their studies. This would have effected change, which hopefully would lead to a generation of college athletes with degrees.

It would have been the first time that the colleges would have announced to a whole generation of future Michael Jordans, "Look, kid, if you don't study, you don't get to be Michael Jordan."

But for such a radical change to be enacted, educators would have had to stand strong against the money that motivates college sports. Educators would have had to fight against the overemphasis on college athletics that has pervaded our society. Of our spiritual leaders, only Arthur Ashe, the tennis player, has consistently recognized the need for Proposition 42, the need to make the current generation of high school athletes study first, play ball second.

So why has there been such an outcry from these coaches, which in effect condones the status quo? Because it is in their best interests to do so. The overemphasis on college athletics, fueled by the millions of television dollars poured into the college sports factories, have made these coaches the most powerful in America. They make more money than any of the pro coaches. They are the only class of coach to make as much as some of the pro players. Why should they emphasize academics when athletics is making them so much money? With this infusion of large sums of money comes a warlike mentality to protect the system that is making them rich.

Writing about college basketball is a lot like what I always imagined writing about the Mafia would be like. In researching this book, I saw the look of fear wherever I turned. Players—even those who had left the N.C. State program—were afraid of being blackballed from the game. One player had me call his father, who informed me his son would not speak because the coach had the power to "ruin his career."

Professors expressed a fear of being fired by the college administration. Even students refused to speak on the record without assurances their identity would be protected. Some sources were nervous. Others were petrified. One, whom I met in Raleigh, insisted on meeting me at the pay phone outside the Kinko's Copy Center at eleven in the morning. As I waited, he snuck up from a back alleyway, tapped me on the shoulder and, like a spy in a John le Carré thriller, I whispered to him my motel location and the room number. We arrived in separate cars; once inside my room, we talked. He knew I had interviewed others, but what he didn't know was whether the coach, Jim Valvano, knew of my involvement in this project, and he was afraid that Valvano was having me followed and that he would be seen with me. When we were done he crept away as secretly as he came. As bizarre as all this intrigue sounded, when he left I, too, was having thoughts of white-hooded visitors coming to my room in the middle of the night to drag me away.

And yet there was real reason for my concern. You will notice that at the end of the book one of my sources, John Simonds, has his shoulder dislocated by one of the coaches. The coach somehow found out Simonds was considering being involved in a book about the N.C. State program and, to keep him from talking, attacked him, dislocating his shoulder. I know who did it, but I am not naming him—deliberately. The fact is, Simonds, who is not a timid person, is very much afraid of this guy. And he should be.

It is that fear that has kept more sources from speaking out. Another former N.C. State player told me, "I am afraid. I don't want to get hurt."

As a result, I told each of the sources that they were

free to deny publicly that they had spoken to me. I promised that if the area was sensitive, I would protect them and write, "Said one player . . ." something I hate to do but in many cases the only way I could impart the information and at the same time protect the source. Almost every conversation I had, I taped. The tapes are in a safety deposit box.

So why did so many people talk if they were so afraid? The players talked because to a man they felt betrayed. The sizzle to come to N.C. State, it turned out, was always juicier than the steak itself. The players I spoke to had been high school All Americans who had come to college with a dream—to be a star and to play professional basketball—only to have that dream shattered. Apparently this is a common occurrence among the country's college basketball players, who are promised the moon and the stars and a shot at the pros to get them to enroll, only to find out that they are merely pawns in a multi-million-dollar game orchestrated by the coach and approved by the athletic director, where the main beneficiary is the coach, where the secondary beneficiary is the university, and where the players often are the losers.

Here's what too many athletes learn from their college education: the Art of the Big Con 101. The coach makes a million or so for himself. The college makes millions for its athletic treasury, plus gets millions of dollars of free publicity. And what does the player end up with many times? No education, no degree, no skills, no money, no pro career, and no hope.

N.C. State, like many other basketball powers, is rated highly because the coach is a great recruiter. His kids are culled from top-prospect lists in the national basketball magazines. They are so talented that despite the psychic scarring of many of them, the team still wins a lot of basketball games. The players come because Valvano—and many other coaches as well—sells The Dream: to play on a national championship team. Each hopes, moreover, that the coach will train him and give him the opportunity to be a professional basketball player. Part of the come-on delivered to each player is that if he comes to the school, he will start and star and be in a position to turn pro. Coaches are forced to make such promises because few kids would come without them.

Of course, that a kid buys into this is partly the kid's fault. The coach is only telling him exactly what he knows the kid wants to hear. The most talented players, tall or talented or both by age thirteen, choose the schoolyard over the school books. And when it comes time for the college recruiters to come calling, they listen for the siren song: "We're going to be national champs. We're going to be on television. We're going to be famous. We're going to be number one."

The kids who ultimately fall by the wayside never think to ask, "What kind of education will I be getting?" Because they really don't care. And because the coach really doesn't care either, the result is a corruption of the admissions process and a corruption of the academic process, with the "student athlete" often given higher grades than he deserves just for being on the team.

If the reality turns out to be far different from the expectations, a corruption of values occurs as well. Players begin to see the value of using others for personal gain. As they sit on the bench and rot, they become bitter. They begin to see what college basketball is really all about: big money, using people, getting publicity, stepping up that ladder on the shoulders of others—them.

And so some of these players have chosen to talk about what happened to them and to their teammates.

From talking to these college players, it is clear that college basketball's system of recruiting can be as fraudulent as Three Card Monte. A college coach—that character-builder of modern-day lore—has license to promise anything to get a high school prospect to come to his institution. But once a player signs on, suddenly he discovers what army recruits quickly discover—civilian standards no longer apply. A coach is not bound to keep his promises even though the player must commit four years of his life to that coach. For the player, it can be a bargain made with the devil.

The player finds he is forced to accept his lot in sports life. There is nothing he can do about his situation, no one he can turn to. This may be hard for the public to accept, because college basketball players are usually very tall and so much in the public eye. But they are the Silent Ones—no matter how badly a player is cheated, lied to, screwed over, or ruined by a coach, there is literally nothing he can do about it. He can't sue for breach of contract. He can't go on strike. He can't do any of the things other workhands can do in American society—except transfer.

But the NCAA makes transferring very risky by decreeing that the athlete who transfers must sit out an entire year, a long period of stagnation that often erodes the player's skills. Rather than do that, most stay, accepting their fate.

And so they keep silent. All athletes subscribe to something called The Code, an unwritten but oft-stated law of the locker room that whatever happens to them or to their teammates and coaches during the course of a season is taboo as a subject of conversation with anyone except another teammate.

Who knows when it started, but it has always been there, and certainly was first promulgated by a coach, because it is a most effective device, giving the coach free rein to do as he pleases with his players, right or wrong. As long as the players follow The Code, the coach knows his dirty laundry won't be aired in public.

Part of The Code, as passed on to players by the coaches, is that the press is the enemy. Throughout the entire 1986-87 season, Valvano reportedly stressed, "Fellas, the people from the press are barracudas. They'll distort anything you say, so make sure what you say is clear, that it can't be taken two or three ways. And guys, don't ever rag on me, cut up your teammates, or rag on the other team."

And so, beginning as freshmen, the players are wary of the press. Reporters become people to shun, for fear that if the player were to say something under his breath, he would become banner headlines the next day.

As a result, if a player sees things he finds questionable, objectionable, dishonorable, or beyond his understanding, he says nothing—to anybody. He has to file it away and forget about it. He won't even tell a friend, for fear that the friend will tell another friend and a reporter will overhear and start an investigation and trouble.

Players who are unhappy or who feel lied to or cheated rot inside as their dissatisfaction festers. They may opt to accept the petty perks of the experience—perhaps cars, money, jewelry— feeling that if they aren't going to achieve their dream, then at least they'll get something out of it. Their values erode further.

It is the fear of breaking The Code that allows amoral coaches to mislead players and get away with it. Without The Code, they would have to face their accusers. And worse, they would be forced to look at themselves in the mirror and admit what they are doing to the kids who put their faith and trust and hopes in the coaches' hands.

It's one reason the powers that be at N.C. State don't want to see *Personal Fouls* published. Nothing about them in this book is so terrible per se. They are doing nothing more than what is being done all over the country. But though they are doing what they are doing, I suspect they don't want to admit it—to themselves most of all. Coach Valvano probably tells himself that his players really do like and admire him, that he really is giving his all for them, that coming to N.C. State has been good for them. And for some of the players, it probably has. But then there are the others. How can he explain to them his lack of caring about them as people? How can he explain to them how the reality of their experience was so far removed from what they had been promised?

Ira Berkow in the New York *Times* wrote: "It has been said that a chain is only as strong as its weakest link. With the glorification of sports, it turns out, the edification of students is diminished.

"And if education becomes our weakest link, and entertainment our strongest, then there is trouble festering."

And yet, despite the warning, there is talk of televising high school games and making a national high school college basketball championship. The result will be to begin the process of corrupting ideals even earlier.

It's time for someone with real power to stand up and shout, "Stop. We have gone too far. We have created a snakepit for our youth, and we must change the system and close it down." The colleges have become demeaned. The kids are demeaned. To what end? A basketball tournament as exciting as any competition on earth. But is it worth it?

The question everyone involved with education—college administrators, faculty members, the NCAA, state legislatures, Congress—should be asking themselves is: What should we do to protect the kids? What can we do to make the administration of college-revenue sports less selfish and self-serving?

Though the events in this book pertain to one university, they are certainly not unique to that university. The Walters-Bloom trial was proof of that. Ronnie Harmon of Iowa and Mark Ingram of Michigan State were not in school for their diplomas, but rather to play football. I personally was told by a teammate about one college football superstar who got $65,000 a year to play. One of the State players told me three other colleges offered him money to come and play.

In the context of college basketball, it makes more sense to me for the player to take the money than not. The player sees everyone else involved rolling in dough. He wants his piece. Putting aside the testimony that they were using mob muscle to keep their clients from deserting (the reason they were really convicted), was Walters and Bloom's giving college athletes money in exchange for their representation so terrible? Is it any less terrible than players getting money from friendly boosters?

One of two courses of action should be taken immediately. I suspect none will be—ever.

The first suggestion is made out of cynicism and anchored in reality. The colleges should be allowed to do what they are doing now—running their sports programs independent of the academic institutions—with one change: They should pay their players their market value. It's the players who put the fans in the seats. It's the players who go to the NCAA tournaments. It's the players who make the money come flowing in. And the players should get something in return: money, up front.

If Patrick Ewing is worth $3 million a year to the New York Knicks, he certainly was worth $500,000 a year to Georgetown University. The income he generated, I'm sure, was far more than that. How much was Michael Jordan worth to the University of North Carolina? What was Steve Kerr worth to Arizona, Danny Manning to Kansas? If the colleges were forced to bid for their services, we'd find out.

At least if the athlete got paid, he wouldn't be left with an empty bag if the coach screwed him over. He could sit on the bench, stewing about the lack of playing time but comforted by the cash in his bank account.

As a corollary, players should be allowed to promote products. Why should a coach like Jim Valvano get $150,000 from Nike for having his players wear Nike products exclusively? Why shouldn't the players get a large chunk of that money? They're the ones wearing the products.

What is the alternative? It's the idealistic approach. It posits that colleges be seats of higher learning where every student is academically qualified. It posits that college sports return to what it once was—part of the university, like the chemistry or music department, rather than what it has become: a cash cow for the athletic department and a minor league for the NBA. I would propose the following steps to return sports to its rightful place on campus, to maintain academic integrity within the universities, and to return basketball players to mainstream college life. (Michael Albanese should take some credit here.)

1. *Eliminate freshman eligibility*. A player should spend his freshman year acclimating himself to the college environment, spending all his time attending classes, getting remedial tutoring if need be for the purpose of helping him pursue a course of studies that would lead to graduation.

2. *Any student accepted by the university under Proposition 48—those students accepted with less than a C average in high school and under 700 on the boards—must maintain a 2.0 average in college or be expelled.* The university must tutor such students, and the student must study, like any other student at the university.

3. *Eliminate athletic dormitories*. Let the athletes have the same social experiences as the rest of the students. Integrate them rather than segregate them.

4. *Schedule games on Friday and Saturday only*. Athletes spend far more hours on the basketball court than in the classroom and library. The week should be dedicated to class, study, and practice, not basketball competition.

5. *Split the TV money among all NCAA schools*. Take away the financial incentive for a team to be on TV all the time. If all schools split the money, the major finan-

cial incentive for building basketball powerhouses at any cost would be eliminated. If you eliminate the $2-million grand prize for winning the NCAA championships, you also get rid of an awful lot of cheating.

6. *Outlaw booster groups whose sole purpose is to raise money for the athletic department.* An athletic director with unaccounted millions of dollars in his war chest by definition has more power than the chancellor. In fact, he may have more power than the governor. A basketball team doesn't need millions of dollars to run a sound program.

7. *As an alternative, decree that all money raised by booster groups be given to the general treasury,* not straight to athletic directors.

8. *As a third alternative, make the booster club balance sheet public.* Where does this money come from? Where does it go?

9. *Give coaches tenure.* Treat a coach like any professor. One of the reasons the coach wants to win so badly is that he doesn't want to get fired, and who can blame him? The job of a tenured coach would not be in jeopardy if his record were sub-par. As long as the coach is building character, teaching the game, doing the best he can with the kids he's got, he shouldn't have to worry about losing his job.

10. *Outlaw sneaker and clothing manufacturer contracts for coaches.* These contracts serve neither the university nor the players. Players should be allowed to wear whatever brand of sneakers is most comfortable, and the university should pay for them, just like they buy football cleats and baseball uniforms.

11. *The NCAA should inform the NBA it will no longer be a minor league to the pros.* University presidents should instruct the NBA to form its own farm system, like baseball. That way, high school players with no academic leanings could go to the pros without having to masquerade as students.

And if the NBA should refuse, the NCAA should inform the NBA that it will tighten its standards for athletes further. Eventually the NBA will capitulate.

Something else should be done for the players. I have a great job for Vice President Quayle. President Bush should appoint him ombudsman for college athletes. If a college athlete feels he is being screwed or something heinous is going on at his college, he should be able to inform Dan. A coach may be powerful, but he isn't as powerful as the United States government.

As I am writing this, I am grimacing because deep down I am aware that the current system will never change. The competition leading to the Final Four has become a TV draw on a par with the World Series and the Super Bowl. And in today's society, TV calls the shots. It's money that dictates the tune: Win at any cost. In 1989, as a result, we saw Seton Hall recruit a young Australian player, Andrew Gaze, who took courses and swore he was at the Hall for an education but then returned to Australia the day after the final game, skipping the last month of school. Does propriety mean nothing any more? Which coach will be the first to import Russian pros to his college to learn English and play basketball?

After reading this book, a small percentage of readers are going to say, "These players were so naive, they deserved what they got." You are wrong. That's too cynical for my blood. You have to remember that these players are just kids—they are seventeen and eighteen years old. They are at the mercy of the recruiters and the coaches. They don't deserve anything less than honesty and integrity from appointed representatives of these seats of higher learning, institutions that are supposed to exist to train our youth for the future. The players at colleges like N.C. State are taught, all right. Exactly what they have learned the reader will have to judge for him- or herself.

The first people I wish to thank are the basketball players, administrators, and students of N.C. State who cooperated despite their fears and anxieties. A special thanks to John Simonds, a courageous man who has already been identified as a major supplier of information. I can only hope that someone with some power to change things will care enough to act and that some day your courage will result in the end of a system that hurts so many youngsters and causes them to be so fearful.

I wish to thank the library staffs at the Library of

Congress in Washington and at N.C. State University for their cooperation, and also the staff of the *Technician*, the N.C. State college newspaper.

Finally to Kent Carroll and Herman Graf, my publishers, and to Alan Neigher and Neil Reshen, without whom this book never would have been published. Also to Bill Taylor, who aided in my research, and to Dick Gallen, for his discerning suggestions. Thanks also to R and C and S and M. You know how much you mean to me.

—Peter Golenbock
April 1989

1

Coach V Wows Raleigh

The new coach stood in the media room in the Case Athletic Center before a small cluster of reporters from Raleigh, Durham, and the small towns of the surrounding North Carolina countryside. A local Raleigh television camera crew also was there, recording his introductory press conference. James Thomas Valvano, a fast-talking, wise-cracking young man of thirty-four, after resigning his coaching job at Iona College, had been named coach of the North Carolina State University basketball team by Chancellor Joab Thomas, and he was snowing the press with a rich sample of the New York shoot-from-the-hip, street-smart style he would be bringing into this Southern hotbed of tobacco, education, and basketball.

Valvano was different—fresh, young, and breezy. He did not seem to be the usual basketball coach—taciturn and serious. His answers were usually barked out with the wit of a high school kid who answers the teacher with a smart remark in order to impress the blond stunner in the third row.

The men in attendance loved his quick humor and the way he threw in an occasional swear word without feeling self-conscious about it. The women liked his broad smile and his resemblance to Dustin Hoffman and Joe Namath. The comparison to Namath, the New York Jets football star, was one he was asked about often and he had a stock answer that always left his audience chuckling.

"The difference between Joe and me," he said, "is when you make the money he makes, they say you're ruggedly handsome. When you make the money I make, they say you have a big nose."

A reporter asked Valvano about his contract. His answer was evasive but clever.

"When I came here for the interview, I played very hard-to-get," said Valvano, pausing for effect. "I told 'em I wanted a multi-week contract." Everyone in the room laughed at his self-effacing comment. The subject was deftly turned aside.

He was asked about having to live in the shadow of Dean Smith, the legendary coach of archrival University of North Carolina, fifteen years his senior.

"I don't intend to live in anybody's shadow," Valvano replied. "I know there's a fellow named Smith at that place over there." He paused. "And besides," he adlibbed with a smile, "I'm going to outlive him."

When the laughter subsided, Valvano turned serious. He discussed his coaching philosophy, stressing the importance of a coach being tight with his players.

"I have a close relationship with my players," he said. "A lot of the players at Iona called me 'V.' I enjoy the relationship with my players. I look forward to it. When they leave, I want us to be friends. If they don't feel comfortable having dinner with me, then there's something wrong."

On his philosophy concerning athletes and their education, Valvano told the press that he didn't want basketball players whose sole concern in life was playing hoops. The players he was going to be recruiting would be students, too. "In fourteen years of coaching, I've only had three kids not graduate." The reason for his emphasis on education, he said, was that there were more important aspects to life than the game of basketball. "In the grand scheme of things and compared to what they're going to accomplish in their lives, basketball is insignificant," he said.

He added that he would attempt to bring to his basketball program at N.C. State men of character. It was important for State to bring in athletes who were "quality human beings," he said.

"I will ask our kids to be three things; the best students, the best athletes, and the best people they can possibly be. I honestly believe if our young people strive for that, we're going to be successful, regardless of the wins and losses."

He then struck just the right chord for his new Bible Belt constituency: "We want our players to try to reach the potential that the Lord has given them."

Finally, Valvano talked about the new spirit he was going to bring to N.C. State. Everyone in the room knew he had gone to little Iona, a nobody of a team, and with some razzle-dazzle recruiting in a very short period of time had built the school into a national basketball power. Everyone in the room sensed what bringing Valvano to State could mean to the State basketball program.

The reporters wanted to know about his plans for the program. Valvano looked at them with his riveting stare.

"When I took the head job at Iona," he said, "I started a program I called 'Dare to Dream.' Three years later, we went to the NCAA tournament. In three years, I intend to do it again, but this time I will not settle for anything less than a national championship.

"In fact," he said, "I guarantee it."

Not a soul in the room doubted that this man—this great man—would do just that.

2

Making It Big at Iona

Jim Valvano was born on March 10, 1946, and raised on Alstyne Avenue in Corona, a section of New York City's borough of Queens, sandwiched between Jackson Heights to the west, Flushing, home of the Mets, to the east, Forest Hills, once site of the U.S. Open, to the south, and LaGuardia Airport to the north. He received an elementary school degree in street smarts before moving with his family to Seaford, Long Island, a town on South Oyster Bay, about ten miles across the City's border into suburbia.

Valvano arguably was the best athlete ever to come out of Seaford High School. He played basketball, baseball, and football, winning a total of ten letters, the only Seaford athlete ever to do so.

He was recruited into college by Bill Foster, the basketball coach at Rutgers University. During his entire college career, Valvano was a defensive specialist, one of those bulldog white guys who grabs onto his opponent's jock and never lets go. Though overshadowed by his backcourt partner, Bob Lloyd, a scoring machine for the Scarlet Knights and a bona fide All American, when Lloyd got hurt and missed a game, Valvano poured in 38 points to lead the team.

As a senior Valvano was named captain and led Rutgers to a 22–7 record and a third-place finish in the National Invitational Tournament of 1967. He was named to the all-tournament team.

At only age twenty, following graduation, Coach Foster named Valvano Rutgers' freshman coach, the start of a career that took him next to the University of Connecticut in Storrs, where he was assistant coach, and then to

Johns Hopkins University for one year, where his 10–9 record as head coach was Hopkins' first winning season in twenty-four years. He then went to Bucknell University, where for three years he floundered around .500. Based in the small town of Lewisburg, Pennsylvania, on the western branch of the Susquehanna, fifty miles upriver from Harrisburg, Valvano might as well have been coaching in Nome, Alaska. Blue-chip basketball players don't often choose to make the trip to Lewisburg.

In 1975, Valvano finally got a job where his recruiting skills would bear fruit.

The institution was Iona College, in New Rochelle, New York, a short car ride from the City and a Catholic school that was routinely getting clobbered by such ecumenical powerhouses as St. John's, Fordham, and Manhattan. The president, Brother John Driscoll, was sick of watching losing basketball. It upset Brother Driscoll that his school was thought of as a weak sister in athletics. The year before Valvano came, the Gaels had finished 4 and 19.

"We were getting to be everybody's homecoming game," Brother Driscoll said.

Keenly aware that most of the students who went to Iona, New York metropolitan–area kids, were basketball junkies, Brother Driscoll sought to hire a coach who would bring him a winning season, promising all the support he could as far as recruiting and scholarships.

"I believe we have the best librarian around," he said at the time, "but that doesn't get us any publicity. A national ranking is a big calling card. Top-notch basketball is very important to Iona College."

During Valvano's audition for the job, Brother Driscoll took him into the 3,000-seat bandbox in which the team played and told him, "I don't want a pious loser. I want you to do it within the rules, but I want you to do it."

They shook on it. It wasn't the most prestigious coaching job in the world, but the move freed Valvano to be where the action was, back to a branch of the Big Apple tree and within commuting distance of more familiar ground, his backyard, that hotbed of hoop, Long Island.

The major problem Valvano faced was his meager recruiting budget of $7,500 a year. He apparently decided that to build a winning program, he would have to convince some local blue-chip high schoolers that they should come to Iona to lead the Gaels to glory.

In his third recruiting year, after two so-so seasons, Valvano hit the jackpot. His first big score was in convincing Glenn Vickers, a six-foot-three-inch forward from Babylon, Long Island, rated the best player on the island, to come to Iona. Vickers had led Babylon High to two straight Long Island championships and was being courted by Southern Methodist University, the University of San Francisco, and several schools in the Ivy League.

Valvano's tactic was to recruit Vickers' father, William, as hard as he did the son. Valvano promised William Vickers that his son would be the player around whom his entire program would be built. He also convinced the senior Vickers that it would be in the son's best interest to go to college near home.

"I pushed Glenn to Iona," said William Vickers. "Glenn almost went to SMU, but I said, 'Hey, what if one of us got sick? How would you be able to get home? What if you got sick? We couldn't just get on a plane and come see you.' "

That an eighteen-year-old in the prime of his life should get so sick his parents would have to come visit him seemed a remote possibility, but Valvano apparently had convinced Vickers' father it was an important consideration, and Glenn Vickers enrolled at Iona.

Once Vickers signed up, Valvano was able to recruit a bruising young six-foot-ten center with a body of granite by the name of Jeff Ruland. Ruland, a senior at Sachem High School in Ronkonkoma, Long Island, averaged 29.5 points a game as a senior. Ruland later said that he respected Vickers' game so much that he wanted to play college ball with him.

First, though, Valvano would have to sell him on Iona. One of the ways he did it was to convince the boy that as coach he would be like a surrogate dad. Ruland's own father, Kenneth, once had been a talented baseball player, but the two were never close. The father died of a stroke in 1967, when Jeff was nine.

"My father was in construction," Ruland once said. "He built cesspools. Somebody had to do it." There was real bitterness in his voice. He had been let down by someone he was supposed to trust, his father, and he would never forgive him for it. Valvano rushed in to fill that void. In so many words Valvano promised that if Ruland came to Iona he would be the dad Jeff Ruland never had.

As with Glenn Vickers' dad, Valvano played on the natural parental urges. He convinced Ruland's mom that if her boy went to Iona, close to home, he would be well taken care of, better than if he went to one of the faraway colleges that wanted him: Kentucky, Indiana, Notre Dame, and North Carolina.

"I never said anything about it," said Anita Ruland Swanson, "but Jeffrey knew I wanted him close. He's my baby, and if he went away for four years, I couldn't survive."

Valvano told her, "The scholarship is good, even if he breaks his legs tomorrow." Said Mrs. Ruland Swanson, "Valvano cared about him as a person. You can't con me or Jeffrey."

Ruland, it turned out, was far the greater-impact player than Vickers. By his sophomore year, Ruland was rated by one professional scout as perhaps "the best college center in the country" and a "sure-fire first-round NBA pick."

The two boys' freshman year was a success but still a disappointment, because Ruland seriously hurt his ankle and missed part of the season. Also, some of the upperclassmen rebelled at the special treatment accorded the two star frosh recruits by the coaches. Both started, and it didn't sit too well with the returnees, who also complained that Vickers and Ruland were getting all the publicity.

After Iona lost to Holy Cross in a game marked by bickering among the Iona players, Ruland went home and told his mother, "We're dropping out."

Vickers and Ruland were planning to transfer together to one of the Ivy League schools that had recruited Vickers. It was a serious enough move that Valvano went before the rest of the squad and told them the two were leaving the team.

But that night he was saved by his parental admirers. Mrs. Ruland Swanson and William Vickers met with their sons at her workplace, Ernie's Tavern, named after her fourth husband, and at the meeting, Ruland's mom told her son, "I didn't raise no quitter. Now you two get back to Valvano, or I'll break your legs." Her loyalty may well have saved Valvano's career aspirations from being short-circuited.

With his two stars back, Valvano acted quickly to heal the schism on the team. With Iona playing an exhibition game against the Australian National Team, Valvano had Vickers and Ruland sit out the game—he told the rest of the squad they were hurt. After Iona was badly beaten, outshot and outrebounded, the other team members, while still dismayed by the star treatment Ruland and Vickers were getting from the coaching staff—Ruland especially—at least had a fuller appreciation of what their teammates meant to the team's success.

"The rest of the squad realized we couldn't win without Rules and Vick," said Valvano. The end-of-year tally read seventeen victories and ten defeats, and though Iona didn't make any postseason tournaments, Valvano was fortunate to have his team intact for the 1977-78 season.

And yet, a reader following Iona's fortunes in the press would have thought Valvano was having a love-in with his players. Tony Kornheiser, a reporter for the New York *Times*, went to visit the Iona campus on Christmas Eve 1978. About a half hour before midnight he was riding with Valvano and the coach's wife, Pamela, in their car when Valvano turned onto North Avenue in New Rochelle. When the car stopped at a light, another car, with Vickers behind the wheel, drove past.

"There goes Vick," said Valvano. "Must be a study break."

Shortly after, another car, this one driven by Ruland, pulled alongside. Three teammates were in the back giggling.

"Where'd you go?" Ruland asked Valvano.

"Scouting in Jersey," Valvano said.

"See any good players?"

"Pretty good."

Ruland motioned toward the guys in the back seat. "Got some pretty good players in here," he said.

"Yeah, sure," said Valvano, dismissing his evaluation.

"[Blank] off," said Ruland, laughing.

Valvano started to laugh until it became a "roar." Kornheiser and Valvano had been discussing whether Valvano could run the same kind of program at one of the big basketball factories in the South. Valvano had had offers from Jacksonville and St. Louis University and had turned them both down. With his contract at Iona due to expire, he asked Kornheiser, "Do I belong in the South, where the referees wear crewcuts and say things to the coach like: 'Hi there, C.T. Mighty fine team y'all got heah. How's the wife? The kids? How's that prize pig of yours?' "

Wrote Kornheiser, "Now Vickers and Ruland have given him the answer. That's why Valvano is roaring."

"Can you imagine a player telling his coach to buzz off at a place like Georgia?" Valvano asked Kornheiser. "It's almost midnight, and my two best players are out on the town. And you know what? I love it. I wouldn't have it any other way. I tell my kids to have fun, to dream. I tell 'em my dream is to put my butt on the bench at the Final Four. But I don't want to do it if I have to stop laughing."

In that same article, Vickers praised the Iona business program to Kornheiser, calling it cake and playing in the shadow of Madison Square Garden "the frosting on the cake." Ruland told Kornheiser he loved Valvano, loved Vickers, loved his mom, and then Ruland said, "Hey, Kentucky won without me [Kentucky won the NCAA championships in 1978], so why shouldn't I go somewhere where I can help build a program? I must be right up there with the best of them, 'cause when I'm on the court I'm kicking tail, and nobody's kicking mine. I'm having the time of my life."

In their sophomore year, Ruland and Vickers led Valvano's team to a 23–6 record and to an invitation to the National Collegiate Athletic Association tournament.

The next year it was 29–5 and another NCAA bid. But despite the successful record, Ruland was becoming disgusted with the lack of national recognition accorded Iona and himself. After beating number one–ranked Louisville by 17 points in Madison Square Garden in early 1980, Iona was only ranked nineteenth in the national polls.

Said Ruland, "We didn't just beat [Louisville], we

kicked their asses. That week we were ranked nineteenth in one of the polls, and even though we didn't lose a game, the next week we were gone. So it turned out it was all for nothing."

Ruland was also becoming disillusioned with Valvano, whom he felt was no longer there for him. During his freshman year, while he was nursing an ankle injury, Rules lived in Valvano's house. Valvano's kids pushed two beds together so that Ruland could sleep comfortably. Valvano phoned Ruland's mom nine times to keep her apprised of her son's condition.

By Ruland's junior year, however, it was, as Valvano himself described it, "a different time, a different program."

When Ruland injured his hand that year, his mother read about it in the newspapers. Valvano admitted that five times he told Ruland's mom that he would drive out to see her, to get a bite to eat, and to discuss her son's future. But by Ruland's junior year, not only was Valvano the school's athletic director, but he had a radio show, a cable TV show Sunday nights, and he was making so many public appearances he had little idle time to spend with his players.

The conversation with Mrs. Ruland Swanson about her son's future never took place.

About a week after Iona lost in the opening round of the NCAAs, Louisville (the team Iona beat by 17) won it all, and two days after that Valvano—despite everything he had said to Kornheiser—convened the team for dinner and announced that he was leaving Iona and going to one of those big Southern schools, to North Carolina State University, to become its basketball coach.

Ruland and Valvano hugged. Both cried. But Ruland was badly hurt by Valvano's defection. It was the last time he spoke to Valvano. The year before, when Valvano had been offered the head coaching job at Providence College, he told the press, "Jeff Ruland could have gone anywhere in the country, but he decided to give four years to me. It wouldn't have been fair to him or to the other players for me to leave. It would have been contrary to what I preach."

One year later, Valvano was gone from Iona, with Ruland, Vickers, and the rest of V's boys left behind.

Valvano's assistant, Pat Kennedy, was named the new coach.

Valvano's departure from Iona took place on March 26, 1980. One month later, Iona was abuzz with speculation that Valvano had jumped ship just before an imminent collision with a looming iceberg.

On April 25, 1980, Brother Driscoll announced that after an internal investigation, Iona's star, Jeff Ruland, was ineligible to compete his senior year. According to Brother Driscoll, Ruland had signed with an agent, Paul Corvino, the father of an Iona alumnus, at the beginning of his junior year, making him ineligible under NCAA rules to maintain his amateur standing.

It was an affair coated with sleaze and shrouded in mystery. The issue first arose when news of the arrangement was leaked to the local papers. Who leaked it remains a mystery. Only two people know for certain, Ruland and Corvino. Valvano denied knowledge, but he admitted meeting with Corvino just a month before the scandal.

Ruland didn't want to leave school. He knew how badly his mom wanted him to get his diploma, and when he met with President Driscoll, he said that he badly wanted to remain for his senior year.

Researching his article the year before, while Ruland and Valvano were still enjoying their honeymoon, Kornheiser discussed the possibility of Jeff's leaving early for the pros with Mrs. Ruland Swanson. Kornheiser asked her what she would say if he came and asked her permission to leave school before graduation to join the pros.

"Jeffrey," she said, "it don't turn me on. You going pro wouldn't make me happy; it would make me very unhappy. This house isn't much, but what do I need? I've already had a Cadillac, and where am I gonna wear your mink coat? In that crummy gin mill? Forget about it. Get that piece of paper, Jeffrey; let me see it before I close my eyes. It don't take me much, Jeffrey; you go back to school, or I'll knock you on your tail."

Kornheiser repeated this to Ruland. He smiled. "She'd do it, too. That's why I'm staying."

But when Brother Driscoll asked Ruland whether he had signed a contract with an agent, Ruland truthfully admitted that he had signed a document making Corvino his agent. Ruland also told him that Corvino had been giving him pocket money from time to time "so I could do my laundry."

Brother Driscoll had no choice but to declare him ineligible to further compete in college athletics. Ruland's alternative was to declare his eligibility for the NBA draft. Mrs. Ruland Swanson's boy would not be getting his diploma.

Brother Driscoll called a meeting of the rest of the squad and told them to expect the worst: a loss of $100,000 from television revenues, nullification of the team's second-round advance in the NCAA championships, and a possible reversion of its 29-and-5 record to 0 and 34.

For his part, Paul Corvino denied everything. Before Ruland admitted the existence of an agreement, Corvino denied that there was any kind of contract making him Ruland's agent. He claimed he and Ruland were but friends. "Why can't a friend help another friend?" he said. "Is there some kind of law that says a friend can't help another friend?"

After Ruland made his admission, Corvino told reporters, "I didn't break any laws. I don't belong to the NCAA."

According to Ruland's friends, Corvino had been pressuring Ruland to skip his senior year and turn pro. They expressed an opinion that by leaking the existence of their relationship to the press, Corvino would have been the one to benefit had Ruland kept him on and signed with the pros.

Oddly, however, Ruland didn't blame Corvino for the leak and the subsequent end to his college basketball career—he blamed Valvano. Perhaps it's one reason Ruland hasn't spoken to Valvano to this day.

Said Ruland, "A lot of things happened that I had nothing to do with, but I got the bad end of the stick. He [Valvano] saw the boom was about to come down, and so he jumped ship."

What happened to Ruland after he was forced to declare himself available for the NBA draft becomes only more confusing. He was clearly the best center available, certainly better than his competition, collegiates Joe Barry Carroll, Kevin McHale, Mike Gminski, Kiki Vandeweghe, and Ricky Brown. He should have been picked high in the first round.

But at Iona there were rumors of investigations to come, one by the NCAA and another, a more serious one, by the FBI, as charges of free money and game fixing swirled around the Gaels team. The NCAA charged that payments of thousands of dollars were made to their basketball players in violation of the rules.

Among the lesser allegations, it was alleged that players could sign at three locations on campus for drinks and meals, with the school picking up the tab. Two of those locations were Fonz's, which was owned by Joey di Fonzo, and The Railroad, which was owned by di Fonzo and, according to Iona players, also by Valvano.

It was also alleged that the players were allowed to hail a cab and ride as far away as Manhattan, billing the fare to the school. Athletes also were alleged to have the use of telephone credit cards for private calls.

When the story of Ruland's agency agreement was leaked, an angered Ruland immediately dumped Corvino as his agent. Corvino reacted by saying that Ruland was "cuckoo" and "not too bright."

Ruland then hired Larry Fleisher, respected in basketball circles and later the head of the NBA Players Association. But just before the draft, Fleisher dropped Ruland as a client. Perhaps it was the specter of the NCAA wrongdoing and FBI game-fixing investigations. Fleisher wouldn't say.

Even more curious, when the NBA draft came around, Ruland wasn't picked on the first round. All the other big men, Carroll, McHale, Gminski, Vandeweghe, and Brown, were picked ahead of him, and when Golden State picked him at number twenty-five, he was immediately traded to the Baltimore Bullets for a draft pick. Curiously, he didn't play that year in Baltimore. He played in Barcelona, Spain.

The NCAA and FBI investigations did not lead to indictments or to findings of wrongdoing. The next year Ruland returned to the Bullets and had a productive, lucrative career.

But once Ruland left Iona, he would not forgive Valvano for betraying him. Several years out of college, Ruland said of the recruiting job done on him by Valvano, "I got fed a bunch of bull, and I believed it."

Brother Driscoll and Mrs. Ruland Swanson both blamed Valvano for breaking his obligation to Ruland, of putting his career ahead of the wants and needs of his players. They accused Valvano of being oblivious to the harm to a boy that comes after making him a surrogate son and then deserting him without so much as an "I'm sorry" —even if that boy is six feet ten inches tall.

Valvano, for his part, was contrite. "Maybe I did go wrong, as far as personal relationships. Obviously, at times, maybe I didn't realize the strength of a relationship you have with the youngsters," he said.

"A part of me had to stop doing part of the personal things. What I should have been able to do was the things that got me where I was. That's a tug-of-war. What price do you pay? To miss your own professional opportunities? That's the question you ask. That's the question I'm asking myself."

Back in Raleigh, where Valvano was preparing for his first season as head of the Wolfpack, the storm of controversy swirling around New Rochelle brought barely a whisper of scandal onto the serene campus of N.C. State. And if anyone knew, apparently no one seemed to care.

3

1983 NCAA Champs

When coach Norm Sloan left N.C. State for Florida at the end of the 1979-80 basketball season, his departure was unexpected. The usual "I left for a better opportunity" was cited. Rumors of a rift between Sloan and Athletic Director Willis Casey were bantered about, as was speculation that the "college administration," whoever that might have been, was dissatisfied with him.

Perhaps it was dissatisfied because one of Sloan's players, Clyde (The Glide) Austin, had been accused by the NCAA of getting two cars valued at $20,000 from alumni close to the basketball program, in violation of NCAA rules. How a poor college kid without a job could have gotten those two cars short of his winning the lottery was never satisfactorily explained. Nevertheless, the NCAA cleared him of wrongdoing.

Whether the investigation was the cause of the strife leading to Sloan's exodus was never made clear, but despite his having a talented nucleus at N.C. State, with one game left in the regular season, Sloan announced he was heading off to the Sunshine State, leaving his seventeenth-ranked Wolfpack behind.

Athletic Director Casey's first choice for the position was Morgan Wooten, the head coach of DeMatha High School of Hyattsville, Maryland. Wooten's teams were annually rated among the top in the nation, and he had a reputation as a molder of young men. Of the three megatalented sophomores left behind by Sloan at State, two of them, Sidney Lowe, a playmaker, and Dereck Whittenberg, a talented shooting guard, had graduated from DeMatha. Both would ultimately end up in the NBA.

Wooten, a career educator, turned down the job. He told Casey that he was happy where he was, doing what he was doing, and furthermore, he did not wish to uproot his five young children.

When Wooten said no, Casey's next choice was Valvano, who had recorded a 52–11 record in his last two years at Iona. So it was Valvano who inherited both Lowe and Whittenberg and also six-foot-eleven-inch sophomore center Thurl Bailey.

Valvano completed his first year at 14–13, and the next year hit the recruiting jackpot, landing two talented forwards, Cozell McQueen and Lorenzo Charles, to complement his three stars left over from the Sloan era. State went 22–10 in 1981–82, losing to Tennessee-Chattanooga in the opening round of the NCAA tournament.

The next year Valvano added Ernie Myers, one of the greatest penetrating guards ever to come out of New York City, and Terry (The Cannon) Gannon, a long-range shooter, to back up his stars, and by his third season at N.C. State, Valvano had the manpower to challenge for the NCAA championships.

Two Atlantic Coast Conference rules changes influenced the outcome of the 1982-83 season. The first was the advent of the thirty-second clock. A team had to shoot the ball within thirty seconds of taking it out of bounds or else lose possession. The other rule ended up winning it all for the Wolfpack: the 3-point shot. If a player shot outside nineteen feet, the basket would count for 3 points. Dereck Whittenberg was perhaps the greatest 3-point shooter in college ball at the time. Terry Gannon wasn't far behind him.

State began the season rated number sixteen in the nation. With three games left, the Wolfpack was 16–8, but only 7–4 in the ACC. If the team had a weakness, it was that Bailey, though six-foot-eleven, was more a forward than a center, and he had trouble stopping monster middlemen like Ralph Sampson of Virginia and Ben Coleman of Maryland.

Another reason Valvano felt the team didn't do better was a serious ankle injury to Whittenberg, who missed twelve games. However, Whittenberg's replacement, Ernie Myers, who had sat on the bench most of the early part of the season, came in and averaged 18 points a game.

With three regular-season ACC games left, Whittenberg was declared fit to play. The question everyone was asking was, "Who will Valvano start, Whittenberg or Myers?" One of Coach Valvano's philosophies apparently is to choose his top five players and to play them for most of the game. So it was an important decision. Whoever was not chosen would warm the bench.

Valvano felt that Whittenberg, the senior, would be more productive than Myers, the freshman. When Whittenberg returned, Myers returned to the bench, invisible the rest of the way.

With Whittenberg back but rusty, the Wolfpack lost two out of three, to finish the regular season 17–10, 8–6 in the ACC, fourth behind Carolina, Virginia, and Maryland. State was rated number sixteen at the end, the same as at the beginning. Nobody was expecting State to win the ACC title, never mind the NCAA championship.

Valvano, for his part, always kept up his humorous public face. A few days after a stinging loss to archrival North Carolina, Valvano told reporters, "This fellow wrote me that if we lose one more game to North Carolina, he's going to come up and shoot my dog. I wrote him back that I appreciated his interest but I didn't have a dog. A couple days later, the guy sends me a dog."

In another press conference, Valvano asked reporters if they knew what the N.C. State dental plan was. When reporters all shrugged, he said, "We either win or the alumni bash out our teeth." Laughter filled the room.

Valvano suspected that State would have to win the ACC championship to get a bid into the NCAA tournament.

In the ACC tournament, North Carolina State beat Wake Forest by a point in the opening round when Lorenzo Charles converted one out of two foul shots, upset Carolina in overtime in the second round when All American Sam Perkins of Carolina missed a corner jump shot at the buzzer in regulation to win it, and won Valvano's first ACC championship by beating Sampson and Virginia 81–78. Norm Sloan's big three—Thurl Bailey, Sidney Lowe, and Dereck Whittenberg—led the Wolfpack in scoring. Lorenzo Charles pulled down 12 rebounds. Ernie Myers played two minutes and didn't score.

To win the NCAA championships, a team must win a total of six games. It is a grueling ordeal, and only the most talented, deep teams end up victors. Rarely does a team win the NCAA on a fluke, though a little luck along the way does help.

At Corvalis, Oregon, North Carolina State beat Pepperdine in double overtime in the opening round. Pepperdine star Dane Suttle blew the game when he missed four free-throw opportunities in the last twenty-nine seconds of regulation. So began the talk of the 1982-83 State team being the "team of destiny."

In the next round, against the University of Nevada at Las Vegas, State won by a point, despite trailing the Running Rebels by 12 points with less than twelve minutes to go and despite 27 points by Sidney Green of Vegas, who before the game had said of Thurl Bailey, "He doesn't show me very much." Green was wrong. Bailey scored 25 points and had 9 rebounds to win the game, scoring 15 points in the last nine minutes.

The level of excitement around Raleigh rose a couple of decibels as the team flew to Ogden, Utah, for the two games of the NCAA Western Regionals.

Against Utah, Derreck Whittenberg scored 27 points, and State hit 79 percent of its shots in the second half in a 75–56 rout. State caught a break when its opponent in the regional finals was Virginia. State had played the Cavaliers three times already and was more relaxed than it would have been if playing a power it hadn't seen before.

With the score tied and only about a minute remaining, Virginia's Othell Wilson, only a fair shooter, was deliberately fouled. He made one, missed the second. Dereck Whittenberg passed off to Lorenzo Charles, who was fouled with twenty-three seconds left. Charles hit them both. State led by 1.

Virginia missed a final shot, Cozell McQueen got the rebound, and North Carolina State was on its way to

Albuquerque and the Final Four. The nicknames for the team abounded: The Kardiac Kids, Destiny's Darlings, the Cardiac Pack, the Team of Destiny. State was two games away from becoming national champions.

The team came back to Raleigh to practice. The NCAA set up a press conference, hooking up the coaches of all four finalists— N.C. State, Georgia, Louisville, and Houston—for interviews.

"Are there any questions?" From Houston came a sober "Houston passes." From Louisville, "Louisville passes." Before anyone else could respond, Valvano jumped in with a savvy bridge reference, "Raleigh bids three spades." Valvano was puncturing the pomposity of the occasion with his wit, and everyone was taking notice. Jim Valvano was proving a master at generating goodwill with the media.

Four thousand fans showed up to watch practice in the Reynolds Coliseum. Two days later, the team left for Albuquerque. Having the fans around was too distracting for the coaching staff.

When the bus left for the airport, the crush of fans lining up side by side along the interstate to see them off was so great that one would have thought it was the forerunner to Hands Across America.

Once in Albuquerque, the hottest topic of conversation was Valvano and his Cinderella team. Unlike most coaches, Valvano encouraged his players to be cooperative and open with the press, and the press responded by writing upbeat stories about the Wolfpack and their energetic coach.

"Valvano is an electric personality who encourages his players to be themselves," wrote Mike Downey of the *Detroit Free Press*, "unlike those who believe basketball is most efficient when engineered by robotics."

N.C. State had to beat the University of Georgia in order to get to the NCAA finals to face the winner of the Louisville-Houston game. This was the first time Georgia had ever reached the Final Four, so the Cinderella aspect of State's story line was downplayed temporarily.

Whittenberg and Bailey scored 20, and Lowe had 10 points and eleven assists, and though the lead dropped from 18 to 6 with five minutes left, State never lost control.

N.C. State was in the finals. Thurl Bailey told reporters, "We've come a long way this season, all the way to the final two teams. People dream about where we are. It's truly a remarkable experience."

In the afternoon's other semifinal, Houston, led by Akeem Olajuwan, outmuscled Louisville in an explosive offensive display. The number one–ranked Cougars won 94–81. It was their twenty-sixth straight victory. No one gave N.C. State a chance. All the experts were saying the same thing; that the game was a mismatch, David against Goliath. The mismatch story line was a great opportunity for some talented writers to unleash their wit.

"North Carolina State's best chance is a bus wreck," wrote Charlie Smith of the *Tulsa World*.

Wrote Joe Henderson of the *Tampa Tribune*, "Blindfold? Cigarette? Last words? Sayonara, N.C. State.

"State will probably be escorted by armed guards and priests mumbling the 23rd Psalm as it comes out for tonight's National Championship game against the Houston High Phis. There'll be no reprieve. The noose drops at 9:12 P.M.

"Rain would make it perfect. It always rains at an execution."

Dave Kindred of the *Washington Post* said it so well that Valvano later took the quote and affixed it to his office wall for permanent display. Wrote Kindred: "Trees will tap dance, elephants will ride in the Indianapolis 500, and Orson Welles will skip breakfast, lunch, and dinner before State finds a way to beat Houston."

Even the coaches were philosophical. Said Dana Kirk, coach at Memphis State, in the *Dallas Morning World*, "If I'm North Carolina State, the first thing I do is get Lou Ferrigno. You know the guy who's the Incredible Hulk? I get him and put him in the middle. Then I try to run a quick draft and get about seven draft picks.

"And then I pray.

"Pray hard Sunday. Early mass. I just can't conceive of North Carolina State winning, to be honest."

The game started with State taking the lead, and at the half State led 33–25, but Houston, led by Olajuwon, went on a 17–2 run in the second half, putting State down by 7. Houston then went into a stall, but Valvano countered by having his players deliberately foul, and when the Houston players kept missing the free throws, State was able to come back and tie the score at 52 apiece with a minute left.

Houston's freshman point guard, Alvin Franklin, went to the free-throw line and missed; State got the ball and, with forty-four seconds left in the game, called time out.

Valvano told Sidney Lowe, "Make something happen." The plan was that as soon as the clock ticked down to ten seconds, Lowe was to take the ball into the middle. Whichever side the pressure came from, that was the side he was to throw the ball. Either Lorenzo Charles, on the left, or Dereck Whittenberg, on the right, would be open. Thurl Bailey wasn't an option, because Olajuwon would be on him.

Houston applied hard pressure, and the play got all fouled up. Bailey, in the corner, ended up with the ball, and with the seconds ticking away he fired it back into the middle to Whittenberg out above the top of the key. Whittenberg let fly from thirty feet. It was way short.

But Lorenzo Charles picked it off near the basket, reached up with both hands, and dunked it—a breath before the final buzzer sounded.

Jim Valvano had done it. Only twenty-six coaches had ever won a national championship, and Jim Valvano was number twenty-seven.

In that glow of nostalgia that marks the N.C. State national championship, one of the scenes that is remembered most vividly is Jim Valvano running all over the court after the game, looking for someone he seemingly never found. The national television cameras followed him that afternoon as he ran this way and that, then back again, his arms waving madly.

Valvano's explanation is also remembered, for its hilarity if not its substance. The following is what he told the press in its entirety. He has subsequently performed this monologue in front of countless audiences who never seem to tire of hearing him talk about how State won the national championship back in '83.

Valvano told the reporters that day:

"So there I was when Lorenzo Charles dunked the ball

. . . I told him in the time-out, 'Lo', make believe anything that comes near the rim is a hubcap' [rimshot] . . . and I know we have won it, the national championship, and I am going to enjoy this and be famous so I start to run. Where was I running? I was running around looking for Dereck Whittenberg to hug. Because I have dreamed of this moment all my life, and I know I am only the twenty-seventh coach in history to win it and sixty million people are watching, and I have been hugging Whitt after all of our games because he is my designated hugger, and I know the cameras are on me, and I am thinking, 'V will make history here.' No question about it. Every Sunday of my life I have tuned in 'Wide World of Sports' and heard 'the Thrill of Victory and the Agony of Defeat' and watched that skier come down the mountain . . . boom, schuss, boom, splat . . . and somewhere in France some poor woman is going, 'Look, Pierre, here comes *mon père*,' and I know all they have ever had to show on 'Wide World' is the Agony of Defeat and now I, V, will be the Thrill of Victory. No question whatsoever. I know the cameras are zeroing in on me running in slo-mo like this [he feigns running in slow motion], and the crowd is roaring . . . Aaaahhhhhh . . . and I am running, and Whitt is running, and 'Chariots of Fire' is playing in the background, and it is going to be history! Me! Whitt! Slo-mo! 'Wide World!' Thrill of Victory! History! Me! Whitt! Together! Hug! 'Chariots of Fire!' And I will be on TV forever. No question.

"And then I get out there in the middle of nowhere, and there's Whitt . . . *hugging somebody else*! [Pause for laughter, as alums fall off their chairs in glee.]

"So I run left looking for somebody to hug. Everybody is hugging somebody else. I run right, looking. Everybody is hugging. There is nobody left to hug! I have just won it all. History. Twenty-seventh coach. Sixty million watching. And I got *nobody to hug!*

"Where am I running? I finally find our athletic director, Willis Casey, a bit old and fat but a nice man. My boss. Gave me my break. He grabs me. He hugs me. Wonderful. Great. Finally, a hug. He's not Whitt. He's old and fat, but a hug's a hug. Slo-mo hug. 'Chariots of Fire' hug. History. No question. And then Willis Casey *kisses me square on the mouth!* [A pause as the rest of the alums prostrate themselves on the floor in hysterics.]

"I have just won the national championship, twenty-seventh all time to do it . . . sixty million have watched me running around like a maniac . . . and then I fall into the arms of a fat old man who kisses me square on the mouth! The guy watching in Dubuque puts down his beer and says, 'Mabel, come look at this.' And me, V, the champion-of-the-world coach, running slo-mo, history forever, I feel the Thrill of Victory and the Agony of Defeat all at the same time! No question about it."

4

The Washer

Despite the dramatic, popular success of the North Carolina State basketball team, there were rumblings of dismay and disgust coming from a minority of faculty members and administrators whose emphasis was education first and sports second—educators who were concerned that the reputation of the university was being sullied by Coach Valvano's disregard of school standards in his recruitment of players.

If Valvano heard the criticism, he made it clear he didn't care. Valvano's goal, as it was at Iona, was to get his team to the Final Four, and past experience had taught him well that the only way to get there was to recruit the finest basketball talent the high schools had to offer. He demonstrated that he was determined to go after the best talent—regardless of academic ability or character.

In a speech in the spring of 1982, Valvano declared he would recruit as he saw fit and asserted that no one in the university had the power to stop him even if they wanted to.

Stated Valvano, "We're not even really part of the school any more, anyway. I work for the N.C. State Athletic Association. That has nothing to do with the university. Our funding is totally independent. You think the chancellor is going to tell me what to do? Who to take into school or not to take into school? I doubt it."

Valvano's statement was cited on the editorial page of the New York *Times,* which asked, "How many scandals must erupt before the reputation of higher education, or at least of individual schools, is compromised?"

* * *

The first Valvano recruits who raised professors' eyebrows were two players from his first recruiting class, key members of the 1983 NCAA championships, Cozell McQueen and Lorenzo Charles, the former six feet ten inches, the other six feet eight inches, towering masses of muscle but highly suspect in terms of their suitability for a college curriculum.

McQueen, described as a "lovely guy" by friends, was functionally illiterate. On the day after the death of Maryland star Lenny Bias, Cozell sat with his roommate, trying to read the newspaper about Lenny. He asked his roommate the meaning of one word after another, getting stuck on so many words that finally his roommate took the newspaper and read the rest of the article to him. Cozell had loved Bias, a friend, and as the roommate read the account of Bias's accidental death from a drug overdose, Cozell cried.

Lorenzo Charles publicly embarrassed the university as a result of a lapse in social etiquette. The hulking giant was loitering in one of the university's public parking lots with a few of his friends when he noticed a Domino's pizza delivery boy taking two large pepperoni pizzas to one of the dorms. The talk around campus was that Lorenzo accosted the delivery boy and told him, "Hey, pal, give me those pizzas, or I'm going to beat the shit out of you." "Sure, man, just don't pound me," responded the deliveryman. Said Charles, "Give me those pizzas, you punk," and he took them and departed.

The delivery boy called the Raleigh police and based on his description—black and about as tall as a skyscraper—it wasn't difficult for the authorities to figure out the identity of the culprit.

In court, the charge was dropped when Charles entered a felony diversion program. He was required to serve 34 hours in jail, perform 327 hours of community service and participate in a counseling program.

Members of the North Carolina State administration and faculty were mortified that one of their students would gain national attention for the university in this manner.

Valvano tried to put a positive spin on Charles' behavior, declaring that the incident "may have turned his life around." Valvano cited Winston Churchill. " 'Greatness,' " said Valvano, quoting Sir Winston, " 'also brings on great responsibilities.' Lorenzo has learned that because he is an athlete, he must be responsible for his actions and, because he is an athlete, his actions will receive more attention."

He did not discuss his responsibility in bringing Charles to the university. If a coach recruits a player who has a high school reputation for avoiding the books and for hanging out with a bad crowd, no matter how tall or talented he is, trouble for the university lies right around the corner. Wasn't he concerned that Charles' behavior was a reflection on his win-at-all-costs philosophy?

Apparently not, because embarrassment was to repeat itself with the recruiting of another gigantic, talented academic Sahara by the name of Chris Washburn. Washburn, considered the single most promising high school athlete in the entire U.S. of A., stood six-foot-eleven and weighed 255 pounds as a high school senior. He was an unusually mobile athlete for a manchild of his size, cobralike on defense and able to dribble in traffic and dunk over his outmanned opponents, leading his first high school, Hickory, to a two-year record of 48–5, moving on to Fork Union Military Academy, where he led that team to a 22–5 record his junior year, and then finishing at Laurinburg Institute with an 18–2 record—a four-year record of eighty-eight victories and twelve losses.

Despite his switching from one school to another, the experts and scouts managed to keep up with him, as Washburn was named to the *Parade* magazine All American team for three consecutive years, only the fourth high school player in history to achieve that distinction. As a senior he averaged 30 points, 17 rebounds, and nine blocked shots a game, was named Co-Player of the Year, and was selected for the prestigious McDonald's All Star Team.

Chris Washburn knew at an early age he would go to college and ultimately to the pros—at age nine to be exact. That's when he got his first letter of college recruitment. From that time on, he was the target of hundreds of colleges, even though all along he displayed a marked lack of interest in doing any school work. He wasn't stupid or slow. In fact, he had a sharp mind and at times displayed a charming wit. He simply refused to study. To him, learning was not related to his goal—playing professional basketball. Washburn reportedly had to leave Hickory High after his sophomore year because he failed driver education and phys ed during summer school, making him ineligible to play his junior year.

He moved on to Fork Union (Virginia) Military Academy, where he again performed dismally, and so again he changed alma maters, to Laurinburg (North Carolina) Institute, where questions were raised about his academic eligibility and where jaundiced eyes wondered who had bought him a new $10,000 Subaru.

Because Valvano had won the NCAA national championship, he could make Washburn a promise no other coach could make him: If you come to North Carolina State, you will start at center and you will have an opportunity to lead State to *ANOTHER* national championship.

If anyone doubted Valvano could get any student he wished into N.C. State, those doubts were put to rest when Chris Washburn was accepted as a student. When he was admitted, rumors among concerned faculty members were rampant that a figure high in the school administration had ordered Washburn's admittance. Later it would be revealed in court that Washburn had scored but a 470 combined on his SATs! Concerned faculty members were appalled and embarrassed.

Washburn's lack of knowledge was appalling. At State, Washburn was getting tutored for a geography test. The tutor asked, "What is the country directly south of the United States?" Washburn thought a minute and said, "Canada." The tutor said, "No, they speak Spanish. Maybe that will help." Washburn responded, "Spain?"

When he was asked what country was directly north of the U.S., his answer was, "England?"

The NCAA looked into Washburn's recruitment. It, too, wondered whether Washburn's car had something to do with his choice of college, but it failed to turn up evidence of any violations.

Though Washburn and another of Valvano's prize recruits, Nate McMillan, a junior college All American transfer from Chowan Junior College in Murfreesboro, North Carolina, were joining Ernie Myers, Lorenzo Charles, and Cozell McQueen, Valvano knew that the inexperience of the team would probably keep it from reaching the Final Four in 1984. His big three from the Sloan era—Thurl Bailey, Sidney Lowe, and Dereck Whittenberg—had moved on, but Valvano was confident that from Washburn's sophomore season on, his recruiting efforts would be paying off. He was certain he'd get so many blue-chip high school All Americans to commit to him that the Wolfpack might be the next UCLA, winning the national championship year after year.

"For one year it will be a struggle; we'll be on hold," said Valvano just before Washburn's freshman year in November of 1983. "These young kids will develop and will be joined by some real great prospects. I think we'll be in the Top Ten for at least the next four years."

The problem for Jim Valvano was that Chris Washburn was a social deviant, and at almost seven feet and 260 pounds, he was a danger to Raleigh society. The catalyst that set him off, as the students around him well knew, was cocaine.

Early in his freshman year he strolled into one of the dormitories and rode the elevator to a girls' floor. The students who saw him said he looked "as high as a kite." He wandered into one of the girl's rooms, unplugged her telephone, and attempted to walk out with it.

The girl, who stood up to about his waist, went running up to him and screamed, "I don't care who you are, you'd better give me back my fucking phone or I'm going to have your ass in the slammer."

Washburn was so impressed with her moxie, he handed her back the phone.

A couple weeks later Washburn beat up a coed, was arrested, convicted, and placed on probation.

Despite his social difficulties, Washburn started at center when the basketball season began in November, and with his six-foot-eleven frame sandwiched between the six-foot-ten McQueen and the six-foot-eight Lorenzo Charles, the Wolfpack looked like an NBA team as it opened the season beating Houston by 12 in a rematch and then going on to win six of its first seven games. All he had to do was remain eligible, and N.C. State would have a real shot at another NCAA championship.

On December 18, 1984, Washburn visited the ground-floor room of William West, a sophomore football player with whom he had gone to school at Fork Union Military

Academy. West lived down the hall from Washburn at the College Inn, the dormitory for North Carolina State's athletes. Washburn noticed West's five-piece stereo system and asked him how much it had cost. West replied, "About eight hundred dollars." Said Washburn, "Don't forget to take it home during Christmas vacation."

The next night, according to police, someone opened up the window to West's bedroom, climbed in, and removed a turntable, amplifier, tape deck, and two large stereo speakers. When West's roommate, Jeff Davis, returned about midnight, he saw that the stereo system was missing and noticed footprints the size of Bigfoot on the ledge outside the open window.

The roommate called the Raleigh police, not the North Carolina State campus police. Had he done the latter, Washburn might have avoided the trouble that was to follow, as the investigation might have remained internal. But because West called the Raleigh police, the incident was written into the night log, fair game for snoopy reporters.

When the Raleigh police arrived, they took a cast of the gigantic footprint on the windowsill and fingerprints from the room. The foot and fingerprints belonged to Washburn.

In a twenty-seven-minute interrogation, the nineteen-year-old Washburn at first denied knowledge of the theft. But police investigator D. A. Weingarten countered by calling him a liar. He told Washburn, "Chris, I'm telling you like it is. This is the real world now. Coach Valvano can't protect you." After Weingarten convinced Washburn he had enough evidence to prove his guilt, Washburn finally admitted he had taken the stereo, calling the episode "a stupid prank."

"I was going to give it back," Washburn said. "I was playing a joke on a friend."

But when asked where he had taken the stereo system, Washburn told Weingarten, "I took it to a guy in Durham. I can get it back."

On December 23, powerless to get Washburn out of his mess, Valvano suspended his star from the team for the rest of the season. Valvano made no mention of the burglary charges, saying only that Washburn had "personal problems" that made it inappropriate for him to continue on the team.

Valvano discussed the impact Washburn's loss would have upon his team.

"Before this happened," said Valvano, "we were a legitimate top ten team. Now we're mediocre. We're exactly back where we were last year." In discussing the year-long suspension, Valvano made himself seem the stern disciplinarian by saying, "I didn't do this to appease university or county officials. This was my decision.

"I could have waited until the January hearing and let him play all season. But I know Chris. I realize that he has yet to mature. He needs to understand where he is and where he's going. He needs to realize that he doesn't walk this earth alone, that his actions affect many other people. Chris needs to step back from the spotlight."

On January 8, 1985, Judge Narley Cashwell rejected a defense motion for dismissal, despite the contention that Washburn stole the stereo equipment in order to "play a joke" on West. He also refused to reduce charges from second-degree burglary—a felony—to something less. Washburn was facing a minimum sentence of fourteen years, with time off for good behavior. The possibility existed that Washburn would not only miss the season, but most of his prime as well.

The case went to trial, creating embarrassment for both Washburn and North Carolina State—including the revelation that Washburn had scored a dismally low combined total of 470 out of 1600 on his SATs (you are handed 400 points for signing your name). Washburn's attorney struck a deal with the prosecution. Washburn pleaded guilty to three misdemeanor charges and was sentenced by Wake County Superior Court Judge J. Milton Reid to forty-six hours in the local jail—to be served on the first anniversary of the theft—given a six-year suspended sentence, and placed on five years probation.

In return, Washburn agreed to the following conditions:

1. Pay $1,000 to the state's victims' compensation fund.

2. Undergo mental health counseling by a practitioner appointed by the court.

3. Undergo drug and alcohol therapy and thirty hours of confrontational therapy. (No mention was ever made of his drug habit throughout this entire episode, and even after he was ordered to undergo drug treatment, no one thought to ask why.)

4. Donate two hundred hours of his time to a center for mentally retarded children.
5. Perform one hundred hours of "heavy housecleaning tasks" at a home for persons on parole.
6. Do maintenance work for twenty hours for the Raleigh police department.
7. Surrender his driver's license for ninety days.
8. Allow himself to be subject to an ongoing search warrant "at reasonable times."
9. Avoid use or possession of illegal substances and stay away from other users.
10. Be gainfully employed the next two summer vacations.
11. Make a visit to the state prison.

Even without Washburn, the 1984-85 N.C. State basketball team was a powerhouse. Guards Ernie Myers and junior college transfer Spud Webb, a five-foot-seven-inch midget who could outrace anyone while dribbling a basketball, handled the ball, while seniors Lorenzo Charles and Cozell McQueen were joined by sophomore Bennie Bolton to give the team strength under the boards and a lot of scoring up front.

Valvano's Wolfpack finished the year 23 and 10, tying for the ACC regular-season title. The team lost in the second round of the ACC tournament to Carolina, but beat Nevada-Reno, Texas-El Paso, and Alabama before losing to St. John's in the finals of the Western Regionals of the NCAA.

Valvano's freshman recruits, moreover, were his finest class since his arrival on the N.C. State campus back in 1980.

With Cozell McQueen and Lorenzo Charles finishing their careers at State, Valvano badly needed athletes to team with Washburn, sophomore forward Bennie Bolton, and returning senior guard Ernie Myers, and he got them. Oh yes, he did.

Of the six youngsters coming to State, five were named high school All American in one poll or another. All had been recruited by the cream of major basketball powers. Two, Charles Shackleford and Teviin Binns, stood six-foot-ten. Shackleford had been recruited by Maryland, Duke, North Carolina, Houston, Louisville, DePaul, and Kentucky. Binns, a Junior College All American from

Midland Junior College, was reputed to be a scoring machine. He had been recruited by 150 major colleges. Walker Lambiotte, a six-foot-seven-inch guard with an uncanny shooting eye, was named the MVP of the prestigious McDonald's High School All Star Game and was rated among the top ten prospects in the nation.

Valvano, moreover, had induced Mike Giomi, the best rebounder on the Indiana University varsity, to come to State, after Giomi had been tossed off the Hoosier team for skipping too many classes. In high school, the six-foot-nine-inch Giomi had been named Ohio High School Player of the Year.

Not satisfied with adding two six-foot-tens and a six-foot-nine-inch tower, Valvano also convinced a former member of the Greek National Basketball Team, Panagiotis Fasoulas from Thessaloniki, Greece, to join the Wolfpack for the 1985–86 season.

It was a dazzling array of talent that Valvano managed to bring to Raleigh, and with his potential college All American Chris Washburn returning, the N.C. State campus was abuzz with talk of the possibility of another national championship.

5

Valvano Becomes A.D.

Even before America discovered that Chris Washburn had been accepted into N.C. State after scoring only a 470 on his College Boards, the members of the State faculty who regarded Jim Valvano as a blemish on its academic reputation were conducting a study of N.C. State's admissions practices with regard to its athletes.

The Faculty Senate's investigation in 1984 disclosed that the administration had given Valvano and his coaches carte blanche to fill a certain number of spots at will.

"Basically speaking," said one of the faculty members who conducted the investigation, "the admissions process was a joke."

What was revealed was that the coaches themselves were acting as a separate admissions committee for the university. Valvano and his coaches were virtually admitting some athletes even *before* they took their SATs.

Said one of the investigators, "The coach went out and recruited a kid, announced in the newspaper that so-and-so had signed a letter of intent to attend the university, say on a basketball scholarship. That coach was tantamount to admitting that person to the university."

The report produced by the Faculty Senate revealed that the athletes admitted into the university had embarrassingly low SAT scores and extremely low high school grade point averages compared to the general student population.

None of this created a ripple of media attention until three-quarters of the way through the Faculty Senate investigation, when the Chris Washburn trial revealed his 470 SAT score. Then suddenly, to the chagrin of Chancellor Bruce Poulton and the athletic department, America's press began having a field day.

George Vescey of the New York *Times* interviewed N.C. State Assistant Vice Chancellor Hardy Berry, who said, "The history of American sports is tied in with education. Who can forget that Amos Alonzo Stagg helped give an identity to the University of Chicago, one of the great institutions in our country?"

Wrote Vescey, "The University of Chicago long ago divested itself of big-time sports, but somehow remains one of the finest schools in the country."

Hardy's boss was Bruce R. Poulton, the chancellor. What was Poulton's role in the admission of these academically deficient students? Did Poulton have the clout to order a player like Washburn into school? Was Poulton embarrassed over the Washburn revelations?

When the uproar subsided, little changed. The one significant outcome of the Faculty Senate report and the Washburn embarrassment was a recommendation to support the NCAA's Proposition 48, which called for any athlete who had less than a C average and less than a 700 on his College Boards to sit out his freshman year and hit the books instead. In itself, Proposition 48 was hard for the educators on the faculty to swallow because it was such a small step. The average nonathlete entered N.C. State with about a B-plus high school average and around 1100 combined on the SATs. Was it so much to ask a student athlete to come in with at least a C average and a paltry 700 on his College Boards? For many coaches around the country, it was, going back to the philosophy of so many high school basketball stars that studying was irrelevant to their lives. For those coaches, Proposition 48 was hard to swallow because potentially it could inhibit the participation of their recruits. But at State, the athletic department bowed to the pressure and publicly agreed to abide by Proposition 48 guidelines.

The Faculty Senate also recommended that the university admit students based upon their academic qualifications and not upon their athletic prowess. This dictum was ignored.

Another result of the activity of the Faculty Senate was the appointment of its chairman, Dr. Roger Clark, a professor in the field of architecture, as the faculty's representative to the Athletics Council for the 1985-86 academic year.

The NCAA requires that every college have an Athletics Council, a body comprised of a majority of faculty but including students and alumni, to oversee the athletic department and make it accountable to the university. The seven faculty members are selected by the school's chancellor, the three alumni by the alumni association, and the three students by the student body president.

Since he had just headed the Faculty Senate's study on academics, Dr. Clark assumed he would be given a spot on the council's Academic Policies Committee, the watchdog concerned with athletes' grades. He was not. Instead Dr. Clark was put on the committee overlooking the athletic facilities. After all, the veteran council members told him, he was an architect by trade and best suited to survey the athletic plant.

From the beginning Dr. Clark was viewed by the senior faculty members on the council as an outsider. Clark's intention had been to follow the mandate as set down by the NCAA, to be an overseer, to uphold the academic standards of the university with regard to athletics.

But he quickly realized that his fight to be a watchdog would be futile because, as he discovered, the majority of the council members had been provided with great seats to games, access to players, and access to Valvano. The real role of the Athletics Council, Dr. Clark discovered, was to act as an arm of the athletic department—a protector, apologist, and lobbyist.

When Clark attempted to pass the resolution "Athletes must go to class or they don't play," the Academic Policies Committee's chairman, Fred Smetana, a professor of mechanical engineering and a long-time member of the Athletics Council and supporter of Valvano, did not allow the resolution to come up for a vote by the full council.

Earlier, when both Clark and Smetana had been members of the Faculty Senate, that body had voted on a resolution declaring, "Students who come to the university ought to be qualified." Reportedly, the only faculty member on the Faculty Senate to vote against the resolution was Fred Smetana.

Council meetings were tightly controlled. Secrecy was

stressed, as though national secrets, not collegiate athletics, were involved. The watchdogs, according to one council member, were kept in the dark about drug problems, and grade deficiencies were discussed in only the most general terms, as in "A swimmer is in academic trouble." The reason cited was a law designed to protect the privacy of the students from having their grades publicized.

The athletic budget, which at State comes solely from ticket sales, television revenues, and money donated by the Wolfpack Club, was revealed to the council members but kept secret from the public or press. At the yearly council meeting to discuss the budget, a copy would be distributed to each member, and at the end of the meeting it reportedly would be collected.

Said a council member, "The council would give its rubber stamp, and it would be passed."

For all but the most innocuous of noncontroversial topics, secrecy was called for. No other campus committee closed its meetings to the press. Moreover, the members of the Athletics Council routinely were warned by Chairman Richard Mochrie not to talk to reporters about what went on at the meetings. Again, one would have thought national security was at stake. Or that the athletic department was trying to hide something.

Council Chairman Mochrie, a professor of animal science, a nationally known official in the world of track and field, and a strong supporter of Valvano, often warned the other members that if the press had any questions about what went on at meetings, the proper procedure was to send the reporter to him.

When the student newspaper, the *Technician,* demanded that it be allowed to send a reporter to the council meetings, Chairman Mochrie was adamantly opposed.

In trying to justify the policy of secrecy, Mochrie told the paper, "I really think it's better in the long run. When you are batting things around, I can't see cluttering up the press with what's going on."

The council went so far as to solicit the opinion of the chief deputy attorney general of the State of North Carolina, who proclaimed that the Athletics Council was exempt from the state's Open Meeting Law "because it does not satisfy the law's definition of a public body."

Chairman Mochrie further justified the policy by citing

his boss, saying, "Chancellor Poulton has asked that these meetings be closed."

When the reporter went to see Poulton, the chancellor told him, "If the majority of the committee wanted to open the meetings, I guess they could." Fat chance of that happening. He had appointed the members.

It was apparent to faculty members and students that under the Poulton administration, whatever Valvano and his athletic department wanted to do, they could do—and that if anyone dared buck Valvano, he would have to take on Poulton as well.

Dr. Bruce R. Poulton, with the rugged good looks of actor Robert Mitchum, had arrived at N.C. State in 1981, a year after Valvano, and immediately formed a close bond with the basketball coach. Standing at six-foot-seven, the towering Poulton had once played varsity basketball at Rutgers, Valvano's alma mater. He earned his bachelor of science degree in animal sciences in 1950, a master's in nutrition in 1952, and his doctorate in endocrinology in 1956, all from Rutgers.

Like Valvano, Poulton climbed the stepladder from campus to campus before his arrival in Raleigh. After beginning as an instructor and associate professor at Rutgers, he was an administrator at the University of Maine, was a fellow at Michigan State, then returned to the state of Maine to become administrative assistant to the governor of Maine, James Longley. After a political baptism, Poulton was named as the first chancellor of a consolidated New Hampshire University system before finally landing the top job at N.C. State.

In Poulton, Valvano apparently had found his champion. "Poulton sees Valvano as a motivator, someone who won a championship, and he sees nothing bad about him," said one faculty observer. "Valvano's high-strung, ambitious, seems to have all the right values, and I'll tell you, he brings a lot of money to the university. That's the bottom line."

Said a faculty critic of the Valvano-Poulton association, "Chancellor Poulton is very close to Valvano, and nobody can say whether he's intimidated by him or just agrees with him, but regardless, Valvano has his run of what he wants to do. He's got Poulton around his finger, and since Poulton appoints the council members, if there's enough pressure, any vote is going to pass."

Said a member of the council, "We give our rubber stamp to everything that occurs in the athletic department."

Faculty members who will discuss the relationship between Poulton and Valvano say they don't know why Poulton is such a devotee of Valvano, but one former faculty member may be shedding light on it with the following account.

Said the former faculty member, "One time I noticed that one of the players had failed three courses and that two weeks later the F's had been changed to D's. I was so upset I went to see Chancellor Poulton to tell him I was concerned that Valvano had put pressure on other professors to change the grades.

"The thing that really disturbed me was the fact that Poulton told me, 'Valvano is a very popular personality, and he is good for the university, and he could buy or sell me, so there's no need to get into a hassle.' "

[Poulton, in a prepared statement, has denied the conversation ever took place. The former professor, in rebuttal, replied; "The truth is the truth."]

The issue that brought home Poulton's unqualified support of Valvano was Valvano's push to become athletic director at N.C. State. Valvano had been A.D. at Iona, and he was used to having his way. As basketball coach, he didn't control the budget for his team, didn't make the schedule, didn't arrange for television and radio, didn't make the travel arrangements, and didn't have complete control over recruitment. The A.D. was top dog, and Valvano wanted the job.

Soon after Willis Casey, the incumbent athletic director, announced that he was going to retire, the Athletics Council impaneled a search committee, headed by Chairman Mochrie.

Valvano's power move toward the athletic department directorship began with the kind of backroom maneuvering Lyndon Baines Johnson would have been proud of. Soon after Casey announced his retirement, a rush of sixty applicants from around the country applied for the prestigious, high-salaried position. But a petition began to circulate, signed by all the coaches, demanding that Valvano be named the new athletic director.

When the petition was handed to Mochrie, he stopped the evaluation process in its tracks. Some of the other candidates had informed him, he asserted, that so great was their respect for the N.C. State basketball coach that they did not want to be considered as long as Valvano was a candidate. As a result, Mochrie averred, the Search Committee would be forced to deal with whether or not to hire Valvano before it could continue the search any further. The Valvano steamroller was under way.

The Search Committee then interviewed Valvano, said it was impressed by him, and summarily brought forth his name as athletic director for approval by the entire council.

On a cold Thursday in February, the Athletics Council met to vote on Valvano's nomination. Three of the council members, two students, and Dr. Clark, spoke in opposition to Valvano's appointment.

Dr. Clark was the most outspoken. He cited what he characterized as "Valvano's disregard for education." "He couldn't care less," said Clark. "He brings people to be at the university who are unqualified. He doesn't care whether they go to class or not. He doesn't care whether they perform academically or whether they graduate. The athletic director is the one person who is supposed to be the watchdog. Why in the world are we turning around and putting the person who is doing the worst job of that in the whole athletic department and making him the athletic director?"

When Clark finished, Chancellor Bruce Poulton spoke. Poulton vehemently denied everything that Clark had said. The chancellor then said, "I move for a vote on the question." The tally was 10 to 3 in favor, with two students and Dr. Clark voting against Valvano.

The last step to Valvano's appointment as A.D. was his ratification by the university's board of trustees. Two days after the Athletics Council meeting, it was announced during halftime of the basketball game against the University of Kansas at Reynolds Coliseum that the board of trustees had named Valvano to be the college's new athletic director.

This was no surprise to those involved in Valvano's selection. One week earlier—four days before the Athletics Council meeting—the agenda for the trustees meeting listed an item: "approval of the athletic director appointment." Since the only candidate being considered was Valvano, it might as easily have said "approval of Jim Valvano as athletic director."

The voting process was "rigged," said one observer.

In the school newspaper, the *Technician*, Valvano was quoted as saying he was planning to use the dual role of basketball coach and athletic director to "project a new image about the university's athletic program."

He told a reporter, "To be honest with you, we've had some problems here since I've been here the last several years. I think it's important that we start spreading the good news about North Carolina State athletics and the success we've had here."

Poulton was quoted in the article, saying the advisory committee had "enthusiastically endorsed Valvano."

With Poulton solidly in his corner and the faculty opposition effectively silenced and neutralized, Valvano was now in total control of the athletic department. With respect to athletics, he was overseer of finances, could influence the independent and highly lucrative Wolfpack Club, arrange the TV schedule, arrange the schedule of games, and he would have absolute control over the entire basketball program. And he would need every ounce of that power to keep Chris Washburn and any of his other nonacademic stars in uniform.

There is a postscript to this story. When Dr. Clark's term on the Academic Council expired, the Faculty Senate commended him for the job he did and recommended to Chancellor Poulton that Clark serve a second term. Poulton, who has the ultimate authority over the council, did not reject Clark's nomination outright but ordered the Faculty Senate to submit more than one recommendation.

The Senate submitted two names, Dr. Clark and Dr. Keith Cassel, to Chancellor Poulton. Dr. Clark's tenure on the council had come to an end.

About two months after Valvano was named athletic director, the N.C. State student newspaper disclosed that the red Cadillac Poulton drove around in was actually provided to him free by the Wolfpack Club. The school's chancellor, it turned out, had been provided with a car by the Wolfpack Club for the past twelve years.

The Wolfpack Club, denying any impropriety, argued that their gift was saving the state and hence the taxpayers of North Carolina money.

To critics, Poulton's free Caddy gave the appearance of being an inducement or a reward for cooperation with the athletic department. To educators, it indicated where Poulton's priorities lay.

Red-faced, Poulton returned the red car.

6

Protecting His Investment

On October 9, 1985, Chris Washburn, who remained in school and on scholarship during his one-year suspension from the basketball team, was reinstated to the team by Valvano.

The student newspaper, the *Technician*, showed just the right amount of Wolfpack spirit by trumpeting in an editorial, "Welcome back, Chris."

Valvano told reporters that Washburn had not only finished his court-ordered community service work but had made sufficient academic progress to return to the team. Chris has "learned from his mistakes," Valvano declared.

By midseason Washburn was telling reporters, "In many respects what happened to me made me a better person because it made me mature and wise up and realize a lot sooner that the childish things that I've been doing have to somehow be put in the past. It's time for me to start acting like an adult."

It was all PR. Despite the hours of community service, the pious statements, and having to report to his state-appointed counselor every month, Chris Washburn, according to his teammates, remained a walking time bomb.

In practice he reportedly enjoyed abusing Assistant Coach Tom Abatamarco, the man who had helped recruit him to State. After practice Washburn would grab Abatamarco, who was a hundred pounds lighter, and wrestle him to the ground. He would throw basketballs at him from the blind side. One time Washburn, angry because Abatamarco was critical of him during practice, kicked the assistant coach hard and reportedly screamed, "Get away from me, you little motherfucker." Abatamarco tried to reason with him. He said, "Chris, I'm your father. If it wasn't for me, you'd be nowhere." Washburn replied, "Get out of here, you stupid bastard."

His teammates were all afraid of the seven-foot, 260-pound mammoth. Said one, "Nobody would ever say anything bad about him, because Wash was the kind of guy who would flip out and come back and get you. He's seven feet and two hundred and sixty pounds. That's a big man." Said a teammate, "Wash would steal you blind and was dangerous. So you didn't want to get him mad."

Toward the end of the spring semester of his sophomore year, Washburn discovered his girl friend was seeing another guy and reportedly beat her up so badly that he broke her nose. It was set privately so the incident wouldn't get out to the press.

A large part of what accounted for Wash's behavior was the fact that he had resumed his love affair with the white powder.

"Wash would play games on coke," said a teammate. "The first half he'd play great, and then the coke would wear off, and in the second half he wouldn't do a thing." To get by the three-times-a-year drug tests, Washburn reportedly once went into the urinal with a hidden container of clean urine provided by a friend, stepped up, and instead of peeing, poured the clean urine into the test cup.

Another time he tried a less conventional means of passing the test. He sprayed cologne into his urine sample, shook it up, and handed it in.

"He went 'chhh chhh' into the cup," said a teammate, who watched. " 'This ought to do it,' Wash said."

Did Valvano know that Wash was on coke? Did Valvano ever receive a positive drug test from Wash? If an illegal substance was found in Wash's urine, was anything ever done about it—either for or to him?

Washburn's behavior was abhorred by some teammates, but what disturbed them far worse was the favored treatment he was getting. There were two sets of rules at State, one for them and another for Wash. It was a repeat of what had gone on at Iona, where Jeff Ruland

and Glenn Vickers got the "star treatment" that caused resentment among the other members on the team.

"Chris was the star," a teammate said, "and without Chris in the middle, State wouldn't have been that good." He paused. "Valvano did things for Chris, I'm telling you, that you wouldn't believe. Schoolwise, Chris never went to school. He'd come to some classes, but he was never there enough times to pass. But V gets you through school if he wants to. I believe that ever since Chris got to State, I would be surprised if he ever passed a class. And he still managed to play.

"I know this: Chris was the only one who didn't have to go to study hall. Why? I don't know why. Everybody else had to be there, but Chris didn't. He'd do what he wanted. He'd come late for practice, meetings, hold up the bus.

"I remember we were going to Maryland, and Chris wasn't there. V said, 'Come on, let's go, forget him.' But V didn't really mean that, because if we went up there without Chris, we would have probably lost.

"We drove up the hill from the College Inn, and at the top of the hill, Chris was in his car at the stoplight, getting ready to come down to meet the bus.

"V said, 'Chris, what are you doing?'

"He said, 'I overslept, man. I overslept.' And he parked his car and walked onto the bus. He was Chris Washburn. He had his own little room at the end of the hall at the College Inn. He came from a poor family, but he had all these different doodads, stereo stuff—the baddest room I seen at the Inn. He had a big old bed.

"They gave him a new car, a white Datsun 300ZX, and he used to play the music all loud with his shades on. And Chris always had a pocket full of money. He was never broke. And Chris had gold all over his hands. Somebody in town was getting him some jewelry.

" 'Boy,' I thought, 'someone is really taking care of him.'

"And the thing was, he knew he'd play his minutes. I'm not saying he shouldn't play, but once you know you're going to play, you don't have nothing to worry about. You go out there like a chicken with your head cut off, and still you know everything is going to be all right. He was Chris Washburn. In practice, he would loaf, and V would never say nothing about Chris. Chris would be in the room while we were watching game films, and he'd be sleeping. V wouldn't say nothing. If it was anybody else, he would turn on the light and yell, 'Get up. What do you think this is, watching a fucking movie?' But he would never say nothing to Chris. Chris would come in late with them shades on, and you knew when he was wearing shades, something was going on. He'd come in all the time with those shades."

The players knew Washburn used cocaine, but no one said anything to him about it. "He was living and doing the things that he wanted. He was one of the best centers in the nation. Everybody heard of Chris Washburn. That's how it was," the teammate said.

The sin was, nobody considered the long-range effect of a drug addiction on Chris Washburn. Nobody said to him, "You are ruining your life. You are ruining a million-dollar career." Nobody said, "Stop."

Said a teammate, "Nobody said, 'Chris, we're going to do this our way. We're going to take you in and do the right thing.' Yeah, V had to know, but he was Chris. V didn't want the franchise to go down. He wanted to win. And coaches will do anything to win, believe me. V told us time and time again, 'I don't care. When the game comes, I want to win.' That's all. Period."

Said another player, "Why should Chris do what he didn't want to do? He had the coaches by the balls. He was a franchise player, so they had to keep him happy. They had to cater to him. They had to let him call the shots, which is outrageous. The shoes are on the wrong feet here. The athlete is running the show. But if Wash had gotten upset, that would have meant the press getting involved and threats to transfer, and V couldn't have dealt with that."

And so Chris Washburn managed to survive his sophomore year, playing every game, proving his excellence on the court, leading State to a 21–13 record and earning recognition as one of the dominant players in the college game with a scoring average of 17.6 points and 6.7 rebounds a game.

With Washburn leading the way, the Wolfpack almost achieved Valvano's goal, reaching the Final Eight of the

NCAA championships. They beat Iowa, then Arkansas-Little Rock in double overtime, and in the Western Regionals beat Iowa State before losing to powerhouse Kansas.

State was up by 5 points with only eight minutes to go, but Kansas shot State out of the game, and the Wolfpack was eliminated.

7

The Class of '86: Drum and Andy

High school seniors looking at North Carolina State were aware that State had advanced to the Final Eight of the NCAAs. They recognized that Chris Washburn was perhaps the most dominant center in all of college ball, with freshman Charles Shackleford, the six-foot-ten power forward, showing both catlike agility and awesome power to the basket. The twin giants made the Wolfpack very tough to stop offensively. Valvano, moreover, had yet to make full use of his other talented young recruits, forwards Teviin Binns and Chucky Brown, and guards Walker Lambiotte, Quentin Jackson, and Kelsey Weems. But Valvano had the reputation of preferring to play upperclassmen, and everyone eagerly anticipated the time when they would be unleashed.

It didn't take a genius to see that all Valvano needed for a 1987 national championship was a point guard to run the offense and one more outside shooter to spell—and ultimately replace—senior Bennie Bolton.

The point guard Valvano set his sights on was a little hunk of gristle named Kenny Drummond, the star of Sacramento Community College, the top junior college basketball team in the country. Though only six feet tall and weighing perhaps 175 pounds, Drum, as he was called, was so fast down the floor that if you blinked he could beat you to the basket and dunk on you. He could also hit a 3-pointer from downtown, and on defense, not only did he attach himself like Elmer's, but if you gave him an opening to the ball, he would flick it away for the steal and an easy basket. Sacramento finished its season

27–7, defeating San Francisco City College for the JUCO championship. That year Drummond scored 848 points, an average of 25 points a game, and he had 208 assists and an incredible 204 steals.

Equally important, Kenny Drummond had the right approach to the game. He played hard, forty minutes a game. He even practiced hard. Every day before practice, he would run the dozens of stairs up and down the football stadium, keeping in racehorse shape.

He was religious and he was a team leader. He knew the value of never giving up, for Drummond had actually gone to college without even graduating from high school. Growing up in Peoria, Illinois, Drummond had been a hoop star as far back as the eighth grade, when he was playing for the Hairston Elementary School. The coach of the local Catholic school, Academy Spalding of our Lady Institute, saw him, was impressed by him, and offered him a scholarship to come and play basketball.

When he told his mother of the scholarship offer, her response was, "Don't you want to go to Manual High School with all your friends?" But Kenny Drummond knew it was an unmatched opportunity. He told her, "No, I think I'd rather play against them."

Drummond starred at Academy Spalding his ninth, tenth, and eleventh grades, but then he had a falling out with his coach. When Bradley University suggested he go to a prep school his senior year, he did, transferring to Oak Hill Academy in Virginia. But Drummond became homesick, dropped out of Oak Hill, and instead of returning to school, moved west to Sacramento, California, to live with his sister.

Drummond got a night job as a security guard at Sacramento Community College. During the afternoon, he went into the gym, shot baskets, and sometimes played in pickup games with the varsity players. The Sacramento basketball coach, Mike Syas, noticed him, asked him who he was and where he came from, and invited him to play on the team.

In California, you don't need a high school diploma to go to junior college. But you do have to take a full course load to compete in athletics, so Drummond enrolled, took a full load, and played basketball. He also studied and passed a high school equivalency examination.

Drummond didn't play much his first year at Sacramento. He was a role player, filling in when the starting point guard needed a rest or when a pressing defense was called for. But under Coach Syas's direction, Drummond got an education, both on and off the court. Syas drilled into him what he would have to do to be productive in society.

Syas, who had fought in Vietnam, emphasized academics. He drilled his players into believing in the importance of education. "Nobody is going to give you anything in this world," he told them. He demanded that all of his players graduate, and they did. Drummond was one of his best students, finishing the two years with a degree in criminal justice and a 3.5 grade point average.

On the basketball court his second year, Drummond was designated by Coach Syas to be his floor leader. No one worked harder. No one fought harder. Syas, who is black, had an all-black team. He demanded camaraderie from his players, and they became like brothers. The tallest member of that Sacramento team was only six-foot-five, but nobody could run with them. As soon as a member of the team pulled down a rebound, he'd make an outlet pass to a guard, and everyone else would fill a lane and head for the basket. They ran as if someone homicidal were chasing them. It was tiring to watch them play.

And when the team needed a basket, Kenny Drummond—uncannily accurate from twenty feet—inevitably provided it. Drummond impressed the scouts from the major colleges so that despite his diminutive size, they predicted a bright future in the National Basketball Association.

Drummond began getting mail from major colleges. There were the schools from the West—USC, New Mexico, Oregon, and UNLV—but Drummond's reputation had spread across the country and he also heard from Purdue, Wisconsin, Minnesota, hometown Peoria's Bradley University, who had wanted him out of high school, and North Carolina State.

Drummond was made the same offer by all the schools: two years to play, three to graduate. To land Drummond, the difference had to come in the brochures and the quality of personal contact by the coaches.

It was hard to best North Carolina State's literature.

Just about every day during the recruitment period, Valvano's staff sent something out—a flyer, a brochure, a calendar, a news clip, a schedule of games, a color poster of Reynolds Coliseum filled with 14,000 screaming fans to put on the wall, or a schedule of televised appearances.

It was the lure of appearing on national TV that captured Kenny Drummond's attention. As a youngster he had watched his favorite basketball stars on TV, and he wanted to be on national television like them. One brochure sent to Drummond included the schedule of seventeen N.C. State games that were going to be televised either on a television network or on ESPN. This was his chance to be seen all over the country by his friends and by the professional scouts. He well knew that getting into the pros sometimes required more than talent, especially for a small guard. You also had to be seen. Fully a third of N.C. State's games were going to be televised nationally. N.C. State had Drum's full attention.

Tom Abatamarco, Jim Valvano's assistant coach and chief recruiter, had worked for Valvano at Iona and moved to N.C. State when Valvano beckoned. A short stocky man with a thick mustache, Abatamarco had a quick wit, like Valvano, and could talk a blue streak. As a recruiter, he was considered a genius. Abatamarco had the ability to sense what it was the prospective athlete wanted to hear and then tell it to him. Abatamarco had helped recruit Vickers and Ruland at Iona and had played a role in landing Washburn, Lambiotte, Shackleford, and all the other top-rated N.C. State prospects.

When Abatamarco first called Drummond, Drum was flattered to hear from him. Abatamarco wanted Drummond to know that at N.C. State he could be part of a national championship. He told Drummond that if he worked hard enough, he would play. He told Drummond he would be on TV a lot. And he told Drummond that Coach Jim Valvano really wanted him to come to State.

The next time Abatamarco returned to Sacramento to see Drummond, he brought Coach Valvano with him. "I was honored," Drummond said later. He was awed. Drummond remembered seeing Coach Valvano on television running around like a crazy person after winning the 1983 NCAA championship. Drummond often had watched

Valvano on national television. He remembered one time seeing Valvano dive onto the floor after the referees made what Valvano considered a bad call. Before their meeting ended, Drummond asked Valvano for his autograph.

Valvano told Drummond there were two other point guards on the team, Kelsey Weems and Quentin Jackson, but said that in his opinion, Drum was quicker and better suited to the role of point guard than they were.

In the spring of 1986, Kenny Drummond signed a letter of intent to attend North Carolina State University. He had but one reservation. Sometimes when other coaches asked him where he was going and he responded, "N.C. State to play for Jim Valvano," the coach's reaction would be, "Are you sure you want to go there?" Drummond always said, "Yes, sir, I am sure." But it did make him wonder.

The outside shooter that Valvano particularly celebrated recruiting was a Mississippi high schooler reputed to be the second incarnation of Pistol Pete Maravich, the former LSU and NBA star. His name was Andy Kennedy and, like Maravich, he was skinny, white, and a scoring machine. In addition, like the former LSU legend, he had a flair for the game, playing with great intensity—cussing, ranting and raving at himself, driving himself to perfection, and at the same time exciting and entertaining the crowd. By the time Kennedy graduated from high school he had scored 2,400 points in his career.

Kennedy grew up in the town of Louisville (pronounced Lewisville), Mississippi, population 12,000. In his senior year, he averaged 29 points and 11 rebounds a game despite having to play every game against a box-and-one defense in which the opposing coach would have four of his defenders play either a 1-2-1 or a 2-2 zone, with the fifth defender, usually the team's best, playing one-on-one against Kennedy.

Kennedy began his education as a first grader in an all-white private school, and he went to that school through the tenth grade. He was six-foot-four that year and averaged 30 points a game against what he considered inferior competition—white kids. He knew that if he was going to become a college player and then a professional, he would have to gain more experience by competing against the best—blacks—so, bucking the rigid divisions of the Deep South, Andy transferred from an all-white private school to the 70 percent black public school, Louisville High School, a football power that had won three straight state championships but had finished 1 and 23 in basketball the year before. At Louisville High, Kennedy was one of four white basketball players in the entire conference.

Because Kennedy was coming from private school, critics scoffed at his 30-points-a-game average. "Who was he playing against? Nobody!" was the refrain. He also heard the bad rap being whispered behind his back: "He's good, but he's too slow to play with the black boys."

In his first public school game, against a predominantly black team, Andy Kennedy proved himself to his black teammates, his coach, and his critics. He was 22 for 27 from the field. He scored 54 points. This was before the 3-point rule. If that had been in effect, he would have scored over 60 that night. Whenever people said that the white players couldn't play, Kennedy took it personally. Most times he would go head-to-head with the other team's best player, a black player, and end up with the better statistics. That year, his junior year, he averaged 31 points a game, leading Louisville High to a sixteen-victory season and into the district finals.

Complicating Kennedy's career was the fact that he had to play for four different coaches in his four years of high school. He had a freshman coach in private school, and then in tenth grade played for the varsity coach. When he transferred, he was playing for a third coach who left "for personal reasons" at the end of the year, and the school principal was forced to hire another coach.

In choosing that coach for what was to be Kennedy's senior year, the principal, who was also the football coach, really gave the basketball team the shaft, Kennedy felt. Applying for the job were coaches with twenty years' experience, men panting to switch to Louisville High just to be Kennedy's coach that year. If nothing else, the new coach would have the opportunity to meet some of the most famous college coaches in the nation, who had flocked to the school gym to watch Kennedy play his junior year and were sure to return. High school coaches know that sometimes, if a college wants a player badly enough, it will take the player's coach along as an assistant. That's how some college coaches move up. And Kennedy was good enough to make that a possibility. But the principal/football coach picked as a coach a man who had never coached at the high school level. Coming into a new situation is tough enough, but the new coach was coming into a situation where the eyes of the college basketball world were upon him and his team. What new, inexperienced coach wouldn't feel intimidated? But with Kennedy leading the way, Louisville still managed to finish 22–6, reaching the state finals before losing, and Kennedy was being touted as Pete Maravich reincarnate.

Kennedy was named Converse Top-Ten All American. He was a Parade All American. He was named to the Gatorade Circle of Champions and proclaimed Player of the Year for the state of Mississippi. Kennedy was chosen for the Dapper Dan Tournament, a three-day affair with the top twenty-five high school basketball players participating in a three-day tournament.

Kennedy was also a good student, averaging 3.2 out of 4. On his ACTs he scored a satisfactory 18. Kennedy could have gone to any college in the country.

He had received his first recruitment letter when he was in the ninth grade. It was from Georgia Tech. The possibility of his getting a scholarship was raised by Coach Dale Brown of LSU when Kennedy was in the eleventh grade. Scholarships can't officially be offered until senior year, but the letter made it clear the scholarship could be available for Kennedy when the time came.

The summer before his senior year, Kennedy attended the B/C All Star camp in Millersville, Georgia. B/C stands for Bolton and Cronover, the two entrepreneurs who own it. The B/C camp, like the Five Star camp in Pittsburgh and the Athletes for Better Education camp in Princeton, New Jersey, allows high school basketball stars to come together in one place for three days and play against each other, not only to gain the experience but to allow college coaches and their assistants to sit on their kiesters in one spot and evaluate a large selection of the best high schoolers available to them. There was no teaching at the camp. It was just a showcase for talent.

Kennedy didn't really want to go. At $320, it seemed too expensive a tuition for the privilege of going to a meat market to play in hundred-degree heat and sleep in bunkhouses that weren't air-conditioned. Still, he knew that if he didn't go, he would risk not getting mentioned in the national scouting report services, which are read by all the college coaches.

If he hadn't gone to the camp, he still would have played college ball, but chances are he wouldn't have ended up All American.

There were 425 basketball players in camp—it *was* a meat market. Hundreds of college coaches and assistants and other free-lance bird dogs were in attendance. Four games a day were scheduled. Every kid had a number. Kennedy's number was 62. After three days, everyone was talking about number 62.

At the rousing finale of the camp session, an all-star team comprised of the top twenty kids is chosen, ten players for each side, and each player gets to perform in either the first and third or the second and fourth quarters. Among the players in that game were Eric Manual, who went to Kentucky; Felton Spencer, who went to Louisville (pronounced Louieville); and Larry Rembart, who went to the University of Alabama at Birmingham. All twenty players in the game ended up at major colleges.

Kennedy scored 17 points, led his team in scoring, and was named the Most Valuable Player of the game. After that came the deluge.

Kennedy had always dreamed of being recruited. He had heard stories about coaches calling kids fifteen times a day. He never believed those stories—until he got home and the phone didn't stop ringing. A coach would call, he'd hang up, the phone would ring again. It was another coach on the line. His dream was turning into something less. It was like getting a job at a chocolate factory.

He was also being deluged with mail—from 120 different colleges. Iowa was sending him a letter every day. He was getting hand-written notes from all the colleges in the Southeast Conference.

Three of the colleges offered him something other than

a scholarship. One told him they would give him an unspecified amount of cash, a new car, and a summer job at $22 an hour. Another told him, "Andy, we'll take care of you. When you get up here, we have a guy who can give you a deal on a new car."

Another school offered a new car and payments of $200 a week.

The offers were tempting, but Kennedy figured, "If they offer me something, they can just as easily take it away." He wanted to go to the situation that was best for his basketball career, not go for the money.

Kennedy's considerations were always very pragmatic. The two most lied-about things in the world, Kennedy concluded, were sex and recruiting. It didn't take all that much effort to write him a letter or to call him, he decided. For him to consider a college, the coach first would have to come to one of his games or to his home to visit him in person.

Eleven coaches came to see him at his home: Jim Valvano of North Carolina State, Bobby Cremins of Georgia Tech, Larry Brown of Kansas, Bob Boyd of Mississippi State, Wimp Sanderson of Alabama, Dale Brown of LSU, C. M. Newton of Vanderbilt, Norm Stewart of Missouri, George Raveling of Iowa, Lee Hunt of Old Miss, and Bill Foster of the University of South Carolina.

Kennedy was skeptical about going to Kansas, because he was afraid that Coach Larry Brown would leave town before he graduated. Brown told him he had promised his star, Danny Manning, that he would stay until Manning left, but since Danny was a sophomore, Andy was afraid Brown would leave him hanging for two years.

His reservation about Mississippi State, only twenty minutes from his home, was that he wanted to go to college away from home. But there was a lot of in-state pressure. Andy had been going to Mississippi State's basketball camp since he was in the eighth grade, and he knew everyone would be saying, "If they can't get Andy, who can they get?" Mississippi basketball fans were taking it for granted that Andy would be going there.

Kennedy's reservation about Georgia Tech was his fear of the consequences of going to college in a big city. He was coming from the boonies, and he didn't want to get distracted by the lights and the action of Atlanta. Also,

Atlanta had the Braves, the Hawks, and the Falcons, and Andy wanted to play for the only ticket in town.

Kennedy had always resented the fact that football ruled in the Southern states of Mississippi, Alabama, and Louisiana. He resented his principal for hiring an inexperienced basketball coach—to him a blatant attempt to keep the basketball team from taking some glory away from the football team. He resented that during his basketball games fans were asking each other, "Who's going to be playing quarterback next year?" He wanted to get away from the Auburn versus Alabama football rivalry and from Mississippi State football. Andy Kennedy decided he wanted to go where basketball was king.

He narrowed his choice to universities from Indiana, Kentucky, and North Carolina—basketball country.

Kennedy didn't think he could take the abuse that Indiana coach Bobby Knight dished out to his players, and when he saw that Kentucky had signed up high school star Rex Chapman, he knew they would no longer be interested in him, since he and Chapman would be playing the same position, shooting guard, and were similar-type players.

The state of North Carolina remained. Coach Dean Smith runs the show at the University of North Carolina, and it's a rare player who doesn't heed the siren song when Dean Dean beckons, but with Kennedy, Smith made the mistake of waiting until too late in the game. When Smith asked him. "Would you like to come to Carolina for a visit?" Kennedy hesitated. Athletes are allowed to visit five schools, and Andy had committed to four already; he wasn't sure whether Carolina should be his fifth. So his response was, "Let me get back to you." The Carolina people apparently felt insulted. Said Kennedy, "After that they were nice, but they felt, 'If you don't want to come to Carolina right off the bat, we don't want you, because we can get whoever we want.' "

That left North Carolina State. If the coaching staff could convince Kennedy that N.C. State was right for him, they would pluck one of the juicier plums in the recruiting orchard.

State had made the important good first impression, and they had made it early. Assistant Coach Tom Abatamarco had contacted Kennedy right after his MVP performance at the B/C camp. He then bombarded Kennedy with calls and letters. The calls were never long, five to ten minutes, but the goal was to make Andy Kennedy a buddy. "Hey, Andy, what's going on? I was thinking of you," Abatamarco would say. "I wanted to call to let you know that." The avalanche of letters told Andy what they had told Kenny Drummond: that N.C. State was a fine academic institution, that it had a large gym filled with screaming fans, that the team played on TV a lot, that it had a winning tradition, and that Coach Valvano was one of the best coaches in the country—a winning coach with a winning attitude, a coach who cared about his players.

Abatamarco visited Andy's home a half dozen times, telling him, "We play in front of great crowds. You'll go to Duke and Carolina and play before twenty-two thousand people. Every game is exciting. We have two hundred people come to our practices."

Abatamarco told Kennedy, "We are going to challenge for the national championship next year. We have Chris Washburn coming back, along with Charles Shackleford, and we have Mike Giomi coming in from Indiana." Kennedy mulled that six-eleven, six-eleven, and six-ten front line, with all three of them legitimate pro prospects. He whistled. He had to admit it was some front line.

Abatamarco also impressed Kennedy with State's schedule of televised games. Seventeen times the Pack was going to be on national TV. Seventeen times pro scouts could watch him play from the comfort of their living rooms.

Abatamarco also told Kennedy the one thing he wanted to hear. "Andy, if you come to State, you'll play."

More than anything else, that's what the recruit wants to hear, that he's going to play. In a recruit's mind, the issue of whether he's going to play or not is paramount. If he doesn't get to play, nothing else matters. If he doesn't get to play, being on TV means nothing, playing for championships means nothing. If he doesn't get to play, he doesn't make it to the pros.

When Coach Valvano visited the Kennedy home, he picked up on that theme, employing his enthusiastic, rat-tat-tat oratory. He told Kennedy, "You'll get to play on a national contender. We play in the ACC, play on national TV all the time, and both our guards, Nate McMillan and Ernie Myers, are graduating. You'll get the chance to play a lot of quality minutes as a freshman, something a lot of players don't."

Kennedy was sitting on the edge of his chair, spellbound. He liked Valvano's intensity. He liked the way Valvano related to his parents. He especially liked what Valvano was telling him. It was what Kennedy wanted to hear. N.C. State appeared to be an ideal situation for him. Kennedy, an avid basketball fan, knew the names, classes, and statistics of most of the players from the top college teams. Behind McMillan and Myers, Kennedy knew, were Walker Lambiotte, who at six-foot-seven played more like a small forward, and Vinny del Negro, who never played either his freshman or sophomore year. Kennedy had watched State play on TV fifteen times the year before, and he had never seen del Negro take off his sweatpants. Kennedy told himself, "If they're not playing him, he obviously can't play."

Valvano told Kennedy, "Vinny isn't going to be a player here. He's just a good kid, the kind of kid we want in our program, a good guy who isn't going to cause any problems."

Kennedy was impressed that without saying it in so many words, it appeared that Valvano was telling him he would be starting at the shooting guard position if he came to N.C. State.

Valvano and Kennedy went outside to shoot hoops into the basket in the driveway. Valvano could still hit a shot, Kennedy noticed. It was a reminder that he had once been a very good college player. As they shot around, they bantered and joked, and Andy could see that Valvano was a player's coach, the type of coach he could be tight with.

Kennedy asked Valvano about the Chris Washburn stereo theft incident. Valvano assured him that it had been blown way out of proportion. "He went into a football player's room and borrowed his stereo, used it for six days, and didn't return it," Valvano said. "That's all. It wasn't like he was stealing it. He just borrowed it."

After a three-hour visit, Valvano left. Kennedy told himself, "Let's be realistic. There's Bennie Bolton and Walker and Vinny. Maybe I won't start, but I should play fifteen to twenty minutes a game, and we should win the national championship. Nobody will be able to touch us."

As noted, under NCAA rules, a high school player is allowed to visit five college campuses, and Kennedy arranged to visit N.C. State, Mississippi State, Georgia Tech, LSU, and Kansas, in that order.

When Kennedy visited N.C. State, he got the royal treatment. It was mid-October. He attended an N.C. State football game with several of the players, and it was like a dream come true to see the fans in the football stands coming over to ask the players about the coming basketball season.

After the game, most of the players on the basketball team went over to Coach Valvano's home. It looked to Kennedy like a big party, and he was impressed that Valvano and the players seemed so chummy, that if a player had a problem, he could go to Valvano, have dinner with him, and talk about problems.

That evening Valvano took Kennedy to visit Reynolds Coliseum. As they stood at midcourt, in the shadow of 12,000 empty seats, a lone spotlight shone on the pair. Wafting down from the public address system came the sounds of a basketball game in progress.

Kennedy, gazing at the empty fire-red seats and picturing them filled with fans rooting for him, was listening to the final minutes of a North Carolina State–North Carolina basketball game for the ACC championship.

Only seconds remained on the clock. The score was tied. With the ACC championship at stake, the announcer was describing how the Wolfpack was rushing the ball upcourt, trying to get one last shot off before the final buzzer.

Kennedy heard the announcer say, "With a chance to win it all, Bolton passes into the middle to Washburn. Washburn throws it into the corner to Andy Kennedy." The chills began a fast climb up Kennedy's back. The announcer continued, "Kennedy lets fly from way out. I think it is . . . it is. It's GOOOOOOOOOD! The Wolfpack win it. The Wolfpack win the ACC championship. Andy Kennedy has done it." And it was almost as though

Andy Kennedy *had* done it. He stood there grinning while the sounds of Packmania roared through his head.

The rest of the visit was a blur. There was a frat party into the night. Kennedy, from a town the size of a packed house at Reynolds Coliseum, felt as though an entire town had been stuffed into that frat house. His hosts that evening—Mike Giomi, Walker Lambiotte, and Vinny del Negro—seemed like great guys. The girls who came over to say hello seemed like great girls.

The following morning, a Sunday, Valvano met Andy at the airport for breakfast. As a parting inducement, Valvano told Kennedy, "If you come to N.C. State, we won't bring in another player to play your position until your junior year."

On the plane home, Kennedy thought, "The facilities are nice, the guys are cool, and they say I'm going to play." He felt "up" about State.

The next week he visited Mississippi State, and the week after that Georgia Tech. He then cancelled his visits to Kansas and LSU. The recruitment grind had gotten to him. He hadn't intended to commit during the November signing period, but he was sick of the late-night phone calls from coaches. Also, his senior-year basketball season was about to start, and he felt he needed to get back into the gym.

Kennedy had to commit to a college between November 14 and November 21 or else he would have to wait the entire basketball season and sign at the end in April. There were added pressures on him to sign up from the college coaches, who didn't want to have to keep up the pressure for another six months. There were good arguments for him to sign early. He was being offered a four-year scholarship unconditionally. What if he hurt himself during his senior-year season? What if he had a sub-par season? Most important, what if State found somebody else?

During the recruiting process, a coach makes up a list of four or five players he wants at each position. If a college goes after five top shooting guards, the first one that commits is the one the college accepts. Hypothesize that N.C. State is recruiting both Andy and Rex Chapman. Maybe the coach wants Rex because he's a tad better. But if Andy commits first, the coach has to take

Andy, because if he refuses Andy, there's always the possibility that Rex will go to another college, and then the coach is left holding an empty sack. Likewise, if the player waits too long and one of the other players on the list signs up first, then the player is no longer desired by the coach. It's cat and mouse, though sometimes no one is quite certain who is the cat and who is the mouse.

Considering all of the alternatives, Andy Kennedy—shrewd, knowledgeable, and intelligent—decided to sign a letter of intent with Jim Valvano and North Carolina State during the fall signing period.

Kennedy told himself, "I believe in Coach Valvano. He's going to give me my chance."

Drum and Andy Kennedy weren't Valvano's only prizes. In addition, The Wolfpack signed Brian Howard, a six-foot-six-inch 200-pound forward from Winston-Salem, North Carolina, A *USA Today* honorable mention All American and named by the *Basketball Times* as one of the top twenty small forward prospects in the nation; and Avie Lester, a six-foot-nine, 220-pounder from Roxboro, North Carolina, another monsterchild in Chris Washburn's mold, a bull who could dunk on anyone. Lester was listed by the *Basketball Times* as one of the top twelve power forwards among the high school ranks.

Valvano's talent pool for 1986-87 would be awesome. He'd have two entire teams of high school All Americans. He'd have talent rarely seen on a college basketball court. He'd have a team everyone would be talking about for years.

8

Wash Burns State

When Kenny Drummond and Andy Kennedy arrived at the North Carolina State campus to begin their initial year at State, whatever hopes they were harboring for a national championship took a serious hit when center Chris Washburn decided not to return to school and to head for the NBA instead.

Since coming to N.C. State two years earlier, Washburn must have kept Valvano and his coaching staff up nights worrying what their star would get into next and how to keep him out of trouble, out of the press, and out of jail. Valvano did as much for Chris Washburn as one human being can do for another, guiding him, harboring him, protecting him, fathering him, keeping him happy. But despite all his best efforts, and reportedly after dozens of affirmations by Washburn to Valvano that he would stay in school and finish out his college career at State, only days after N.C. State lost to Kansas in the Final Eight of the NCAA championships in March 1986, heavy speculation began that Chris Washburn would skip his junior and senior years at State, take the hard cash, and turn pro.

One teammate suggested that Washburn's departure resulted from his disappointment at the loss in the NCAAs. State had led by 5 points with only eight minutes to play, and after Kansas hit basket after basket, unanswered by State's exhausted defenders, the Wolfpack was defeated. As Valvano's style was to play the starters most of the way in the big games, by the fourth quarter they were huffing hard. At the five-minute-to-go mark, reportedly they were running up and down the court at barely three-quarter speed. Nevertheless, Valvano apparently was hesitant about taking the starters out, even for a short rest. He must have felt the other players were untested, and he was loath to use them. One of the players commented, "If he had used some other players for just two or three minutes, let everybody else get their rest, then maybe we could have won it." But he didn't, the team lost, and Washburn, for one, apparently was angered at the loss.

After the N.C. State players returned to Raleigh and resumed classes, it was obvious to his teammates that Wash had disappeared from campus. Nobody saw him for about a week and a half. Then all of a sudden he and his parents arrived in a truck, backed it up to the driveway of the College Inn, and proceeded to load all his possessions into the truck. That's when his teammates knew for sure that Chris Washburn was leaving.

The next day Washburn's mother called Valvano and told him he was turning pro. And that was the last his teammates saw of Chris Washburn—until the summertime.

Freshman center Charles Shackleford had tried to talk Washburn out of leaving. Shackleford knew that N.C. State had the potential to go all the way if Washburn stayed. But Shackleford's efforts came too late.

Washburn was feeling the pressure to turn pro. He was being advised that it would be in his best interests to leave college and turn pro, that if he turned pro he could make millions of dollars. He was told he would be one of the first three picks in the draft if he turned pro. All of which was accurate. He was also told, "If you get hurt playing in college, you'll lose all that money." Which was also true.

All Valvano might be able to counter that with was, "Chris, stay for me. You owe it to me," although whether he ever said that is anyone's guess.

But Washburn thought like a pro. Loyalty to his coach or to his teammates wasn't as important as trailing the cash. That was where it was at. Ever since the ninth grade, Chris Washburn had thought like a professional, with his eyes on that bottom line, going wherever he could be helped the most.

Moreover, he had to know that his coaches and advisers had always treated him as a professional, that he was a commodity. Going to the pros was just one more step in his professional career. Except this time the reward would be a contract worth seven figures.

Washburn was chosen third by the Golden State Warriors in the 1986 NBA draft, behind Brad Daugherty of Carolina and Lenny Bias of Maryland.

Only twenty years old, Washburn signed a multi-year contract worth $750,000 a year. A teammate remembers Washburn's triumphant return to Raleigh that summer after he signed his contract and received his signing bonus.

"Wash returned driving a hundred-and-ten-thousand-dollar black Mercedes," the teammate remembered. "It had windshield wipers on the lights, a four thousand–watt stereo system, a red telephone to go with the red interior. Aw man, he had a computerlike calculator that he carried with him that opened the doors, controlled the lights, turned on the stereo, from anywhere. We would be walking upstairs, and he would be messing with the radio. Boy, I have never seen a Mercedes like that in my life! He told me he paid one hundred ten thousand dollars. It was brand-new. It had no license tags, just the thirty-day sticker on the back. He drove it from New York, where he got it. We couldn't believe it.

"It was huge. You know how most Mercedeses have numbers on them like 450SL or 300D. This one didn't have any number on. He took us for a spin—we went to St. Augustine College to play a game; the seats warmed up and vibrated. When we arrived, everybody knew it was Chris. He had a crowd of people looking at that car. That car was bad. *Bad!* If you had seen his car, you'd know what I'm saying."

With a $110,000 car, newfound wealth, and the cities of San Francisco and Oakland as his playground, Chris Washburn had the free time and big money to feed his drug habit. Soon after reporting to the Golden State Warriors, he reportedly began showing up late for practice and then missing games, then when he tested positive for cocaine, he was suspended and sent—finally—to a drug rehabilitation clinic.

The Warriors gave up on him—a team doesn't trade the number three pick in the nation unless you believe the cause hopeless—trading Washburn to the Atlanta Hawks, where again he showed awesome ability and again tested positive for cocaine. The jury is still out on

Chris Washburn. A serious question remains whether The Washer, still in his prime, will ever live up to his magnificent potential.

In addition to Washburn, another N.C. State fixture left the scene before Kenny Drummond and Andy Kennedy arrived on campus. Tom Abatamarco, Valvano's right-hand man and chief recruiter since their days together at Iona, took a coaching job at Lamar University. Abatamarco had kept after Drum to go to State and had written or called Andy every single day for a month. But when he left, neither recruit ever heard a word from him again. From Abatamarco's position, there was no reason for him to call. He was moving on to another school, leaving his old associations behind. To him, basketball was a business. Drummond and Kennedy were old business. But to the two recruits, Abatamarco had set himself up as a "buddy." And their buddy had snubbed them, and that hurt, even if just a little.

9

Getting in Shape

Toward the end of August, the members of the North Carolina State varsity basketball team began dribbling back to school for six weeks of conditioning, to begin officially September 1. When Andy Kennedy arrived, he was surprised to find that unlike some conditioning programs, which are run with the precision of military training, the N.C. State program consisted only of mandatory sessions of running sprints and longer distances four afternoons a week under the direction of Assistant Coach Ed McLean. State had a weight coach, named Wright Wayne—some of the players mistakenly called him Wayne Wright—but there was no mandatory weight training. The only aspect of training that was mandatory was a requirement that each player at the end of the training period be able to run three miles in under twenty-one minutes. If a player failed to do that, the penalty was that he would have to run the distance again.

The playing of basketball during this period was voluntary. The players came down to the old Carmichael Gymnasium in the mornings for informal, but hard-nosed five-on-five pickup games of mayhem, where everyone, including—especially—the big men, tried to play like Michael Jordan. Charles Shackleford, the six-foot-ten-inch sophomore center, would bring the ball up the court, dribble between his legs, and shoot twenty-footers. Opposing players would constantly get into fierce shouting matches, because the defensive team was responsible for calling fouls. Inevitably a defensive player would make a call that an offensive player thought niggling or wrong, so when the ball changed hands, the other team would even the score by cheating on the next call and insisting that their play be honored.

Kenny Drummond was taken aback one morning when Quentin Jackson got into a shouting match with Mike Giomi, the transfer from Indiana. Jackson, a junior with a sharp tongue and a quick wit, made a call that offended Giomi, and Giomi called Jackson all kinds of names. As Jackson went to throw the basketball at him, Giomi pushed him hard in the chest and sent him reeling into the wall under the basket. Drummond, who had come from a team where all the players on the team liked and respected one another, saw this bickering as an ominous sign.

Andy Kennedy found out what it was like to be the hotshot new kid on a team. Whenever he played in the pickup games, the other players checked out his game, trying to find out what he could do and what he couldn't do and what kind of person he was. When he and Quentin Jackson found themselves in the same game, Jackson, at six-foot-one, demanded that he guard Kennedy, six-foot-seven. Whenever Kennedy took him into the post, Jackson bumped him, fouled him, and kicked him, talking bad to him the whole time, trying to take his heart, trying to make Kennedy give up so he wouldn't be a threat to him. Kennedy was seeing the same thing that Drummond was seeing: At N.C. State, the emphasis didn't seem to be on team spirit, as it was on other teams. Rather, it was every man for himself.

In the afternoon came conditioning, and a typical session began with calisthenics—jumping jacks and stretching exercises, which were done at half speed, if at all. Then came jumping rope. Here were talented athletes, guys who wanted to play in the pros, and most of them were unable to swing the rope around without getting hit in the back of the head. Coach McLean would yell, "Fellas, it's real simple. Just twirl it. Twirl it and jump," but players only managed to inflict red welts on their necks. After about thirty seconds, he'd yell, "That's it, forget it," and skip to the running part of the program.

Helping Coach McLean was a student volunteer by the name of John Simonds. As a high schooler from Durham, Simonds had been a basketball star until the ninth grade, when he found his true love, running track, and by his senior year he had become the finest prep cross country runner in the state of North Carolina. He had been training on the sly with the Duke University track team since his sophomore year, fully expecting to matriculate at Duke and run varsity track, but in December of his senior year, a young girl in a yellow VW bug ran a red light and smashed into the side of his car at fifty miles an hour as he was driving to school, injuring his back so badly he could no longer run cross country. His doctors expressly forbade him to run track, but they didn't say he couldn't play basketball, so Simonds, six-foot-three, joined the basketball team of his tiny Christian academy (240 students) as its playmaker. He led it to a 22–4 season, including a spectacular upset of Wake Christian Academy of Raleigh, the biggest private school in the area (1,500 students).

Simonds went to N.C. State, not Duke, because it was cheaper and also because his only possibility of participating in college athletics was in basketball, and N.C. State had the basketball team that had captured everyone's imagination. He never forgot the night in March of his senior year when State beat Houston's Phi Slamma Jamma to win the 1983 NCAA championship. He told himself, "I want to play basketball for Coach Valvano," whom he idolized. Simonds knew that as a player Valvano had been a scrappy, smart guard, an overachiever who led Rutgers to a great record when it had no right to be that good. Simonds had just done the same thing in high school. Simonds knew that Valvano was his kind of coach.

At State, Simonds spent hours in the gym, shooting on his own, looking for a way to become involved with the team, with the ultimate daydream of convincing Coach Valvano that he was a good enough player to put on the team. It was a goal he never shared with anyone, because he knew its likelihood was slimmer than the new moon and just as far away. Admirably, he came within a whisker of achieving that dream.

Simonds' circuitous route toward achieving his goal began, unknown to him, when he was chosen resident assistant of Metcalf dormitory. He spent his sophomore year playing big brother to forty freshmen. At the end of that year, he attended summer school, and because of his experience, continued as dorm R.A. Coach Valvano, meanwhile, had rented Metcalf dormitory for the three weeks of his basketball camp; purely by coincidence, his campers were assigned to Simonds' dorm. Coach McLean, who was in charge of Valvano's camp, needed someone to make sure all the campers were assigned dorm rooms and got their keys. Simonds was the one he chose for the job.

The two hit it off immediately. Simonds worked hard in the dorm and impressed McLean with his character and his basketball ability. For the second week-long camp, Simonds was hired as counselor as well as dorm monitor. He was paid $150 a week—for a student, that was a lot of money.

By the third week, Simonds and Coach McLean had become close. They went bar hopping together, and during talks, John told McLean about his track experience and about what had happened to him. By the end of the third week, Coach McLean had invited Simonds to be part of the basketball program in the fall. As a start, he asked if Simonds would be interested in helping him train the players. Simonds was ecstatic. It was a dream come true—rather, part of a dream. He told McLean, "I have to tell you. I want a chance to play." McLean told him, "If you work hard, you can practice with the team, and though it might not be this year, the following year we'll give you a shot at making the team."

Simonds told himself, "All right, John. You're on your way."

Simonds, the track star, was shocked at how poorly the varsity basketball players ran. In the forty-yard dash, only one player, Kenny Drummond, was fast. He ran a 4.3. Sophomore Walker Lambiotte ran it in 4.5, and junior Vinny del Negro ran a 4.7, acceptable times. Everyone else was over 5 seconds; Charles Shackleford did it in 5.5 seconds. Thought Simonds, "He's one step faster than a dead man." Teviin Binns and Mike Giomi were just as slow. Simonds' evaluation: "If one of them got in a race with a pregnant woman, he'd finish third."

With Simonds standing beside him, Coach McLean would time them, all the while shaking his head. "It's just so hard," he'd say. "It's such a struggle to get these guys into shape. We have the worst athletes in the ACC. V is going to go nuts. These guys are going to come out for practice October 15, and they're going to die, and he's going to go crazy."

Drummond and Kennedy discovered something else about their new teammates during the conditioning program: Most of the players didn't take it seriously. In fact, they didn't take much in life seriously.

One time sophomore Chucky Brown stepped up to the line to run the forty. The other thirteen players were bunched up behind him. Everyone was joking, laughing, poking each other, trying to push Brown off the line. Bennie Bolton, the senior veteran, sneaked up behind Chucky and got his toe right on the back of Brown's running shoe. Chucky was an intense competitor, and he was down in a crouch, waiting for the whistle. Coach McLean was trying to hold back a laugh, because he knew what was going to happen. He shouted, "Go," and Chucky took off, but his shoe didn't leave with him. The shoe went flying up in the air, and Chucky went flying spread-eagle on his face onto the track.

Everyone laughed so hard Coach McLean had to call off practice. They spent the next fifteen minutes lying on the track laughing, beating their fists on the ground. The football players, who were practicing nearby on another part of the field, were looking at them, shaking their heads. Coach McLean was shaking his head, too. "It's so hard," he said. "It's such a struggle."

Another time, Coach McLean had the players running up a fairly steep hill through the woods. They had to work hard to get up it, but you would have thought they were running up Mount Everest, they were complaining so hard. "Coach Mac, you're trying to kill us," Kelsey Weems, a sophomore guard, yelled at him. "Yep, Kelsey," said McLean, "I think you're going to die. I don't think you'll live to play this year. You ought to just go home right now. Call your mom and tell her to come get you."

On the way down the hill, they put on a show for McLean. "I'm going to show Coach McLean this time," Quentin Jackson yelled. The next time they ran up the hill, they were running even slower. "I can't make it one more time, coach. I'm going to quit," Kelsey said. McLean laughed. "Okay, turn your stuff in when you get back," he said. "We'll get somebody else."

The first time the players were timed in the mile, Vinny del Negro did it in five minutes, with Walker Lambiotte twenty seconds behind him. Andy Kennedy and Mike Giomi were able to finish. Kenny Drummond finished, but his time was pathetically slow. Charles Shackleford couldn't complete a half mile. Neither could Teviin Binns, Chucky Brown, Kelsey Weems, Quentin Jackson, Brian Howard, or Kenny Poston.

Coach McLean told them, "V is going to run you guys into the ground because you're not in shape. You're just not making the effort. It's only a mile. It's not that hard to do."

The players didn't seem to care. They stood there, panting and giggling, poking each other, stepping on each other's sneakers.

The capper came on the day the players had to run the three-mile course. They knew that Coach McLean was going to give the times to Coach Valvano. That afternoon all of the players piled into a van, and Coach McLean drove them around the hourglass-shaped course. He pointed out exactly where they were to turn because, as he told John Simonds, "You have to spell it out to them."

McLean assigned Simonds the task of waiting at the key intersection to make sure the players knew exactly where to turn. He said, "John, when they come up to you, tell them to take a left." McLean left Simonds at the spot, and while Simonds waited for the players to make their appearance, he walked over to a nearby apartment complex and borrowed a lounge chair from the deck of one of the units.

About fifteen minutes later, the first group of runners came into view. Vinny del Negro, Walker Lambiotte, and Andy Kennedy were neck and neck, with Mike Giomi ten steps behind them, puffing hard. They were sticking to the course, and as they ran by Simonds, they slapped him five and made the left as they were instructed.

About 240 yards behind came the black players, who knew there was no way they could finish in the time allotted if they stuck to the course. Instead, they created shortcuts wherever they could, running through a cow pasture owned by the agricultural school. As they neared Simonds, he could see them cutting through backyards, running through swing sets, running low through grass three feet high, trying to keep the white guys from seeing them and looking around for Coach McLean in the van.

Quentin Jackson was leading the way as they came through the field, and Simonds could hear everyone yelling about watching out for cows. Someone else yelled to watch out for pigs and dogs. Someone else warned of snakes and bees. All of them were bent over and laughing.

When they got to Simonds, who was sitting at the neck of the hourglass, instead of turning left and attempting the second, longer loop, they cut directly across the neck through King Village, the married and foreign students' housing, cutting about a mile and a half off the run. They had a little time to kill while they waited for their teammates, and most of them stopped in front of a tall bush in the middle of the housing complex to urinate. Here were a half dozen skyscrapers wearing sweatshirts with "N.C. State Basketball" on them, standing in front of that bush and watering it with impunity as moms and their kids and students passed nearby.

After they finished, they hid behind a row of cars, waiting for the white guys to start back toward the finish line. In time, they could see the white players come puffing past at a distance. Simonds stood on the road, cheering them on. As soon as they passed, the black players piled out from their hiding places. It was three-quarters of a mile back to the finish line, and they took off running, again cutting corners, running across a creek, anything to save a step or two.

And notwithstanding all that, they still barely made it. The last two in were Charles Shackleford and Teviin Binns. The twin towers, Shack and Tev, crossed the line in less than twenty-one minutes, but Coach McLean knew they had cheated in some way because they were barely sweating. Still, when Coach McLean looked at his stopwatch, it read: twenty minutes, fifteen seconds. He never thought they would make it, but they did. He couldn't believe it! There had to be an explanation. He turned to Simonds and said, "John, did they cut any corners?"

Shackleford and Binns both looked at him hard. Simonds said, "Coach, I told them, 'Turn there, and they turned.' "

They had turned all right, but right through King Village. McLean kept asking Simonds, "Are you sure they turned?" Simonds kept saying, "Yeah, coach, I saw them. It was unbelievable, coach. You wouldn't have believed it!" All of which was true.

Everyone went in and took showers, and they were all slapping Simonds high fives. Shackleford and Binns offered to take him out to dinner. They were loving the idea that they didn't have to run that far and, even better, that they had pulled something on McLean and hadn't got caught.

Coach McLean sent the times in to Coach Valvano. Valvano must have been thinking, "Boy, do I have a team that is ready to run, run, run."

10

V Comes Back to Town

For those first six weeks of training, John Simonds and the rest of the players saw Coach Valvano only once for a ten-minute team meeting. From mid-August to mid-October, Valvano was out on the road, flying around the country, visiting his top high school prospects. Under NCAA rules, Valvano wasn't allowed to conduct basketball practice until October 15.

The players had a fall break from October 10 to 15. From October 10 to 12, Nike, the company that manufactures basketball shoes and apparel, hosted a sports clinic at N.C. State. High school coaches paid $300 to stay for three days to hear lectures on the sport of basketball from the masters, dozens of the top basketball coaches, the Big Name Coaches. About the only names who weren't there were North Carolina's Dean Smith, who is affiliated with Converse, and Mike Krzyzewski of Duke and Bobby Knight of Indiana, who are with Adidas.

Coach McLean recruited Simonds to play host and chauffeur to the visiting coaches. One of the coaches he took to the airport after his lecture was complete was Lou Carnesecca, the coach of St. John's University in Queens, New York. During the ride, Coach Carnesecca was in a festive mood. Valvano hadn't shown up yet, and Carnesecca wanted to tease him a little. He told Simonds, "When you see V, tell him I said to keep more meatballs and provalone cheese on the bar in the hospitality suite."

"Coach, I'll tell him," Simonds promised.

Simonds dropped Carnesecca off at the airport and drove back to the clinic, returning to the hospitality suite to down a few beers with the other coaches, including Eddie Sutton of Kentucky, Jim Boeheim of Syracuse, and Abe Lemons of Oregon State. Simonds was feeling the buzz of the beer and the Big Time when Valvano walked in the door for the first time.

Valvano immediately singled out Dick Vitale, a former coach and now a commentator for ESPN, and began ragging on him. Valvano said, "I remember this about you, Dick, the losingest coach in the NBA, and here you are commenting on television, after you got fired in the NBA. What do you have going for you, you old glass-eyed rascal?"

Vitale made a silly comment about Coach Valvano's nose, and Valvano went over to the bar and filled a glass with Sutter Home white Zinfandel, his favorite table wine. He then walked over to the roast beef and was attacking it with the serving fork when Simonds walked over to say hello. Valvano had met McLean's recruit during the basketball camps and had liked his attitude and his dedication, and it gave Simonds great pleasure whenever Valvano ran his a hand through his hair and hollered, "Johnnnnnnnny," whenever they passed.

Unfortunately, Simonds had been pounding the Bud too hard. As he approached Valvano, he put his arm around the coach's shoulder and, in an overly loud voice, said, "*Lou* told me to ask you, 'Where are the meatballs and provalone?' "

It was as if someone had farted in church. All the coaches who had been chattering and bantering suddenly halted in midsentence. When Simonds said "Lou," the fork Valvano was using to stab the roast beef stopped in midair. He looked at Simonds and asked, "What did you say?" Simonds repeated it: "*Lou* told me to tell you . . ." and when the veins started popping out in Valvano's neck, Simonds realized he had made a faux pas. "Oh my God, I just spat on the Devil," he thought to himself.

Valvano looked at Simonds and then looked back at his friends. He said, "Fellows, keep talking," and they did. He said to Simonds, "Do you want to work for me?" Simonds said, "Yes, sir." Valvano said, "You want to play for me?" Simonds said, "Very much so." Valvano said, "If I ever hear you call one of my friends by his first name again, you will rue the day you ever saw my face."

Simonds looked ready to cry. Valvano then started to laugh. He said, "I cannot believe that you called Coach

Carnesecca Lou. I don't even call him Lou. I can't believe it. One of my own guys calling him Lou, like you and he were fast friends all your life."

For a few days after that, Simonds assiduously avoided Valvano. Once practice started, if Valvano walked over to his side of the court, he walked to the other side. The players knew it, too. Mike Giomi had been in attendance that day at the clinic and told the rest of them what had happened, adding a little spice to the story, telling them Simonds had offered Valvano a beer and then had delivered the fateful line: "*Lou* said . . ." Giomi supplied all of Valvano's hand motions, and while he told the story, the other players fell on the floor laughing.

After that, if Simonds was out on the court and Valvano walked by, as Simonds tried to make himself invisible, one of them would yell, "Hey, Lou, come back. Where are you going, Lou? Hey, Lou! LOU?"

Kenny Drummond, Andy Kennedy, and the other two freshmen, Brian Howard and Avie Lester, got a taste of Coach Valvano's flair for the dramatic when the official start of practice was celebrated the evening of October 14 with what was called Midnight Madness. Valvano had scheduled a 9:30 P.M. exhibition game at Reynolds Coliseum between the NBA's Atlanta Hawks, with former N.C. State star Spud Webb playing against the Cleveland Cavaliers and former Carolina star Brad Daugherty. The 12,400-seat arena was sold out.

After the game, which ended minutes before midnight, the crowd remained in its seats. The band blasted out the school fight song, the local TV cameras rolled, and exactly at the stroke of midnight, Jim Valvano and the fourteen members of the N.C. State basketball team ran out onto the floor and played a twenty-minute scrimmage. Everyone got to play. Everyone played run and gun. Everyone on the team was happy. It was the first, and last, time all season long.

11

Practice Begins

Everyone was on time, taped, and ready that first day of practice. That was also to be a first and last. At four o'clock sharp, Coach Valvano swaggered in, wearing flaming red sweat clothes made by Nike and, like a drill sergeant meeting his new recruits, trying to look mean. Following closely behind him, like puppies behind their master, were two of his assistant coaches, Dick Stewart and Ray Martin.

Coach Valvano wasted little time. He began, "All right, everybody on the line," meaning the endcourt line, and he had the players sprinting full court, back and forth. He then broke them into two lines and had them pass the ball back and forth as they bolted down the court and back. All the while he kept up a line of chatter. He said, "All right, fellas, we have a new season. We're going somewhere this season. Last season, it was the Final Eight. We were up by 5 points against Kansas. Wash had a chance to put us up by ten, and I'm thinking to myself, 'We're going to the Final Four,' but he misses a shot and the Kansas fans, they start chanting, 'Rock, Chalk, Jayhawks,' and the next thing I know, we're finished, and we're flying home."

He continued, "That's hard for me to swallow, guys, real hard. We gave that game away. We gave away our chance at the Final Four. That's what I work for every season, and this season it's going to be different. We're going to work hard." Then he used a phrase he would use over and over again. He said, "We're going to run the floor." And then he used another one: "And we're going to fill the lanes." He said, "I want you to think when you go to bed at night, 'Run the floor.' And when you get up, I want you to think, 'Fill the lanes.' We're going to run the floor, guys, we're going to run the floor," meaning that this year the team was going to sprint up and down the court all game long, trying to run the other team into the ground.

John Simonds stood on the sidelines listening. He knew what kind of condition the players were really in. He thought, "We're going to run the floor? We don't have five guys who can run half a mile, never mind run the floor for an entire basketball game."

That day, October 15, Valvano had his team practice for two and a half hours. He told the players, "Fellas, Tark [University of Nevada at Las Vegas Coach Jerry Tarkanian] practices for three solid hours, but I don't believe in that. We'll practice two and a half hours every day, and you'd better be able to give me one hundred and ten percent that whole time or you just won't play for me."

In the background, veteran players Charles Shackleford, Teviin Binns, Quentin Jackson, and Kelsey Weems were all cutting up, pushing and shoving each other, giggling, and not paying much attention to what Valvano was saying. And he didn't pay any attention to them either. The new players thought that odd.

Valvano continued his tough stance for the first few days. Practice was so rigorous the only thing the players were concerned with was making it through. Except for Kenny Drummond, Vinny del Negro, and Walker Lambiotte, who were in top shape, the rest of them were really sucking wind.

After running and passing drills, Valvano would stand in the middle of the court screaming, "Run the floor, fill the lanes," like a drill sergeant. He incessantly accused everyone of being lazy.

He screamed, "This game is so hard, guys; it's a hard game to play. But if you just listen to me, I'll make it easy for you. And what's our key theme? Guys, we're going to run the floor this year. We're going to fill the lanes. I'm tired of us playing hard for just one half. We come out and play strong for one half, and then we sit back on our butts for the whole second half." Some of the veteran players knew that Washburn's cocaine addiction had been one reason for this, but nobody said anything. Others who had sat on the bench the year before thought to themselves, "If you got more of your players into the game, your starters wouldn't be so exhausted in the second half."

The first week of practice consisted of running and passing drills, something every team does. The next week, the team began working on plays. Learning the plays can be difficult, even for veteran players, and considering that this team had exactly two vets, the players thought Valvano would have had more patience in the way he went about it. He had five different set plays he initially wanted them to learn, and he spent exactly three days teaching them. The first day he covered all five of the plays in about an hour. No one was picking them up. Charles Shackleford, who had played forward the year before, was playing center this year, and he spent the afternoon running around aimlessly on the court trying to look as if he knew what he was doing, while the other guys were laughing at him. Even at the end of the season, said teammates, Shackleford didn't know some of the plays. Teviin Binns, the other six-tenner, stood around looking lost. Kenny Drummond, at the point, could fake it the best, since he had to be at the top of the key most of the time no matter what the play called for. Guard Kelsey Weems hadn't a clue where to go, but he was so quick and so good an athlete that when he saw an opening, he could cut for the basket and score.

After practice that day, the players were down in the locker room, and Teviin Binns said, "Man, I just can't follow it." Andy Kennedy said, "Can you believe this? I don't know where to go."

The next day things didn't improve. Valvano told them, "When I hold up a fist, we run Play One." And then he explained the play. The squad was divided into two teams, the red team and the white team, and one team would run the play three times—slow, then medium speed, then quickly. Valvano immediately went on to the next play. "When I cross my wrists, that means Set Two." And he demonstrated that one—slow, medium, and fast. And he went on to the next play.

After demonstrating all five plays, he instructed the teams to scrimmage each other. As the red team, the team composed of probable starters, brought the ball up the court, Valvano crossed his wrists, indicating Play Two. Unfortunately, most of the players could only remember the previous play they had gone over, with but one player remembering Play Two correctly and another one free-lancing entirely, so five guys were running helter-skelter, a mad carnival of mayhem.

Valvano, frustrated, shook his head. "It's such a hard game to coach," he said. "Guys, you're just killing me. Guys, what's the problem? It's such an easy game to understand. I just went over the play a couple minutes ago. It's just a simple play."

And it was a simple play, but the fact that he had combined it with four others all in one shot made it impossible for anyone to remember. Making things worse, the players on the white team, the probable subs, angry that Valvano didn't consider them good enough to be on the red team, played an aggressive man-to-man defense against the struggling red team players. As practice droned on, the red team seemed to become more and more confused, and Valvano's temperature seemed to rise higher and higher.

"Guys, what's the fucking problem?" he screamed. "Shack, do you even know what we're playing?" Shack didn't say anything, but the other guys began giggling, because Shackleford was trying to act as if he had it down, even though it was clear from his movements that he didn't know one play from another.

Valvano barked, "Okay, let's try it again. It's real simple. You just go here, and you go here, and you go here. The pass goes here, and boom! All right?"

Drummond took the ball out and waited for Valvano to call the play again. But this time Valvano called a different play! Everyone had concentrated on remembering the play Valvano had just outlined, and now they were faced with having to remember one of the other plays. As Valvano changed plays, one could almost hear the wheels turning inside the players' heads. Again each player randomly selected a piece of one of the five plays, with Shackleford and the two forwards ending up in the same corner. Valvano was so mad he punted the basketball almost to the high ceiling of the gymnasium. The players were impressed.

Valvano reportedly screamed at Shackleford, "Charles, are you going to play? What are you thinking? Do you have shit for brains?"

Everyone was supposed to be taped and ready to practice at four P.M. sharp. Valvano was never available until then, because as athletic director he had meetings, plus he was still making trips to see recruits, plus he was in constant demand as a luncheon speaker. As a result, his time was valuable, and he flew off the handle whenever one of the players was late for practice.

Charles Shackleford, the center, was invariably five or ten minutes late, if he showed up at all. Andy Kennedy noticed that Shack usually missed the stretching, and that Valvano would scream at him but never punish him. Teviin Binns was often late and so was Kelsey Weems, and their lateness would inflame Valvano.

One afternoon Valvano was standing on the court shaking his head, saying, "Fellas, I fly all over the country during the day. I stay up late at night working. And I get to work about five-thirty every morning. But I'm at practice every day on time. You guys have one thing to do, and that's go to school and be at practice. What's so hard about being here at four o'clock? Every one of you guys gets out of class by one-thirty. How come you can't make it?" He then turned to Mike Giomi, the senior transfer from the University of Indiana. Valvano said, "Gee, tell the fellas what it was like playing for Coach Knight. If practice was called at four, what time were you taped up and on the floor?"

Giomi said, "If you weren't on the floor by three-thirty, you'd better have a serious medical excuse."

Valvano said, "Was anyone ever late for Coach Knight's practice?"

"No one would ever dream of it," Giomi said.

"What the hell does that say about me then?" Valvano complained. "I mean, I can't even get my own guys to come to practice."

* * *

As the days passed, it was apparent that learning the plays wasn't all that important, because Valvano rarely called for them. The team had several outstanding pure shooters—senior Bennie Bolton, soph Walker Lambiotte, and the new kid, Andy Kennedy—but for some reason the N.C. State offense didn't stress special plays calling for screens or double picks to free those players for open shots. Rather, the State offense preferred to utilize the natural abilities of the players, which were considerable. It played run and gun, and with Kenny Drummond at the point guard, either he would bring the ball down the court and fire away from twenty-five feet or he would throw it in to Shackleford, who would make a move to the basket. If Shackleford was closely guarded, Shack would throw it to one of the other players, who could then show off his one-on-one offensive ability. The players penalized most by this type of offense were the pure shooters, especially Bolton, who if given an opening could score with regularity from twenty feet. The problem was, if he was closely guarded, he wasn't quick enough to score on his own. Lambiotte and Kennedy, disciplined players in high school who were used to set offenses that called for them to shoot most of the time, had difficulty with an offense that called for improvisation in a crowd.

During practice Valvano would stand in the middle of the court, and the players would run up and down all around him. They would use him for a pick, sending the defensive player into him, and Valvano would be swearing as the other players tried hard to suppress laughter. Most of the time, Valvano kept up a nonstop patter as play swirled around him, yelling at the players, talking about the concepts of winning. For him, this appeared more important than plays.

"You have to have goals," he told the players one afternoon. "We have to win twenty games so we can get into the NCAA tournament." And he segued into "Run the floor" and "Fill the lanes," while the players carried out their business as though he weren't even there. Each player played his own game, fitting himself into the offense as best he could, and if it fitted into what Valvano wanted, fine, but if it didn't, the coach would scream for a little while and then they'd go and do their thing over again.

To the dismay of the freshmen on the white team, after the first few days only the members of the red team were taught new plays. The starters, the red team, would run them, and it was the whites' role to play defense against them. Each week the players on the white team had to pick up new plays solely by observation.

For some players, like Andy Kennedy, who were capable of playing more than one position, this really put them in a bind. Andy had to watch to see where all the players on the red team were going for each of the three positions on any one play. It wasn't humanly possible. Through the first few weeks of practice, he ran around the court in a daze. He hadn't learned a play since high school, and the plays were difficult to pick up just by watching. Making it even tougher was the fact that the red team players did what they could to keep the white teamers from learning the plays. One time Kennedy asked Quentin Jackson, "What do I do if I'm on the wing on a break?" Jackson told him the wrong thing, apparently on purpose. The next time the situation came up, Kennedy did what Quentin had told him and looked like an idiot.

"You wanted to win games," Kennedy said later, "but everyone was out for himself."

Valvano screamed a lot during practice, but the players knew he was in a good mood on the days he was yelling at them, so they didn't mind. On the rare days he wouldn't talk to anyone, that's when the players knew to lie low.

One afternoon Valvano had the players work on pushing the ball up the court. Shackleford didn't show and a couple of the players had minor injuries and sat out, so John Simonds got an opportunity to put on a uniform and work out with the team, as Coach McLean had promised. Simonds was supposed to pass the ball from the out-of-bounds line under the basket to Valvano, who was standing just beyond the top of the key. From there Valvano's task was to throw a long bomb pass.

Brian Howard, the freshman forward, was standing right next to Simonds, and he also had a ball. When

Valvano yelled, "Pass it," Simonds let fly and so did Howard. Valvano had turned his head to look upcourt, and when he turned back to find the ball, he saw Howard's ball, which he caught, but Simonds' ball bonged off his head.

"John," screamed Valvano, "what are you trying to do, kill me?" He swore. "My own boys are trying to kill me. They hate me." Everyone else was laughing openly.

"Okay, let's try it again." This time Howard was standing farther down the court, and he got another ball. When Valvano called for the ball, Simonds again threw one ball and Howard another. This time Howard's ball hit Valvano, but Valvano nevertheless blamed Simonds.

"Simonds, you fucking buffoon!" Valvano shouted. "Are you trying to kill me? If you hate me, say so now so I know, because I can't keep taking this. You're banging them off my head." He then heaved the offending basketball up into the stands. He mumbled, "Goddamn, I just don't know what to do with these people any more." The other players were on the floor with laughter. Howard stood on the sideline, trying to be serious, but it was apparent he thought the scene hilarious. Simonds looked pained. At his small Baptist high school, Simonds had been regarded as a model student. The faculty had awarded him the school's highest honor, voting him "the student with the most Christlike personality." Simonds was not used to being treated in any way but respectfully by faculty members. At N.C. State he was being called a "buffoon" by the coach he adored in front of the entire varsity basketball team.

After practice, in the locker room, Simonds was just on his way back from showering when Shackleford poured a pink, sticky Gatorade-like sports drink on him. Everyone thought it hilarious. Simonds was forced to go back and take another shower. But this was his initiation into the Big Time. Inwardly, he was thrilled to be in a position to get screamed at by Coach Valvano and to have a varsity basketball player think enough of him to pour a sports drink all over him. This was going to be an education he would never forget. He just knew it.

Practice ended every day at five-thirty, then the coaches left the gym. Vinny del Negro, Walker Lambiotte, Mike

Giomi, Andy Kennedy, and Simonds, the "ivory five," together with Chucky Brown and Kenny Drummond, usually remained, shooting jumpers and foul shots and working on their games. The rest of the players would either leave, or they'd work on something goofy, like Shackleford and Teviin Binns perfecting their 3-point shots. Or else all hell would break loose.

The ruckus usually started between Shackleford and Quentin Jackson. Shack was the tallest player on the team, Quentin the shortest. Quentin was very bright and extremely vocal. Shackleford was not good at repartee. But if they were having an argument, Shackleford knew he could always fall back on one phrase guaranteed to make Jackson lose his cool. Jackson has a large head, so Shackleford always called him "Helmet Head." When that happened, Quentin would start a barrage of name-calling, or he would comment on Shackleford's lack of brains or rag Shack for never brushing his teeth and always hanging out with fat girls.

Shackleford's response was pretty much limited to a string of "Helmet Head, Helmet Head, Helmet Head," which further inflamed Jackson, sometimes to action. Quentin would grab a basketball and sneak behind Shackleford when he wasn't looking, and from about four feet away he'd bank a throw off Shackleford's head. As soon as Shack's head cleared, there would be a free-for-all.

Once the first blow was struck, the others in the gym either got out of there or else ran and grabbed a basketball. Just because it began with Quentin and Shackleford didn't mean it stayed between those two. As the mood in the gym grew more playful, the game turned into a vicious form of dodgeball, with the players throwing basketballs as hard as they could at each other.

Shackleford would try to go after Jackson, but he never could get him, because Jackson was fast and quick and smart and Shackleford not so fast and not so quick and not so smart. So Shack would turn on someone else. He and the other players would stand in the middle of the court, each holding a basketball, some holding two, and—it was hard to tell who made the first throw—in no time basketballs would be flying all over the gym as the nonparticipants ran for cover. It was dangerous out there.

Shackleford could only bench press 150 pounds, but he had long arms, and when he came across and delivered that ball with all his might, George Brett would have had trouble hitting it.

Valvano inevitably found out about these scenes because the next day, when the team returned for practice, out of two dozen balls, two would be on the court and the rest would be scattered way up in the stands.

If there was horseplay, Shackleford inevitably was in the middle of it. Shack enjoyed waiting for a teammate to shower and towel himself off before pouring the pink, sticky sports drink all over him and making him go and shower all over again. He also got a big kick out of pulling the towel off a teammate and sticking heavy-duty adhesive tape across his behind. When the teammate screwed up his courage to pull it off, it would hurt like hell.

Shack once got a tube of muscle balm, put a glob of it on a tongue depressor, and rubbed it into Chucky Brown's hair. In retaliation, Brown broke out a can of the sports drink and poured it all over Shackleford.

Still, the activity Shack—and Teviin—enjoyed most was "Bombs away!" with the basketballs. One time Mike Giomi was standing out on the court practicing his shots, when Shack, Tev, Kelsey, Chucky, and Quentin each grabbed a ball, ran up behind the six-foot-nine Giomi, threw the balls at him in unison, and then hightailed it out of the gym.

Another time the players ganged up on the Gum Man, an elderly bespectacled man Valvano had hired to dispense Doublemint to the players. When a player finished chewing the gum, he routinely threw it on the floor, and it was the Gum Man's job to pick it up. This particular afternoon after practice, Shack, Tev, and the other bombers nailed the Gum Man with basketballs, breaking his glasses. The next day Valvano chewed out his players as Shack and Tev grinned and chuckled.

There was another facet of the team's personality that made itself evident the first couple of weeks: If you left your sneakers out, it was probable that someone would grab them. Over the course of the season Nike gave each player about fifteen pairs of sneakers for free. Retail, the sneakers went for about $72. If a player left his sneakers unattended or in an unlocked locker even for a second, the likelihood was that they would be gone when he returned, as though they had disappeared into the Twilight Zone.

Naturally, the first victim of the season was the rawest rookie. After practice on the opening day of practice, the new kid Simonds opened his locker, took out his sneaks, and left them on the bench in front of his locker while he went to the bathroom. He slapped the players high fives as he went; they were laughing and joking with each other, in large part because they all knew he had stupidly left his sneakers for the taking. He was gone less than a minute. When he returned, they were gone. He had worn them exactly once.

Simonds asked everyone sitting around him if they had seen who took his sneaks. The answer was unanimous, "No, man, I didn't see a thing."

Simonds was forced to go to Coach McLean for new ones. He said, "Somebody stole my sneakers." It was a litany Coach McLean heard often. McLean knew it was usually a scam, but it was tough for him to do anything about it. He knew that some of his players would do anything to get a new pair—their friends would pay $40 for a new pair of Nikes, because they were expensive sneakers and because they were the sneakers the ballplayers wore.

Coach McLean said, "All right, John. This one time. It's such a struggle. You have to watch your shoes."

One afternoon Simonds watched as Shackleford nailed a pair of Kelsey Weems's sneakers. It was after practice. Simonds watched Shackleford scan the locker room and notice that Kelsey's locker was ajar. While Kelsey was in the shower, Shackleford darted over to the locker, opened it real quick, snagged his teammate's sneakers, hustled back to his own locker, dumped them in, slammed it—boom!—and locked it.

When Kelsey came back, he pitched a fit. He started yelling, "Shack, I know you stole my shoes." Shackleford feigned being hurt and then acted angry. He said, "No, man, I wouldn't steal your shoes. I wouldn't take anything from you, man, because we're tight." By the first practice game three weeks later, Kelsey had had three pairs of sneakers stolen. Coach McLean then had to call Nike and ask them to send more shoes.

McLean was always telling the players, "Come on, guys, lock your lockers. I know that nobody on this team ever takes them—everyone in here is honest as a nun—but, fellas, lock your lockers, because somehow these things are walking out of here."

12

Shack

Charles Shackleford grew up in the city of Kinston, North Carolina, seventy-five miles southeast of Raleigh down Route 70. He was the youngest of fourteen children. Of his eight brothers, Cote, Alfonzo, Doug, Mike, Bobby, Tom, David Lee, and Dan, Jr., not one of them was an athlete.

Charles' father, Dan, was a cement finisher. He poured concrete for driveways and laid foundations. The Shacklefords didn't have a lot of money, but there was always enough to get by.

At age fourteen, after finishing eighth grade, Shackleford attended Coach Valvano's summer basketball camp. He stood six-foot-eight, and he demonstrated the agility that would soon put him among the best high school players in the country. During that camp, Valvano told Shackleford he had the talent to play college basketball, and soon after camp ended, Valvano began sending Shackleford letters, fostering his interest in playing at N.C. State.

Shackleford, from the ninth grade on, knew he was going to play college ball, and he believed he would go on to star in the pros. When you're six-foot-eight in junior high school, you believe you are Superman, impervious to harm on a basketball court and free from the toils of the everyday world, including school work, that smaller and less talented ninth graders must face.

Shackleford, from ninth grade on, was convinced that one day he would play in the NBA. He knew he had the talent. Valvano, for one, had told him so. Even before his high school years had passed, dozens of other people—coaches, fans, strangers, girl friends—had told him the same thing. He began spending most his spare time on basketball courts, and spent very little time at his school work. As he said much later, "I didn't give anything else another thought, because I knew I was going to make it."

In his sophomore year, Shackleford went right from his freshman team to a starting role on the varsity. He was the only sophomore starter on the Kinston team.

Shackleford played for a coach named Paul Jones, a white man. Shackleford, who is black, didn't have any trouble with Jones because he always played the whole game, but according to Shackleford, several of the other black players felt that Jones played inferior white players over them, and the team was rife with dissension. Team members were jealous of each other and rooted against each other. It was every player for himself, he said.

Shackleford, growing to six-foot-ten by his senior year, was a scorer of rare talent. Because it was every man for himself and the guards didn't pass him the ball as much as he liked, he said he had to score most of his points off rebounds and loose balls; when his teammates did get him the ball inside, he could dribble between his legs, drive hard, change direction, and slam over his head, sending the Kinston rooters into paroxysms of hoop ecstasy.

Shackleford averaged 22 points and 14 rebounds a game in his senior year, and he was named North Carolina Player of the Year by the *Greensboro Daily News*. In a game against archrival Rocky Mount High School, Shackleford scored 35 points and pulled down 31 rebounds. He was also named to McDonald's All American team as an honorable mention and was named third-team All American by *Street and Smith* magazine.

Despite his awards, Shackleford was convinced his personal records should have been grander. The problem: his teammates and Coach Jones. "I wasn't really getting the ball like I should have," he said. "With the right coaching, there'd have been no limit to my scoring potential."

In high school, Charles Shackleford was a celebrity. Everyone—sports junkies, big-eyed girls, even teachers—wanted to be his friend. As he explained it, "They see you on TV, and they think, 'Man, I wish I could have him.' " His teachers helped him get through, even though he did little work. He admitted, "Yes, it did help." He paused. "A lot."

By the beginning of his junior year, the colleges were knocking on the door of the Shackleford residence. He filled two huge cardboard boxes with letters from every major college basketball power in the country. He heard from Maryland, Duke, North Carolina, Houston, Louisville, DePaul, Kentucky, and, of course, North Carolina State, which had been in contact with him since he was a freshman.

Shackleford narrowed his finalists to DePaul, Maryland, and N.C. State. The only school he visited was N.C. State.

According to Shackleford, Valvano's assistant, the ubiquitous TomAbatemarco, sent Shackleford 1,500 letters during his high school career. In the fall of his junior year, before the November deadline for committing to a college, Abatemarco was on the phone to him every night. As usual, it was "How are you doing? What's going on?" Tom Abatemarco had become a part of Shackleford's everyday life.

During one visit to Shackleford's home, Abatemarco brought with him a tape of an ACC finals game between North Carolina State and North Carolina. In the room with Abatemarco and Charles while the tape was being played were Mrs. Shackleford and four of Charles' siblings. Everyone listened intently as the announcer intoned, "With only seconds remaining in the game and State down by a point, Shackleford gets a pass from Chris Washburn in the corner, shoots a jumper, and IT'S GOOOOOD!" The good feeling flowed over Charles Shackleford. He thought to himself, "Ah, man."

Shackleford described his reaction to hearing the tape: "You get little goose bumps running all down your spine, and you be all happy, and you feelin' good, you're excited, you got good vibrations, and it's just real exciting."

Valvano attended several of Shackleford's games, and when he visited the Shackleford home, he told the tall youngster that if he came to State, he would start as a freshman and would become a star and go on to the pros.

Also, Valvano convinced him that there was a real possibility that the combination of Washburn and Shackleford just might win the NCAA championship. "That was another good reason to sign," Shackleford said. "We had a lot of talent, and I wanted to win so badly. I signed because we had Chris. Because I didn't want to play center. He was going to be the center, and I was going to be at power forward."

Shackleford, too, was impressed that N.C. State played on TV so often. He was a North Carolina boy, and it was his chance to have all his friends watch him on the tube often.

And Shackleford genuinely liked Valvano. "I liked him enough not to take official visits at any other schools," he said.

The icing on the cake, the ploy Abatemarco and Valvano both used to their best advantage, was that when they romanced the boy, they also romanced the mother. In addition to convincing Charles, Valvano and Abatemarco also convinced Mrs. Shackleford that N.C. State was the school for her son. "Once they convinced her," said Shackleford, "they convinced me."

So when the early signing period arrived, six-foot-ten Charles Shackleford made four years of work pay off for Valvano's staff. He signed a letter of agreement to attend North Carolina State for the 1985-86 school year. The signing ceremony in the Shackleford home was attended by Valvano and covered by local reporters and by radio and TV. From the start, Charles Shackleford got the star treatment.

When basketball season began, Charles Shackleford made immediate headlines. It was the year after the Washburn stereo-theft debacle, and with the Faculty Senate having made a big stink with their investigation of academic policy in connection with athletics, Chancellor Bruce Poulton announced on September 8, 1985, that Charles Shackleford and three football players did not have a high enough combined grade point average and SAT score to be eligible to play sports in their freshman year.

In the first five games without Shackleford, N.C. State beat Western Carolina and Furman, lost to Loyola of Chicago by 2 points, beat Clemson by 3, and lost to Wake Forest by 1 point.

Game Six was against the University of Kansas in

Greensboro on national TV. Proposition 48 in theory may have been all well and good, but State needed its freshman phenom in the game against Kansas. Shackleford was surprised when he learned he would be eligible to play. When asked why he suddenly had become eligible after Chancellor Poulton had declared he must miss his entire freshman year of basketball, Shackleford said, "They told me they wanted me to play against Kansas."

A member of the college administration who knew the background of Shackleford's "rehabilitation" said, "The Kansas game was actually played during the exam period," and suggested that someone high in the college administration must have given Shackleford permission to play.

With Shackleford magically rehabilitated academically, he teamed with Washburn and helped transform N.C. State into a dominating force, winner of thirteen of its next seventeen games. The four losses came against nationally ranked teams. With the two working hard in tandem, N.C. State got to the Final Eight and that infuriating loss to Kansas in the last five minutes. If only Washburn hadn't left State for the pros, State would have been the favorite to win the national title in 1986-87. But with Washburn gone, Charles Shackleford was forced to don Washburn's mantle as the franchise player. He would have to shift from power forward, a position he loved, to center, a position he wasn't bad at, but since he wasn't as physically intimidating as some of his opponents, he was often at a disadvantage there, and it frustrated him.

To help Charles—to whom Valvano now referred in the media as "Sir Charles"—feel better about having to make the switch, by the beginning of his sophomore year, Shack was getting the special attention Washburn had gotten the year before.

Quentin Jackson, for one, reportedly noticed the difference in treatment between Shack's freshman year and sophomore year. Like Washburn the year before, Shack didn't have to do anything he didn't want to do. Quentin laughed about it all the time and was heard to say, "Hey, Shackie, you're getting the Wash treatment."

Said Simonds, "The coaches went out of their way to make sure Shack was always happy and kept out of trouble. V called the rest of us by our last names, called us idiots in public, but when he talked to Shack, he'd ask, 'Sir Charles, are you going to practice with us today?'

"I was thinking, 'Here's a guy who can barely read, brushes his teeth once every five days—honest to God, the guy has breath that can melt the tires on a car—and V was calling him 'Sir Charles.' Basketball was not what I thought it would be."

Another teammate noticed that Shack was never without money.

"He always kept a little wad with him," he said. "His sophomore year he started wearing gold, and you knew when he started wearing gold that he was being taken care of but good.

"We'd say, 'Hey, Shack, they hooking you up, right?' He'd say, 'You know it. You know it.' He'd smile and say, 'Yeah, yeah.' "

The man who was responsible for fulfilling the needs of the black players was a handsome, impeccably dressed black man named Charles S. Logan, known as C.Lo. No one knew what he did for a living, only that he was wealthy enough to drive a late-model, expensive Mercedes Benz. No one knew what his relationship with the team was, only that he had enough influence with the NCSU athletic department to have seats directly behind the N.C. State bench. Before and during games the coaches and players could be seen giving him a respectful nod. It could have been a scene out of *The Godfather*.

If Shackleford, or the other black players, needed something, C.Lo was the man to call. If a black player, for instance, wanted spending money or stereo equipment or Hydrochlorothiazide, the little pink diuretic to mask drugs for a urine test, or new clothes—just about anything but a car—he need only call C.Lo, and C.Lo would call his connections, and in the middle of the night a couple of tough-looking dudes using the aliases of Pobie and Ernie would pull up in front of the College Inn in a Cadillac and make a house call. It was all very hush-hush.

After the season was over C.Lo would arrange exhibition games for State players once their eligibility was up, paying them $500 a game to play in the games.

Exactly what C.Lo got out of his Big Daddy role other than a chance to rub elbows with the varsity basketball players no one thought to wonder nor apparently cared. C.Lo was keeping the players happy, and that's all that seemed to really matter. Though C.Lo was known for his connections to the drug world, no one apparently was bothered enough by his presence to ask him to stop associating with the players.

C.Lo, according to a close friend, originally came from Newark, New Jersey and was a student and basketball player at St. Augustine College in Raleigh, where he was hired for several years as an assistant basketball coach. C.Lo and Valvano reportedly first became involved in the early 1980s when Valvano hired him to be a coach at his basketball camp. It is an association, sources say, that those close to Valvano are loath to discuss.

According to one source, an investigator recently called one of the administrators of Valvano's NCSU basketball camp on the telephone to ask if he knew the whereabouts of anyone named C.Lo and then asked, "Who wants to know?" The investigator said he was representing a four-year-old girl who had been badly hurt in a traffic accident. He said he needed to find the sole witness to that accident. Charles Logan was that witness, he said. Without him, the girl might not collect the money she would need to recover from the insurance company.

According to the investigator, the camp administrator angrily replied, "Fuck that four-year-old girl." The investigator thought to himself, "Nice people I'm dealing with." The camp administrator then softened and said he would agree to meet with the investigator if he made an appointment.

The investigator asked, "Why should I make an appointment if you don't know a C.Lo?"

The camp administrator hung up on him.

C.Lo, according to his close friend, has been a cocaine user and has been in a drug rehabilitation center. At the time this book was going to press, C.Lo was a fugitive from the state of North Carolina. There is a warrant out for his arrest. He is believed to be living somewhere in Georgia.

Cars were supplied by others.

Shack had been boasting to his teammates that he was going to be getting a car, but had told them it would be another Subaru, so they were surprised when Shack announced one day, "My car is here," and outside in the College Inn parking lot stood a fully equipped, souped-up, late-model Pontiac Trans Am.

Exactly where it came from nobody knew. Nobody ever knows, except the player and the person who gives it to him. The car was in Shackleford's girl friend's name. But one thing his teammates did know: she hadn't bought it. She reportedly worked as a secretary, making about $15,000 a year, and it was absurd to think she could afford either the $16,000 Subaru coupe he had driven as a freshman or the $23,000 Trans Am.

Said a teammate, "Some people were saying Shack's girl friend bought it for him, but we knew better. It was brand-new. I thought to myself, 'Oh Lord, that came right off the truck.' It still had the price sticker right on it. It read twenty-three thousand dollars. I said, 'Damn, Shack.'

"But what was funny, on the back it said, 'I Got Mine at Boomershine,' a car dealer in Atlanta, Georgia. Why Atlanta, Georgia? We were thinking, 'Shack's got some car.' He would drive that thing ninety miles an hour like it was nothing."

Though he felt he fully understood why Shack got the car, his teammate was a tad jealous. "I thought to myself, 'Shack got himself a ride and I'm walking.' "

But there was no denying the teammate admired the car.

"That Trans Am had a race motor," he said dreamily, "and every morning we would hear Shack pumping it up, 'Bruuuummm. Bruuuuuummm. Bruummmmm.' I always knew when Shack was getting ready to leave."

Because the car was put in Shackleford's girl friend's name, if anyone came snooping around or if it got stopped, it wasn't his but his girl friend's.

The presence of Shackleford's fancy new car did, however, make certain members of the faculty very suspicious. Said one, "His family situation wasn't all that good financially, and I don't care what kind of summer job he had, he wasn't going to make enough money to buy that car. It never did add up in my mind."

The first part of the season, Shackleford drove his Trans Am without license plates. Where the license plate should have been was the dealer ad plate announcing, "I Got Mine at Boomershine."

Coach McLean and John Simonds were in the basketball office one day when Shackleford, who wasn't in the mood to practice that day, pulled into the parking lot to drop Kelsey Weems off. As the gray Trans Am sat idling in the parking lot, Coach McLean looked out the window and noticed that there was no license plate on it. "Good God," he said to Simonds. "How long has it been like that?"

Immediately, Coach McLean got on the phone and set it up for Shackleford to get license plates for his car.

13

Scrimmaging

The last three weeks of practice were devoted to finding a starting lineup. Valvano divided the team in two, with the red team—the starters—scrimmaging against the white team—the subs. At most schools, scrimmage time is for working on plays and learning defenses. At N.C. State, scrimmages were more like war, because the talented players on the white team were so angry they weren't starting that they scrimmaged with a fierce abandon not usually seen in practice. The reason they were angry was that every player on the squad had believed he would either have a starting berth on the team when he got to school, or at least a "substantial role" with plenty of "quality time." Since only five players could start, the others seethed through most of the season. Making the problem worse was Valvano's philosophy of playing the five starters most of the time, so the white team players who were promised a starting berth weren't really subs, they were in fact benchwarmers.

With the advent of scrimmaging, Valvano had to settle on an initial starting five. At center he started Charles Shackleford. Shack had enough height for center, and he had the ability to be a phenomenal scorer—in games when he'd catch fire, he would make fade-away, arching shots without seeming to look at the basket, or loosey-goosey shots in traffic, where the ball would appear to be going over the backboard but would instead catch the right angle and go in. The one question about Shack was whether his skinny frame could take the abuse of the bangers.

Senior Bennie Bolton was penciled in to start the season at the small forward spot. Bennie had sat his freshman and sophomore years. As a starter his junior year, everyone had expected great things from him, but what he could contribute was limited because of his lack of speed. Because he was slow, he was unable to put the ball on the floor and drive to the basket.

If he could get open, he was a great shooter, but because Valvano didn't often run plays to get him an open shot, Bennie didn't shoot as much as he might have, and when he got the ball he wasn't open very often. Bennie had to do it on his own or it didn't happen, so if Bennie was guarded by a tough defensive player, he wouldn't get many points. But if his man was lax on defense, Bennie was capable of scoring 20.

At the power forward spot, Valvano started Mike Giomi, the senior transfer from Indiana University, who was finally eligible to play after sitting out for almost eighteen months. Giomi had been selected Ohio High School Player of the Year in 1982, and as a sophomore at the University of Indiana he had helped shut down Michael Jordan and then hit the clinching free throws in the Hoosiers' 78–68 win over North Carolina in the second round of the 1983 NCAA tournament.

Indiana coach Bobby Knight had dropped Giomi in the middle of the 1984 season, and though he looked a little rusty, everyone at State was figuring him to be a strong rebounder and an enforcer for the Wolfpack.

Giomi's departure from Indiana had been something of an enigma. Giomi was such a picture-perfect forward that Coach Knight had used him in his instructional films.

The official story on Giomi's departure was that Giomi had broken Knight's hard-and-fast rules about how many classes a player could skip, so Knight dropped him.

Giomi disdained talking about his experience at Indiana. When asked about Knight, his usual reply was, "I see things differently from him, and I'm going to be happy here."

One thing Giomi did comment on was the difference in approach between Knight and Valvano. At Indiana, Giomi once observed, "Some days we'd go to the gym without a ball. The whole two-hour practice was defense." At N.C. State, it seemed that the only time Valvano practiced defense was as punishment.

After reading *Season on the Brink*, John Feinstein's

book about Knight, an N.C. State teammate asked Giomi, "Man, how can you take that verbal abuse so much?"

Gee said, "You wouldn't dare grab him, because he's so fucking mean-looking and he's big. He's six-foot-four, two hundred twenty. You wouldn't dare challenge him."

The one story Giomi did tell was about the day he and one of his Indiana teammates had played badly against Minnesota. Knight refused to let them fly home with the team. "We had to fly back on a charter jet with the alumni," Giomi said.

Giomi was a fundamentally sound, hard-working player. He ran the floor well and was tireless. The question from the start was whether he could come back after being away from the competition for so long.

At the shooting guard spot, Valvano went with six-foot-seven sophomore Walker Lambiotte, the McDonald's All Star Game MVP in his senior year in high school. Walker had been promised the moon by Valvano, and he did start in his freshman year, but he didn't play as well as was expected. His high school coach had nurtured and pampered him, designing plays just for him, so he wasn't used to having to play under an offense that forced him to fend for himself. He had been used to getting double screens to free him for shots, but at State he was getting the ball with defensive pressure, and he was having trouble adapting.

Walker had never understood his role in the State offense. In addition to being a good shooter, he had done his best work as a slashing-type scorer, making quick moves to the basket, leaning on his man, getting rebounds and putting it back up. In his freshman year he was told to be a shooter, so he didn't get to employ his other skills. This year Valvano moved him to guard, again to take advantage of his shooting ability.

At point guard Valvano chose Kenny Drummond, the star JUCO transfer. Drummond's selection caused severe strains in team unity from the outset. Guards Quentin Jackson and Kelsey Weems hated Drummond's presence from the first.

Jackson, a junior, had sat on the bench the season before while senior Ernie Myers played, and he had to be figuring that 1986-87 would be his year to start at point guard. But Valvano apparently didn't think Jackson could maintain a high enough level of play to do more than go in on defense for a couple minutes.

Weems, a sophomore, had sat behind Nate McMillan. Kelsey had been a superstar in high school, an All American from Atlanta. He was a racehorse—no one could dash down the court faster with the ball. He sometimes played out of control, occasionally taking the ball to the hoop on one-on-three situations and sometimes bouncing passes off his teammates knees, but to be successful he had to find his rhythm by playing, and despite Valvano's promises, he had played little his freshman year. He had anticipated much more playing time in 1986-87, as had Jackson, until it was announced in the local papers that Valvano had recruited Kenny Drummond to be State's starting point guard.

The animosity between Drum and the other two guards was evident from the start. In one of their first conversations, Drummond sought to establish his leadership role by announcing to his new teammates that he was going to be running the team.

Quentin, never at a loss for words, told Drummond, "I feel betrayed, man. Coach V promised me that he wasn't going to bring in another point guard until after my junior year."

Drummond replied, "He didn't tell me that." But Drum knew that Quentin was telling the truth.

With Shackleford, Bolton, Giomi, Lambiotte, and Drummond selected as the initial starters, the red-white scrimmages got under way, and they were brutal.

Avie Lester, the mammoth freshman center, wasn't a good shooter, but if he got the ball close to the basket, he could dunk with the best of them. He played hard, but he fouled an awful lot. Lester resented having to play with the subs, because like the others he had starred his whole high school career, and he didn't like being considered second best.

Quentin and Kelsey resented Drum; and Vinny del Negro, the high school All American from Springfield, Massachusetts, and Andy Kennedy, the freshman star from Mississippi, resented having to play shooting guard on the white team behind Lambiotte. Each felt they should be starting and that Lambiotte belonged at small forward.

Del Negro, a junior, had sat on the bench through his freshman and sophomore years despite promises by Valvano to the contrary, and it appeared he was going to be sitting again this year. Most of the team members felt that Vinny should be starting at point guard, not Drummond.

When Vinny became a senior, *Sports Illustrated* did an article on him, explaining how he had patiently waited in the wings, keeping his own counsel, waiting to live out his dream, until the day he finally got his chance and became a star.

According to teammates, nothing could have been farther from the truth. For the first two years, Vinny reportedly called home often, asking to be allowed to transfer. Some days he would be crying. The article described his father as telling him, "Son, stay there and work your butt off," but in truth his dad was furious with Valvano. Reportedly the only reason Vinny didn't leave was that Valvano was so persuasive with promises to del Negro, Sr., that his boy would be playing "soon."

Teammates said that Vinny and his father had had numerous heart-to hearts with Valvano over Vinny's lack of playing time, and that several times Vinny made the threat to transfer, only to have Valvano promise him more playing time in the future—promises never kept. Del Negro's father reportedly became so frustrated for his son a couple times that he threatened Valvano. It was said he once told Valvano, "If you don't play my boy, I'm going to kick your ass." And still Valvano didn't play him.

The candidates on the white team behind Giomi at power forward were freshman Brian Howard, a real bull, named North Carolina High School Player of the Year by the *Greensboro News and Record*; hardworking sophomore Chucky Brown, six-foot-eight, a talented, hardworking, serious player on the court, but a funny, laidback guy who wore slippers and a coonskin cap wherever he went outside; and six-foot-ten senior Teviin Binns. Binns was perhaps the most bitter team member of them all.

14

Tev

Teviin Natoega Binns was named by his mother after the historical Roman figure Octavian. His friends all call him Tev. As a boy he grew up on the streets of University Heights in the Bronx, not far from the uptown campus of NYU before it was taken over by Bronx Community College.

After his ninth grade at John F. Kennedy High School, Teviin was playing in the Holcomb-Rucker summer leagues. He was six-foot-seven, but he could barely read and write, so distracted was he by the life on the street. After one of the summer league games, his coach, Evander Ford, the coach of Benjamin Franklin High School, asked Tev if he would be interested in going south to finish his education. Carl Walker, the president of Georgia Christian High School in Valdosta, Georgia, a small private Christian school, had been visiting friends in New York, had attended the game, and noticed Teviin and another basketball talent, Andre Brittain, who had been playing at Benjamin Franklin. If Tev accepted, he would get room and board and a chance for a better education, away from the streets of New York.

Tev didn't want to go, but he was realistic about street life, so he accepted. The first day he arrived in Valdosta, he was homesick and wanted to go back to New York. The Georgia country life was so different. At JFK he was an anonymous face—albeit atop a very tall body—among 5,000 students. At Georgia Christian, he was a person among the 240 students. He wasn't used to teachers watching him, making him study and go to Bible classes. It took him time to adjust.

But he stayed. The coaches knew that if they could

nurse Teviin along until the start of the basketball season, he would never want to leave, because returning to the basketball team was six-foot-six forward Kevin Ellis, along with a six-foot-five small forward to team up with Tev and Brittain, a flashy guard.

Georgia Christian would be a powerhouse.

Tev did stay, and for his three years at Georgia Christian, the team did not lose. Teviin Binns' high school record read: games won 96, games lost 0. The closest Georgia Christian came to losing in his senior year was in a 7-point game in the state tournament, which they won. They beat some teams by 100 points. In one game, Tev scored 35 points and pulled down 18 rebounds. He'd have had more, but he only played the first half. Sometimes, after the pregame dunk drill, the opposition simply gave up.

At the end of his senior year, Teviin got scholarship offers from a handful of major colleges, including New Mexico and Idaho State, but he felt he would have a better chance of ending up at a major power if he went to a two-year junior college first. He decided to go to a junior college in Texas, figuring that the best junior college basketball teams in the nation came from Texas. He wanted to be seen in a program where he could make an impact and get noticed by the majors, and he chose to go to Midland Junior College, after getting letters from Midland and then reading an article in *Sports Illustrated* about Spud Webb and his teammates at Midland. The article told how Midland had just won the junior college national championship.

Teviin told himself, "Damn, it's in *Sports Illustrated*. I know it must be a good school."

In Tev's freshman year, Midland went 20–15 and lost in the regionals in Midland's gym. He averaged 16 points and 9 rebounds a game, was named all-region and all-conference, and in one game against Odessa, scored 35 points and had 14 rebounds.

In his sophomore year, Teviin became a dominating force in junior college basketball. Under coach Jerry Stone, Midland played run and gun and dunk, with Tev doing a lot of the dunking, as the team finished with a 31–6 season. Teviin that year shot 56.8 percent from the floor, averaged 20 points and 9 rebounds a game, and led the conference with a record 127 blocked shots.

He led Midland to fourth place in the national tournament, was named to the all-tournament team, and was also named first-team junior college All American by the *Basketball Times*, *Basketball Weekly*, and the National Junior College Athletic Association.

This time, instead of a handful of offers, over 150 major colleges were writing him. The mayor of Lubbock, Texas, wrote him to suggest that he attend Texas Tech. A man who owned a shoe company in Memphis, Tennessee, wrote to tell Tev that he would make it worth his while if he came to Memphis State and replaced Keith Lee. Bankers and businessmen wrote him, touting the benefits—both academic and financial—of going to their college of choice.

Villanova, which had won the national championship the year before, promised Tev a starting job, but at center, and he declined. He felt his ultimate position, the one he would play in the NBA, was at power forward, and he wanted to go to a team that would prepare him for his pro career. He turned down Maryland because they didn't come to him until late in the recruiting year.

Oral Roberts, the TV evangelist whom Tev used to see on television, was also recruiting him. He flew him to Oral Roberts University in his private jet, and when Teviin deplaned, Oral took his hand and kissed it.

Tev paid a visit to Seton Hall University in New Jersey, because the brother of Mike Brown, the assistant coach there, had lived in the same apartment building as the Binns family. Tev had been impressed during a Midland game against an opponent in the tiny town of Clarendon, Texas, way up in the mountains, to look up in the stands and see Mike Brown sitting there.

The most important consideration to Teviin was going to a team that stood a chance to win the NCAA championships. After going undefeated in high school and almost winning the national junior college championship at Midland, Teviin had become used to winning. So he decided to go with a sure thing: North Carolina State.

There was only one college recruiter who had been recruiting Teviin in the Bronx *before* he went south to Georgia: Tom Abatemarco. Abatemarco had met Teviin when the youngster was in the ninth grade, and already back then was pitching the benefits of going to college at

N.C. State. When Tev headed south, Abatemarco kept up with him. When he went to Midland, there was Abatemarco. Tev liked Abatemarco. Binns told himself, "Tom is very funny, and if Tom is funny, Valvano must be funny."

Tev, moreover, had been a close friend of Ernie Myers, the legendary Tolentine High star, who went on to play for State. He had also been impressed that former Midland star Spud Webb, the five-foot-seven dunking guard, ended up at State. Teviin could have gone to N.C. State right out of high school, but Abatemarco and Valvano suggested he go to junior college instead. Binns' grades were really bad, and the coaches were afraid he would quickly flunk out. "They wanted me to go to Midland and grow up and improve my skills," said Binns.

On one trip to Midland, Abatemarco brought his tape—N.C. State against Carolina. Teviin heard himself playing against Michael Jordan and Sam Perkins, and when he heard himself hit the winning shot with a second left, Tev thought to himself, "That could be me."

Tev, too, desperately wanted to be seen on TV, and no one was on TV more than N.C. State. "That's what high school boys dream of, playing on NBC or CBS so your friends can watch you play. That's one reason I wanted to go there: to be seen on TV—all the time," he said.

And so after visiting Villanova and Seton Hall, Teviin's third and final visit to a college was made to N.C. State. He flew with Spud Webb's parents to watch the senior guard play in his final college game against Wake Forest the next day. Abatemarco and Assistant Coach Ray Martin were waiting for him. They drove him to the College Inn to meet the players, went to the movies, and then took him to a couple of the nightclubs on Western Boulevard.

The next day he had breakfast, lunch, and dinner with Valvano. Teviin had one concern: He wanted to be assured that if he came to N.C. State, he would play. Valvano several times told him, "No matter what, you're going to play." Valvano told him he was impressed with his quickness, range, and scoring skills, and to take advantage of his skills, he intended to use him at small forward, even though he was six-foot-ten.

The coach surprised Binns with his honesty when he

told him that they were dissatisfied with the play of their two returning small forwards, John Thompson and Russell Pierre.

"Thompson can't shoot," Valvano said. "He doesn't have a jump shot, and as for Russell, we don't like his offense. They can't do the things you can do. You will be able to fill right in and play."

Valvano also told him, "Come in, and if you do well, you'll get the publicity you need to make it to the pros."

He also promised him he would not sign another shooting forward until after Teviin graduated.

After dinner, Valvano took him to the Reynolds Coliseum to watch the team play Wake Forest. Tev was introduced to Chris Washburn, who was sitting at the end of the bench in his civvies because of his yearlong ineligibility, and pictured himself playing side-by-side with Washburn on the 1986 NCAA championship team.

After the game, he went to the locker room, and when he saw the reporters and the TV cameras, Tev thought, "I could be the one in front of those cameras."

When it came time for Binns to sign his letter of intent to go to N.C. State, he was still concerned about his playing time. Because he was a minor, his parents had to sign the letter, and on the phone from Midland he told Valvano, "If I'm not going to play twenty minutes a game, I'm not going to let my parents sign."

Valvano traveled to the Bronx to get the required signatures in person, and during his conversation with Mrs. Binns reportedly began talking about his own father, who had just passed away. Valvano began crying, and with tears flowing down his face looked Mrs. Binns in the eye and promised that Teviin would play twenty minutes a game. She signed the letter of intent.

Tev was going to N.C. State.

When it was announced that Teviin Binns was coming to N.C. State to play small forward, Russell Pierre immediately transferred to Virginia Tech. Valvano reportedly had promised Pierre that he would start and star at State, and with the heralded six-foot-ten-inch JUCO scoring machine coming to campus, Pierre decided it would be best for his career to leave. John Thompson also felt betrayed, but he would not transfer until after the fall term.

Even before Teviin arrived on campus, Valvano broke one of his major promises to the boy, not to bring in another power forward until his junior year. After the recruiting year was over, Teviin knew his main competition would be coming from Charles Shackleford. But then, "from out of nowhere," as Teviin described it, Valvano added to the team a member of the Greek National Basketball Team, Panagiotis Fasoulas, a seven-footer with curly hair, little court sense, an inability to speak English, and only one year of eligibility left, which meant he could play basketball that year even if he never went to a single class, which, his teammates say, he never did.

Teviin was irate. "He just appeared on the scene one day," said Binns. "We already had fourteen players. We were loaded at every position. Anybody on our bench could have gone to another college and started. What did we need this guy for?"

When practice began in Binns' first year at State, Washburn was in the middle, Nate McMillan and Ernie Myers were the guards, freshman Walker Lambiotte was starting at one corner, and Tev was starting at the other. Valvano was full of praise for his new JUCO transfer.

And then, before the first scrimmage game, Teviin went up for a rebound in practice and came down on the foot of Mike Giomi, who was ineligible to play in the games but practiced with the team all season long. Teviin's ankle blew up to three times its normal size and turned black and blue. Teviin suffered a severely sprained ankle and missed the next four weeks of the season. When he returned, Charles Shackleford was playing power forward, and Teviin became a fixture on the bench.

Once his ankle healed, Binns desperately wanted to play, but he didn't comprehend that under Valvano's system, one man plays most of the time, and everyone else sits, no matter what promises have been made.

"I was first-team All American junior college," said Binns. "I was coming off one of the best years I've had, and I just knew I was going to play. Except that I didn't."

Teviin would go into Valvano's office, and he'd say, "Coach V, why ain't I playing? I'm doing good in practice?" Valvano would tell him, "Yeah, Teviin, I think you should be playing. I think you and Chucky Brown both should be playing more than you are."

Teviin didn't play ten minutes a game. Valvano had promised Tev's mother that her son would play twenty minutes a game, but the closest he came was the nineteen minutes he played against Duke, when he scored 11 points and had 5 rebounds.

After that game, Valvano brought him into his office and told him, "Tev, I liked the way you played today, and from now on, you will be playing twenty-plus minutes."

The next game was against Virginia. Teviin played two minutes.

"Two minutes!" said Binns. "And he told me in my face that he was going to play me. And that's when I lost a lot of respect for V, because time and time again he would tell me I should be starting, but that he wanted to try this or that, so he wasn't going to do it yet.

"There were times before a game, he would say, 'Teviin, you're going to play,' and I wouldn't get into the game."

If Binns did do something good, it seemed that Valvano then took him out. And Binns would be angry, and he would let Valvano know it.

"When you tell me things and they don't happen on the court, I get mad," said Binns. "That's just me. I wouldn't say nothing, but I would stare at him, and he couldn't even look me in my eye. That's how rude he was. It was terrible."

Binns discovered that Valvano was a professional in the true sense of the word, in that little else mattered to him except winning the game—not promises kept nor hurt feelings nor having the respect of his players.

"He was dirty," Binns said, "that's why I didn't respect him. He would just lie to you, in your face. My junior year my father came down plenty of times to talk to V, and V would tell him, 'Tev is going to play.' Or he would say, 'Right now Tev isn't doing what he's supposed to do,' and he would change everything around and say, 'we need a power player, and Tev isn't a power player.' "

When Binns reported for practice his senior year, Valvano called him into his office. Valvano told him, "You're going to start this year, Tev. I want you to grab loose rebounds, put in garbage baskets, use your finesse, because that's what you are, a finesse player. I want the seniors, you and Bennie, to start this year at forward, along with Shack, Lamb, and Drum."

Why Valvano kept making these promises not even Teviin pretends to understand, but when the 1986-87 practice season began, Valvano started Mike Giomi on the red team at small forward, and Tev was back working out with the scrubs.

Adding to the injustice Binns felt was his enmity for Giomi.

"First Giomi breaks my ankle, and then the next year he comes in fresh, spanking, never played before, and he takes my spot. V was giving all my time to Giomi, and I couldn't stand the guy. It was like V was saying, 'Here, Gee, take Teviin's time.' It wasn't right. It wasn't right at all."

The six weeks of practice for the 1986-87 season concluded with three red-white scrimmages before sold-out crowds complete with referees and time clocks. In the first scrimmage game, Teviin scored 22 points. In the finale at home at Reynolds Coliseum, he poured in 42 points in an impressive offensive display. He fouled Giomi out of the game, and no one, not Chucky Brown nor Shackleford, could keep him from scoring.

During the scrimmage Valvano kept saying to him, "Yeah, Tev, that's it, that's it. You're really filling it up," and Tev was thinking to himself, "This is my senior year. I got to go out in style."

After the game the fans were saying to him, "I didn't know you could play like that." He replied, "There are a lot of things you don't know. If I just get the chance, I'll show you."

Even Valvano was impressed. He said, "I didn't know you had it in you, Tev." Binns said, "Coach, if I get the chance, I'll show you some more."

With the practice period at an end and the regular season about to begin, Teviin's positive outlook returned. He had just scored 42 points in a scrimmage and had impressed Coach Valvano. Tev told himself, "I know I'm going to play. I just know it. There is no way he is going to sit me on the bench."

15

Rumblings

Athletic Director Valvano had arranged a schedule for his team that anticipated the hulking presence of Chris Washburn in the middle. Overlooking the schedule-stuffers, the guaranteed wins against such weak-sister colleges as East Tennessee State, Western Carolina, Duquesne, UNC-Asheville, Tampa, Winthrop, and Brooklyn, games that could be won with the last five players from the bench, no college team had a tougher schedule. N.C. State had to open against nationally ranked Navy, led by super center David Robinson, and before the season was over, it would have to play a series of nationally ranked teams including Kansas, Oklahoma, DePaul, and Louisville, plus the toughies from the ACC—the University of North Carolina, Duke, Clemson, and Virginia.

Valvano had planned to use the last of the team's three intersquad scrimmage games to work on its plays for Navy, but when Valvano spotted one of the Navy assistant coaches in the arena, he reportedly ordered the team not to run them because he didn't want the opposition coach to see what he was going to do. His players weren't fazed by this. They suspected he had no intention of running them during the game anyway.

The matchup of Navy center David Robinson against Chris Washburn would have been a classic, but The Washer had skipped to the NBA, and his replacement, Charles Shackleford, seemed outclassed by the seven-foot midshipman. Shack had hurt his right wrist during practice fooling around while working on his dunk moves, and there was a question whether he would even be able to play.

After Shack had hurt his wrist, the trainer had put it in

a light cast. Shack could have worked out—ran, kept in shape, shot foul shots, and studied Navy's offense—but his effort was halfhearted, infuriating some of his teammates who envied his physical skills—his height and quickness. It was his motivation they questioned.

"If Shack had had a good game against Robinson, he would have been set," said one teammate. "Everyone would have said, 'If he can do it against Dave Robinson, he can do it against anybody.' "

But Robinson scored 36 points and had 10 rebounds. He was the whole Navy team. Shack had 7 points and 6 rebounds.

And yet, as much as they grumbled about Shackleford's lack of dedication, the player team members bitched and moaned about most was Kenny Drummond. They were furious at Drummond.

Drum was talented. Most of them admitted that. Against Navy he scored 18 points, including the game-winner. But they felt he played as though he were the only guy out there—in the same fashion he had for Sacramento Community College—running and gunning but not passing, and his teammates were unanimous in their criticism of his style of play.

Valvano would signal a play from the sideline. Drummond would echo his signal and then do something totally different—a made-up free-lance play that usually ended in Drummond's shooting the ball. His teammates would be out of position and lost out there as Drum ran his game, ignoring everyone else.

The in-bounds pass would come into Drummond, who would dribble up the court as fast as he could and then either take a twenty-five-footer or drive one on four. What he didn't do was pass the ball very much.

Forward Bennie Bolton got the ball enough to score 20 points, but Mike Giomi and Walker Lambiotte, Drum's most vocal critics, were unhappy, feeling that Drum had largely ignored them.

Afterward Drummond said, "I was wide open from the outside, so I shot. I passed to Giomi, and sometimes he scored, and sometimes he didn't. Lambiotte was hurt. Why give the ball to someone who's hurt?"

The star of the game turned out to be Vinny del

Negro. With seven minutes to go in the first half and State struggling, Valvano put Vinny in to a standing ovation. (His players said they suspected the only reason Valvano put him in was that the game was being played in Springfield, Massachusetts, del Negro's hometown, and the coach wanted to save face with the crowd.) Del Negro—virtually without experience during his first two years at State—came in and hit three 3-pointers for 9 points at the half, giving State a 15-point halftime lead and forcing Valvano to play him again in the second half.

State blew its lead, and with fourteen seconds left in the game trailed by 2 points when Drummond threw up another of his long bombs for 3 points. "Coach Valvano told me to take the last shot. And everything he tells me to do, I do," he said.

Drum then deflected a Navy pass into Shack's hands, Shack got fouled going to the basket, and when Shack hit one free throw, State had a 2-point lead that held up when Navy missed from halfcourt at the buzzer.

The State fans were ecstatic. They loved the way Drummond played the game—fast, exciting, and with a real flair, shooting from the hip from anywhere. Only his teammates had reservations.

Teviin Binns didn't start, but Valvano did play him. He scored 10 points, including four Alley Oop dunks, and he was particularly pleased because the game was being played on ESPN. After the game, Binns went up to Valvano and said, "Thanks, V, for the playing time. I really appreciated it."

Valvano said, "There will be more, Tev. There will be more."

When the players returned to Raleigh for a week of practice before playing in the Great Alaskan Shootout in Anchorage, Alaska, the grumblings about Kenny Drummond continued. Valvano had built him up in the papers, he had been the Most Valuable Player of junior college basketball, and he had just walked into his starting job—and the rest of the guys were very unhappy.

The day after they returned from Springfield, Walker Lambiotte was leaving practice with John Simonds, Mike Giomi, Vinny del Negro, and Andy Kennedy, when in his Southern drawl, Andy said, "Gooddddddammmmittttt, Kenny just about killed us against Navy."

Giomi responded, "Yeah, he's going to hurt our team." A couple days later, as Quentin Jackson was getting changed for practice, he said to Drummond, "Hey, Drum, are you going to try to kill us today?" It was a snide remark to get his feelings out into the open. On the college level, if one player didn't like another's game, he didn't keep it a secret.

Drummond attempted to make Weems and Jackson understand—he was a teammate, and if he scored 2 points, the 2 points would be credited to N.C. State; if he got a steal, it was an N.C. State steal. Drummond explained to them that at Sacramento no one cared if you scored 50 points and they scored none, or vice-versa, as long as the team won. He tried to tell them it wasn't a question of who was a star and who wasn't, but whether the team was winning.

Weems and Jackson were unmoved. "And what hurt me," Drummond said, "was that I couldn't get them to see this. I prayed for them. I couldn't do anything else."

Drummond, scarred by their resentment, turned inward, retreating into his own shell. "After a while, I would just go to practice, do what I had to do, and then go to my room and watch television."

He knew there was a problem, and to help resolve it, he sought to arrange a meeting with Valvano.

Drummond felt, "I'm here at State all alone. I have no relatives to talk to. I can't talk to my friends on campus about the basketball program, because they can't do anything about it. Only Coach Valvano can do something about it."

Four times he went to see Valvano. Four times Valvano's secretary made an appointment for Drummond to see the coach, and four times when Drummond arrived for the meeting, Valvano wasn't there—the secretary didn't know where Valvano was. And Valvano never got back to him.

"I was kind of there all by myself," Drummond said. "And I didn't want to be there all by myself. But I was."

After the Navy game, Kenny Drummond was a pariah on the team. "I was by myself," he said. "I basically had nobody."

Part of what separated Drummond from the others was his perspective. He had the athlete's arrogance that he was starting because he deserved to be starting. He trusted Valvano's judgment, and Valvano was telling him that he was playing excellently and that he should keep doing what he had been doing.

At the same time, he felt the others weren't starting because they weren't as good as he was. As a logical result, he felt Jackson and Weems should have been satisfied with their backup roles.

"If everyone had the attitude, 'I'm a role player. I'm going to do what the coach asks me to do and that's it,' then everything would be fine," said Drum. "But on this team everyone wants to start. Everyone wants to make it in the NBA." Trying to put his difficult situation in understandable terms, he said, "If there's a good player and everyone knocks him, then everyone else's chances are that much better."

The problem with his logic, of course, was that Weems and Jackson had both been star players in high school, had been promised starting roles by Valvano, and resented Drummond for taking jobs they felt rightfully belonged to them.

For his part, Drummond sought to win the respect of his teammates through leadership. On a team renowned for its laxness of play, especially in practice, Kenny Drummond killed himself. While Shack, Teviin, and Giomi ran listlessly up the court during practice, Drummond pushed himself as hard as he could, one time running so relentlessly that he fell on the floor with exhaustion.

When he saw Shack ambling down the court or saw Teviin watch his man get the ball, then turn and shoot a jumper right in his face without Tev's making a move to stop him, Drummond would say to himself, "These guys should have played for my junior college coach. They would be totally different players."

It didn't bother him so much that Teviin didn't hustle. He understood that Tev had lost some of his drive because of the way Valvano had handled him the year before. Even Drummond had to laugh the time Valvano stopped practice and yelled, "Teviin, what the fuck are you doing? Are you going to guard your man or not?"

Tev turned around and, serious as a heart attack, said, "Coach, if I want to stop him, I'll stop him."

Valvano's lower lip hit the floor. He turned to Coach McLean and said, "Coach McLean, what did he just say?" McLean replied, "Jim, he said, 'If I want to stop him, I'll stop him.' "

Valvano was so flabbergasted, he said, "Well, okay, I have a team of geniuses here. Let's play." And he put the ball back in play as the rest of the players busted up.

That Shackleford didn't hustle bothered Drum tremendously. "Damn!" Drummond said. "Guys dream to be six-foot-eleven. And here's a guy who could go somewhere and make some big money just playing basketball, and he won't take it seriously. I don't understand that at all."

In practice, Drummond tried to goad Shack into better performance. In one practice, when Shack pulled down his first rebound, Drummond told him, "Congratulations, you just got one more rebound than a dead man." But Shack wouldn't take that from this outsider. He replied belligerently, "Who the fuck are you supposed to be?" Drummond just walked away.

When some of the other players began making their feelings toward Drummond known, he defended himself in the way he knew best—by attempting to become even more dominating on the basketball court. As the season wore on he continually sneered at the teammates who complained they weren't getting the ball enough. He rationalized his tendency to hog the ball by saying, "A lot of the times I would pass the ball, and nobody would catch it. That would be a turnover for me. I was hitting. So I started shooting more."

Which only increased the tension.

Once the first game was behind them and everyone knew who the starters were, the players began playing dirty in practice. When there are ten men on the court and everyone believes he should start, the resentment of the subs for the starters grows day by day. Worsening the situation was the knowledge that the likelihood of a starter losing his job for a reason short of serious injury was unlikely, so the subs rooted for the starters to get hurt; sometimes they did what they could to inflict the injuries themselves. Practices became battles.

Players would set picks that were really brutal. A player would go through the middle and get punched in the kidneys or the nuts and wouldn't even know who had punched him, the action was that fast, the culprits that smooth. A player would pop his opponent and then spin away or turn and pretend to be looking for the ball, and the victim would never catch him.

One time when a couple players missed practice, Valvano allowed John Simonds to fill in, and when Simonds ran through the middle, Shackleford hit him right in the chest with his elbow. Simonds couldn't breathe. He turned red in the face and started gagging. A day after Kenny Drummond guarded him, Simonds woke up with black spots all over his body, small bruises where Drummond had been popping him on his arms, legs, and even his stomach.

Kelsey Weems always seemed to be getting beat up in practice. He was always complaining that Shack played dirty inside. Shackleford would take his hand and smack Kelsey in the face on the way through the middle or poke him in the eye or the nose, making his eyes water. When Kelsey came flying through the middle after Drummond, Shack would stand there and bust him in the face with the back of his hand. Or he would stick his knee out and pop Kelsey in the thigh. And Kelsey would come back out to the top of the key screaming, "Shack, I'm going to get you for that."

It was serious business out there. The guys who weren't starting wanted those jobs. And Drummond, who always played hard, would defense Kelsey Weems to death. Kelsey would be bringing up the ball, and Drummond would be pulling on his shorts, grabbing his shirt, punching him in the body—anything to gain an advantage.

Drummond, in turn, took a lot of cheap shots from Quentin and Kelsey. But it was not in Drum's nature to acknowledge what they were doing. When they knocked him down, he just got up and patted them on the butt. He knew that hurt them more than if he had retaliated.

Not surprisingly, the white squad of benchwarmers usually beat the red team during practice. After all, the red team had to run plays and the white team didn't, and most of the time the red team didn't get the plays right. Avie would bully Shack, and Shack wouldn't want to play, and Andy Kennedy would hit some shots, and Teviin would work his offensive magic, and with Kelsey and Quentin running the offense and playing tough defense, the white team would be ahead until Valvano, for the benefit of any press and fans in attendance, blew his whistle and ordered the white team to play zone defense, enabling Bennie Bolton, Walker Lambiotte, and Drum to shoot the eyes out of the basket for the red team and get back into the game.

In addition to the rivalry between the red team and the white team, there was another polarization splitting the team: white skin versus black.

Only a few coaches—for example, John Thompson of Georgetown and Jerry Tarkanian of the University of Nevada at Las Vegas—do not have to deal with racial disharmony. That's simply because they recruit almost all black players. Most college teams have black and white players, and it is always the role of the coach to keep the racial problems at a minimum.

The biggest problem for a coach is the charge of favoritism. With a black coach, it is the white players who level the charge. With a white coach, it is the black players who are unhappy.

On the N.C. State team, black players felt slighted, charging that Valvano, who is Italian, always favored Italian players. The black players all felt that his Italians—Mike Giomi, Vinny del Negro, and Walker Lambiotte—got preferential treatment. (Never mind that Lambiotte wasn't Italian. He was grouped with Gee and Vinny and hence considered to be Italian.)

Valvano unknowingly made the situation worse, because in the press he would always brag about his penchant for his Italian players. Valvano would say, "I don't play him because he's Italian. I play him because I'm Italian," and he would always get a laugh. But whenever the black players heard that, it made them furious, because they translated his statement to mean Valvano didn't have the same respect for the black players he had for his Italian players.

On this N.C. State team, some of the black forwards were particularly galled that Mike Giomi was starting.

Said a black teammate, "Giomi would mess up, and there would be no consequence for him. He'd just come back and [V would] play him again. He'd mess up, and [V would] play him again. Gee sucked like a big lollipop. We used to call him 'Frankenstein.' He didn't have no coordination. He didn't have finesse, no kind of moves, no post-up moves. The boy couldn't even dunk that good. And I seen him get ate up on defense, back-doored, and V would just overlook it. I mean, Giomi stunk! But V'd just overlook it and go on with Giomi. I mean, he gave that boy so many chances. It was like Giomi had to play."

Lambiotte also came in for criticism from the black players. Said one, "Walker wasn't a flashy, hard-nosed player. He didn't bang or bruise. When he got into the game, he would be real nervous. We'd be thinking, 'What the hell is he doing in the game? He can't play.' But his freshman year he played a lot. Everyone would say, 'The only reason V's playing him was because he did so good in that McDonald's High School All Star Game.' We knew he was overrated. But V kept sticking him in there, saying, 'He'll come around.' It's like these Italians. He'll play his people. Walker was V's boy."

Vinny del Negro, unlike Giomi and Lambiotte, didn't come under criticism from the blacks. In fact, quite the opposite. They felt that del Negro should have been a starter—over Drummond.

Said a black teammate, "Vinny was pretty cool, and we all knew Vinny could play. When I first laid eyes on Vinny, I said, 'That white boy can play some ball.' And look how long it took V to recognize him—till the end of his junior year. He didn't play at all. He couldn't even buy his way into a game. And nobody would ask any questions. Nobody would say, 'Hey, V, why isn't this person playing?' "

The general feeling among the black players was that they were better athletes than the whites—more talented, more physical. The whites believed themselves to be better basketball players, thought they were smarter and had better court sense. At practice or in the locker room,

Quentin Jackson, Kelsey Weems, or Chucky Brown might make a light crack about Valvano's playing the white players. Quentin would say to Andy Kennedy, "The crackers got a lot of time today, didn't they, Andy?" And Kennedy, also light-heartedly, would comment, "If you dumb niggies would just try a little harder . . ."

Whenever a black player talked about "V's boys," or "the crackers" or "the whiteys," he was talking about the white players.

The talk could get rougher during scrimmages. If Avie Lester, rough and mean, crashed into Giomi and then Giomi elbowed back, Avie would curse, "You big wophead motherfucker!"

Lester, the freshman hulk, was often in the middle of the action. Avie was a wild man, a very physical player. When he fouled you, you knew you were fouled. Avie was one black player who held a dislike for Vinny del Negro, but it had nothing to do with Valvano. Avie believed that Vinny never passed him the ball because he was black.

One day during practice, del Negro went running through the middle and Avie saw him coming. Avie had his back to Vinny and, just as Vinny came by, swung his elbow out and nailed Vinny right across the jugular. Vinny dropped. When he was able to breathe again, he went after Avie. The other players had to pull them apart.

A couple plays later, Vinny went back into the middle, and this time Avie smacked him right in the face with his fist.

This time Valvano called time and stopped practice. He reportedly called Avie a "no-account, motherfucking jerk, less than a man," and then he called him "a boy."

The rest of the black players noticed. Even though Avie was clearly the instigator and in the wrong, they said to themselves, "Vinny is Italian. He's V's boy. So Vinny gets away free and Avie gets blamed. V is one prejudiced guy."

Said a black teammate, "Valvano was just trying to protect Vinny. He was always doing that. It just got on my nerves."

During another practice the red team was practicing its

21 defense, with the guards out on top. If the forwards didn't stay tight on their men, the defense was worthless, and as play went on, Kenny Drummond noticed that Mike Giomi wasn't hustling.

Drummond looked back at Giomi and shouted, "Why don't you play defense, man?" Giomi replied, "Shut the fuck up." Drummond shot back, "You shut the fuck up."

Valvano blew his whistle, walked over to Drummond, and grabbed him by the uniform strap. "You shut up," Valvano said to Drummond. "This is my team, not yours. Play your position and mind your own business."

Drummond was mortified and hurt. He felt that as point guard it was his job to be team leader. It bothered him that Giomi wasn't hustling, and since no one was calling the guy on it, Drummond felt it was his duty to do so. When Valvano took Giomi's side, Drum felt betrayed.

"I was just telling the guy to play defense," he said. "I wasn't telling him to go to hell or cursing at him. I just said, 'Why don't you play defense, because we're out here working our butts off. Your man comes up and gets the ball every time, so we're just wasting our time.' But Valvano grabbed me. I didn't understand that. I'll never understand that."

Adding to the disharmony was the belief on the part of the black players that because the team was based in Raleigh, North Carolina, in the heart of the Old South, Valvano felt pressure from wealthy alums, the landed gentry, and the members of local society to have at least two white players in the starting lineup.

"Our friends would tell us that there had to be a certain amount of whites, two or three, out there," said one black team member. "The black football players would say it. Our friends on campus would say it. Even though they didn't deserve to be out there. This is a white-dominated school. The whites get a lot of breaks on this campus and in this state. I guarantee you that. There are damn few blacks in the administrative offices of N.C. State. What does that tell you?"

At the same time the blacks felt, "Without us, he wouldn't have much of a team."

It wasn't surprising then, that when the team went on the road, the blacks hung out with each other, and the whites hung out with the whites. There were exceptions. Bennie Bolton sometimes hung out with Andy Kennedy, although usually he kept his distance and was a satellite unto himself. And Kenny Drummond usually stayed by himself. Kelsey Weems, too, sometimes crossed over. Usually, though, the segregation held.

Said one of the black players, "It's the way people are brought up. We would all hang out together, and they would go their way."

16

North to Alaska

Valvano's N.C. State Wolfpack had a reputation for being renegades. When the team went on the road, the way it dressed and comported itself only added to that mystique. Coaches of certain teams, the Duke Blue Devils for instance, insisted that the players wear jackets and ties on the road. The State players didn't wear jackets *or* ties. Instead, they wore sweat clothes—made by Nike, the sponsor that paid Valvano $150,000 a year, in part for his players to be walking billboards for its products. During the season Valvano did not permit any player to wear sporting clothes made by another manufacturer.

At the beginning of the season, Valvano said, "We're a basketball team. We should look like a basketball team." What he meant was, everyone had to stop wearing different style sweatsuits. He wanted uniformity—fire-red N.C. State sweatsuits—made by Nike.

To get to Alaska for a three-game Thanksgiving weekend tournament in Anchorage, the team had to fly from Raleigh to Chicago, then from Chicago to Seattle, and then from Seattle to Anchorage.

On a foggy and rainy Thursday morning, the bus met the players at the gymnasium. The airport was only twenty minutes away, but the coach suspected that if they met there, half his players would be late and they'd miss the plane. The bus left at seven. The first day of the trip would be spent in the air.

Everyone got on the bus. There were fourteen players and fourteen Walkmen. Each player was listening to a different station or to a personal tape, singing along to his own private music. Bennie Bolton was one of the louder singers. Bennie loved his music and didn't care where he was when he sang. Bennie even sang on the airplane while the passengers looked at each other, wondering who he was. Because he was six-foot-six, rarely did anyone say anything.

Daylight broke just as the bus pulled into the airport. The players got on the plane headed for Chicago. It was packed—not a spare seat. They scrambled to be first on the plane, because the goal, especially for the supertall players, was to sit on the aisle so they could stretch their legs out. Shackleford, the tallest player at six-foot-eleven, was the most aggressive in his quest for the elusive aisle seat. Since he always had money, he had an advantage. One time he reportedly offered Quentin Jackson thirty dollars for his seat. Just to get Shackleford angry, Quentin turned him down. "Nah, Shack, I like this seat too much." Shackleford sometimes had to resort to conning old ladies out of their aisle seats. Glib and charming when he wanted to be, he was usually successful.

The players would get riled when they had to sit in the middle or by the window and one of the managers or a friend of Valvano's was assigned an aisle. Any time John Simonds got the aisle, the players would try to remove him bodily and take his seat. Brian Howard, in particular, hated to see Simonds on the aisle. He would try to push him onto the floor while Simonds strapped himself in and held on for all he was worth.

Shackleford, the diplomat, would try a different tact. "Come on, John, let's switch," he'd say. "We're good friends. We're tight."

With Shack on the aisle, the lives of stewardesses were made difficult. He would throw his size 19 sneaks out into the aisle and be sound asleep, snoring with his big mouth open, his head tilted to the side, his Walkman blasting music by Phil Collins through the earphones, preventing the stews from getting their food cart past him to feed the rest of the put-out passengers.

The flight to Chicago was turbulent. Walker Lambiotte, for one, was nervous as a snake. Teviin Binns was afraid to fly under the best of conditions. Any time the plane bumped, Teviin would start talking out loud, "Hey, man, be careful with this plane." The other passengers looked at each other, smiling benignly at Teviin's behavior. They understood.

When the players weren't dozing, they acted like little kids, popping each other on the back of the head with their knuckles, pestering the stewardesses for more peanuts, and throwing the peanuts all over the cabin.

When the plane finally landed in Chicago, everyone had to hang around the O'Hare terminal an hour to wait for the connecting flight. It left the players enough time for some good, clean mischief.

Valvano, as was his custom upon deplaning, headed for the pay phone. Right behind him were Shack, Tev, Kelsey, and Quentin. As Valvano began pecking out his credit card numbers, they could be seen circling him like vultures, trying to pick up the sequence of numbers as he punched them into the telephone.

Said Simonds, "Valvano was using the athletic department credit card number, and the snoopers knew that if they could get ahold of that number, they probably could call free all over the world for the rest of the year and never get caught."

Walker Lambiotte warned Andy Kennedy, "Man, don't let anyone find out you have a telephone credit card. 'Cause if they ever get that number, you are going to get a bill that they will send you in a box."

Kennedy had a phone in his room in the dorm. He always kept his room locked when he went out. He feared that Shack or Tev or Kelsey would sneak in there and call their friends in Sydney or Katmandu.

After failing to get the credit card number, the black players went off by themselves, walking down the corridor of the airport terminal in a long strand, taking it slow amid the Thanksgiving weekend mob, a string of tall dudes with Walkmen on their heads, chilling, walking the baddest walks in town as they scoped out the women walking by.

Shack and Kelsey Weems were the masters. Shack would walk up to a female stranger and say, "Hey, baby, I know that you like me." The girl would say, "No, I don't." He'd say, "Yes, you do. I'm a basketball player, a big star. I'm going to play in the pros one day. Don't you want to spend some time with me? Don't you want my phone number?"

Shack and Kelsey were always asking girls, "What's your name? How can I call you?" Shack would say, "I'm coming back through this town. I'll be faithful to you."

The white players looked on entranced—and more than a little envious. Said one, "We never would have had the nerve to do something like that."

The flight from Chicago to Seattle was a dream. The plane was a 747 jumbo jet, and few passengers other than the State team were aboard. Everyone stretched out, drank soda, and watched *Top Gun* all the way to Seattle. Teviin, stretched out across four seats, was in his glory. He made a toast, "Alaska, here we come."

Along with the coaches and the players, the Wolfpack also took along its two radio announcers, Wally Ausley, who does the play-by-play, and his color man, Garry Dornburg. They announced the games on WPTF, "Home of the Wolfpack." They were favorites of the players for two reasons: They were terrific announcers, and together they weighed about 700 pounds and were easy targets for the players' juvenile humor.

On the flight to Seattle, Dornburg got up to go to the bathroom. Teviin Binns was in line behind him. The bathrooms in a 747 are extremely narrow, and after Dornburg opened the bathroom door, he discovered that he couldn't fit through.

To Teviin, it was a funny sight watching a grown man turn one way, then another, and pull in his ample stomach in order to squeeze himself into the bathroom. Dornburg had to go, and he must have been uncomfortable, but he just couldn't fit through the door. The other passengers watching the scene sympathetically kept themselves from laughing.

Teviin Binns couldn't control himself. He began laughing so hard tears came down his face, and he ran back to where the other players were sitting to tell them of the unfolding drama.

Teviin yelled "Gary's too fat to get into the bathroom. You ought to see that white nig." The whole plane was in an uproar. "You should have seen him," Teviin cracked. "That fat rascal couldn't back into the bathroom."

When Dornburg returned to his seat, still unsuccessful in his attempt to negotiate the space leading into the bathroom, the players were screaming, "Ahhhhh, Gary!" laughing out loud. They knew he hadn't been able to go, so when the plane finally rolled to a stop and the cabin door opened, they made a big show of making way for him yelling, "Get out of his way. Gary has to *go!*"

The third plane, from Seattle to Anchorage, was small and packed and uncomfortable over a five-hour flight. As the flight droned on, outside the windows all the players could see below was snow, one snow-capped mountain after another. The sun shone off the snow so brightly that even from 30,000 feet, it was hard for them to keep from squinting. As the plane circled to land in Anchorage, the players looked down to find that even the runway appeared to be made of ice. They wondered, "Are we going to land on that?"

They did. After the plane skidded to a stop, the players grabbed their gear. They were standing in the aisles when Vinny del Negro, who had traveled with the team as a freshman two years before, was heard to mumble under his breath, "Fucking Alaska. I'm back here again. I can't believe it. Fucking Alaska."

It was three o'clock in the afternoon when the team arrived at the Captain Cook Hotel. It was dark. While the players lay around their rooms waiting for practice at five, John Simonds went with Mike Giomi to scout out the best restaurant in the hotel. Valvano believed in his team going first class, so there was no meal budget. Simonds had only been with the team a short while, but already he had discovered one of the benefits of traveling with Valvano's basketball team: unlimited free food. Whoever said there was no such thing as a free lunch—or breakfast or dinner or between-meal snack—didn't play for N.C. State.

For every game that was scheduled, each player received $8 in meal money. But it was money the players put in their pockets because they didn't have to spend it. All a player had to do after ordering a meal was sign the tab. The N.C. State athletic department picked it up. The only things taboo were room service and alcoholic beverages. Since the athletic department budget was overseen by Valvano, the players knew that even if they took advantage, running up huge tabs, chances were no one would say anything. Players may have griped about what was going on on the court, but no one ever complained about the accommodations. Valvano called the shots, and for his team it was top drawer all the way.

The Captain Cook was a huge complex. It had three eight-story towers for guests, and six restaurants. Simonds and Giomi determined that of the six restaurants, the best was a fancy French restaurant on the top floor.

The two went up to the restaurant and made a reservation. Simonds, who was feeling more and more a part of the team, did what any other team member might have done. He told the maitre d', "We want a table for five at about ten tonight." He picked out a table in the corner with a view of the city overlooking Anchorage Bay.

The maitre d' inquired as to what they wanted to eat. Simonds, who knew something about U.S. geography and indigenous foods, quickly replied, "King crab." And then, considering the four giants he was eating with, he said matter of factly, "In fact, we want all you've got."

"Very good, sir," said the maitre d'.

All the way from Raleigh, Simonds had been telling Andy Kennedy, Walker Lambiotte, Vinny del Negro, and Giomi, "In Alaska, you have to eat king crab." Lambiotte, who was from a small town in Virginia, had never heard of king crab. Simonds told him, "King crabs are about three feet long, and they taste better than lobster." Since all Walker had seen were Maryland crabs, he thought Simonds was making it up. Walker told him, "Sure, Simonds, and I have some swampland I want to sell you down in Florida."

Practice was uneventful. The players ran a couple of wind sprints and then shot around. Everyone was very tired. Valvano told the players, "Get to bed early."

After practice everyone headed back to the Captain Cook. The black players went down to the coffee shop and ordered three or four cheeseburgers each, fries, and several rounds of shakes, and they took them up to their rooms where they played blackjack until long into the morning.

Giomi, Lambiotte, Kennedy, and Vinny del Negro, along with their ringleader, Simonds, elevatored up to the French restaurant. Without ever once looking at the menu, they began with fresh orange juice and large salads, followed that with "finger food," and after that Simonds told the waiter, "Bring on the king crab."

The waiter brought out two silver trays with the king crab just as Simonds had described it. The chef had already cracked the crab, so all the players had to do was reach in, pull out the meat, and dine. It was culinary heaven.

Lambiotte loved the king crab, and he felt beholden to Simonds. He said, "John, we believed you all along. We had confidence you weren't going to do us wrong." For the next thirty minutes nobody said a word. Before they were done, they ordered two more silver trays of crab. Then they ate German chocolate cake and custard and eclairs for dessert.

Simonds, in particular, felt on top of the world. Simonds had begun the season as an assistant to Coach McLean, but in his heart he'd always felt himself a player first, a coach's assistant second. His dream had been to play on the N.C. State basketball team, and though this year his job was to put in time as a practice player and Valvano's assistant, he knew that in another year he would be a player, along with these other guys. Simonds was proud of what he had already done for them. First, he had saved half the team from having to run in the three-mile run, and now he was leading the other half of the team in an eating orgy. He was getting what he had craved—acceptance by the players. He thought to himself, "If only this evening would never end."

After the crab orgy and dessert, everyone was stuffed and in a giddy mood. Vinny del Negro had picked out a custard, and he looked at it, and he said, "Hey, you guys, do you know what this looks like?" He held up the shimmering custard for the others to see.

Andy Kennedy immediately knew what Vinny was getting at. "Aw, Vinny, no. Don't say it."

Avie Lester—big, bruising Avie—had one of the worse cases of acne the players had ever seen. When Avie got hit in the face during practice, puss would start oozing on his face, and the other players would point to Avie's face and laugh.

Vinny, who had no love lost for Avie, told the others,

"It looks like Avie's face." Tears rolled down their cheeks, the five were laughing so hard.

Until the bill came. The waiter handed it to Simonds. He looked at it. Silent words formed on his lips. "Five, five, zero, point, zero, zero." He exhaled. "Five hundred and fifty dollars," he whispered. He thought to himself, "My God, we have really had it. This is more than a little bit over budget—even though we don't have a budget."

Del Negro asked, "How much is it, John?" Simonds couldn't say it. He handed the bill to del Negro. Vinny, in his understated way, said, "Oh, shit. We're in deep now." He handed it to Andy Kennedy. Andy said, "Goddddammmmmnnn. How are we going to explain this one?" Walker said, "This has to be a mistake. It says we ate three hundred dollars worth of crab."

It wasn't a mistake. Orange juice in Alaska costs $20 a glass.

Giomi said, "We might as well pack up and go home now, because we are going to be on V's shitlist."

"What are we going to do?" the players asked each other.

One of the consistent aspects of an athlete's personality is that in his own mind he is never at fault in any situation. If there is a crisis, the athlete seeks out someone to blame. Four pairs of eyes landed as one on Simonds.

Vinny said, "Great move, John. You really got us into this. You hooked us up all right, but good. This is the last time we're listening to you."

Walker said, "I knew we couldn't trust you to do anything right. For some guys, it's such a struggle. Ever since you hit V in the head that day, you just haven't been one of us."

The four of them pounded him hard verbally. Simonds tried to defend himself. Faced with sudden ostracism, he knew he needed a way out. Suddenly, he came up with a solution. His roommate at the hotel was Toby Brannan, another of the team trainers. Simonds suggested, "What if we sign Toby's name to the whole thing?" The nodding came furiously. Simonds added a 20 percent tip to the bill and signed, "Toby Brannan."

Their mood again lightened. They left the back room of the restaurant, laughing all the way. As they entered the front room, sitting three feet away from them were the N.C. State coaches—Valvano, McLean, Stewart, and Martin. All eyes met. The players looked at Simonds. He was once again their spokesman. Whenever a yellow flag went up, they resorted to being dumb players again.

Valvano said to Simonds, "What the hell are you guys doing here?" Simonds, hired by Valvano, was back in the middle again. His choice was to tell the truth, to squeal on the players and himself, or to cover up for the players and himself. Again, in a tight situation, he took the players' side.

Simonds said, "We came up to grab some food, but we saw how expensive it was, so we just grabbed a couple of burgers instead." Valvano wasn't buying it. He said, "Sure. I'll bet that's all you had." Simonds said, "Honest, coach. We didn't know it was this expensive," and looked behind him for confirmation. He discovered he was all alone. While he was discussing the situation with Valvano, the players slid out of the restaurant one at a time.

During the month Simonds had been with the team, he and Valvano developed a real affection for each other. He had become Valvano's jack of all trades. He drove Valvano to the airport, sometimes took care of his kids, helped send out recruiting information, even went on a couple recruiting trips to nearby North Carolina towns. He played in practice sometimes. John Simonds was more than a manager. Valvano called him, "My assistant, John Simonds."

Before Simonds could make his exit, Coach Ray Martin said, "John, I need you to do me a favor. When I packed this morning, I forgot to pack my underwear. Take our car. Here's some money. Go down to J.C. Penney's and get me some drawers."

Simonds didn't want to go but couldn't get out of it. At ten at night, he drove the coach's car through the ice and snow, skidding all the way, to get Martin some underwear. When he got back to his room, the players laughed at the idea of his going out into the freezing cold to buy Coach Martin skivvies. Simonds didn't care. Anything to be with Coach V.

Friday was a lazy day. The opening round of the tournament wasn't until Saturday. At ten o'clock the sun came up, big and beautiful. And by two-thirty it was pitch black again. There was nothing to do except play cards and watch TV. Vinny continued mumbling, "Fucking Alaska."

While the whites played hearts, the blacks continued playing blackjack for high stakes and eating burgers, fries, and shakes. Quentin Jackson was smarter than his competition, so he could sweet-talk Shack, Tev, and whoever else was foolish enough into playing with him and then take them for all the dough they had. Quentin reportedly came home from Alaska $350 richer. Shack, who left for Alaska with $500, reportedly left broke.

And while the white players very quietly dealt their hands and played, until someone got nailed with the queen of spades or shot the moon, the kibitzing and second-guessing was continuous in the rooms of the black players, as were the charges of cheating and stacking the deck and dealing from the bottom. Periodically, one could hear Shack yell out, "You helmet-headed motherfucker," as Quentin happily raked in the dough.

When the white players tired of hearts, they turned to playing poker for pennies. None of the four—Vinny, Giomi, Kennedy, or Lambiotte—had much experience with gambling. None of them had much experience with anything except basketball.

As they played, Giomi was dipping Copenhagen chewing tobacco. Lambiotte said, "Hey, give me some of that." Walker had never done snuff before, and Copenhagen is strong. He stuffed about a half tin's worth in his mouth, then went on playing his cards, as Giomi stared at him with wide eyes.

After about five minutes, Walker began to slide off his chair. His head began bobbing and his eyes turned watery. Vinny asked, "Walk, what's wrong?" Lambiotte said, "Man, I'm so wasted, I can't even see." Walker had such a buzz, he could not stand up. The others laughed at him all night. Kennedy said, "Walk, you are a stupid bunny rabbit. You come up here and you start dipping and you can't see straight. Walk, what are we going to do with you?"

Meanwhile, over in the rooms of the black players, a steady influx of college-age, *zaftig* girls began. It seemed that whatever black female students were in the city showed up on the basketball players' floor.

The next morning Kelsey Weems told his white teammates, "Shack had a girl on his bed, and Tev had a girl on his bed, and they was naked doing what they were doing with those two heifers while all the other guys stood around and watched them and laughed."

The white players were bug-eyed. None of them had the balls to share with Kelsey and the other black players the tale of *their* great adventure: watching Walker get blitzed on snuff.

17

The Great Alaskan Shootout

Friday night, they got to play basketball. State's first-round match was against the University of Texas. The host arena seated about 5,000 fans. About 125 crazies showed up. Since the game was being broadcast nationally on ESPN, the players didn't care how many came. Back in North Carolina, everyone could watch them.

Texas should have been a pushover, but some Wolfpack players were so flat from the inactivity—and others from the activity—that Texas outplayed N.C. State and was ahead by 5 points with only two minutes left.

Valvano looked down the bench and brought in Andy Kennedy, cold. Kennedy's primary skill was his shooting ability from long range. Valvano said it often, "That boy can shoot the ball." But in the season opener against Navy, a team that played a zone defense the entire forty minutes, Valvano never once put Kennedy in.

Texas coach Bob Weltman was a disciple of Bobby Knight. His team plays Bobby Knight–style tough man-to-man defense, so Andy didn't figure even to get into the game. Making his situation worse, in practice the day before, playing in a gym with no heat, Andy went in for a layup and one of his teammates kneed him in the leg and gave him a severe charleyhorse. Before the Texas game, he could barely walk through the warm-up drills. Kennedy tried to disguise the hobble, but his thigh hurt a lot. It was hard for him to walk, never mind play.

And so, as Texas was kicking State's butt, Valvano began pacing up and down the bench looking for an answer. Kennedy had previously decided that as long as he had to sit on the bench, he would sit right next to Valvano, to learn whatever he could. So that's where he sat every game. He also hoped that by sitting next to Valvano, his proximity would help get him into a game. Through his entire life up to his arrival at State, Kennedy had not only played every minute of every game, but he had been the star on whom the rest of the team depended. He was not used to having to watch others play. During the entire Navy game, Kennedy stared right into Valvano's eyes, hoping Valvano would tap him on the shoulder and send him in.

Against Texas, whenever Valvano looked at him, Andy looked away. His leg was hurting so badly he didn't want to go into the game.

Two minutes remained. Valvano looked down the bench and barked, "Andy, go in there for Bennie."

Andy knew that if he said he was hurt, Valvano would never call his name again. Kennedy went into the game, as nervous as he'd ever been in his life. The game was on national TV, his mom and dad were watching from Mississippi, it was his first college game experience, and Texas was threatening an upset of significance.

Kennedy was feeling numb, he was so nervous. His leg hurt the first time down the floor, but his adrenaline was pumping and he quickly forgot about the injury. Texas had the ball and, after holding it for forty seconds, shot and missed. Kennedy got the rebound. Coming up the court on offense, Kennedy passed the ball inside to Shackleford, and in a rarity, instead of shooting it himself, Shackleford passed the ball out to Quentin Jackson. Meanwhile, Kennedy got boxed out, and as he was trying to shake free, a Texas player elbowed him in the throat, dazing him momentarily. Free finally, Kennedy was standing way outside the 3-point line when Quentin hit him with a pass. Without hesitation, Kennedy let fly, and as he did so, Valvano made a face that said, "Good God, what have I done?"

Kennedy's lunar probe of a shot finally came down, and it hit nothing but net to close the gap a point. Valvano and the State substitutes leaped off the bench. Valvano called time out. He pulled Kennedy out of the game and put Bolton back in.

As he sat back down, Kennedy thought to himself, "Maybe I've proved that I'm a player."

The game came down to the final shot. State had the ball, down by a point. Drummond came down the court with the ball, threw up one of his thirty-footers and missed, but Lambiotte got the rebound. He went to shoot with less than a second left, and got hacked by a Texas player. The whistle blew as the final buzzer sounded. The referees, ruling he was fouled before the shot, awarded Lambiotte one and one.

Both teams came off the court. Every fan sitting frozen in that arena was rooting for Texas. N.C. State never got the cheers in neutral arenas. Fans who didn't care instinctively rooted for the Wolfpack's opponents. They all wanted to see Valvano and his renegades lose. The fans close by the State bench were shouting obscenities at Valvano, and they were razzing Lambiotte, who was white as a ghost.

During the time-out, the players sat on the bench while Valvano screamed at them for playing so poorly. "It's all you guys' faults. You haven't done anything right all day. But we have to win this game. We can't lose to these guys." Valvano never said a word to Lambiotte. He didn't even look at him.

Walker went out to the line. He was the only player out on the court, along with the two referees.

Texas called another time-out. As Walker returned to the bench, he looked like snow. His teammates were all thinking the same thing, "I'll bet he needs to find the men's room."

He went back out to the free-throw line, shooting one and one. If he missed the first shot, State would lose. If he hit the first one, he got to shoot a second one for the victory.

Lambiotte had not played a good game, and he was not a great free-throw shooter—he shot the ball at the wrong spot on the rim. Walker was still sick from his experience with the Copenhagen. Walker was shaking, he was so nervous. But Walker *was* a gamer. He let fire his first free throw. It bounced several times on the rim . . . *bongity, bongity, bongity* . . . before going in, *plop*. The score was tied.

Walker took a deep breath. The referee bounced him the ball. He spun the ball in his hands, bounced it twice, and this time he hit nothing but net—*swish*! The State players, blacks and whites, ran onto the court and mobbed him. He had saved the day.

On ESPN, during his interview with Dick Vitale, Valvano talked about how great it was to win the game, but when he got back to the locker room he berated his players in terms they wouldn't have allowed even on cable. When he entered the locker room, he caved in the team doctor's bag with a hard kick, sending it flying across the room. He picked up an eraser and bounced it off a wall and onto Teviin's head, where it left a long white streak. Teviin protested, "Come on, man."

"Shut up, Tev," Valvano told him.

For twenty minutes Valvano raged on, stressing how badly his team had played, complaining that they had wanted to lose. About fifteen minutes into the harangue, Valvano stopped and said, "You know, Walker, that's the kind of situation that every one of us dreams about since they're a kid. Game's on the line—one and one, no one else on the court, no time left. And you hit both of them. The first one was a little shaky, but both of them went in, and we won the game. Great job, Walk. You really pulled through for me." And then Valvano resumed his raging.

When finally Valvano said, "Let's get out of here," the players grabbed their gym bags and left before he could change his mind. Afterward the players noted that Vinny del Negro had been played sparingly. After his performance against Navy, they couldn't figure out why V didn't play him more.

Teviin had sat on the bench the entire first half, repeating an imaginary conversation with Valvano: "I played good against Navy. What did I do? Come tell me something." He went in the game in the second half and quickly scored 5 points, but Valvano took him out and didn't put him back in, and Tev was angry.

The next day, Thanksgiving day, Valvano made the players all go to study hall. Shackleford spent the entire time listening to Phil Collins sing "In the Air Tonight." Shack had taped it over and over on a ninety-minute tape, and though he was listening to it through headphones, he was playing it so loudly that Phil could be heard singing throughout the room. Making things more raucous, Shack sang along at the top of his voice. And Shackleford sings badly.

The players on the other side of the long tables were laughing about each other's first-grade-level work. Most of them were still trying to pass English 111, the basic freshman English course that must be passed to graduate. Kenny Poston, who was on the team mainly as a practice player, was taking English 110, which was one level below basic English. Poston was reading *Animal Farm* by George Orwell and when he stumbled over a three-syllable word, he leaned over to Quentin Jackson and said, "Hey Quentin, what's this word?" Quentin looked over and with a straight face said, "Cat. Kenny, that's cat. C-A-T. Say it." Shack continued his warbling and the rest of the players laughed until the end of study hall.

That afternoon State had to play the University of Iowa, led by All American guard B. J. Armstrong. For thirty-six minutes the Wolfpack played stellar ball, leading by 12 points with four minutes left. And then the team fell apart. Valvano had used his starters most of the game, and they died. With only a couple of seconds left in the game, Iowa tied it. State had a final possession, but Bennie Bolton missed a wide-open jumper at the buzzer.

State lost by 1 point in overtime. Drummond missed a thirty-five footer, again at the buzzer. There were tears in his eyes as he walked off the court.

Valvano was despondent. In the locker room afterward, he told his players, "Guys, I just can't believe this. You beat this team last year in the NCAAs, and then you come out and blow a big lead. I don't know what we're going to do. If we keep playing like this, our season is as good as over."

Nobody said anything, but several of the players thought to themselves. "This is the third game of the season. What is V talking about, 'as good as over'?"

Teviin Binns was furious with Valvano for another reason. Valvano had the habit of telling a player, "Here's a mind check to see if you're in the game," and then he would put the player in for two minutes and then take him right out. He wanted to see if the player had what it took to go into the game cold and still play well. The players never understood this thinking, and whenever it happened to a player, the main result was that the player would come out of the game spitting fire in anger at Valvano.

Early in the Iowa game, after a dead-ball situation, Valvano put Teviin in the game. Teviin took the ball out from under his basket. He threw it a little wide of Walker Lambiotte, who mishandled it, and the ball went out of bounds. Valvano immediately took Teviin out. Walking back to the bench, Teviin asked Valvano, "What did I do?" Valvano didn't respond, but Teviin didn't play again.

After the game, Teviin asked Valvano, "What did I do, V?" Valvano said, "Tev, I'm just trying to win. Just doing anything I can to win. You have to spare your personal feelings when we're on the court."

Binns said, "Come on, V. You can't tell me that." But there wasn't any more to be said. After the Iowa game, Teviin had trouble looking Valvano in the eye, because after that game, he refused to believe anything Valvano told him.

Despite his clutch 3-point shot against Texas, Andy Kennedy didn't get in against Iowa. He was mystified. He couldn't figure out what was going on.

The consolation game was played the next day, Sunday. To competitors, consolation games are like shucking corn. It's just no fun, even though State beat Utah State badly.

Vinny del Negro got to play some quality minutes, and he played well. His competitor for the shooting guard spot, Andy Kennedy, was put in the game for defensive purposes. Valvano had him guarding Utah State's star, Reed Newly. Newly had hit five 3-pointers, so State went to a box-and-one, with Kennedy playing man-to-man on Newly while everyone else played zone.

Newly took a shot, and Kennedy blocked it. Kennedy grabbed the ball, dribbled to his end and dunked the ball. He then hit a 3-pointer for a total of 5. And then Valvano took him out; he didn't play another second. Kennedy told himself, "This doesn't make any sense. Why is he doing this to me?"

18

A Different Drummer

Kenny Drummond scored in double figures against Navy, Texas, and Utah State, and the Wolfpack was victorious in each game. Drummond was pleased: His defense was tough, his shooting accurate, and the team had taken three out of four. Valvano was also pleased with the way Drum was playing.

The rest of the team was ready to mutiny over the way Drum was playing. The big guys all felt that Drum was a hog. They gave him credit for his shooting ability, but Drummond wasn't playing run and gun at the junior college level any more. He was playing the Big Time, and all his teammates had been high school All Americans. All his teammates had been used to getting the ball, and Drum wasn't sharing the rock.

By the time the team returned to Raleigh at the end of the Alaskan Shootout, they had experience playing alongside Drummond. Only on the rare occasion, they realized, would he pass the ball. As a consequence, the other players, especially the subs, began to take Drummond's rare pass and, instead of looking to pass it somewhere else, would shoot the ball, figuring, "My only chance to stay on the court is to make a shot." So up it went. They were feeling, "He's going to be out there thirty-eight minutes no matter what. I'd better take care of number one."

A couple of the forwards noticed that when Drum did throw the ball in deep, the pass would be late. In top-rated college basketball, everything depends upon split-second timing. For a big man to be open for a shot, the big man has to come off the pick and get the ball during that split second while the defender is still fighting through the block. If the pass comes in one second too late, the defender will be through, and the big man will be guarded and have to pass the ball back out.

The forwards found themselves calling, "Ball," and getting Drum's passes so late that they would have to pass the ball back to Drum, who would then shoot from twenty-five feet—unless the forward got so angry at Drum that he would force the shot with the defender draped all over him, just to keep the ball from going back to Drummond.

Throughout the games, the forwards kept yelling at Drummond, "Get me the ball, dammit," and Drummond would either reply, "I'll get it to you," and then ignore the forward the next time the situation arose, or Drum would reply, "Let me play my game."

The other thing that bothered his teammates was that Drummond was a loner, choosing to remain in his room and watch TV rather than go out with them. They hadn't considered the slights the sensitive guard had felt when he first arrived on the team. Also, they rarely invited him. They considered him arrogant and selfish. Behind his back, his teammates whispered that the only reason he came to State was to use the exposure to demonstrate his shooting ability to pro scouts by gunning away, and the rest of them be damned.

Drummond heard all the criticism, but in his own mind felt that his teammates were simply jealous of his status as team quarterback. He resented that his teammates never said, "Nice shot," when he hit a 3-pointer, and he noticed that his teammates never gave him a pat on the back after a game, even after he scored 20 points or more. Whenever he played what he thought was a good game, all he heard was the criticism that he shot too much, that he was a detriment to the team. He kept his composure by telling himself, "We're winning, and I'm playing good enough to play in the NBA."

The other player causing dissent on the team was Mike Giomi. He had come to State from Indiana with a fine reputation, but he was playing so poorly that some of the players didn't think he should be playing at all. On offense he was slow, and on defense he rarely hit the boards. They wondered about his intensity, his desire. There was no fire in his game.

The black players especially resented that he was playing. Chucky Brown reportedly resented the minutes Giomi was taking from him, and Avie Lester, the freshman, was heard constantly complaining about the "Italian connection" at State.

At dinner one night, as the black players ate together, Avie was railing about Giomi's lackadaisical play. "Man, he sucks. He's a sorry dude. He shouldn't be playing."

Kenny Drummond interrupted him. Drummond, despite being a loner on the court, preached team unity off it. He said, "Hey Avie, we're on the same team, and he must be doing something right to be playing.

"Damn, man, I don't understand you guys," he continued. "We're all on the same team and, first of all, Giomi isn't here. Why don't you wait until he comes in and then say what you want to say? And maybe he'll work harder next time."

Drummond was trying to still the internal unrest. What he did was turn the black players against him.

Replied Avie, "Kenny Smith [from North Carolina] is better than you are."

Said Drummond stiffly, "Everyone has their own opinion."

In practice the next day, Valvano spent the entire session screaming at Avie Lester, almost to the point, the other players felt, of unfairness. Avie wasn't a smooth player, but he did work hard, so the other players couldn't figure out why Avie was Valvano's scapegoat so much of the time.

As practice was drawing to a close, Drummond made a disparaging comment about Avie's game. "Fuck off!" Avie told him. Drummond, a wise, street-smart kid who wouldn't back down from a bulldozer, said, "Why don't you do something about it, you pimply-face nig."

Avie, sensitive about his acne, went at Drummond. They squared off, but the other players got between them before anyone threw a punch.

Coach McLean told Simonds, "It's a good thing that got stopped, because Drummond would have killed Avie." Avie was six-foot-eight and strong as a bull, as opposed to Drum being six feet and thin as a wire.

Avie walked toward the locker room, with Drummond

right behind him. In the locker room, the shouting began heating up again. This time it was Coach McLean who arrived in time to keep them from fighting.

McLean shouted, "This is going to stop right now. This is not going to happen on my team. We're not going to act like a couple of high school juniors. We're a college team, and I'm not going to put up with this shit."

In his own mind, Drummond thought Avie was all talk and no action. "The bigger your mouth is," Drummond thought, "the smaller your heart."

Kenny Drummond was becoming more and more isolated on the N.C. State basketball team.

19

The Mutiny

The Wolfpack played its first game back from Alaska against East Tennessee State, a small, schedule-stuffing team. East Tennessee was quick but short, and State scored 104 points in a rout. The next game was against Western Carolina, another patsy.

In practicing to get ready for the game, Valvano told the players, "Aside from the ACC games, we have two really tough non-league games on the schedule, Western Carolina and Tampa."

He said, "For the past ten years, Western Carolina has always come to our place, because they didn't have a home court. Well, they just built a new five thousand–seat arena. We are the inaugural game for them, and they are going to be psyched. Fellas, this is going to be a 'cause game' for them." He said, "They want to beat us worse than anything in the world. Their whole season is this one game. That arena is going to be so loud, with all those Catamount fans packed in there, all those redneck mountain people. They are going to be pumped about tearing you guys from limb to limb."

The players weren't buying it. They figured it was going to be East Tennessee all over again. So we're playing in their barn. Big deal.

Valvano was right about one thing. It was incredibly loud in the arena. Valvano couldn't even be heard in the huddle. The rowdy fans threw cups of ice, hot dog buns, and popcorn at the State players. The Catamounts competed for thirty-five minutes, keeping the crowd animated, but in the last five minutes State kicked their butts, winning by 20.

A third-straight schedule stuffer, Duquesne, visited Raleigh, and Drummond led the team in scoring in yet another rout. With State up by 25 points late in the game, Valvano put Andy Kennedy in for the first time. With only minutes left, Kennedy hit a 3-pointer, and when he ran off the floor, Valvano came up to him and said, "You know, Andy, you're going to be a great player here. Hang in there."

The Wolfpack was 6–1, and to outsiders the team was doing great. To insiders, it was just a question of when everything was going to blow.

The explosion came at home against the fourth push-over opponent in a row, the University of North Carolina at Asheville. Asheville had a couple of decent players, but average height and no depth, and with Shack and Drummond leading the way, State won by 16. Andy Kennedy got to play with only minutes left in the game. He took a bad shot off a late pass from Drummond, and Valvano yanked him back out and put the starter, Walker Lambiotte, back in the game. When Kennedy came out, three other game-long benchwarmers—Teviin Binns, freshmen Avie Lester and Brian Howard—moved down toward the end of the bench by one chair.

With twenty seconds left on the score clock, Charles Shackleford launched a dunk that brought the crowd to its feet. While the Pack fans roared their approval, Brian Howard, who was sitting on the end, said to Avie and Teviin, "Come on," and the three stood up, slammed their towels down, and left their seats, walking along the sideline, out of the noisy arena, and into the silent locker room as the final seconds ticked away.

Not many fans noticed this major act of defiance because of Shack's dunk. But Valvano noticed.

In the locker room after the game, after Valvano had critiqued the game, he said, "You three guys, and you know who you are, got up and walked off the bench. Don't think I didn't see that. That really pisses me off. Nobody walks off my bench and embarrasses me in my barn. Nobody. Everybody here thinks they are special. I've been coaching basketball twenty years. I'm not going to put up with this shit." Then he added, "If anybody messes with me, I'm going to call my uncle from Long Island to come down here."

And he stalked out of the locker room.

Binns thought, "He isn't talking about Vinny or Walker or Giomi or Andy. He's talking about us." Looking back, Binns regretted not saying something to Valvano in the locker room that evening.

The next day Valvano didn't show up for practice. The players got taped and were shooting around when Coach McLean came into the gym and said, "Everybody gather around." He said, "Jim is really upset about what happened last night. He's over in his office right now, and if you have a beef, you go over and talk it out with him."

McLean continued, "Coach V doesn't want to ever see this happen again. He's sitting there, and he wants to listen. And, fellas, this is going to be the starting point of our season. If we don't get it out in the open now, all these tensions about who's playing and who's not and feelings that V's playing favorites with the whites or the blacks, we'd better get them out now or otherwise we are in for a long season."

He said, "If you don't have a beef, practice is over."

The players all stood around, pondering what to do. Bennie Bolton was heard to say, "I've been here four years, and I've never had a meeting with V one-on-one, and I can't see any reason to start now. There's no point. First of all, he does all the talking. Second, what V tells you in his meetings doesn't go along with what happens on the court."

Bolton reportedly had come to State because of Ray Martin, Valvano's assistant coach and a former Notre Dame star, who was in charge of recruiting black players. Because Martin was on the N.C. State staff, Bolton had assumed that he would have someone he could relate to if he had a problem. Said Simonds, "Only when Bennie got to school did he discover that Martin's skill was recruiting, not relating." Bolton, who never smoke, drank, or cussed, was an idealist who believed that blacks always got the short end of the stick in American society. He was an intelligent man who believed in right and wrong. He believed Valvano often to be wrong, especially when it came to race relations.

Bennie's teammates thought him odd. He enjoyed wearing army fatigues, and it was rare to have him give a straight answer to a question. In the middle of a conversation having nothing to do with basketball, Bennie would blurt out, "V is a prejudicial dude, isn't he?" His teammates would wonder, "Where did that come from?" They all knew that Bennie didn't like Valvano as a person, didn't like the fact that as athletic director Valvano had almost no blacks in his administration, didn't like the way he treated his players, resented his meat-market approach to recruiting, and didn't like his coaching tactics. In sum, there was little about Valvano that Bolton did like. Anytime something positive about Valvano appeared in the local paper, Bennie would say, "That's a crock, isn't it?" He once told Simonds, "He's a con man, not a coach."

Bolton refused to see Valvano. He left the gym, followed by Quentin Jackson. By nature, Quentin did not like to make waves. Kelsey Weems was another player who reportedly was very unhappy. Weems, a nice kid with a load of talent, desperately wanted to play, but Drummond was getting all of his minutes.

Teammates felt that Weems could have been a star if someone had taken his raw talent and molded it, but Valvano was not a teaching coach, so Weems was perpetually in the dark as to what he had to do to improve sufficiently to play. Worsening his situation, Weems was one of Valvano's whipping boys. In practice Valvano ragged on Weems endlessly whenever he made a bad pass or was in the wrong spot at the wrong time. Valvano never had a good word for him.

"Kelsey, why don't you talk to him?" asked one of his teammates. Kelsey turned with sad eyes and said, "It won't do any good. He isn't going to listen to me." And he left.

Mike Giomi was the next to decide. Giomi was reportedly unhappy because he wasn't fitting into Valvano's system—he didn't really understand what that system was. It seemed to him that State's offense consisted simply of Drummond's bringing the ball down the court and shooting. At Indiana, as throughout the Big Ten, the style of basketball was more physical and more structured. Big Ten teams ran plays to perfection. Giomi was used to knowing exactly where he was supposed to be at all times on the court. At N.C. State, the offense was a whirlwind of improvisation. The ACC was an improvisational league, with North Carolina's Michael Jordan the prototype ACC player. So Giomi was lost and his NBA aspirations were sinking fast as he struggled just to get up and down the court in time. It was starting to be the team joke that "Mike Giomi is the worst player in the ACC," even though State hadn't begun its ACC schedule and even though Valvano was still starting him.

When asked if he was going to see Valvano, Giomi said, "Let me tell you. We are all just pawns in a big chess game. I know that the only reason I'm here is to put a basketball through a bucket so I can bring people in here to pour money into this program. I don't care what happens to this team. I'm out for one thing. I want to play in the pros, and I'm going to do everything I can to play in the pros. If the team suffers, that's fine. But I don't have time for this nonsense, to talk to a bag of wind when he's not going to listen to me. I got better things to be concerned about, mainly the pros."

Teviin Binns also refused to go see Valvano. Hearing Valvano threatened to sick his "uncle" on him, Binns decided that his relationship with Valvano was over. He didn't want to have anything more to say to him. Valvano had promised Teviin's mom that he would play twenty minutes a game, and here he was in his second year at State, and he hadn't played twenty minutes in a game even once. Teviin didn't want another meeting in which Valvano would tell him, "We're going to go with you in the future," only to continue to sit him on the bench.

Teviin had started the season with hope, taking a seat right next to Valvano on the bench. As the season wore on, he began moving farther and farther away from Valvano, until by this time he was down with Brian Howard and Avie Lester on the end. Ernie Myers, a former Wolfpack player and an unpaid assistant to Valvano, told Teviin, "Don't worry about it, Tev, he has to play you." But Tev knew Valvano wasn't going to. And he never did.

Teviin left the building and went home.

Kenny Drummond went to see Valvano. He wanted to talk to him about the jealousy of his teammates and the tough time he was having with Quentin and Kelsey. But Drummond never got an opportunity to speak.

Valvano began by telling Drummond what a good person he was, that he was working hard, doing a great job.

And he told Drummond that if he kept up the good work, he would have a great career at N.C. State.

What could Drummond say? The coach was telling him how great he could be. Drummond thanked him for his support and left.

The other players knew that Drummond had gone to see Valvano, but no one cared enough to ask him about the conversation. By this time everyone was bad-mouthing Drummond, convinced he was dragging the team down, and they didn't want anything to do with him. The white players, especially, verbally roasted Drummond at every opportunity.

Andy Kennedy, who was unhappy at playing so little, went to see Valvano. Kennedy was considering leaving the team, transferring at Christmas. A player may leave in the first semester as long as he doesn't play more than eight games, and the Asheville game was the Pack's eighth game. Andy wanted to let Valvano know how he was feeling.

Kennedy told Valvano, "Things aren't working out. I'm not playing as much as I thought I would."

Kennedy had twice before had this conversation, and in the past Valvano had told him, "Kennedy, goddamn it, you are so selfish. You should be thinking about the team, not yourself. You're part of a team." And both times Kennedy came away feeling guilty, and angry.

This time, when Kennedy mentioned that he was thinking of transferring, Valvano sang a different song. He promised Kennedy that if he stuck it out, he would become a star at State.

Valvano said, "Listen, hang in there. We've only played eight games, and you're still learning. You can do it. We're expecting great things of you. You're going to play—a lot. Please be patient."

Kennedy thought that this time Valvano would take him seriously and maybe he would get to play.

After the meeting, Kennedy returned to the gym to shoot baskets.

Brian Howard, one of the three who had walked off the bench, also went to see Valvano. He returned to the gym and was standing with Kennedy when he unleashed his anger at Valvano.

Howard mumbled, "I'm a great player, and I can't get to play because V doesn't know anything about the game."

As Brian was raging, Andy came to a realization. He said, "Brian, you know what? I'm transferring. I'm leaving this program. I got all the promises made to me—I was hoodwinked into coming here, and now I'm getting jerked around. I told Valvano I was staying, but if I don't leave now, I promise I'm through at the end of the season. I'm out of here. I'm a good player, and I don't care what he thinks. I'm outta here."

Brian Howard replied, "Yeah, me too. I've had it. I'm going somewhere else and be a fucking superstar, and fuck V."

20

Promises, Promises

John Simonds didn't go see Valvano because he loved working for him, but as final exams neared, he was beginning to realize that working for the basketball program had become a full-time job and his school work was suffering seriously. He was facing every schoolboy's nightmare, going into finals without having done the necessary studying to pass.

On a car ride to drive Valvano to the airport, Simonds broached the subject of his grades. He said, "Coach V, I love working for you. I love this program. I like you. But I have to tell you, I'm failing my classes."

Valvano said, "John, I know you're working hard for me. You're a good man. I like you. All the coaches like you, and I want you to be a big part of this team. I want to take care of you, because you're a good man. Don't worry about your grades. I'll handle it."

Simonds didn't question him further. He didn't ask Valvano how he was going to "handle it" because he knew the coach had the clout to keep him in school, no matter what, and he figured Valvano's word would be good. Simonds breathed a sigh of relief and said, "Thanks, coach. I really appreciate it."

Simonds took his finals. He passed only one class. Still, he wasn't worried about his grades. Valvano was "taking care of it."

He did have another problem, however. Once he began traveling with the team, he realized that he no longer had time to hold down his job as resident assistant in the dormitory. That job provided him with room and board. His work with the basketball team was strictly volunteer. Though his heart was with the basketball team, he realized that quitting his dorm job would mean putting himself in a serious financial bind.

Shortly after returning from Alaska, Simonds went to see Coach McLean to discuss his dilemma. He said, "Coach, if I quit the dorm job, my board will no longer be taken care of, and I'm going to be short of money."

McLean told him, "John, you're a big part of this program. We're going to try to put you on scholarship with the team." If that happened, Simonds didn't have to worry about money. Simonds blindly assumed the scholarship would be forthcoming and quit his dorm job. He moved out of the dorm to share an apartment off-campus with a friend.

To help make ends meet until the scholarship came through, Simonds got a job teaching Nautilus weight training at the Raleigh YMCA. He came in three days a week at six in the morning, worked until ten, went to class, and then showed up for basketball practice at four in the afternoon. For his toil at the Y, he got minimum wage, $3.35 an hour. After taxes, that came to about $60 a week. His expenses—rent, gas, and food—came to about $80 a week.

Each week Simonds waited for his scholarship, hoping he could cut down on his hours at the Y. He kept thinking, "It should be any day now." But by the end of the term, it hadn't happened, and he was so broke he was eating noodles and rice every meal.

It got so bad that one evening his girl friend took him down to the Food Lion and bought him loaves of bread, peanut butter and jelly, and canned goods like fruit cocktail and tuna fish. As Christmas break neared, the food was running out. John Simonds was living on hopes and dreams.

Christmas vacation saved him. Finals ended on December 17, the day of the Asheville game, and all the students left for home—except the basketball players. A game against Tampa University was scheduled for December 27, and Valvano demanded that the team practice until December 23. "Then you can leave," he said, but added, "You have to be back Christmas day, because that night we have practice, and the next day we have to fly to Tampa."

The players were furious, because most of them lived

too far away to go home for just one day. For them, canceling plane reservations for the flights home for Christmas was a downer. The only solace was Coach McLean's gracious invitation to his home for Christmas dinner.

For Simonds, having to stay on campus with the basketball team meant that he would get $37 a day meal money. Every day from December 18 until January 5, Simonds and the other players got a perdiem of $37 for a total of over $700. Like the players, who were happy to spend somebody else's money in a heartbeat but squirreled their own money away like misers, Simonds got to keep most of that money, spending $5 a day on food and using the rest for rent and gas. He'd go to the Food Lion and buy six Mr. P's pizzas at 49 cents a pop. For dinner he'd eat three of those and drink a glass of milk.

Meal money was his recompense for working so hard for Valvano.

21

Music Class

Christmas vacation must have been a time of serious panic for Valvano. Charles Shackleford and Kelsey Weems had done so poorly academically that they were going to be ruled ineligible to play spring semester. Without Shackleford, the season would be a disaster.

One of the classes Shackleford and Kelsey had failed was Music 200, taught by Dr. Frank Hammond. Ordinarily, it's an easy class to get a C in. The student reportedly listens to music and learns a few general philosophies in class, and the C is his. Said Simonds, "If the student is on the basketball team, Dr. Hammond, who loves hoops, has been known to give A's to players who attend class and show some interest."

But Shackleford and Weems apparently never attended class. So Hammond failed them. Valvano made an appointment to see Dr. Hammond personally.

Dr. Hammond, sympathetic with Valvano's plight, agreed to give Shackleford and Weems a crash course from the start of Christmas vacation to the beginning of the spring semester. If the players passed the test, they would get B's.

But Hammond threw in a catch. "You," he was reported to have told Valvano, "have to take the course with them."

Valvano was fuming when he returned from his meeting with Hammond. Here was Jim Valvano, the athletic director and basketball coach of N.C. State, being told by a professor—of music, no less, and making a paltry salary in comparison to his—that he would have to take a crummy music class with two of his intellectually uninterested ballplayers.

But Valvano had little choice. He needed Shack. So he agreed and dutifully attended the classes, which Dr. Hammond was gracious enough to hold in the basketball offices. When the players arrived for their chalk talks, they'd find the chalk board covered with musical notes. When Valvano arrived to talk basketball, he'd erase the notes without a word and begin talking.

Like Shack and Kelsey, Valvano also had to write reports. Coach Stewart also went to the music classes and took notes for everybody. Stewart then typed out the notes and passed them out to Valvano, Shackleford, and Weems.

One day Stewart asked John Simonds to go to the library and check out some books on Tschaikovsky for a book report Valvano had to write. He said, "I need you to get some simple, easy-to-read books, because we have to plow through this real quick, find out the basic information, so I can write this book report for V." Simonds was sure Stewart was going to ask him to write it.

Simonds went to the library and checked out three books on Tschaikovsky. Stewart took the books and said, "Thanks, I'll turn the books back in after I write the report.' (Stewart never returned the books. Simonds had to pay a $15 library fine at the end of the year.)

Valvano, of course, tried to keep it quiet that he was also taking the course. Said one of the few players who knew, "It was so funny. Here was a nationally renowned basketball coach taking a make-up music class with a couple of real boneheads."

One day about the second week of class, as the players were stretching on the floor Valvano was heard complaining about "how it's a hard game" and how being a coach was so tough. Bennie Bolton looked up and said deadpanned, "Hey, coach, how about that classical music?" Valvano stopped dead in his tracks. With the others snickering, he calmly replied, "Well, you know how it is when you're in with Shack and Kelse. It's a laugh a minute."

The other basketball players felt that the make-up class was a charade. Not one of them expected to see Shackleford ineligible the second semester. Said a teammate, "Everybody knew that wasn't for real. They were trying to play people like, 'They're doing a course, so you know they're going to pass now.' "

Said another teammate, "We knew Shack was going to be eligible. Because V couldn't afford him to fail. He was the only big man we had. We knew that if Shack didn't play, we weren't going to win. Shack knew that. *He* knew he wasn't going to fail."

John Simonds, recalling the incident, remembered thinking to himself, "Holy mackerel, there are a lot of kids who flunk out of school here because though they try hard, they can't quite make it, or they have to work their way through and they just don't have enough time to study, and here are two guys taking a special class who are going to pass and stay in school because they play basketball."

22

Tev Wants Out

On Christmas day, Teviin Binns asked his girl friend for advice. Should he quit the basketball team? He had considered transferring after his junior year, and he was angry that he hadn't. He was angry that Washburn and Shack had gotten the star treatment with all the perks while he hadn't. But more important, he was bitter that they had been given the chance to show their skills and he hadn't. He had been promised a significant role, but that role had never materialized. The fall term of his senior year was coming to a close, and by all appearances his chances to be a college basketball star were passing him by, all because he had put his faith in Coach Valvano, who had reneged on promises made to him and his mother.

His girl friend, who had endured his pain throughout one and a half seasons of basketball, told him, "Teviin, do what you feel is right for you."

The next day the rest of the players were milling around the court, getting ready for practice to begin, when Teviin called Simonds over and handed him an envelope. He said, "Wait until practice is over, and then give this to Coach Mac." Coach McLean was the only one of the four coaches Teviin liked or trusted. If Tev would miss anyone beside the players, it would be Coach Mac.

Simonds didn't wait for practice to end. He sensed what the note was about and immediately handed it to McLean, who opened it up, whistled low, and said, "Jim isn't going to like this." No matter how often it happened—and during Valvano's tenure as coach it happened often—if there was one thing Valvano dreaded, it was bad press over one of his players leaving the program.

A month earlier Teviin had told a local newspaper

reporter, "I'm thinking about transferring because Valvano isn't up-front with me." Valvano had cornered him in practice and told him, "The reason I don't play you is that you don't play defense." Binns shot back, "Everybody on this team don't play no defense. You can't tell me that." Teviin no longer believed anything Valvano told him. Valvano warned him, "Don't dog me in the papers, and I won't dog you."

When the other players found out that Teviin was quitting, they lost whatever spark they'd had during practice, because everyone loved having Teviin around. Teviin had a zest that they enjoyed, and whenever practice was boring or Valvano was being heavy-handed, they could always count on him to come up with something light to keep everyone sane.

They knew something else: that he could play. Said Simonds, "When he felt like it, in practice he would become a scoring machine, slamming on the defense, bounding up the court full-speed, taking out his frustrations."

Teviin called his father and asked him to contact some other colleges. His father called Villanova, who had recruited him out of Midland Junior College. He called his Midland coach, who was now coaching at the University of Texas at Arlington. Teviin didn't care that Arlington was a small school. He just wanted to go somewhere and play.

The next day Valvano called him into his office. Coach McLean was sitting there, too. Valvano had seen Teviin's letter and had talked to his father on the phone. Valvano told him, "Do you know that you flunked out and you aren't eligible to transfer?"

Teviin was shocked. He said, "I haven't flunked out."

"You're about to," Valvano said. "Your grades aren't good."

Teviin was boxed in. His option to transfer was cut off. His only hope in basketball was to continue at N.C. State.

Valvano had become his savior by default.

Valvano said, "Teviin, your father told me I better take care of you, and since I told him I would, I'm going to have to talk to some people and see what we can do to keep you in school."

Teviin had joined Shackleford in the same leaky academic lifeboat. The only way Teviin would get to play basketball was to rely on Valvano to find a way to keep him in school the spring semester. Teviin had no choice but to return to the basketball team.

Valvano said, "If you stay, I will make sure everything is okay, and you will play."

Teviin believed the first half of Valvano's promise. But he knew the second half of the statement was no truer this time than it had been any other.

23

Tampa

The basketball team practiced Christmas night, after dinner over at Coach McLean's house. In the locker room after practice, the players were cracking on each other, making fun of the presents they got. Quentin Jackson, picking on his favorite target, said, "Shack got a big present. He found out who his dad was." Everyone went "Ooooohhh, Shack," and Shack got angry and replied with his usual "Helmet Head" retort. Drummond uncharacteristically joined in, saying, "Teviin got a pair of knitted socks for Christmas," which made most of them laugh, because the players were cool about their socks, and knitted socks were definitely not cool.

In two days State was scheduled to play Tampa, a Division II school that figured to do about as well as East Tennessee, Western Carolina, or Asheville had done. In other words, Tampa had no business playing on the same court with N.C. State. That State would win the game was all but preordained. State was favored by 15 points easy.

The next morning everyone got up and left for Tampa. The players were pissed off because Valvano had made them stay through the vacation to practice, and when they arrived at the bus, they were told he was too sick to go with them, which made them even madder. One player grumbled, "He's home eating turkey while we have to go to Tampa to play some crummy Division II school."

In twenty years of coaching, Valvano had missed exactly one game, and the story was that he had come down with the flu and had a temperature of 104, and his doctor told him it would be risky for him to fly. All week Valvano had warned the players that this would be another "cause game," that Tampa would be psyched playing in its own arena, and he expressed worry that the players wouldn't take Tampa seriously because it was only a Division II school. On that score he was right. The players didn't think Tampa would be any better than Asheville, the other "cause game."

The players were delighted that Valvano couldn't make the trip. Everyone was light-hearted. The only ones walking around with a tight feeling were the assistant coaches, because they knew they were on the line. If they lost, they had Valvano to answer to.

When the team arrived at the Tampa Hyatt the afternoon before the next day's game, John Simonds got the surprise of his life. He had been assigned Valvano's suite. When he opened the door to his room, he saw a hallway a mile long. The bed was big enough for professional wrestling—six pillows rested across the headboard. The bathroom was as big as Texas. Inside there was a refrigerator stocked with booze, food, and caviar. Simonds wondered if this is what Valvano meant when he said, "I will take care of you."

Simonds called Andy, Vinny, Giomi, and Walker to see his room. Vinny volunteered, "You stay with Gee, and I'll move in here." Walker said, "You room with Andy, and I'll move in here." Simonds declined both offers.

Simonds and Walker spent the evening watching television in Simonds' suite. The rest of the players went across the street from the hotel to a nude bar. Coach McLean had told them, "Fellas, we don't want you going in there." To this team, that was the wrong thing to say. As soon as it got dark, the players headed for the Tanga Lounge.

At two-thirty in the morning, there was a pounding on Simonds' door. It was Mike Giomi. He could barely stand up. Staying out until the sun came up was common for most of the players. There was nothing to do the next day until about five, so it was not at all unusual for the players to stay out all night and sleep until four in the afternoon. Giomi went straight for the refrigerator. He said, "Man, I'm starving." The way it worked, whatever was eaten or drunk from the refrigerator was billed to the room. Giomi took out his army knife and started popping holes in the bottom of Pepsi and beer cans, sucking them dry upside down, and then putting them back in the refrigerator so that it looked as if nothing had been used. He ripped open the bottom of a container of dip, scooping the dip from the bottom and whipping it on crackers he had extracted through the bottom of the box. Singlehandedly, Giomi cleaned out the refrigerator.

The real excitement of the night occurred at about three in the morning. The fire alarm went off on the twelfth floor, where the basketball players were being housed. The handful of players who were asleep were awakened by the incessant clanging of the alarm bells. Almost immediately, doors opened and heads were popping out into the hallway. "What is it?" "It's a fire." "FIRE!" A stampede to the fire stairs began. Players came barreling down the hallway in their underwear. Chucky Brown's eyes were bulging with fear, his mouth wide open. The "boom, boom, boom" reverberating from pairs of large, pounding feet hitting the metal stairs could be heard as the players flew from floor to floor down to the ground.

In the lobby, most of the guests of the large hotel were standing in pajamas and nightgowns. The fire trucks arrived, but the firemen were unable to locate what had set off the alarm. The police went to the players' floor, but they didn't find anything either.

The players looked around the lobby. "Where's Shack and Tev?" Chucky Brown asked.

Back in their rooms, Shack and Tev were smoking—what Teviin cryptically described as "fat cigars." Shack apparently was concerned the smoke would set off the alarm, and according to Teviin, Shack took off one of his size 19 sneakers and began whacking one of the smoke detectors as hard as he could.

"Shack, man, leave that alarm alone," Teviin told him. "Shack replied, 'Let me just see if the lid'll come off.' And *pop*, it broke, followed shortly by 'Wooooooo woooooooooo.' "

Shack and Tev could hear the announcement on the loudspeaker to evacuate the building.

Said Tev, "We agreed: We ain't going nowhere." When

the officials came up to the room, they feigned being asleep, stifling giggles under the covers.

Everyone slept in until right before game time the next day. Simonds remembered Shackleford's long walk to the bus. Simonds wondered what Shack was on.

Said Simonds, "Shack came out of the lobby elevator walking very slowly, wobbling and wearing a stupid grin. He walked through the glass doors to the outdoors and aimlessly wandered out into the parking lot, where he searched for the bus to take the team to the arena. The bus had been parked behind the hotel, and as this six-foot-eleven giant with size nineteen sneakers and wearing a Walkman on his head was slowly meandering around, in search of the lost bus, his teammates finally figured out where he was, and from around the corner of the building, they began yelling, 'Hey, Shack, back here.'

"Shack nodded, changed direction, and walked slowly to the bus. As he went to step up into the bus, he fell down lengthwise in the stairwell as his teammates laughed at him. He grabbed the first object that didn't move and pulled himself up into the bus. He then stood and marched to the back of the bus, sat down, turned on his Walkman, closed his eyes, and didn't budge until the bus got to the arena. If the coaches noticed, they didn't say anything."

While the rest of the black players were listening to what the whites called "niggie music"—rap music—Shack was chilling out, listening to his "In the Air Tonight" recording by Phil Collins, white-bread rock and roll, taped to repeat itself over and over and over.

Four thousand Tampa fans packed their arena for the game. State was up by 8 at the half, and the game should have been in the bag. The focus of amusement for the players was the power struggle going on between Coach McLean and Coach Stewart. Valvano, back in Raleigh, had directed McLean to run the team on the court. McLean was the more knowledgeable coach—he was the X's and O's man on the team, the strategist. He was the one who sat next to Valvano and counseled, "Jim, go to a two-three zone," and Valvano would yell, "Two-three zone," without even questioning it. Then McLean would say, "Shack's tired. Call a time-out." Like a puppet,

Valvano would call, "Time out." As far as the players were concerned, Ed McLean was the man, the heart and soul of the team, the one coach who would come over when a word of solace was needed and say, "Keep your head up."

Coach Stewart was vying with Coach McLean to see who would run the team. The players reportedly saw Stewart as Valvano's hatchet man. He was also seen as a tattletale. During practice, Stewart was the one who would say, "Coach V, Avie isn't hustling," and then Valvano would come down hard on Avie. Stewart was Valvano's best friend, and he was so pumped up about wanting to win the game for the Gipper back home lying in his bed that he couldn't contain himself.

Once the game started, whenever McLean called time and began to say a few words, Stewart would jump in, saying, "We have to win this one for V. He's taken care of us. He lets us stay in first-class hotels. You gotta come through for him this time. You can't let him down. He's such a good man. He gives up everything that we've got." Which may well have been true in Coach Stewart's case, but most of the ballplayers were feeling less than charitable toward Valvano by this time, so Stewart's cheerleading was met with stony contempt.

The players' enmity was on their faces. The last thing most of them wanted to do was win a game for Valvano. It was not what they needed to hear.

As usual, State was playing run and gun, and though it led at the half, the team played poorly. Walker Lambiotte was missing most of his shots. Drummond was throwing up his long bombs—whenever the ball was passed back to him after the first pass, he always shot it—so everyone else figured, "I've got to shoot rather than pass it back to Drum." Even Kelsey Weems was shooting jump shots, and that was just not his game.

When the second half began, State turned flatter than an empty pita. In the second half, Shackleford was standing, as one teammate described it, "like a dang monument." In the first half, he had played average, or perhaps a little below average, but after the halftime break, the other players noticed that Shack wasn't even making an effort. Nothing. He was missing shots he normally made, from close in, firing them hard off the backboard. One time he turned around from the side of the backboard to shoot from close in and bounced the ball hard off the wrong side of the board. On defense, the smaller Tampa players were slamming on him time and again.

Meanwhile, as the game neared its conclusion, with State slowly falling behind the moderately talented Division II school, Coach Stewart took over completely from Coach McLean. Stewart took players out after they hit shots, shuffling them in and out willy-nilly.

Late in the game Walker Lambiotte hit a couple of jumpers and was immediately yanked. When he came out of the game, Walker was overheard asking anyone within hearing distance. "What the heck is the coach doing?"

On the bench, Stewart was screaming at the top of his lungs—shouting, yelling, cursing, trying to stop the tide of events. Once after he called time the players waited for instructions for an out-of-bounds play, but Stewart had only one thing on his mind: "Guys, please, for Christ's sake, think about the Gipper. Think about the V Man laying on his bed, listening to the radio, pulling for us. Win one for him."

When Stewart said that, a couple of the players made a face of exasperation, and spit on the floor, *ptttui,* and muttered, "Goddamn it." The last thing they wanted to hear was a "Win one for the Gipper" plea.

With the score 63–62 Tampa, Shackleford missed a free throw. John Jones, who scored 30 points for Tampa, then hit a jump shot with seconds left and made two more free throws for a 5-point Tampa victory.

In the locker room after the game, Coach Stewart was so angry he just sat on the bench, staring at the players and shaking his head. He said, "Guys, I can't believe we just let Coach V down. After all he has done for us, you guys let him down." The players thought for a moment he was going to cry. He said, "Imagine the V Man sitting back home having to listen to this on the radio. Boy, you guys, we owe him everything, and we just let him down." The players were almost ready to break the door down to get away from him. They didn't want to hear that.

The players didn't say a word. They dressed quietly and got ready to return to the hotel. Coach Stewart said,

"You guys have some soul searching to do. I don't want to talk to you." He left. The other coaches left.

Brian Howard, who hadn't played much, smashed his locker door shut. He was heard mumbling, "Let them down, shit!" Andy Kennedy said, "We didn't have a coach tonight. We don't have a coach anyway." Everyone grabbed his stuff and headed for the bus.

Chucky Brown was heard to say, "Hell, I'm leaving right now. Where's the bus?"

When Coach Stewart said, "Think about the V Man," Teviin Binns, who hadn't played a minute against Tampa despite having his entire family fly down to watch him play, said disgustedly, "Let the V Man suck my fat one."

24

A Night on the Town

With the game out of the way, it was time for the night owls to go out on the town. Walker stayed back at the hotel to watch movies on Simonds' large TV set, in the room originally reserved for Valvano. Vinny, Giomi, and Tev went out with relatives, who had come down to see them. Andy Kennedy and the rest of his teammates hopped into a cab and set off for some big-time nude bar action in the black section of downtown Tampa.

Not all of them made it through the entrance door. Bennie Bolton forgot his ID. Chucky and Andy were underage and couldn't get in. But Shack and the others who made it inside moved right up to the edge of the stage, where the action was. They ordered drinks and ogled the young girl gyrating her lithe body, their eyes as big as pie pans. Then the girl bent over low, rubbed her hand on her crotch . . . and wiped her damp hand across Shackleford's face. While everyone else thought this hilarious, Shackeford suddenly became angry, and reportedly he swung and tried to hit her.

The bouncers, quicker than the Tampa guards, rushed in, grabbed Shackleford, and threw them all out.

Back out on the street, Andy Kennedy looked around and noticed that he was the only white face there. Hundreds of people were milling about, enjoying the breezy Florida night, just hanging out. Chucky and Kelsey walked down the street and parked themselves on a bench to watch the girls walk by. It was two in the morning.

A scuffle broke out down the street by the bar they had just been thrown out of. A "pop pop" was heard, though no one could be sure whether it was a firecracker or gunfire. As Chucky and Kelsey sat on the bench, they could see a herd of people racing toward them. Leading the mob were Shack, Quentin, Avie, and Kenny Poston, outracing everyone in town, running like the wind to keep from getting shot at.

Andy and Drum, who hadn't bothered to run, suddenly found themselves left behind. They went to hail a cab, but none came. Cab drivers aren't eager to head for that part of Tampa at that hour of the morning. There was no traffic on the street, not a car in sight.

The two players walked more than a mile to the interstate and put out their thumbs to hitch a ride back to the Hyatt. It was five-thirty in the morning. They only had two hours to make the plane. When a car finally stopped, they told the driver where they wanted to go, but he didn't want to take them. Drummond promised to pay the driver twenty dollars if he would take them back to the hotel. The driver agreed. But when he stopped in front of the hotel, the two players got out of the car, walked off, and left him sitting there. Said Kennedy later, "We didn't have any money. What was he going to do?"

That morning the plane from Tampa to Atlanta was delayed by fog for six hours. Everyone knew Valvano was stewing back at home, waiting for the players to arrive so he could chew them out. The delay was not going to help his disposition any.

Finally, the plane landed in Raleigh and the bus returned them to the school gym. And sure enough, Valvano was waiting. He said, "I want to see everybody in the locker room."

In the locker room, he started blasting away. "Guys, I am so disappointed. You lost a game that I was counting on us winning. We're getting hammered in the press for losing to them. I wish I could have been there." And then he said, "Even though I wasn't there, it's still my fault."

Said one teammate, "No one was listening. Most of the players had had about an hour's sleep and were exhausted, and they were so disgusted with the entire basketball program that they didn't have the patience to listen to another lecture."

As Valvano talked, Shackleford's head began bobbing, and before Valvano had finished, Shack was sound asleep. The rest of the players sat staring at their sneakers, kicking each other in the back of their chairs, dying to get home and get some sleep.

25

The Stakes

Valvano had a good reason for being so upset over the team's loss to Tampa. His players were messing up his grand plan for the season. As athletic director, one of Valvano's goals—and the goal of most athletic directors—was to mine the gold at the end of the college basketball season: the $520,000 per team given to each of the four teams to reach the Final Four of the 1986-1987 NCAA national tournament.

He had said it often. "All that matters is getting to the Final Four. That is what I live for."

College basketball used to be about school spirit and cheering for the boys and beating the archrival, but with the age of television and now the superfund age of cable television, there is simply too much money being tossed around for any athletic director to ignore it.

Before TV, it used to be that all an athletic director had to do was field a representative team; you'd still draw full houses in your home arena. But with television doling out millions of dollars for the best teams to play on the tube, being representative is no longer good enough. Just as most high school players want the chance to be seen on national television, athletic directors want their teams to be seen on national television. There are two reasons. The first is that television visibility enhances recruiting tremendously. The second is that a team playing often on national TV stands to gain hundreds of thousands of dollars for its war chest. A team that makes it to the Final Four of the NCAA championship . . . well, there's riches in them there networks.

When Valvano composes his schedule, reportedly he is trying to figure out how his team can end the season with twenty wins out of the twenty-seven games it plays during the regular season. For with twenty wins, the team is guaranteed to get an invitation to the NCAA championships. If the team fails to win twenty games during the regular season, it can make up the difference in the Atlantic Coast Conference championships. If it wins seventeen games or less, to get to the NCAAs it must win the ACC championship outright, since the ACC winner automatically gets a bid to play in the national championships.

Valvano once explained his grand plan to John Simonds. According to Simonds, Valvano figured that in the ACC his team would probably lose twice to Carolina, once to Duke away, once to Georgia Tech away, and also to several of the national powers he routinely schedules in order to keep the Wolfpack on national television: Navy, Oklahoma, Louisville, Kansas, and DePaul. To win the magic twenty, the team had to win half of its tough games and roll over all of the pushovers including East Tennessee, Western Carolina, Duquesne, Asheville, Winthrop, Brooklyn College, Chicago State, and Tampa.

Losing to Tampa threatened his grand plan.

It is not easy to know how much money the N.C. State basketball team earns for the athletic department and for Valvano.

The athletic department budget comes solely from revenue-generating sports (basketball and football) and from donations to its Wolfpack Club, the alumni- and civic-sponsored group that funds scholarships and repairs facilities. Not a nickel of state funds goes to N.C. State athletics. Since the funding isn't public, the books are not open to the public.

While budget information is kept as secret as budgets for CIA covert missions, Valvano once discussed the subject with Andy Kennedy. He made it clear that basketball, not football, was N.C. State's meal ticket, the one sport that supported the rest of the athletic program.

"We used to have long layovers in the Atlanta airport," said Kennedy, "and sometimes Valvano would talk to us. I can remember that our football team had just gone eight, three, and one and played Virginia Tech in the Peach Bowl, the best record they ever had—ACC football stinks—but we were winning games and were ranked eighteenth in the country. And yet, with all of the fans we drew and the money we got from the bowl appearance, Valvano said we only cleared maybe five hundred ninety-five thousand dollars, because the football team has one hundred fifteen guys on scholarship, you have to feed them all, buy equipment for all of them, transport them to the games, and you can see it costs so much because of the sheer numbers.

"Well, there are fourteen of us on the basketball team. That same year Valvano said that on just our TV contract and our gate at Reynolds, we cleared over two-point-six million. We made five times more money with eight times fewer players."

And that doesn't include the torrent of money that comes pouring in from the 11,000 loyal members of the Wolfpack Club, which raises millions for N.C. State athletics.

The Wolfpack Club was founded in 1936, and it does the same thing similar organizations on college campuses all across America do—it funds scholarships for the athletes and does what it can to "promote and support the athletics program."

At the universities where such clubs don't exist, the donor gives the money to the college, and the college spends it where it needs it most. By giving to the Wolfpack Club—or whatever the local sports booster club may be—a donor can show unlimited generosity to athletics without being concerned that the money might go into the college treasury and be spent for other reasons—say, on education.

The Wolfpack Club has grown so large that there are thirteen full-time paid staff members who handle the operation, and another 400 volunteers who help solicit funds. The Wolfpack Club acts like any alumni fund. The difference is that the money going to an alumni fund provides chairs for visiting professors and scholarships for students. The purpose of the Wolfpack Club is to raise money for the athletic department only.

How much is raised? The guess is that it's in the millions.

When a member of the Athletics Council, the school watchdog over the athletic department, was asked whether it reviewed the Wolfpack Club budget, he said, "I can't remember the budget from the Wolfpack Club ever coming to us, because it's private, separate from the university. They raise the money and use it as they see fit."

The one piece of information that is public is Valvano's basic salary: That is public information because his salary is paid by the state of North Carolina as part of the funding for the college. He is paid $106,000 a year to be basketball coach and athletic director. He does, however, make much, much more than that.

He several times bragged to John Simonds, as though he couldn't quite believe it himself, "I make a million and a half dollars a year."

The biggest chunk of outside dough he gets is from Nike. Valvano makes his players wear Nike shoes and athletic wear during State's games at home and on the road. He gets paid $150,000 for them to serve as walking advertisements for Nike. They get free shoes and clothes.

In addition, Valvano gets money from his weekly hour-long TV show and his daily five-minute radio show, and he has earned revenue by becoming pitchman for Mountain Dew soft drink, Ronzoni, a health club, a bank, South Square Hyundai of Durham, and the public transportation system. He also signed a lucrative contract to give motivational speeches to employees of the North Carolina-based Hardee's hamburger chain at $4,500 per speech.

There's more. Valvano owns a summer basketball camp for 900 campers a summer (300 kids a week for three weeks) at $240 a head, and he gets most of those kids to pay $25 a pop to have their picture taken with him at the end of the week.

After he won the 1983 NCAA championship, he unveiled his own line of "Coach V" sportswear. Offering T-shirts, jogging suits, and color-coordinated sweater, shirt, and slack ensembles made of polyester, his label was carried throughout North Carolina at Belk department stores.

Valvano also has investments that are kept private under his JTV Enterprises. His magnificent home on Glasgow Road in the suburb of Cary is located in an ultra-exclusive section of town and is valued in the mid-six figures.

But like all college basketball coaches, Valvano lives on a tightrope. The money comes surging in only if his team keeps winning. In such an uncertain profession, a coach must keep up the pressure on his players not to let down, lest he end up like so many other former college coaches—even some of the best college coaches—teaching high school and coaching pimply-faced adolescents in the boondocks.

Losing to Tampa, then, meant more than just losing a ballgame to a bad team. It threatened a season he had worked hard to build. College basketball is no longer a sport. It has become a big multi-million-dollar business. It is the coaches who suffer the most under the strain of the pressure. It is no wonder coaches like Valvano are desperate to win.

26

Mourning for Lenny Bias

State defeated a burly, less talented team from Loyola of Chicago and then hosted the University of Maryland, a team shattered by the death of its all-time superstar, Lenny Bias, and by the subsequent firing of its charismatic coach, Lefty Dreisell. After Bias's death and the subsequent witchhunt, Dreisell took the fall, and several of his players quit over his departure as coach. The Terrapin schedule was pared down, and the players were given only two weeks to practice. The new coach, Bob Wade, had the reputation at Dunbar High School for relating to his players, but he soon learned that college ball is not high school ball, that his star recruits were more interested in playing pro ball than studying, and that the alumni didn't care whether his kids liked him so much as whether his kids won ballgames.

Maryland led at the half by 2 points, holding the ball most of its allotted forty-five seconds, slowing the pace. When State got into gear in the second half, it became a 20-point N.C. State romp.

Throughout the game, the players were haunted by the visage of Lenny Bias. He had died the previous June, while most of the N.C. State players were still on campus attending summer school. That night they'd gathered in the basketball offices to watch the evening news on Valvano's giant TV screen, and as they saw clips of Bias soaring, magically moving for impossible baskets, playing defense as though possessed, a song by Night Ranger called "Good Bye" was played as background, and there wasn't a dry eye in the room.

Every player thinks he has the best game running, thinks he's top dog, that nobody can top him. But everybody knew that Lenny Bias was the best. All the N.C. State players loved to watch him play. They worshiped his game, and they loved him as a person, because Lenny Bias believed in all the right values. He worked hard, during the season he didn't drink as much as a beer, and he was polite and respectful. If ever there was a "nice guy," Lenny Bias was it. He had Christian values, a rarity for someone as talented as he was. He had a terrific mom and dad, who kept him humble and didn't let him get a big head. Lenny was always friendly to people and took out time to sign autographs. To his friends and anyone who knew him, Lenny Bias was a special human being.

Bennie Bolton was close to Lenny, and shortly after Lenny died, Bolton dropped out of summer school and disappeared from sight. The coaches hadn't seen him for three days, so Coach McLean reportedly went to Bolton's apartment and found Bennie lying in bed. Bennie, who is an excellent artist, had painted pictures of Lenny as a memorial and placed them around his bed along with lit candles, in mourning for Lenny. Bennie did not utter a word to Coach McLean. Seeing Bennie was okay, McLean turned around and left.

A couple weeks afterward, Bennie, Cozell McQueen, Lorenzo Charles, Quentin Jackson—all friends of Lenny—and John Simonds were sitting around eating pizza in the basketball office, when Bennie mentioned that so much of what had been written about Lenny was erroneous.

"On occasion Lenny would smoke a little pot," Bennie said, "but very rarely. Lenny was the type of guy who if he drank a beer, he'd go out the next day and run it off." Lenny Bias didn't have an ounce of fat on him. He was big and strong, a perfect athletic specimen.

Bennie reportedly also knew the friends who were with Lenny in his dorm room the night he died. Most of the State players knew them. They liked his teammates, Terry Long and David Gregg, but the other friend, Brian Tribble, had a reputation as a drug supplier. He had also been accused of murder in another incident. If an N.C. State basketball player wanted to score some pot or coke while they were playing at Maryland, reportedly they knew Tribble was the man to see.

Bennie told his teammates that he had spoken with Long and that Long told him that what was printed in the paper—that Lenny sat down and did a couple lines of cocaine—was crazy. Because Lenny wasn't that sort of guy, and because he was due to return to the Boston Celtics, the pro team that had drafted him number one in the country, to take another physical, which included drug tests.

According to Bennie, Long told him that he, Gregg, and Tribble were doing cocaine but that Bias had declined. Lenny said, "I'll just do a little weed." But unfortunately for Lenny, the weed he smoked was laced with crack—who laced it nobody knows—and Lenny died of heart failure. "It blew a hole in his heart," Bennie said. Which happens. Except this time it happened to the best amateur basketball player in the world.

What saddened the N.C. State players most of all was their knowledge that when Lenny had his first seizure and fell to the floor, his friends were so scared they started cleaning everything up—the straws, the mirror, the cocaine—and then vacuumed the floor to make sure everything was spotless, waiting thirty-five to forty minutes before calling for an ambulance for Lenny. Had they called the police right away, Bennie said, there was an outside chance Bias might have been saved.

So while State was playing Maryland, the Wolfpack players replayed in their minds the recording of Brian Tribble's voice to 911, pleading, "Don't let Lenny die. Please don't let Lenny Bias die." Lenny Bias was indeed dead, and it was such a shame.

With their victory over Maryland, the Wolfpack finished its fall semester with a record of nine wins and only two losses. The Pack was rated in the top twenty. But Valvano and the players were facing another crisis. Those damn academic requirements were rearing up on the horizon again like carnivorous monsters in a video game. Despite everything, Charles Shackleford, Taviin Binns, and Kelsey Weems all had flunked out of school. The new challenge: getting them back for the rest of the basketball season.

27

Grade Games

After the conclusion of the fall term final exams, Valvano reportedly told the players that "a few of them were in trouble academically," and he warned them not to say anything to the press about it.

He said, "Guys, I just want to emphasize that we are a team. Anything that happens to us, happens to us as a team, and when I say team, that includes the players, the coaches, and the managers. Everyone else is the outside world, and we don't need contact with them. Anything that happens to us as a team, stays as a team."

At practice Coach McLean told them, "I just want to remind you that it's against the law to talk about anybody else's grades, and if anybody asks you, tell them it isn't something you can talk about, that you don't know anything about it, and to talk to Coach V himself."

On most campuses, the less anyone knows about an athlete's grades, the better. Rarely are they a topic in the papers, because the information is limited to only a few people—the registrar, the coach, the player, the advisers—and since keeping a player eligible seems to be the highest priority at certain colleges, academic problems are tightly guarded secrets.

The public learned that three N.C. State basketball players were in academic trouble when a member of the Athletics Council, Dr. Keith Cassell, Dr. Roger Clark's replacement, revealed it to a student reporter from the *Technician*. He told the reporter three athletes had flunked out but were being readmitted under a special procedure.

Under that procedure, any student who flunked out could go before a university admissions committee to plead his case to be allowed back in, regardless of how poorly he had done the semester before.

If Dr. Cassell hadn't leaked the news to the press, Shack, Tev, and Kelsey could have gotten back into school without anyone even knowing they were in trouble. But Cassell's disclosure that more of Valvano's athletes weren't doing too hot academically created controversy as professors questioned whether everyday students had the same chance to be readmitted as the athletes did.

Where Jim Valvano has been most brilliant and innovative has been in the way he's been able to position himself before the public as an educator-coach. Whenever there is a scandal at another university concerning academics, Valvano is usually quick to say, "I wouldn't tolerate such behavior at N.C. State." In talking about education, he declares, "There is a commitment to academics in the N.C. State athletic department."

It's propaganda, nothing more. The reality is, Valvano's commitment to education is deplorable. During the eight years he has been at N.C. State, more of his players have been on academic probation than not.

The academic performance of Valvano's players has become a standing national joke among other coaches. Said Pat Williams, then general manager of the Philadelphia 76ers, in the *Sporting News*, "They had a big scandal at his place—three players found the library."

There is only one time a year that Valvano really has to sweat out a player's grades: the beginning of the school year, when the NCAA comes in and checks to make sure the athlete has passed twenty-four hours of classes the year before. (That translates to seven or eight different courses, depending upon how often the course meets each week.)

But another NCAA rule eases the burden. That rule states that a player cannot be suspended for the first twenty-four class hours of his career at the university. Hence, Valvano does not have to worry about freshmen their entire first year, and he doesn't have to worry about junior college transfers their first year—though they must have enough credits to pass by the end of summer school.

What the students must do is find a mix of courses from which they can attain an average grade of 2.0, or C. In other words, even if a player ends up failing a few courses, if he can find professors to give him off-setting Bs and As, then he can remain eligible for basketball. To accomplish this, the coaching staff closely monitors what courses their players sign up for.

To help keep the players eligible, a number of professors on campus, to one degree or another, aid the athletes in getting through. The academic advisers know who these professors are, and at the start of the semester, if a player is a serious academic risk, the academic advisers reportedly sit down with the player and say, "Based on your grade point average, these are the courses we think you should take." The player signs the class schedule and the adviser fills in the "right" classes for him.

Not all the players are handled this way—only those in danger of flunking out. The other players choose their own courses, but they, too, have a grapevine that informs them which professors are helpful and which ones dislike athletes. "If you get caught with the wrong professor," said one of the players, "you're in a lot of trouble."

Said one of the basketball players, "I say there are teachers at State and professors at State, two different kinds of categories. Professors really teach you and you can't get over on them. And then there are teachers who let you slide."

The players juggle schedules in search of their pet professors, though usually only one favorite can be assigned out of the four classes each player has to take.

According to one former professor, if you're not one of the professors under the spell of the basketball program, the basketball coaches lean on you hard if a basketball player is in your class and needs a good grade. "I saw it happen all the time," he said.

The course that every first-term freshman basketball player took was an offering called Leisure Alternatives. Said John Simonds, "Show up, and the basketball player usually gets an A. Every ballplayer takes this course. It's been a staple, even if the player had planned on becoming a chemical engineer."

There is one professor close to the athletic department who teaches a very technical, scientific course. To pass his course, ordinarily a knowledge of physics and higher mathematics is critical—but not if you're a basketball star. Among some members of the faculty, this professor is renowned for his generosity to the basketball players. When a fellow faculty member was asked why a PE major would take an honors-level scientific course, his answer was, "To get a good grade." When asked, "Isn't this course too hard for your average basketball player?" his answer was, "Not in *his* course."

The faculty member added contemptuously, "[He] will give an athlete any grade that the athletic department thinks is important." Said another school official, "These players go through classes they don't have any business in, that they don't have any chance of passing, and somehow they get credit."

Said John Simonds, "One of the players told me he didn't even know he was in this professor's course until he looked at his report card and saw that he had taken it and gotten an A!"

The professors help out because, like so many other rabid fans at N.C. State, they love sports and feel it's their civic duty to help keep the players eligible. That they themselves are corrupting the educational process doesn't seem to bother them.

Said one of the players, "I had a teacher in speech communication. He was a sports fanatic. Me and Vinny del Negro was in the same class. All he would talk about was sports, and it was times when we could miss some days with no problem. You're on the team, and they know you be away a lot. There are teachers like that. Me and Vinny got a B."

Other players got good grades in that class, too.

John Simonds took a course with an English professor who boasted to him that despite the fact that Chris Washburn was virtually illiterate in English, the year before he had passed him anyway. "Washburn is a good addition to the university," the professor said by way of justification.

And there was the art history teacher who failed one of the players. The player had missed the final exam, so the professor gave him an F. If the grade had remained, he would have been ineligible spring semester. Without the recorded F, his grade point average would have been high enough for him to play. To help out the basketball

Coach Jim Valvano

Vavlano hugs Kelsey Weems after winning the ACC championship against the University of North Carolina

Dick Stewart

Tom Abatemarco

Ray Martin

Ed McLean

Cozell McQueen

Cozell McQueen

Lorenzo Charles

Lorenzo Charles (center)

Chris Washburn

Chris Washburn

Charles Shackleford

(From the left) Vinny dela Negro, Shack, and Bennie Bolton vs. Virginia.

Avie Lester

Charles Shackleford

Bennie Bolton

Chuckie Brown

Quentin Jackson

Teviin Binns

Kelsey Weems

Kenny Drummond

Vinnie del Negro

Walker Lambiotte

Mike Giomi

Andy Kennedy

Bennie vs. Duke

Andy at the University of Alabama at Birmingham
(Photo by George Smith)

Quentin vs. Wake

Chancellor Bruce Poulton

Coach Valvano

Coach Valvano

Valvano

player, the professor agreed to give him an incomplete. The player was then eligible to play in the spring. The player ended up making up the exam, and he still got an F. But because a student need only concern himself with his grade point average at the beginning of the school year, when the NCAA comes around, that player was able to pass enough summer school courses to become eligible to play again the next year.

Summer school has been the savior of university athletic careers—and why so many of the players are on campus during the summer. Summer school classes are notoriously easier than regular semester courses. Also, during the summer there is another loophole: For the truly uneducatable, players can take correspondence courses, leaving a window of opportunity for someone else to aid in the at-home written exams.

With all of the available loopholes, any athlete could pass—if he did some work. But he had to do it. During a regular semester, even if he got an A from a teacher who loved basketball players, he still had three other courses to worry about. An A and three Fs translates to only a 1.25 grade point average. Most of the players who attended most of their classes and took most of their tests did pass, although their grade point averages still were not very high.

In fairness to them, it is very difficult for the best student athletes to find time to study, considering the amount of time spent practicing, going on long trips to play games as far away as Alaska, and thinking about playing.

Explained one of the players, "Say you're playing Loyola of Chicago on national television Sunday afternoon. You've got a big test Monday. What the hell are you going to be doing Sunday? You're not going to be studying. You're going to be thinking about the game. And after the game, the adrenaline is flowing. You have to get on a plane and get back at eleven-thirty at night, and get up for a seven o'clock class to take a test you haven't studied for. So it's tough."

For players like Shack, Tev, and Kelsey, who had counted their whole lives on becoming professional basketball players, it was difficult to study simply because they didn't possess the basic reading and writing skills.

Teviin never did pass freshman English. More to the point, according to teammates, none of them really cared. Shackleford, especially, thought studying irrelevant to his life. Said an N.C. State student, "I'd hear someone say, 'I saw Shack going to class today.' Everyone would get excited and say, 'Wow!' " Said a teammate, "He didn't give a shit about it."

But other teammates were more sympathetic to their star center. They understood that in the basketball society that fosters a philosophy of b-ball first and only, studying was not what Shack was in school for.

"There are a lot of opportunities to play pro ball today," said one. "You can now make thirty thousand dollars a year playing in Germany. You can play in France, Italy, Venezuela, and in Israel. It isn't just the NBA. And that's solely what he's looking at."

Despite Shackleford's severe academic problems, all the players knew he would remain in school. Said a teammate, "Shack was The Man. If Shack was off the team, we were going to lose. Valvano would do that with all his star players. They would be on the team no matter what."

The loophole that allowed Shackleford to remain eligible—and Teviin Binns and Kelsey Weems as well—was the official readmission process. If a student flunked out at the end of the fall semester, he could go before the Academic Review Board and personally petition for readmission.

Each of the failing players went before the Academic Review Board. In addition, Valvano reportedly testified on their behalf that Chancellor Poulton had signed a contract with them giving his approval for them to play in exchange for their promise (1) to attend classes and (2) go to study hall.

At the Academic Review Board hearing, the players came one after the other. The members of the review board sat around a long table, asking questions like, "Do you think you can continue your education here?" "Are you capable of working toward a degree?" "Are you willing to be tutored and get academic assistance?"

Teviin Binns, one of the players who went through it, said, "All you have to say is, 'Yeah, yeah, yeah,' and they let you back in. After they finished asking their questions, I left, they discussed it, I came back in, and they told me their decision.

"They said, 'We're going to let you back in because you have the capability to maintain a passing record.' "

Teviin had had some concern as to whether he would be let back in, because he was not a star player and he also knew how negatively Valvano felt about him. According to Binns, a couple of years earlier, one of the basketball players, George McLain, who had been on the outs with Valvano, was denied readmission after going in front of the board. Teviin wondered whether Valvano would drop him the same way he had dropped McLain. At the same time, Teviin felt his chances of staying in school were good, because if he was dropped the press would be asking questions, something he knew Valvano wanted to avoid at all costs.

As for Shackleford, all the players knew Shack would be back. "Everybody knew Shack was going to make it," said Teviin. "Everybody knew that. And since Kelsey was Shack's homeboy, then nothing was going to happen to Kelsey either, 'cause they had their own apartment, so if they were taking care of Shack, they were taking care of Kelsey at the same time. 'Cause if Kelsey wouldn't have come back, then I think Kelsey would have told the papers what was going on with Shack."

Shackleford hadn't been worried, not for a moment. He told teammates, "Aw, nothing is going to happen. What are they going to do to me? They need me." And he was so right.

According to John Simonds, the white players—Vinny, Andy, Walker, and Giomi—couldn't believe that Shack, Teviin, and Kelsey were coming back to play after flunking out. Giomi was shocked most of all, because at the University of Indiana, where he had come from, that would have been unheard of. He told teammates he thought it morally wrong. To the white players, it was the "dumb niggies" getting away with murder again.

When news of the flunking players' readmission hit the school newspaper, the administration pulled the wagons into a circle. Chancellor Poulton was evasive. He said, "No one is eligible to represent N.C. State as an athlete unless I certify, or the Athletics Council certifies on my behalf, that [the students] are eligible." Which was true.

What he didn't say was that if you were an athlete, you were much more likely to get certified.

Fred Smetana, representing the Athletic Council, told the student reporter that of the sixty-eight students readmitted to the university on appeal, only eight were members of revenue sports teams, as though that was somehow supposed to mean something.

The criticism of the smelly deal came both from educators and members of the student government. Said a member of the Student Senate, "All the athletes got back in, and then there were all those students who had tried hard and for some reason couldn't cut it, and only a small percentage of those got back in. It wasn't right. The chancellor wasn't going to go to bat for them.

"And what was even more ridiculous, the players had failed fall semester while playing a light schedule. They had had an entire semester to do well and to get ready for the real season. They were starting off the new term with a full ACC schedule and going all the way through March to the ACC tournament and possibly playing up through early April. How were they going to do that and carry any kind of academic load?"

28

Shack Gets a Baby-sitter

From the start of the second semester, Valvano apparently decided he wasn't going to take any more chances with sophomore Charles Shackleford's grades. After Shack had gotten this far, Valvano would have real trouble explaining things to the press and the public if Shack had to go before the Academic Review Board two semesters in a row, so he assigned Coach Stewart to be Shack's baby-sitter, to make sure he went to class and studied. Coach Stewart, however, wasn't up to the job. Shack was too slippery for him. Shack would go in the front door of the College Inn while Stewart waited for him, and then he'd sneak out a side entrance, wasting Steward's time and trying the coach's patience.

Valvano finally decided that in order to harness Shack, he would have to hire a full-timer who could stick to him like tar. Valvano could have chosen someone from the university tutoring program, but in keeping with his penchant for secrecy, he hired a man named Bruce Hatcher to be Shackleford's full-time personal tutor. Hatcher got paid good money, but who, the other players wondered, would want the job of having to baby-sit a six-foot-eleven twenty-year-old?

Hatcher told Simonds, "I was hired to make sure that Shack goes to class every day and that he goes to study hall every day and to make sure he doesn't get in trouble." The manager thought to himself, "Good luck to you."

Hatcher was very good at his job, and it used to frustrate Shackleford tremendously. Shack would come to practice, and afterward he would try to sneak out the back door—anything to get away from Bruce—but Bruce rode him like the proverbial camel. Bruce was always trying to get Shack to study; inevitably, Shack always had a good excuse not to. "Bruce, I don't feel too good." "Sorry, Shack." "Bruce, I have to go to see my babe." "No, Shack." "Bruce, just give me five minutes to be by myself." "No, Shack."

Shack would try anything to get away from Hatcher. When he was in his room and Hatcher came banging on the door, Shack wouldn't answer it. Hatcher would be out in the hall yelling, "Shack, I know you're in there. You better open up this door. Shack, ya hear me? Shack?"

Among themselves, the coaches reportedly laughed about Hatcher's job, because they knew how demanding it was, working overtime to keep up with their star night owl. At night Hatcher would drop Shack off at the dorm and then sit in the parking lot to make sure Shack didn't get in his Trans Am and take off out of town.

Hatcher even traveled with the team to away games. He sat right next to Shack on the plane. He tried all the time to get Shack to study, preventing the lanky player from listening to his music and keeping him from desired sleep and from desired play. One time Valvano intervened. He said, "No, no, not on the plane, Hatch. Wait until we get to the hotel." But once the team got to the hotel, Shack was in a better position to disappear.

What made it even harder for Shackleford to take was the ribbing he suffered at the hands of the other players. The mouth, Quentin Jackson, constantly was heard talking about "Shackie and Hatchie." He was always asking Shackleford "if something was going on." Quentin would say, "Hey, Shack, what are you and Hatch going to do tonight?" And then he'd say, "Are you sure there isn't something else going on that you're not telling us about?" Shack would get angry.

"You Helmet Head," he would respond.

29

Operation Bedspread

Having successfully weathered the academic storm of first-semester academic failure, Valvano and his team could settle down and concentrate on what was really important: the rest of the season. With the spring semester just under way, Valvano could point to his 9–2 record with some satisfaction.

State chartered a little thirty-seater from Piedmont Airlines for the flight to Clemson, which is in South Carolina. South Carolina is shaped like the left-side profile of a nose. Clemson is near the tip, close to the Georgia border, nor far from Tennessee.

As the players were getting on the plane, the two announcers, Gary Dornburg and Wally Ausley, also climbed aboard. The players started yelling, "Split them up. We don't want both those dudes sitting on the same side." Dornburg was in front of Valvano, blocking his way. "Get your fat ass out of the way," Valvano barked. The players couldn't hold back their laughter.

After the plane took off, it flew at what seemed like sixty miles an hour and only at about 5,000 feet, close enough to the ground that the players could tell what kinds of cars were being driven on the roads below. It was early January, and inside the cabin it was cold; everyone had to bundle up.

The team stayed at the Clemson Ramada Inn, which had a Jacuzzi, an indoor pool, and beds fitted with down-filled, cushy comforters in each room to keep the guests feeling warm and pampered.

The next day the players checked out of the hotel in the afternoon, a couple hours before game time. After the game, the team was to fly back to Raleigh. After checking out, all the players loaded their suitcases onto the bus and got on. Valvano and John Simonds stayed behind. Valvano wasn't in any mood to be with the players. Simonds remained to play chauffeur.

As Valvano and Simonds stood in the lobby, the hotel manager said to Valvano, "Excuse me, Coach." Valvano, wearing his pregame scowl, barked, "What?" She said, "Two of your players stole the bedspreads off the beds. We are booked for tomorrow, and we don't have any extras." She asked if he would help get them back.

Valvano's face contorted in rage. "Whose room?" he asked, as if he didn't know. The culprits were Shack and Teviin. "Goddammit!" he expostulated. Then he said, "Ma'am, I will get them back for you."

Valvano walked out to the car, with Simonds behind him. When they got in, Valvano said, "John, this is what we're going to do. We're going to go to the stadium. We're going to open up the suitcases and find the bedspreads, and you're going to bring them back. You're going to talk to the manager, apologize for me, and make sure that none of this hits the press, because they will ruin us if it does." Especially on the heels of the Shack and Tev grade fiasco.

During the whole ride from the hotel to the arena, Valvano was muttering to himself. He said, "I can't believe it. I make a million five a year, I'm a big coach, I won the national championship, went to the Final Eight last year, and I got two guys trying to ruin me, stealing bedspreads."

He then said, "John, I can't stand surprises. It always pays to be totally prepared. Don't let anyone surprise you with anything. Know enough, do enough, that you always know what's going to happen to you, so that you're always prepared for anything that's going to happen."

Valvano and Simonds arrived at the Coliseum. Coach McLean was talking to the players in the locker room when Valvano entered. He said, "Dammit, Shack and Tev. I want those fucking bedspreads right now." Coach McLean said, "What the heck is going on, Jim?" Valvano said, "We have a couple of wiseguys who thought they could steal a couple of bedspreads and make us look bad. Guys, don't you ever fucking think? What the hell are you going to do with a couple of bedspreads? If you'd have asked me, I'd have bought you bedspreads, but no, you have to go and steal them."

Simonds went out to the bus, and a few minutes later Shackleford and Binns came out to help him go through the suitcases to find the purloined bedspreads. Teviin was embarrassed. He didn't know what to say. Shackleford thought it was funny, a big joke. It was the same old story: He knew nothing was going to happen to the franchise player.

With the bedspreads in his possession, Simonds headed back to the Ramada. Shack and Tev went back inside for the ballgame.

Shackleford started, further enraging some of his teammates, who were becoming angry at the special kid-gloves treatment he was getting. It didn't matter what he did.

Said a teammate, "He could have insulted V's wife, and he would have played. It's all about wins. V knew he couldn't win without him."

What further enraged his teammates was that they knew full well that if they had stolen the bedspreads, they would have been benched, or worse. "I'd have been on the first plane home," said the teammate. "V would have shipped my ass out."

The players were laughing behind Valvano's back. Said one, "V, what's he doing? How can he put up with that? Here he is, supposed to be one of the most respected, powerful men in basketball. Why does he have to put up with this from a damned twenty-year-old who doesn't give a shit about him or anybody else?"

Simonds, meanwhile, returned the bedspreads to the Ramada. Valvano had asked him to cover for the players. He told the hotel manager, "Here are the bedspreads. I am very sorry about what happened. Freak circumstances sometimes affect players before a game. They get pumped up and do things they don't think about." The manager said, "Okay. Well, everything's fine since I got the spreads back." Simonds asked, "Do I have your word that this won't get out in the press? Because this could do bad things for us?" The manager said, "Yeah, okay."

Simonds was pouring sweat when he left. He got back in the car, but he didn't go straight back to the game. He drove around aimlessly for a little while, trying to regain his composure, because it bothered him terribly that two of the players had stolen expensive property and he was the guy making up a lame excuse to get them out of it.

Simonds thought to himself, "They get pumped up and do things they don't think about, what crap." He didn't like lying to people. He thought, "I'm getting to be like V."

30

Mike Giomi's Waterloo

The Wolfpack lost the Clemson game. Clemson led at the half by 15 points. In the locker room, Valvano was furious. "I know why this is happening," he said. "Because you guys' minds just aren't on the game. No, you're not fucking in the game. We have two guys stealing bedspreads. This is just fucking dandy."

The Clemson fans hadn't helped Valvano's disposition any. The entire Clemson football team must have gotten tickets right behind the State bench, because a row of huge, vocal students spent the game screaming at the players and giving Valvano a hard time.

Every time Valvano got up, one student screamed at him about his ugly suit, calling him, "You dumb Italian." Another monster screamed out, "You greasy guinea." A couple of the State managers considered going after him until they saw how big he was.

In the second half, the team rebounded. Kenny Drummond played brilliantly, scoring 28 points, making four assists and three steals. But with two minutes left and down by 5, Kenny took a couple of forced shots that missed. So did Walker Lambiotte, and State fell just short. Contributing to the sorry play was Mike Giomi, who had a bad game. Said a teammate of Giomi's attempt to guard Clemson star Horace Grant, "Grant smoked him like a cheap cigar."

With Clemson up by 3 and only five seconds remaining, Drummond threw up a long 3-point try that would have tied the game, but the ball hit the front of the rim and bounced away. And that was the ballgame.

After the game, the talk was of bedspreads, not losing.

On the plane ride back to Raleigh, everyone sat silent and frozen.

The following game was at home against Georgia Tech, which came to town with two terrific forwards, Tom Hammonds and Duane Farrell, big, powerful dunkers who played an intimidating game.

At the start of the second half, with the game neck-and-neck, Hammonds unleashed two dunks in a row in traffic. Valvano was livid. He screamed onto the court, "You dumb fucking jerks, don't give him the lane"—sage advice, and Shackleford and Giomi nodded back at him, but not for any reason other than to keep him from taking them out of the game. By this juncture in the season, the State players had already indicated they had no intention of listening to much Valvano was saying. They had their own game to play, and they were going to play it.

Duane Farrell came down the court, caught an Alley Oop pass off the baseline, and slammed it home on three State defenders. Even players on the State bench clapped in appreciation at Farrell's effort. But any time Valvano looked down the bench, they looked down at the floor, particularly the forwards, trying to avoid eye contact. No one wanted to have to go in and guard Hammonds and Farrell, who were having such a field day.

Keeping State in the game this time was Giomi. Against Tech, Mike scored 24 points, hitting twelve of his fourteen shots.

Another important factor in the game, which State won by a point, was the defense spearheaded by Quentin Jackson and Kelsey Weems. Ordinarily, defense was not State's strong suit. What State did on defense was often dictated by what the other team did on offense. Rarely was there a time when all five State players hustled and played strong D. Drummond was probably State's best defensive player, but none of the players at the other guard—not Walker not Vinny not Bennie—was terribly aggressive on defense. Shackleford, in particular, was weak defensively, so usually State played a zone or what could be described as a "loose man-to-man."

But against Tech, when Valvano put Quentin and Kelsey in together at guard and had them press, the team came alive. They were a full-court trap unto themselves. They harassed the Tech guards, forced turnovers, stole the ball, and every time State scored after a turnover, Quentin and Kelsey slapped fives and exhorted their teammates and the home crowd to a frenzy.

After the game, won by a whisker, the ebullient players spent most of the time getting on Shackleford for getting dunked on so often. Even in schoolyard basketball it's a sin for a player to get dunked on. It's the ultimate loss of face. Players don't mind getting beat by 30 points as long as they don't get dunked on. And Hammonds and Farrell were dunking on Shack time and again, mean two-handed dunks, all the while making derisive faces on the way down, taunting Shackleford for not stopping them. Now it was his teammates' turn to taunt him.

Quentin slyly asked him, "Hey, Shack, how did that ball taste coming through the net on you? What did it smell like going by you?" Poor Shack. All he could say was his usual, and then Quentin said, "Hey, Shack, all you have to do is just breathe on him on the way up. He won't ever come back. I promise you." Everyone stopped what they were doing to laugh.

After Quentin got through with Shackleford, he turned on Walker Lambiotte, who was always getting blasted by his teammates for his acrid body odor when he sweated. During practice his teammates would refuse to guard Walker—they'd walk off the court, complaining about his B.O. Said a teammate, "He smells like a skunk."

In the locker room after the Tech game, Walker was sitting in the corner, minding his own business, when Quentin started getting on him. Quentin said, "Maybe we could just put Walker in there and just stink up the place a little bit, and then they definitely wouldn't come back in the middle again."

The other players were snickering, but not too hard, because they didn't want to be next to get busted on by Quentin.

Continuing their ACC schedule, State next beat Wake Forest at home to bring its record to 11–3. State, rated number seventeen in the country, won the game by 8 points. But no one was happy about the game. They knew they should have won by 20. Wake had once been a power under coach Carl Tacy, but the bloom faded and Tacy left, so the next coach, Bob Staak, walked into a program that was going downhill fast. He was starting at rock bottom and having trouble recruiting high school kids, because the best players usually want to go to winning programs and get a shot at the NCAA championship. That it's a private school with high academic standards makes Wake's problem worse. Unlike N.C. State, athletes have to have good grades, or they don't get into Wake.

Wake had one star player, a pro-speed midget guard by the name of Tyrone (Muggsy) Bogues, along with a cast of lumbering white guys. State was never in danger of losing the game, despite the fact that its offense was disorganized.

Kenny Drummond had played poorly against Tech the game before, and for the first time the local sports writers were chiding him for his poor shot selection and cold shooting.

One of the criticisms leveled against Valvano by the State players was that he paid too much attention to what was written about him and his team, and they noticed that against Wake, for the first time, the coaches were beginning to get down on Drum. The players didn't think the timing was a coincidence—the press criticizes, Valvano reacts. But they weren't complaining, because no one else on the team wanted Kenny in there anyway.

Kenny was still trying hard. He always hustled. He always worked hard. But sometimes he looked lost out on the court. No one was telling him what to do. No one was coaching him. No one was helping him. No one was patting him on the back when he did well. When he played poorly, Valvano could be heard saying to no one in particular, "Kenny's killing us. I don't know what's wrong with the kid."

Giomi had also been killing State. He had scored 18 against a bad Loyola team, and his 24 against Tech was a benchmark for him, but despite that effort, none of his teammates wanted him to play any more either. He had been a superstar at Indiana for three years under Bobby Knight. He was the perfect Big Ten player—disciplined, knew his plays perfectly, knew exactly where to go when the ball went in a certain direction, and with his great stamina he could run up and down the court longer than his opponents. At Indiana, he made his shots and played like a professional. Nobody could stop him.

But at N.C. State, he was playing a different brand of basketball. It was free-lance, speed-and-quickness basketball, and after sitting out nearly eighteen months, Giomi had lost his edge and also his confidence, so he struggled from the start. Said a teammate, "Valvano wasn't the kind of coach who built confidence in a player, so Gee suffered." With each game Giomi tried harder and harder and did worse and worse, putting more and more pressure on himself. And his game was falling apart. Behind Giomi's back, Valvano was heard telling the other coaches, "I guess Bobby Knight was right."

In the Wake Forest game, Giomi committed turnovers, bouncing the ball off his feet, looking as if he were running in mud. Giomi didn't have it any more. By the end of the game, Valvano made it clear that Chucky Brown would be starting in his place, and it hurt Mike badly.

After the game Giomi sat in front of his locker with his head in his hands, looking almost ready to cry. He had tried so hard, but hardly anything had clicked. Quentin didn't make Gee feel any better when he came over to him, shook his head, and said, "Hey, Mike, cast iron hands tonight? I got some eggs in my locker. We can fry some if you're in a hurry."

After one practice during which he was really struggling, one of Giomi's teammates had asked him, "Do you think Bobby Knight is checking the boxes on you?" Giomi said, "Yeah, he always checks on his former players." He looked sad. He said, "Coach Knight has seen all the boxes on me, and he's saying to himself, 'I was right about Giomi. I did the right thing.' "

So Giomi felt like a failure. Said Simonds, "He thought to himself, 'I failed Bobby Knight. I failed V. What does that say about me?' "

Some of his more sympathetic teammates felt that the system had failed, rather than Giomi. "I knew he wasn't a failure," said a teammate. "Gee got ruined by Coach Knight, by Valvano, and by the NCAA that makes a player sit out a year when he transfers, even when it's the coach who forces him to transfer.

"Gee was a good guy, but he wasn't able to stick out four years of abuse by Bobby Knight, so he quit. And when that happens, it's Knight's fault, because he better know enough about each kid he recruits before he signs him to know he can pull his shenanigans on him and he'll still be there at the end.

"And then Mike comes to N.C. State, and everyone is thinking, 'He's a Bobby Knight product, he'll score thirty a game,' and he never comes close to that, and so the fans dogged him, booed him, called him 'slow' and 'flatfooted,' without remembering that he hadn't picked up a basketball in a year and a half.

"All he needed was someone to work with him. But V wasn't the coach to do it, so Giomi was consigned to a seat at the end of the bench, disgusted and rejected."

31

A Visit to the Dean Dome

The 1986-87 N.C. State basketball season was really three seasons. During the first season, State rarely lost. During its second season, it rarely won. The first game of its second season came during the third week of January against its hated rival, the University of North Carolina Tar Heels, at Chapel Hill in the 21,426-seat Dean Smith Student Activity Center, more commonly called either the SAC or the Dean Dome, named after Carolina's charismatic living legend, basketball coach Dean Smith.

The N.C. State-Carolina rivalry is among the fiercest in the country. There are several reasons for this. One is the proximity of the schools. Raleigh is only a twenty-minute car ride from Chapel Hill. Another reason is that in the seven years he has coached at N.C. State, Valvano has yet to defeat Dean Smith at Chapel Hill. But the most important reasons are history and tradition.

In North Carolina, there are two kinds of people—Wolfpack fans and Tar Heel fans. Having started out as an agricultural school, N.C. State has always been stereotyped as a "cow college," despite the fact that its engineering program is rated among the top in the country. Tar Heel fans enjoy disseminating the N.C. State stereotype, calling it "Moo U" and teasing State students by asking them whether they always wear overalls and drive a John Deere. The Carolina fans even sing a parody of the "Marine Hymn" about State that includes the line, "As the tractors go rolling along."

To the State fan, Carolina, or Chapel Hill, is peopled

by rich preppies who go to school on the family dole and spend Dad's big bucks. State students look at the Chapel Hill students the same way that Boston College students look at the Harvard preppies, as a bunch of upperclass snobs with a lot of money who drive BMWs, Audis, and Porsches.

State students are also aware, as one Stater put it, that "Carolina has the babes. Everybody knows that for sure. But those girls are preppie and snotty."

In short, jealousy often runs from the State student to the Carolina student, and contempt filters down from the Carolina student to the State student. Basketball games become a class war—economic class, that is.

Tar Heel fans are renowned for their arrogance, which stems from the championship-quality basketball that granite-faced Dean Smith has turned out since he came to Carolina twenty-five years ago. It's an arrogance that comes from rooting for a coach with a record of almost 600 wins and fewer than 170 losses. It comes from knowing their institution is one of the finest in the country. It comes from having more than and feeling superior to the have-nots.

According to State fans, the Carolina fan is to be despised as much for his intolerance as for his arrogance. At basketball games at Chapel Hill, opposing rooters sometimes accidentally find themselves sitting in the Tar Heel rooting section. If an opposing rooter becomes too vocal, the Tar Heel fans will bodily lift the struggling offender out of his seat and pass him, row by row, up toward the top of the arena until he is no longer able to be heard.

Woody Durham, the Carolina radio announcer, is the perfect Tar Heel rooter. If the opponent comes down the court, makes a great move, and slams the ball home, Woody will say, "Layup, State." But if a Carolina player scores, even if it's an easy shot, Woody will make it sound like the world's greatest shot. Woody drives State fans, and all opposing team fans, to distraction.

And should, God forbid, Carolina end up with fewer points than the opponent, as far as Woody's concerned, it is never Carolina's fault, never the Tar Heel players' fault, never Dean Smith's fault. Woody finds an outside factor—usually the referees. "The refs blew the game for us," Woody will moan.

State fans hate Woody Durham. "If I never hear him again, it will be too soon" is typical of how State fans feel about him.

The rivalry extends to the coaches. Dean Smith is so successful that it's hard for an opposing coach not to be jealous. Moreover, his Dean Dome, which was built entirely with private funds, reeks of class, style, and old money. It is beautifully designed on the outside and inside has plush chairs and not a bad seat in the house. Carolina has truly built one of the great monuments to a living human being.

Reynolds Coliseum, where the Wolfpack plays its home games, is called "the house that Case built," referring to basketball coach Everett Case, who coached at State from 1946 until 1964. The Reynolds seats but 12,400, and Valvano wants to replace it with something glitzy—in his own image and with his own name on it. He has in his plans the construction of his own monument at State. When the new arena is discussed, it already has a name: Valvano Hall.

When the players entered the sparkling clean Tar Heel arena to warm up, the first thing they noticed was that everything was Carolina blue, which is just a shade darker than robin's egg blue. The seats were Carolina blue. The floor was Carolina blue. The band. The roof. Even the hair of some of the fans. The other thing they noticed was that on the walls near the ceiling hung huge photos of Carolina's greatest teams alongside the retired jerseys of its greatest stars—Michael Jordan, Sam Perkins, Bob McAdoo, Charley Scott, Phil Ford, James Worthy. A mini–college basketball hall of fame was draped on those walls. And then there were the banners.

Said one State player, "If Carolina farts, they put up a banner." He wasn't kidding. If Carolina won the NCAA championship one year, not only did it put up the championship banner, but there was also a Final Four banner and a Final Eight banner and a Final Sixteen banner, and a Final Thirty-two banner. And if Carolina had the best regular season in the ACC, even if it lost in the tournament, it would have a banner with big letters saying,

"ACC Champs," and in little letters, "Regular Season Winners."

When the players got back to their bench, they noticed that sitting behind them were rich Tar Heel alumni and supporters sitting in what looked like Lazy Boys or Barcaloungers.

During the introductions, the Carolina crowd whooped and hollered, but once the game started, the players noticed that the fans watched the game as if they were at the theater or a movie house. They clapped at the right moments, but with civility. Said one player, "They smoked us so many times that they just assume they will do it again."

State was at a disadvantage because both Shackleford and Chucky Brown had suffered ankle injuries against Wake Forest and couldn't play. Five minutes before the game, Valvano informed Teviin Binns that he would be starting the game at center, facing Carolina's intimidating six-foot-nine, 245-pound freshman center, J. R. Reid.

Teviin didn't have a chance. He wasn't ready to play, physically or mentally. He had been buried on the bench by Valvano for the last two months. Now the coach wanted him to go out and try to guard one of the most dominating forces in the college game. He couldn't do it. Reid scored a point a minute for the first fifteen minutes, as Binns committed four personal fouls by the half. With two minutes gone in the second half, Teviin fouled out. His replacement, Avie Lester, fared no better. Reid was unstoppable, making thirteen of fourteen shots and finishing the game with 31 points. The Tar Heels won by 18. Valvano's streak at the Dean Dome was intact.

Kenny Drummond was the one positive force for the Wolfpack. Drum had 20 points and played Tar Heel star guard Kenny Smith to a draw.

On one of the first plays of the second half, Mike Giomi left himself open to ridicule in perpetuity from his teammates when he intercepted a pass and headed for the Tarheel basket on a breakaway. By the time he got to the key, no Carolina player was even at the halfcourt line. Giomi went for the dunk—brought the ball over his head, he planted his foot to go up for the dunk—but his knee buckled, he lost his footing, and instead of dunking the ball, he pinned it against the front of the rim and fell on his ass in a heap.

The Carolina fans lit Giomi up like a firecracker. They were hollering, "Air ball," and "Can't walk," and one fan stood up behind the State bench and yelled, "Hey, did you just borrow those feet from a duck?"

The harshest barbs came from the State players themselves. When Giomi hit the floor, the benchwarmers first reaction wasn't "Is he hurt?" or "Damn, we lost the two points," it was one of laughter. Bennie Bolton threw his towel up into the air with glee. The rest of the bench held their sides and laughed for five minutes at Giomi's clumsiness.

Said one of the players, "If I had done that, I would have hit the ground and held my knee and said I was hurt, to keep from getting laughed at. We fucked with Gee the rest of the year. We would walk by him and trip, or we'd buckle our leg and pretend to fall. He felt so bad. But it was so damn funny."

Toward the end of the game Dean Smith sent in his subs, but there was no appreciable drop-off in productivity. Carolina won in a rout.

Said a member of the State team afterward, "We couldn't have scored in a whorehouse with a fistful of fifties."

32

Carnage

Duke University, the third team from the Raleigh-Durham-Chapel Hill magic triangle, came to Raleigh to play the Wolfpack. Duke was coached by Mike Krzyzewski, a coach (with a very difficult name to spell) in the same mold as Bobby Knight, a tough, no-nonsense, disciplinarian. When Coach K talked, his players listened. During practice before the game, Valvano sought to show his players what Duke was going to run, demonstrating the structured plays, the double picking, the complicated screens that Duke used. Valvano told them, "When Coach K does this"—he crossed his wrists—"this means Duke is going to run that," and he explained it. One of the State players, aware that State's offense was almost entirely free-lance in nature, whispered, "I wonder what Coach K is telling his players, because we don't run any plays."

And yet, despite Duke's disciplined training, State whipped them by 13, proving once again that the team with the better talent usually wins.

Kenny Drummond—on paper—had the greatest day of his N.C. State career. He scored 26 points against Duke's highly rated Tommy Amaker, beating the Blue Devils to the basket for layup after layup. The team, however, wasn't clicking as a unit.

During the game, Vinny del Negro had the ball on a three-on-one break, with Drum on one wing and Walker Lambiotte on the other. Vinny passed it to Walker for the basket.

During the season Quentin repeatedly complained to Drum, "Man, the crackers only pass the ball to each other." But Drummond always tried to diffuse the situation, saying, 'Man, we're on the same team." But after the Duke game, Drummond also began to feel that the whites did pass only to each other.

"If Lambiotte had the ball, he would pass it to Vinny. If Vinny had the ball, he would pass it to Lambiotte," Drum said.

After the game Quentin remarked to Drummond out loud in front of the white players that the whites only passed to each other. The white players ignored him. Drum said to himself, "The white players know it, and they'll keep on doing it." As for the white players, their feeling was that since Drum never passed them the ball, there was little reason for them to pass it to him.

All through the Duke game, Valvano kept saying, "Fellas, we are just not playing as a team. When are you guys going to jell?" The players looked at each other as if to say, Hold on a minute. The coach is supposed to make everybody jell.

State's next opponent was Kansas, at Kansas. It was Super Bowl Sunday. The State players weren't optimistic. No one was playing well. There was dissension on the team. No one was enjoying himself. No one felt like playing for Valvano. Everyone was irritable.

After State went out onto the court to shoot around, the players came back into the locker room to discuss pregame strategy one last time. Valvano once again discussed the scouting reports, telling his players what he expected each opponent to do and what to look for. Andy Kennedy thought to himself, "We don't know our own plays. We're not going to be able to learn theirs."

Kennedy, who was sitting in the first row, looked back over at Shackleford. Shack's head was bent over to the side. He was knocked out, sound asleep. Kennedy was incredulous. "It's five minutes before a nationally televised game against Danny Manning, perhaps the finest player in college basketball, an All American, against nationally ranked Kansas, and Shack is asleep."

While Shack dozed, Valvano was shouting, "Goddamn it, guys, will you do it? You have to believe in yourselves."

It was 18–2 Kansas before State was able to work up a

sweat. Manning took control of the game. It was no contest after five minutes.

In the locker room at the half, Valvano fumed in silence. Finally, he said, "Guys, you've given up on me. I hate coaching. I don't think I can do this any more. I can't keep going out and getting pounded like this."

Midway through the second half, the tension on the court began to build. As great a player as Danny Manning is, he's a dirty player. "He will hit you with a cheap shot in a minute," said Simonds. Manning hit Mike Giomi a couple of times, and since Giomi was having a tough go of it as it was, getting his shots stuffed back in his face, he was in no mood to be manhandled by a guy who was beating State's brains out.

As Giomi and Manning were coming back down the court, they tossed elbows at each other. At halfcourt they stopped and faced each other, ready to duke it out.

Immediately, Coach McLean, a war veteran, jumped up and said, "Come on, boys," expecting the players on the bench to follow. McLean ran onto the court to defend his player. But when McLean turned around, not a single N.C. State benchwarmer had moved off his chair. Drummond, who loved a good fight, hadn't played much; he was brooding and didn't budge. Avie Lester, the other brawler on the team, didn't stir. Teviin said, "I ain't going out there. Maybe if someone gets hurt, I can play."

Giomi may have stood a good chance of getting his ass beat, but no one on the bench cared. Fortunately, the referees broke up the altercation before any blows landed.

When Coach McLean returned to the bench, he looked down the row of players, shaking his head. He didn't have anything to say. The fact that the bench players didn't go out to help Giomi—never mind that they weren't cheering—put everything in clear perspective.

After the game, in the locker room, Valvano returned to icy silence. And then, suddenly, he began kicking cups, suitcases, and duffel bags and throwing chalk and erasers.

All he said was, "Fuck you all, I'm leaving." And he stormed out.

Manning had scored 30 points. Shack was 3 for 12, Drum 4 for 17. Drum had taken even longer shots than normally. Three times in a row he let fly from outside the professional 3-point line. He was launching intercontinental ballistic missiles. When the press wondered why Drum was shooting behind the pro line and not the college 3-point line, Valvano tried to cover for him: "Kenny must have been confused." The other players didn't believe that, and they were angry at both Drum and Valvano.

In the locker room afterward when he had returned, Valvano was brutal in his frankness about their play. He told the team, "Everyone here wants to play in the NBA, but there isn't a single NBA player in this locker room." He looked over at Drummond. He said, "We have no more Nate McMillans, no more Spud Webbs." Drummond was unfazed. Valvano looked over at Shackleford. "We have no more Thurl Baileys." Shackleford appeared hurt by what Valvano said. Shack had always believed he would end up in the NBA, and now his coach was telling him he wasn't good enough.

After the game Valvano told the press, "It was the worst basketball game played at State since I've been a coach here."

State's record was still excellent, 12–5, but everyone —Valvano, the assistants, and the players—knew the worst was yet to come. Coming up were games against Coach Terry Holland's Virginia Cavaliers at Charlottesville, and then four games against nationally ranked teams: Oklahoma home, DePaul away, Carolina home, and then Louisville away. This was the part of the schedule that Chris Washburn was supposed to handle, but with Washburn in the NBA, Valvano was stuck with a group of disorganized, unhappy, dissatisfied, but realistic players who sensed that they were likely to lose their next five games in a row.

Valvano appeared to be suffering from depression. He was always yelling at the players, often swearing when something went wrong in practice. He was cursing even more than usual. "Get your fucking ass down the court, Teviin." "You fucking cocksuckers," he once screamed at them, "I got a bunch of cocksuckers for a team." The outbursts where he threw or kicked the basketball up into the stands became more common. One time in practice he booted a ball and just missed bouncing it off Chucky Brown's head.

Valvano began blaming his assistants for the poor showing of the team. He accused them of not scouting the opponents sufficiently. In turn, the assistants were complaining among themselves. Coach Martin was heard to say, "V doesn't understand what the team needs."

With the assistants feeling the heat, they were dogging the players more than usual for not working hard enough, which only resulted in the anger of the players coming back on them. During practices, coaches Stewart and Martin would watch the players and act as squealers. "Teviin isn't hustling." "Andy isn't getting back on defense." "Giomi isn't blocking out."

The players wondered, "What's wrong with these coaches? This is crazy." Communication had broken down entirely.

The coach who suffered the most abuse from the players was Coach Stewart. If Stewart was standing on the court and no one was looking, one of the players would throw a basketball and hit him in the back of the head. By the time Stewart had recovered his composure enough to turn around and pick out the culprit, the assassin had blended back into the pack of players.

The players were so down they didn't even feel like practicing. They sat around the locker room, laid back, and when it was time to go upstairs to the gym, no one made a move until one of the coaches ordered them up.

One afternoon the team was preparing for the Virginia game and Valvano wanted Stewart to send the white team out onto the floor to mimic the Virginia offense and defense. No one wanted to be on the white team any more. As Stewart called out names, everyone stood fast.

Stewart called Teviin's name. Teviin didn't move. He called Kelsey's name. Kelsey ignored him. He said, "Come on, Chucky, get out there." Chucky Brown didn't move. "I ain't going nowhere," he said. "I don't see no one else moving."

Stewart shouted, "Chucky, didn't you hear me say, 'Get out there'?" Stewart then said, "You've been on my mind for two weeks. I'm getting tired of your shit." Brown replied, "Man, I don't care. My father's going to come down here and tell you something."

Talk of players quitting was rife. Every day someone was pissed off. Most of the players had been high school All Americans, and they were tired of the way they were being misused—or not used at all.

From this point in the season, some of the players started partying more than usual, staying out late, doing what they felt they had to do in order to keep sane. One night, Andy Kennedy was complaining to Bennie Bolton about how low he was feeling. Bennie said, "There is only one way to play the game here at State, and that's as though you don't care. 'Cause if you play like you care, V's going to shatter you."

Kennedy told himself, "Fuck it, I'm just trying to get through." Basketball at N.C. State was no longer important to him.

33

The Drum-Shackleford Fight

When tempers are short, flare-ups can occur like meteors out of the sky. The team was eating its pregame meal, getting ready to leave for Charlottesville, when Shackleford asked Kenny Drummond if Drum would drive his car down to the College Inn for him. Drum agreed, because he had forgotten his travel bag and had to go back to the Inn and get it. After parking Shack's car, Drum was given a lift to the bus by a friend. At the bus, Drummond handed Shackleford the keys to his car; Shack absentmindedly put them in a coat pocket.

After Shackleford got on the bus, he couldn't find the keys, and didn't remember that Drummond had returned them. Shack said, "Drummond, give me back my keys." Drummond said, "I already gave you your keys." But Shackleford couldn't find the keys and must have figured Drummond was trying to pull a fast one.

All through the bus ride to the airport, the flight to Charlottesville, and the bus ride to the hotel, Shack kept saying, "I know you have the damn keys." Finally, Shackleford lost his temper. On the bus to the hotel, Shack took a swing at Drummond. Drummond swung back, and their teammates waded in to break it up. Valvano began yelling at Drummond, blaming the entire incident on him as opposed to his franchise man, who had the missing keys in one of his pockets all along.

On the way from the hotel lobby to their rooms, Shack and Drummond continued jawing at each other. Shack called Drum more names, and as Shack was putting his key in his room door, Drummond grabbed a fire extinguisher off the wall, pulled the pin out, and went after him. Shack ran into his room, grabbed a table, and threw it through the open doorway at Drummond. Just as Drum was about to punch the button on the fire extinguisher, Coach McLean showed up to take it away.

Valvano reportedly never sought to find out what caused the fight. Instead, he yelled at Drummond for being a "macho man" and told him he was thinking of sending him home. Drummond, who felt betrayed first by Shackleford and now by Valvano, knew he hadn't done anything wrong and was offended that he was shouldering the blame. In tears, crying uncontrollably, he told Valvano, "Hey, go ahead, man. Go ahead."

Later, when Shackleford found the keys and attempted to apologize, Drummond refused to accept the apology. "This was my teammate, my own teammate. That hurt me. It hurt me that he punched me," Drum said later.

Drummond started the Virginia game. He played the first ten minutes and didn't shoot. He was passing the ball when he had open shots, surprising his teammates but angering Valvano. He was in there to shoot the ball. Valvano yanked him and didn't put him back in.

Drum was distracted and his heart wasn't in it any more. He had taken all he could take from his teammates, had played the best he could without any support from anybody. His spirit had finally been crushed by Shackleford's hostility. Drummond told himself, "That's it, I'm outta here. And nobody is going to change my mind."

The game itself was a disaster.

It really looked as if State was going to win it. State led by a point with ten seconds left. State had the ball. Vinny del Negro, State's best free-throw shooter, was on the line for two shots. Virginia called time out.

A new ACC rule had been passed prior to the season, ordering each team to get back onto the floor in ten seconds after the horn blew at the end of a time-out. If the team wasn't out there in time, the referees were to put the ball in play anyway. There is one problem with the rule: In arenas like the one at Virginia, the crowd makes so much noise that the horn can't always be heard.

It was trainer Jim Rehbock's job to listen for the horn,

and while Valvano was talking to the players and Rehbock was listening—in vain—for the blast of sound, the referees walked over to the foul line, counted the mandatory ten, and put the ball down on the free-throw line. The ball was in play.

Just as the ref set the ball down, Valvano noticed what was going on, and he hurried his players onto the court.

There is another rule in college basketball that once the ball is placed on the foul line ready for play, nobody—not even the shooter—may go inside the free-throw circle.

Without thinking, Vinny entered the free-throw circle and picked up the ball. The referee blew his whistle and awarded possession of the ball to Virginia. It was the correct call, but at the time, with pandemonium in the arena, neither the N.C. State coaches nor the players understood why they had lost possession of the ball. To keep the ball, State had but one option: to call time out.

All Vinny knew was that he was being deprived of his two foul shots, shots that would have been game-winners, and the refs had taken the ball away from him. When he tried to find out why, the refs told him to play ball.

There were still ten seconds left. State still had a 1-point lead. Valvano called time out. Valvano sent Kelsey Weems into the game to guard Virginia's star player, John Johnson. Valvano told Weems, "Stay on him. He's going to get the last shot." Coach McLean added, "Guys, don't let Kelsey get picked. Watch the back pick on him."

The horn sounded, and this time they heard it. Virginia threw the ball in to Johnson, and Kelsey was guarding him like a glove. But Shackleford allowed his man to sneak by him, Shack's man blocked off Kelsey from Johnson, Johnson went unguarded to the base line, and with one second left he hit a jumper to win the game.

Valvano lost his composure. He started grabbing the referees, demanding an explanation of why they had taken the ball away from Vinny. Still they wouldn't tell him. With garbage raining down on the State players, the refs just wanted to get out of there.

Vinny wondered aloud what disaster would hit the team next. The next day he found out. The $550 bill plus 20 percent tip for the king crab enjoyed in Alaska showed up in the office of the assistant athletic director.

Vinny, Andy, Walker, Gee, and John Simonds knew it was going to pop up sometime. The only question was when. Timing, they knew, would be everything.

The players were on the floor practicing after the Virginia debacle for their upcoming game with nationally ranked Oklahoma when Kevin O'Connell, the associate athletic director in charge of finance and travel, came running over from his office, his face beet-red. He was holding a small piece of paper in his hand.

John Simonds was the first to see O'Connell coming. He said to Walker, "He's got it." Walker gave Andy the high-sign. Andy whispered, "Goddddammmmmnnnnnnn, we're in trouble now." Vinny said, "Uh oh, here it comes." Only Giomi was cool. He said, "Man, I ain't sweating it."

O'Connell headed straight for Valvano and began talking to him animatedly. Valvano called his coaches over. They all looked at the bill. Valvano screamed, "Toby." It was manager Toby Brannan's name that had been signed to the bill. Brannan came running over, wondering what terrible deed he had perpetrated. Valvano began berating him up and down. He said, "What did you do, take some babes up there to eat?" Valvano said, "This bill is for six hundred and sixty dollars. That's more than my bill, and I had a suite. And here you are, living better than the basketball coach and the A.D. combined. What do you have to say for yourself?"

Brannan, naturally, had no idea what Valvano was talking about. He said, quite astutely, "Maybe somebody signed my name to it."

Valvano mulled that over and screamed, "Simonds, get over here."

"Yes, coach."

"What do you have to say about this?"

Simonds knew better than to fudge it. He said, "Sir, we kind of had this nice dinner and kind of . . . er . . . ate high on the hog, and I guess somebody must have signed Toby's name to it. I don't know who. But I do remember eating crab that night."

Valvano said, "Wait a minute." He thought some more. "I do remember. That's the night you guys came out of that back room saying you had eaten hamburgers."

Simonds said, "Yes, sir. That was it."

Valvano said, "Who else was there?"

Simonds said, "Andy, Vinny, Walker, and Gee."

Valvano shouted, "If you are going to spend this much money on food, you'd better be winning." Meanwhile, the black players were taking all this in and asking each other, Where was this fancy restaurant where those dudes spent $660?

Valvano shouted, "I can't believe it. My players are eating better than I am. Something is wrong in this world. We go up to Alaska and lose, and I got guys coming back here with six-hundred-sixty-dollar bills. I can't believe this. I'm just not cut out for this job any more."

That was the light moment for the week.

The Oklahoma Sooners came to Raleigh. Led by All American Wayman Tisdale, the Sooners were a powerhouse. Once again Valvano had scheduled a game on national television. A full house of 12,400 was on hand at Reynolds.

Oklahoma led by 20 at the half. During the game, Valvano was vicious in his treatment of the players. As soon as a player made a mistake, which occurred frequently against the Sooners, Valvano substituted for him, sat him on the bench, and verbally abused him. "You're a sorry SOB" and "You big, fucking pussy" were a couple of the coach's favorites.

The hometeam crowd, stunned by the Wolfpack's poor performance, didn't treat them any better. As the State players walked off the court, their fans booed them lustily and threw objects at them from the stands.

In the locker room during halftime, Valvano tried ridicule. He said, "You pussies, why don't we put on dresses?" But that was not what the players needed. Their reaction was a blank stare. They needed a coach who could say, "This is what we need to do." So again, all Valvano managed to do was distance himself further from his players.

The players were walking back upstairs when Chucky Brown said, "Come on, fellas, I don't want to lose this game." Quentin began chanting, "We can do it. We can do it. We just got to play good. We just got to." Kenny Drummond was the last one up the steps. Valvano had benched him in favor of Vinny del Negro, and Drum wasn't talking to anybody.

For seven minutes State looked like world-beaters. The Wolfpack outscored Oklahoma 20–2. They were finally playing as a team, making good passes, looking for the open man, making good shots. On the sideline Valvano stopped his usual yelling and screaming. The players had stopped looking at him—the crowd was so noisy, they couldn't have heard him anyway.

There is a noise meter at the top of the Reynolds, with a series of lights going up a tall pole. As the crowd gets louder, lights climb the pole until the red bulb at the top is lit. A lot of fans think the meter is legit, but it isn't. A lever-pusher sits on a platform atop the Coliseum operating the meter. As the crowd begins to yell, he lights a light on the pole. This incites the crowd to yell louder, and he lights another light higher up. Eventually he sucks the whole crowd into screaming as loud as it can in order to get the red bulb lit. When it does light, the noise is so deafening, you have to put your hands over your ears.

With State trailing by just 4 and the red bulb lit, Oklahoma called time out. On the bench Valvano told his players, "I knew we could do it, guys. I had all the confidence in the world in you. I tell you over and over, 'If you just listen to me, we'll get back in this game.' "

But State could not catch up, losing by 4, and afterward Valvano told them, "For the first seven minutes of the second half, you played good, but then you stopped listening to me. And we just couldn't quite get it done."

Realistically, there was much for the players to be proud of. For the first time all year, they had given a superb effort against a tough team. The subs were off the bench, cheering their teammates on, and the electricity was really surging through the arena. But the moment was fleeting.

When they lost, there was a realization that they didn't have what it took to beat a really good team. The players told themselves, "There wasn't any more that we could have done, and we lost."

After the Oklahoma game, the coaching staff quit on its players. The coaches wouldn't speak to them, except to say, "Run this offense," or "Do this drill," during practice. The players took notice that Valvano would see them and say nothing—not even "Hey, how are you doing?" Said one player, "He would walk past us like he didn't even see us."

"They were supposed to be there for us," said another player, "and they weren't. We were down on ourselves. They didn't have to get down on us any more." But after the Oklahoma game, Valvano reportedly told them, "You guys aren't worth a shit."

34

Turning Up the Heat

After the Oklahoma game, the players left the locker room to go back to their apartments. The coaches remained, as did Simonds. Valvano had so much frustration seething within him that he couldn't stand in one spot. Pacing furiously and gesticulating wildly, he said, "I'm on top of a wave, and sooner or later I'm going to fall off."

Then he said to John Simonds, "I need a drink."

Before an earlier game he had once told Simonds, "You know, John, one of these days you ought to do a study. Study the coaches in this country and see how many of them have alcohol and marriage problems." Simonds, trying to be supportive of his coach in a stressful situation, had smiled at him and said, "Yes, sir. I'll do it." Valvano said, "No, John, seriously, I think that you'll find that all coaches have alcohol and marital problems because of the pressures put on the coaches today, with the heavy emphasis on winning—if you don't win, you're out. This drives coaches to the bottle and ends their marriages.

"It's out of control," Valvano had said.

During lunch many days the coaches were in the habit of going down to the Rockola Cafe, about a mile from the basketball office, and having two or three beers. Assistant coach Dick Stewart was particularly distressed about losing.

Valvano once had saved Stewart from a bad situation. Stewart had been an assistant coach at the University of South Carolina when a scandal arose concerning the illegal sale of tickets. Head Coach Bill Foster and all his assistants, including Stewart, either resigned or were fired.

The loss of his job was a devastating blow to Stewart, but then Valvano, who had been his teammate as a player at Rutgers, called and offered him a job as his assistant at N.C. State. Valvano had saved Stewart when he was at his lowest point, so Stewart, more than the others, felt a personal indebtedness to Valvano. When Valvano suffered, Stewart suffered equally. Part of why the players didn't like Stewart was that they knew he was Valvano's boy. Though he knew how they felt, it didn't matter, because his loyalty apparently was to Valvano first, last, and always.

Sometimes at practice, the players enjoyed making sport of Stewart. Said a player, "We'd be doing shooting drills—our guards would come off screens, and he was the one making the passes. He'd be so intense, he'd be throwing chest passes like he was a machine. 'Shoot the ball, shoot the ball!' he'd be yelling, and he'd get carried away, and we would make fun of him.

"Shack used to punt the ball at him. Stewart would be standing on the court after practice, and Shack would stand in front of the exit door, and he'd kick or heave the ball right at him and duck out of the gym. Or Shack would say, 'Everybody,' and we'd all throw balls at him and run and hide. We played games with him. It was hilarious."

With State on a losing skid, Stewart was taking it personally.

It was six in the morning when the bus was getting ready to leave for the airport to go to Chicago to play DePaul, another nationally ranked team. When Stewart arrived, he was in a festive mood, kidding the players, fooling around. When sober, Stewart was usually very serious, never playful. So the players knew he had been drinking.

Said one player, "He used to wear this tight corduroy suit with patches on his arms, and his shirt would be tight, and that vein in his neck would be pumping out, and his face would be red—I mean real red. Red red. One time we thought he was going to blow up. He had a little piece of gum in his mouth, and his little white lips were going . . ."

The DePaul game didn't do a thing to lessen the tension or brighten anyone's mood. This game, too, was on national TV. DePaul's star, Dallas Comegys, took control early, slamming dunks in Shackleford's face, and inside a few minutes DePaul led by 20. On the bench, nobody was clapping. No one cared. They began discussing the relative beauty of the girls in the stands.

Shackleford shot 0 for 9, and Valvano benched him. While he sat at the end of the bench, he found someone to bring him a box of popcorn, and while his teammates were getting creamed, he placidly sat there eating the whole box of popcorn.

In the locker room after the game, Valvano slammed the door, screamed, "Motherfuckers!" threw his jacket, screamed, "Goddammit!" kicked the ice bucket and almost broke his toe. As he was hobbling around the locker room, berating the players, they were silently eyeing each other and biting their tongues to keep from laughing.

Valvano said, "Shack, you are weak. You don't have any strength. You don't have any intensity. You need to lift weights. You need to work on your concentration." Coach Stewart chimed in, "They outrebounded us by fifteen." The players, who saw Stewart's role as that of a tattletale and scycophant, began to laugh. Valvano said, "There isn't anything fucking funny about losing." Said one player later, "He just had so much to say in his mouth. You know how Italians talk anyway. They talk nasty. They curse you out. That's how he was."

The team returned to the hotel. Valvano told them, "I want to see everybody." When the meeting was over, the players had scalded ears.

Valvano took each starter, one by one, and cut him to shreds in front of his peers, a cardinal coaching no-no.

After they left the meeting, Walker was fixing to cry. Giomi was distraught. He said, "I should have stayed at Indiana and tried to fix my problems with Coach Knight." Andy said, "Goddammit, I'm transferring for sure." Vinny was quiet.

As bad as the white players felt, the black players felt worse, because they felt that Valvano had come down harder on them. Kelsey Weems was heard telling Walker, "It's just not fair. You crackers have it too easy. V just hates us."

Bennie Bolton, who was the most critical of Valvano,

had been singled out at the meeting for playing poorly. Valvano reportedly had also accused him of causing dissension on the team, of being an instigator, telling guys not to take their drug tests, telling them to stand up for their rights. Valvano blasted Bennie for being "high and mighty" and trying to be a spokesman and rallying the black players around him to hate their coach. Bennie said, "V said what he had to say, and I don't like it."

In three days the team would have to face North Carolina again. State had lost four in a row and could easily make that five or six, what with the Tar Heels looming and the powerful Louisville Cardinals after them. For the players, the nightmare was real.

35

The Dean

Part of what makes the N.C. State–North Carolina rivalry so intense is the rivalry between Jim Valvano and Dean Smith. It has been said that Valvano harbors some jealousy of Smith, the result of Dean's success, the quality of his program, and the size of his Dome. But if Valvano is jealous of Smith, it isn't nearly as great as the jealousy expressed by the State players for the Tar Heels who get to play under him.

Simonds and several of the State players discussed the differences between Valvano and Smith. The players mentioned the obvious and publicly discussed differences: that Smith teaches a system that the players learn to perfection. That whether the team is up by 10 or down by 10, Carolina runs the same patterns—picking, picking, picking, coming off screens, the ball never hitting the floor, fundamentally sound basketball. One State player contrasted this with the style of play at N.C. State.

"We free-lance," said a State player. "Drum gets the ball and shoots. Shack gets the ball and shoots. We run and gun and do what we can."

They discussed Smith's reputation for recruiting players who study, graduate, and become pillars of the community.

Said one of the State players, "The Tar Heel program is number one in college basketball. Dean Smith recruits the best players, but he always looks at a guy's insides before he looks at his ability. He looks to see how much a player wants it, how much he will be willing to sacrifice individual goals for team goals. He always asks, 'Is he a good kid? Will he go to class? Will he get along with his teammates? Is he going to be a good ambassador for the university?'

"Instead of looking at that, Valvano looks at, 'He's six-eleven, a good athlete, let's sign him,' and he doesn't look at anything else. And that player ends up destroying the team."

They laughed—at the reference to Shackleford, their franchise—and at themselves. They *were* renegades, though they didn't like admitting it.

The players discussed some of Dean Smith's other qualities. "When Dean Smith recruits a high school All American," said one high school All American who went to N.C. State, "he gets to play, and usually he does become a star." Smith is renowned for his freshman stars—the latest: J. R. Reid.

Smith, said Bennie Bolton, genuinely likes his players. "With Dean," he said, "his players come first."

Bennie had played summer ball with Curtis Hunter, who played at North Carolina under Smith. Hunter was supposed to be the next Michael Jordan, but he hurt his leg. One time Bennie asked Hunter, "What is Dean Smith like?"

Hunter said, "Say Dean is in his office with the president of the university, and a player comes in and says, 'Coach Smith, I have to talk to you. It's important.' Dean Smith will ask the president to leave to talk to his player." Hunter said, "That's the way it is at Carolina." Bolton replied, "At State, we can't ever find our coach."

Said another State player enviously, "You look in the Carolina basketball alumni book, and you see all the people who have graduated and gone on to good jobs, and you see he maintains contact with his players. He knows what each one of them is doing. That's what I like about him.

"If you have to sit on the bench for Dean Smith, if you don't go to the pros, at least you're going to get a good-paying job out of it. He has contacts all over the place.

"But if you sit on the bench at State, and your season's up, that's it. You're on your own. That's kind of messed up, when you come to a program you think is one of the best and you find out it's terrible. I'll bet players from ten years ago come to Dean and say, 'I need a job,' and I'll bet you he finds one quick."

Teviin Binns then discussed his high school friend Ernie Myers. Talking about the difference between Valvano and Dean Smith made him bitter.

"In high school, playing for Tolentine High in the Bronx, Ernie Myers was a god," said Teviin. "In one game he scored seventy points. He could come down one on three, shake his three defenders, and score. Everybody knew that Ernie would be in the pros in three years."

Myers had been a McDonald's All Star Game MVP. He was the number one player in the nation coming out of high school. He led Tolentine to three straight state championships.

As a freshman during the Wolfpack's 1983 NCAA national championship season, Myers began the season on the bench, getting little time, as was Valvano's custom, but when Dereck Whittenberg broke his ankle and had to sit out thirteen games, Myers stepped right in, averaging over 18 points a game including a one-game record for an N.C. State freshman, 35 points against Duke. But when Whittenberg returned, Myers again took the bench, and in his next three years, his career went backward. The players say that Valvano, who dislikes flashy players, changed Myers' style of play, slowed him down, made him more methodical and less spontaneous, and by the time he was a senior, he didn't get to start until midway through the season. Myers wasn't even drafted by the pros, and was reportedly devastated. He would say, "Man, all these other high school All Americans, they are all playing in the NBA. What happened to me?" To this day friends say he isn't sure.

Myers was one of three Valvano recruits—Terry (The Cannon) Gannon and Vinny del Negro were the other two—who I could find got their degree at N.C. State. Ernie knew that without that piece of paper, he would have been sunk, because reportedly he knew that Valvano wasn't the kind of coach to use his influence to get him a job.

Said Binns, "V really did him wrong. He could have gotten him a job in the athletic department doing something. Come on, all the people V knows in Raleigh. It's not right. When the players finish their years here, that's it. It's like no more connection. All the players—all of them—go their own way. Nobody would go to V and say, 'Hey, V, I need a job,' because he knows he'll distract him by telling him something that isn't true.

"V doesn't care," said Binns. "When you've finished your four years here, that's it."

36

Blown Out

The morning of the day of the game with the Tar Heels, the *Technician*, the N.C. State student newspaper, ran an edition with a photo of a bunch of fat, ugly nude men posing in seductive positions—with their heads removed and the heads of the Carolina basketball team substituted for them. Star guard Jeff Lebo was pictured naked wearing a kitchen apron with his behind shining outward. Dean Smith was pictured reclining naked on a couch, with a big belly protruding, a basketball covering his genitals, and a foot-long cigar coming out of his mouth. The State students thought it hilarious.

On the day of the game, there was the usual banter between the two student bodies. The State rooters were getting the "tractors and cows" treatment, while the Tar Heels were hearing about "preppies and snotnoses."

Carolina's star player, J. R. Reid, may only have been a freshman, but he had developed into a star, and with his extreme flat-top hairdo, Reid was gaining a lot of attention from the media.

One of the State students, in a rush of inspiration, took a piece of paper, drew dotted lines, and wrote on it, "Fold this into an airplane, and when the PA announcer calls out J. R. Reid's name, throw it at him." The student took the piece of paper to Kinko's Copies across the street from the campus and ordered 2,000 duplicates, charging it to a business without its knowledge, and handed out the 2,000 potential paper airplanes before the game.

When J. R. Reid's name was introduced, the entire student section threw the paper airplanes onto the floor. From the bench it looked like the raid over Tokyo as the paper planes darted every which way before landing, some of them even on the court.

The week before, Valvano had seemed optimistic about the game. One of Carolina's stars, guard Kenny Smith, the sort of player who could beat a team by himself, had had arthroscopic surgery on his knee. Carolina announced that Smith was "extremely doubtful" for the N.C. State game.

The day before the game, the papers said, "Smith will probably suit up, but he won't play." The players were skeptical. They knew that a Carolina ploy was to print phony injury rumors in the papers, hoping to lull the opposition into thinking, "The Heels will be short-handed," only to have them play at full strength and blow out the opposition.

But even at gametime, Valvano didn't think Smith was going to play. He told the players, "Guys, without Smith, I think we can win this game. We can break this slide."

Sure enough, as the teams took the court, walking out there was Kenny Smith. And Smith had an outstanding game, scoring 21 points and playing superbly.

By the half, State was out of the game. J. R. Reid time and again was faking Shackleford off his feet, then making resounding dunks. During a time-out, while Valvano was trying to talk to the players, Quentin Jackson said to Shackleford, "I just can't believe it, Shack. What's wrong with you? Don't you have any pride at all? He's just hammering you." Shack tried to ignore him.

As they did against Oklahoma, the State fans were booing Valvano and his players, throwing ice at them as they went off for halftime losing by 24 points. In the locker room, Valvano told them, "I can't believe it. Twenty years of coaching, and I'm getting booed in my own barn. Fellas, I don't know what to say. We can't play. We can't play with them. Kenny Smith is just killing you."

One of the players thought, "Now it's killing 'you,' not 'us.' V isn't taking the blame for this one."

Valvano continued: "You guys have no self-respect at all. You have no pride. You don't care who you are. All you want to do is eat big meals and get your free sweats and free shoes. You don't give a damn about this team."

He said, "I've been in this game too long. All you guys think you can coach better than me. I don't know what to do. If I could, I wouldn't even show up for the second half."

The players were silent—there was no "We can play" noise from Quentin or Chucky Brown. They trudged back upstairs, returning to the boos. The tide shifted for a couple of minutes while State ran off 12 points in a row, but the Tar Heels maintained a lead at around 18, and even with the Carolina subs on the court at the end, State couldn't get any closer. Midway through the second half, the State fans started their exodus home.

One of the spectators in the stands was George Irvine of the Indiana Pacers. Irvine had come to the game to scout some of the Tar Heel players and take a look at Shackleford.

Sitting next to Irvine was Vinny del Negro's father. They knew each other from college. The senior del Negro reportedly told his son what Irvine had said: "Shackleford would commit suicide if he knew how much money he lost tonight. We had rated him real high, but after watching him practice and play, we don't think he's very good."

Meanwhile, back in the dressing room, Valvano told his players, "Guys, I can't understand it. We were chosen out of all the teams in the country to be put on national television more than anybody else, because we have this magic that any time on national TV we play great and beat great teams. That's what the country wants to see.

"Well, guys, that's it. We've come full circle. Five times on national TV we've gotten squashed by fifteen or more. You guys have really done it to me. Do you think NBC is even going to talk to us next year? Hell, no. What are you doing to me, guys? I'm the one who has to answer to them. On national TV you embarrass the shit out of me. You haven't played at all. One time, I just want you to play your dicks off. Just one time."

He said, "I'm thinking about quitting this game altogether. It's just too hard on me. Because I'm trying, and you guys aren't trying."

With that, Valvano left the dressing room to go out and talk to the national media. When he arrived, he reverted to the smiling, charming rogue TV persona everyone knows. One of the commentators asked him about Kenny Smith, and Valvano said, "Kenny Smith came here; he wasn't supposed to play after surgery, and he scored a game-high on us, had a career game. Next week I got all our guys signed up for knee surgery. If it can do that for Smith, I want everybody on my team having arthroscopic surgery on both knees." Valvano smiled. The commentator smiled. The fans watching at home smiled. Kids across America thought to themselves, "Boy, would I love to be playing for him."

37

Craziness

The N.C. State players didn't get into Louisville until eleven-thirty at night, and their luggage didn't arrive until three-thirty the next afternoon. If they had wanted to practice, they would have had to do it in their suede shoes and skivvies. Because it was so late when they got into the hotel, the only food available was pizza, so they ordered thirty pies and sixty sodas and took those back to their rooms, as everyone was tired from the plane ride. Uncharacteristically subdued, one group of players sat in the inside balcony of the room across from Valvano's, eating pizza and talking quietly.

A choir-group convention was also staying at the hotel, with hundreds of unruly kids from churches and school choirs running up and down the inside balconies of the huge, eighteen-story hotel, with their racket drifting up to the players' floor. Valvano, who apparently thought his players were cutting up again, ran out, came upon the players sitting there, and shouted, "Can't you guys shut the fuck up and go do something else on some other floor? You're embarrassing me. Can't you guys do anything but goof off?"

Before anyone could say a word in his own defense, Valvano stormed back into his room. The players shrugged their shoulders. "Well, that's par for the course," said one of them.

Against the nationally ranked Louisville Cardinals coached by Denny Crum, State once again was on national television. Before the game, television commentators Dick Enberg and Al McGuire came into the locker room to visit with Valvano. They were giving him a tough time about losing. Valvano was overheard saying, "Yeah, I just can't get it done. My ballteam sucks."

In the arena, the Wolfpack players looked up to see the 20,000 Louisville fans holding up a poster of a wolf getting hanged. At the top it read, "Who's afraid of the big bad wolf?" Valvano was heard raging, "Who's afraid of the big bad wolf? Why should they be afraid of us? We couldn't beat Meredith" (a Raleigh school for girls).

State was never in the game. Purvis Ellison made Shackleford look amateurish, and at the half it was the usual story: down by 20.

Valvano tried substituting, something he rarely did. He put Andy Kennedy into the game and instructed him to run a special play he had designed against the Cardinals.

State had practiced exactly one afternoon for the Louisville game. As usual, Kennedy worked out with the subs on the white team, aping the Louisville plays so the starters would have some experience against them in the game. During the chalk talk, while Valvano was explaining the intricacies of the special play, a complicated set of maneuvers, Kennedy didn't pay attention and let his mind wander, because he didn't expect to play.

When Valvano instructed Kennedy to run the special play, Kennedy said to himself, "Hell, I know the Louisville plays. I know what Purvis Ellison is going to do, but I don't know *our* plays. I have no idea what I'm supposed to do."

So Kennedy faked it, and no one said anything, and against Louisville he played twenty minutes, contributing some baskets and some good defense—nothing great but certainly solid. He didn't play again for two weeks.

During the second half of the game Valvano put Avie Lester in to replace Shackleford. Avie went up for a jump shot. It was an ungainly, ugly-looking shot, and the Louisville players started to laugh at his game.

With six minutes left in the game, Avie got fouled. He went to the line. This was on national television, and if viewers were watching closely enough, they could see Purvis Ellison and his teammates laughing. Avie was shooting near the State bench, so the players could hear what Ellison and his Louisville cohorts were saying. Ellison said, "He sure has it bad, doesn't he?" A teammate said, "Yeah, just don't touch him." Suddenly, laughter erupted from the State bench—they realized the Louisville players were talking about Avie's acne. Poor Avie had been hit by some elbows, and as he stood on the line ready to shoot, his face was pussy and bleeding. In a major college basketball game, Louisville was razzing Avie because of his complexion, and nobody from State was doing anything to stop it. Rather, one of the State players yelled out to Ellison, "Yeah, man, you ought to practice with him every day."

Avie was angry and hurt. And he missed the foul shot.

The whole season had fallen in on the Wolfpack. As one player described it, "We were one game better than a dead man."

Back on campus, professors and other students barraged the players with questions like "Do you enjoy getting beat?" or "Aren't you proud of your school?" It hurt them whenever someone asked, "Don't you give a damn that you're getting beat by twenty?" What could they say? The fans complained to them about the grief they had to suffer from students of other ACC schools.

John Simonds continued with the team as an assistant despite not getting the scholarship Valvano promised to him. Nor did he get any indication that Valvano had followed through on the promise to somehow improve his fall grades, and he was failing just about every spring-semester course.

Simonds, along with Walker Lambiotte and Quentin Jackson, had signed up for an English class with a teacher named Mrs. Rich. One day it snowed, so Walker decided not to attend. Quentin and Simonds made it, and at the start of class Mrs. Rich announced a test, saying she would return at the end of the period.

Simonds didn't know much, but Quentin, who sat next to him, nevertheless took down everything Simonds had written word for word. Quentin apparently hadn't studied at all. Simonds completed what he could, balefully acknowledging to himself before he left that it was D-quality work. He turned his paper in and left. Quentin remained, apparently copying as well from another student on the other side of him. When he handed his paper in, it appeared that he was better versed in the subject than Simonds.

The next time the class met, Mrs. Rich returned the

papers. Quentin got a C. Simonds got an F with the jarring notation, "See me." She curtly asked him to meet her in her office the next morning. He didn't know why, but agreed.

When he entered and sat down, she was nervously smoking a cigarette. She seemed agitated. Mrs. Rich said, "Mr. Simonds, I'm going to have you thrown out of school for plagiarism."

Simonds went bug-eyed. She said, "I have evidence that you copied off another person's test. If we take it up before the student court, I can prove it to anybody. It's obvious—word for word."

He said honestly, "Ma'am, I don't know what you're talking about."

Mrs. Rich said, "Oh yes, you do. You know exactly what I'm talking about." She said, "All you players come in here; every one of you thinks he can just blow through my class, that you're going to get an easy A and that you can cheat and get away with anything you want.

"It doesn't work that way in my class," she said. "And you got caught cheating. And I'm going to make you pay."

Simonds hadn't cheated. Quentin had done the cheating. And here Simonds was, facing expulsion from college for plagiarism. He was trying to be calm, though tears began to well up inside him. He considered his response. He couldn't stand the thought of being accused of cheating, but he knew he couldn't blow the whistle on Quentin. Quentin was a teammate. That was against the players' code. He decided to try reasoning with her. He made a convincing case, his strongest argument being, "If I were going to cheat, don't you think I would cheat to make a better grade than an F?" and he pleaded for another chance to prove himself.

Finally, she said, "I still think I should take you up before the board and have you thrown out, but I'm going to believe you. But I better not see one word on your next test that even rhymes with anything else on anybody else's test, or else you're gone. You understand me, Mr. Simonds?"

He said, "Yes, ma'am, I sure do. Thank you."

After he left and got back to his apartment, he collapsed he was shaking so hard. Sweating in the middle of winter, he went outside to cool off. The episode had scared him to the bone, because he had come within an argument of losing everything he had worked for. He thought, "I am getting burned by the system that I am putting my trust in."

At the same time he was furious with his teammate for leaving him to hang out naked to dry. He knew well that had Mrs. Rich tried to toss him out of school, no one from the team—not even Quentin—would have stood up for him. He told himself, "In that situation, V would have saved Shack, but not me," and he knew then that his importance to the team had been largely in his own mind. He knew that had he crashed and burned, Valvano would have said, "John, it was great having you. Tough luck." And he realized then that Valvano could have filled his shoes in the snap of a finger.

"All along I had been thinking I was *the* man—that the players needed me, the coaches needed me—and I was believing a lie," said Simonds. As he sat outside whipped by the cold reality and the equally cold wind, he began to cry, because he knew then that he had dug himself a deep hole and there was no crawling out.

When Simonds told Quentin of his close call, Quentin thought it was a big joke. Simonds said, "Q, I'm really pissed at you." Quentin said, "What are you talking about?"

"You cheated off me word for word. I didn't know you were taking it down word for word," said Simonds. "What's the big deal?" Quentin said. Simonds said, "I got hauled into the office and had the lady accuse me of cheating off your paper and wanting to throw me out of school."

"Yeah, but you're still here," Quentin said. "Besides, hang with the Q Dog; he'll take care of you."

Simonds turned around and walked off, a feeling of disillusionment overwhelming him.

38

Drum Departs

After six losses in a row, State finally won one: against the Winthrop Eagles from Rock Hill, South Carolina. Said Simonds, "Winthrop might as well have been a blind school."

All season long Valvano had been promising the subs on the white team, "You keep playing hard, and I'm going to put you in a game as a unit," but it was only against teams like Winthrop that he would do it. Andy Kennedy had been looking forward to this game. For the preceding week, he had been working out at both the shooting guard and shooting forward positions, expecting a lot of playing time in this game. He had spent the last week watching what the starters were doing at both those positions. But when Valvano put Kennedy into the game against Winthrop, he was put in at point guard; all his study and preparation were for naught.

State played its usual poor first half. The players felt, "What the hell? Everybody else is beating us. Why not Winthrop?" What was going to happen? V couldn't get any angrier.

But by the second half, the Winthrop players began to tire against their taller, more talented opponents, and the Wolfpack rout was on. State won by 26. Despite having to be playmaker, Andy Kennedy scored his season-high 14 points.

The crowd went home happy, having seen a victory and some nice dunks by Shackleford. Only Drummond and Giomi were glum, because they had played little. The lift anyone got from beating Winthrop was negligible. The players felt, "Who did we beat? Nobody." The next day the local papers were critical of the team for even scheduling Winthrop.

The next game was in Reynolds Coliseum against Clemson, which except for Horace Grant, played poorly. But the Wolfpack played worse, got down by 15, and lost by 3 points.

Drummond started the game and took three shots, missing them all. The Wolfpack fans, who had been reading in the local papers of Valvano's and others' criticism of Drummond's shot selection, in unison let out a vituperative flood of booing that hurt Drummond to his toes. And when the fans started to boo and shout, "Get that bum out of there," Valvano did just that, hurting Drummond's pride even worse. Drummond thought to himself, "Damn, who's the coach, the fans or Valvano?"

Teviin Binns, for one, felt terrible for Drummond. Teviin thought, "Everybody loved Drum when we were winning, but once we started losing, they booed him. Why would students do that to their own players? That's messed up, man. I felt sorry for him; they were treating him so bad.

"Valvano should have said, 'This is my player, and I'm sticking by him.' But that's not how he is."

The rest of the players rejoiced that Drummond had been benched. Without him, they had closed the gap to 3, only to lose when a long 3-pointer by Andy Kennedy rimmed out at the buzzer. Quentin and Kelsey and Vinny were heard telling each other, "We can play great when we don't have Drum."

Drum heard them. After the game he went back to his room and had a conversation with God. According to Drummond, God told him, "You don't have to be miserable for anybody. There is someone out there who will appreciate you and your talents." Drum made up his mind: He wasn't going to play at N.C. State any more.

Drum went to practice the next day but decided to skip the practice after that. Instead, after class, he went directly back to his room to be alone. Toby Brannan, the manager, went to see why he wasn't at practice. Drummond told him, "I'm not playing here any more." Brannan told him to go see Valvano and have a talk with him. Drummond said, "Coach Valvano hasn't talked to me in three months. What makes you think I want to talk to him right now?"

Drummond drove over to the Ramada Inn, rented a room, and stayed there for three days. He didn't want anyone, especially Valvano, to try to change his mind. One thing he knew for sure: He no longer wanted to be part of the N.C. State basketball program.

The night he checked into the Ramada Inn, Drummond had another discussion with God. He asked Him, "How could I make this a better situation for me?" And the next morning, when the team was scheduled to get on the bus for the airport to fly to Atlanta for the Georgia Tech game, Drummond wasn't on it. He attended his classes and afterward returned to his hotel room, eating his meals in his room and watching television.

When the team got on the bus to go to the airport and Drummond wasn't on it, everyone started asking, "Where's Drum?" The coaches knew, as did John Simonds.

Simonds was sitting in the front, with Walker Lambiotte a couple rows behind him. Walker asked Simonds the magic question. Simonds mouthed, "Drum quit." Walker's mouth hung open. He couldn't believe that one of N.C. State's star players had quit right in the middle of the season. Andy repeated the question to Simonds. Again Simonds mouthed, "Drum quit." Andy said, "Godddammmnn!" Then Andy said, "Well, it's probably for the best." And then, "Who needs him?" Quentin was exultant. His reaction must have been, "There's a spot for me now."

But when the other black players found out, they were upset and angry. They were of the opinion that Valvano had really screwed him. Chucky Brown was heard to say, "When he was doing good, they were slapping him on the back, but when things started looking bad, he was gone. You don't treat people like that."

Bennie Bolton was particularly upset. He said, "Drum came into the program; he was made all sorts of promises by V about playing, promises he could go and see V any time he had a problem, and then V never followed through on any of them."

Even Kelsey Weems, who stood to gain by Drummond's departure, was down about it. Kelsey told a teammate, "Drum was trying so hard, but he didn't have a coach." And it hurt them, because off the court they had lost one of theirs. And on the court the player Valvano was going to replace him with was Vinny del Negro, the coach's favorite.

After Drum quit the team, the only coach who went to seek him out was Coach McLean. One time he showed up at Drummond's room at seven in the morning and woke him up, just to see how he was getting along. It was Coach McLean who helped Kenny transfer to High Point College.

A short while after Drummond quit the team, John Simonds was driving up the hill from the College Inn to the gym when he saw Kenny walking along the road. Drummond had continued going to classes. He had merely quit playing basketball. Simonds gave him a lift. Drum was sullen and quiet.

Simonds asked him general questions about school, whether he was okay and if there was anything he could do for him. Drum said no. Simonds said, "Drum, I really feel bad for you, because you got burned, and it's not all your fault."

"Yes, it is," Drummond countered.

Drum felt that he should have been smart enough not to fall for Valvano's promises and the glitz and the bull and the lights, smart enough to see that JUCO transfers are more vulnerable than kids who come in as freshmen because a coach has no investment in the transfer and because the fans figure he's a no-brain coming from a junior college, so if he doesn't work out it's his fault, not the coach's. But Drum also knew that he had been without any direction whatsoever, that whenever he had needed Valvano, Valvano wasn't there for him.

Simonds said, "Drum, how do you feel about V?"

"I hate V" was all he said.

39

Captain Ahab

Before the Georgia Tech game Valvano was in a foul mood. The players had gone up to the court for the pregame workout, and he was sitting in the locker room with the other coaches and John Simonds, and he began talking about his problems. The losing was getting to him.

Valvano rambled, "I've got a bunch of guys who just can't play. Kelsey wants to play, but he's not good enough. Walker has completely let me down. He's washed up. He isn't any good. Andy hates me. Bennie keeps everyone else hating me. Shack isn't playing worth a shit. He doesn't care. Teviin's mind is gone." And then suddenly Valvano began chuckling. He said, "In my twenty years of coaching, this is the wildest I have ever seen. I got kids who can't take care of themselves, who get in trouble gradewise and in every other way."

He said, "One of these days, this is all going to come back and haunt me."

Then he repeated something he had said before: "I'm riding this big wave, and I'm going to fall off, and it's going to slap me."

He chuckled again and repeated himself. He said, "Sooner or later, that big wave is going to slap me. I just know it."

40

Glimmers of Hope

State lost to Georgia Tech, even without Drummond. The highlight of the trip for the players was watching the six-foot-eleven Shackleford sneak down the hotel's fire escape to meet his girl friend after Valvano had forbidden the players to go out.

The team returned to Raleigh to play Brooklyn College the next day. Brooklyn College was another team like Winthrop and East Tennessee and Western Carolina and Asheville, a guaranteed win.

Valvano once again had Andy Kennedy playing point guard, after Andy had studied the plays of both shooting positions during practice. He was on the point because none of the other players on the court—Teviin, Avie, Brian Howard, and Kenny Poston, who hadn't scored a point all season—could handle the ball as well.

It didn't really matter. In a game like that, all everyone out there wants to do is shoot, and shoot it up they did. Andy was so happy to be in the game that if the ball touched his hands he threw it up. Each time Valvano called him over to the sideline. "What kind of fucking shot is that? You're 0 for 7." Andy would reply, "I know the next one is going in, Coach," and the next time he brought the ball past halfcourt, he'd let fly.

Bennie Bolton also was letting fly from way out, and the contest was to see who could shoot the longest basket. Shack, with no opposition to speak of, was having so much fun, he'd dribble the ball into the key with four players on him, duck, spin, deek, and take the shot. Two other teammates would be wide open, but Shack wouldn't give up the ball.

When Teviin got into the game, he was like a little kid

being let out of school, he was so happy. There were nights during the season when he went home and cried for hours because Valvano hadn't played him. Against Brooklyn he was playing, and even though the competition was tougher in the team scrimmages, it was still an opportunity for Teviin to show off for the home crowd.

With State ahead by 25 points with two minutes left in the game, Teviin was racing down the court toward the basket on a two-on-one fast break. Teviin got the ball, and as he got to the key, with a defender between him and the basket, he bounced the ball off the floor, hard. As the defender went for the ball, Teviin jumped high over him, caught the ball off the bounce, and dunked it into the basket—backward.

The players sitting on the bench thought the play incredible. They dropped to the ground, lying on the floor in admiration. It may have been the first off-the-floor backward dunk in NCAA history.

Teviin wanted the State fans to see what they had missed by his sitting on the bench for two years. Said Teviin afterwards, "To do that in a game, you have to have some kind of heart, but I took that chance and made it. I wanted to show V what kind of player I could have been."

It was to be Teviin's swan song at State. He didn't get into another game the rest of the season.

After the Brooklyn respite, State went back to playing ACC opponents. The team bused over to the Cameron Indoor Stadium to play Duke in Durham. State had beaten Duke at the Reynolds Coliseum rather handily. Beating Duke at Duke is another story. Blue Devil fans are notoriously brutal to their guests.

Duke is another ACC college that takes its superior image over N.C. State seriously. Duke University probably has the highest academic standards in the ACC, and Duke students are not above letting the N.C. State visitors know just how much smarter they are. Duke students chant, "If you can't go to school, go to State. If you can't go to State, go to jail."

The year Chris Washburn stole the stereo out of a student's room and it was revealed that he had gotten into State with a 470 on his SATs, the Duke fans held up signs that read: "SAT: Sign on the dotted line and get 400 points." Besides that, each Duke student brought a record album cover and when Washburn was introduced, sailed it out onto the floor, a mocking reference to Wash's stereo theft.

The year Lorenzo Charles heisted the two pizzas, the Duke fans fired 8,000 pizza boxes onto the floor when he was introduced. The first year State's Spud Webb went over there to play, the fans threw potatoes onto the floor, covering the court. The Duke fans, indeed, have a sense of humor.

When the State team came out onto the court to warm up this time, Duke students were holding up cards with the message: "Washburn and Drummond, a fine tradition." The week before Washburn had been found to have a cocaine addiction while with the Golden State Warriors. Drum, of course, had quit the team.

Making things even more uncomfortable for State was Cameron Indoor Stadium itself. It's like a big high school gym, with the players sitting in the stands along with everyone else, the Duke students directly behind them, knees in the players' backs, their screaming voices right behind the players' ears.

Some of the Duke fans put on big noses and long-haired, greasy wigs to try to look like Valvano, and all game long whenever he stood up, the fans yelled at him to sit down. Fans were yelling at Shackleford for being stupid. Other fans were calling him "Snap Bean" because he's so tall and thin, throwing raw green beans onto the floor at him.

Andy Kennedy had his own personal rooting section. The Duke student who sat right behind him the whole game kept taunting, "Hey, Kennedy, when are you going to play? You should go pro."

Duke won by 16, State's ninth loss in eleven games. The two wins were against Winthrop and Brooklyn College. Shackleford had scored 13 points in the first half but was so listless in the second that Valvano was forced to bench him. But there was one little glimmer of hope. Against Brooklyn, Valvano had put Quentin Jackson at the point and moved Vinny del Negro to the shooting guard, and together they'd looked sensational. The one question was whether it was because they were sensational, or because Brooklyn was terrible.

Against Duke, Valvano again started Quentin and Vinny, and again they played great together. Quentin gave the team something it hadn't had before, someone to tell the other players where to go and what to do. Quentin wasn't very quick and not fast either, and his jump shot was only average, but he did have one quality that stood out: He never got ruffled. He was a calming influence on the entire team, and when he spoke, everyone listened. He was like a coach on the floor. He was just what the team needed. All season long they had been playing run and gun. With Quentin, the pace slowed way down, and when State ran a set play, often it worked.

The next game was a Sunday contest against Virginia at Reynolds Coliseum. The day before, in an attempt to bring some togetherness to his players, Valvano scheduled an "all-team day"—films at nine, practice from ten until eleven-thirty, lunch together, more films, a tape session, practice some more, and watch a movie.

With tension still at high pitch, however, no one wanted to devote his entire day to basketball. Everyone was still angry at each other, shooting blame left and right, angry at Valvano, angry at losing.

According to the players, when practice began, Coach Stewart had alcohol on his breath and came fixing for a fight. The player he apparently wanted to fight was Chucky Brown, who at six-foot-eight, 210 pounds, would have pounded Stewart to a pulp if he hadn't exerted self-control.

It started when Stewart went up to Brown and said, "Goddammit, Chucky, you haven't gotten a fucking rebound in three fucking months." Chucky sneered, "Fuck you."

Stewart responded by putting his face inches away from Brown's and challenging him to fight. Chucky backed up a couple of steps. The players waited to see what was going to happen. They were hoping Stewart would push Chucky, giving Chucky license, as one player put it, "to beat the fuck out of him." But Stewart's aggression fizzled, and that was the end of it.

State lost to Virginia, but only by 7 points. Quentin slowed the pace down, forcing the team to play with deliberation, something it needed all along, and Vinny del Negro, after three years of sitting on the bench or playing out of position, was finally showing that his All American status in high school was no fluke. Vinny moved through the middle well, drove, penetrated, could stop and pop, and with his nice soft shot—he could throw an egg against a sidewalk soft enough that it wouldn't break—he was becoming a scoring machine.

Finally, the players sensed that State had something going. State wasn't to lose another game the rest of the season, until its final game. It was time for N.C. State's third season of basketball to begin.

41

Andy Rides the Pines

The Wolfpack traveled to College Park to play Maryland, and after five weeks finally won an ACC game, beating the league doormats by 13, thanks to two players, Quentin and Vinny. All of a sudden, the local papers were saying that State wasn't so bad after all, and asking, Where the hell has Quentin Jackson been all season long?

No reporter had the nerve to say to Valvano, "It took you until the twenty-fifth game of his junior year to give this kid a chance. What kind of judge of talent are you?" Instead, the papers were championing V as a coach bold enough to move his players around to find the right combination.

For his part, Valvano was taking all the credit for the team's turnaround. He told reporters, "Well, yeah, I was cultivating Quentin, bringing him along, waiting for that right time to put him in. But you know the press. You guys jump on me all the time. You never give me a second's rest. We lost a couple games, and you're quick to jump on me all the time. Then I plan things out right, according to my well-conceived plan, and everybody praises me. You guys are some two-faced rascals, aren't you?" While he was playing the press for all it was worth, the players were wondering who—Valvano or the gullible reporters—made them puke more.

Andy Kennedy was particularly angry after the Maryland game. During practice a few days before, he had said to Bennie Bolton, "When I was visiting as a high school kid, why didn't you just grab me and say, 'Listen, don't come here'?"

Bennie replied, "I didn't know you."

Aside from Teviin Binns, who apparently had been banished to spend the rest of the season on the bench by Valvano, Kennedy was the only player not to see a minute's time against the futilely playing Terrapins.

Kennedy thought to himself, "We beat the hell out of them, and I don't play. Why?" He couldn't figure it out—until in the locker room after the game Valvano introduced Rodney Monroe, a high school All American shooting guard from Baltimore. Valvano was recruiting Monroe, and to make Rodney think he had a great chance to start as a freshman when he came to State, Valvano apparently had benched his competition, Kennedy. While his teammates were saying, "Hey, Rodney, how you doing, man? You're going to be a great player here," Andy was thinking, "Valvano didn't play me because Rodney Monroe was in the stands. That double-dealing son of a bitch!"

42

Vinny Steals One

All it took was one victory for Valvano to resurrect his dream about getting the big twenty wins and an NCAA bid. State would have to win its final two regular-season games, against Wake Forest away and Chicago State at Reynolds—possible—and then go on to win three games and the title in the ACC championships—impossible.

Wake Forest hadn't beaten anyone in the ACC except Maryland, but by the end of the season Coach Bob Staak had his players at the top of their game, and with Muggsy Bogues and Cal Boyd at guards, Wake was always a threat.

Against Wake, Charles Shackleford indicated his immense potential for the first time all year. He had 28 points and 17 rebounds, playing like he was possessed. With only seconds remaining, however, it didn't look as if Shack's effort was going to be good enough.

Down by 3 points, State had the ball under its own basket. Two seconds remained. To score, State would have to go the length of the court.

The game was on national television in front of a rabid Wake Forest crowd, and their fans could already taste victory. The Wake coach, Bob Staak, was jumping up and down on the sidelines in expectation. Valvano was staring at the clock, knowing a loss would defeat his bid for the NCAA tournament. There were just two ticks left on the clock.

Valvano said to Coach McLean, "Okay, Ed, what do you have for me?"

Coach MeLean pulled out the special play book. He said, "All right, this is what we're going to do. Everyone lines up at the key. At the break everyone goes a different way. Vinny, I want you to go to halfcourt, catch the pass, take about three or four dribbles, turn, and go for it, baby."

The team broke out of the meeting and headed for the court. Bennie Bolton got ready to throw the pass inbounds. Vinny broke to halfcourt, and Bennie hit him with a perfect toss. Del Negro took two long dribbles with big, loping strides, and as the tank was running empty, with two defenders draped around him, Vinny put up a twenty-footer—a 3-point shot and overtime if it went in.

As soon as the ball left his fingers, the horn sounded, the red light ending the game went on, and it was as though everything was in slow motion. Until that ball came down, nobody breathed. When the shot got to the basket, it was perfect. The score was tied.

The game went into overtime, but Wake Forest had blown its chance. State stole the game away.

Kelsey Weems was particularly excited by the win. He had gotten significant minutes guarding Bogues, the five-foot-three tireless cord of muscle, the quickest guard in the ACC, and he had played him tough. Kelsey's defense on Bogues had been instrumental in State's winning the game.

Weems said, "I am so pumped. I finally got Muggsy off my back, and I don't ever have to see him again as long as I live."

It was cold and snowing as everyone got on the bus for the three-hour bus ride from Winston-Salem back to Raleigh the next day, but everyone was in a good mood, even Valvano. They were tired, having stayed up all night playing cards, and soon after the bus left Winston-Salem, everyone was asleep. Shackleford was sitting toward the back.

Suddenly, several of the players were snapped awake by a deadly foul odor in the air. They didn't even have to guess who it was. In chorus they all yelled, "Shack!" The others began waking up, going, "Oh, my God, Shack, how could you?" The players threw open the windows, even though it was freezing outside. Up in the front of the bus, Valvano sat up and said, "My God, was that one of my boys? Shack, how could you do that? My wife and kids are on this bus." After that, everyone was wide awake the rest of the trip.

A motorcade of State fans was accompanying the bus back home, zooming past, honking joyfully, yelling, and waving, and one of the drivers just missed hitting the bus.

"I've seen better drivers in my grandfather's golf bag," said Walker Lambiotte.

There is a full-length mirror—it must be eight feet tall—in the Wolfpack locker room in Reynolds Coliseum. Someone took a piece of soap and, at the very top of that mirror, wrote, "Don't even sleep." Apparently these words of counsel have been there for several years. The janitors clean the mirror a couple times a week because players often spit at it or get sweat on it by flexing their muscles in front of it, but they never wash off that phrase.

John Simonds once asked Bennie Bolton what the phrase meant. Bennie usually doesn't give a straight answer to a question. He will make up something like, "It's a real long story, but it started back with John Brown before the Civil War . . ." And then Bennie will say, "But he told me not to tell you, so I can't."

This time Bennie didn't joke. He said, "All I know is the expression began when the team went to the NCAAs and won it all in 1983." He didn't know who originated it or who wrote it on the mirror. He did know what it meant, however. They all did.

If somebody gets a good grade on a test and tells another person about it, the other person said, "Don't sleep on that grade." If you hit a long 3-pointer, someone will say, "Don't sleep on that three-pointer." Players said it to each other during games. If they were eating a good meal, someone might say, "Don't sleep on this steak."

The final game of the season was home against Chicago State, a team of bruisers. Their center was six-foot-ten, 280 pounds. Playing at home, State took control early, and with Vinny del Negro scoring a career high of 30 points, State kept ahead the whole way, but barely. Valvano was nervous the entire game.

At halftime he said, "Guys, I'm telling you, we're just

not far enough out front. These guys are big. They're pounding you. Shack, are you even in there? That guy is turning on you and outmuscling you. And they are fast, guys. They are a fast bunch of pros. They may not be smart, but they can kill us. I'm telling you, they can kill us."

Quentin kept State poised, and Vinny kept the scoring pressure on. He looked like a machine.

And so, the 1986-87 Wolfpack regular season began as it ended, with a victory. It was time for spring break, and many of the regular students took off for Fort Lauderdale, leaving the basketball players to get ready for the ACC tournament.

The players were pumped. First of all, because the school was closed Friday through Tuesday, meaning $185 in meal money. And they were also pumped because they had won the last three games and were excited about the possibilities.

The team practiced hard. Nobody came out and said it openly, but there was a sense that the players were optimistic about their chances in the tournament. Perhaps they didn't feel they could win it outright—not with Carolina, Clemson, and Duke playing so well—but there was a general feeling: "Come tournament time, don't sleep on us."

43

The ACC Tournament

The Atlantic Coast Conference tournament is a combination basketball orgy and circus. In three days, seven do-or-die games are played, four the first day, two the second, and one the third to decide the champion. Every game is sold out, no matter who is involved, and in the five-state area encompassing the eight schools in the ACC, the majority of elementary, junior high school, high school, and undergraduate ears are glued to a radio if the game is being played during the day, and at night all activity stops as fans from the five states and around the country sit at home and in bars in front of TV sets to watch. What's so dramatic about the tournament is that no matter how well or poorly a team has been playing, it begins the tournament on an equal footing with all the others. Every team is given a chance to start afresh. Whatever trouble and turmoil existed during the season is forgotten; every team enters optimistically. In this single-elimination marathon, the team that's hottest usually wins. Historically, upsets are common and blow-outs few. Upping the stakes is an added bonus for the champion: The winner gets an automatic bid to the NCAA championship tournament.

The State players were pumped up about the coming ACC tournament not so much because of the thrill of competition, but because every player gets four complimentary books of tickets entitling the holder to sit right behind the bench for all seven games. The tickets are so hard to come by that, as one player put it, "It's 'Name That Tune.' " They could figure on earning anywhere up to $500 per book of tickets.

N.C. State players occasionally sold their tickets during

the regular season, but the money they made doing that amounted to peanuts compared to the ACC ticket-book haul they were anticipating. Technically, the only people allowed to sit in the players' seats were relatives and other students. The athletic department attempted to keep track of who was sitting in the players' seats but wasn't fanatical about it. If a player got caught selling his tickets, the penalty was simply to lose some of his ticket privileges for the next year. Players laughed at who sometimes sat in the other guy's seats. "Who's that, Shack?" a teammate would ask. Shackleford would reply, "That's my uncle," and he'd laugh. The man sitting in his seat would be white.

For the next couple of days after the players received their four books of ACC tickets, they sat in the locker room, each with his own local paper, scouring the want ads. Rows of notices advertising "ACC Tickets Wanted" appeared in the Raleigh, Durham, and Chapel Hill papers, all available to the State players. It was all they could talk about. "Hey, look, here's a guy who wants to pay three hundred sixty dollars per."

The whole week Coach McLean kept saying, "Remember, fellas, selling tickets is illegal. You're going to get some good offers, but, gentlemen, it's illegal."

The players would look him in the eye and say, "Yes, Coach. I understand. I wouldn't dream of selling my tickets. Mom is coming."

Everybody on the team sold theirs. One player kept one book of tickets for his father and sold the other three for $575 each. Another sold two to friends for $250 each. A third gave two to a friend who sold them for him. The friend walked into a fraternity house, announced he was taking bids, and walked out with $1,200. Exclaimed one of the bench players, "Finally, finally, I got something out of playing here."

On a Wednesday afternoon, the team flew to Crystal City, Maryland, where the tournament was being staged. They stayed at the Crystal City Marriott, which was, said John Simonds, "as big as Texas." Valvano had Simonds go out, buy him some wine, and bring it back to his suite. "You could run laps in there," Simonds said. "I hadn't seen that many couches in a furniture store." Valvano was hosting a meeting of the ACC coaches, discussing rule and policy changes for the upcoming season.

Another perk of playing in the tournament was that at mealtime the players could treat all the friends and relatives who had come to watch them play. The players from the Maryland area invited girl friends and three or four others, and after running up an $80 bill, they signed the bill without thinking twice about it. The N.C. State athletic department, as always, picked up the tab.

The next day the team went over to the Capitol Center for an hour of practice. They arrived early, and while they were waiting impatiently for the Duke team to finish up, they began running around like little kids, playing tag, slapping each other, causing a ruckus. Valvano stood there, half-heartedly trying to get them to behave, when Coach Mike Krzyzewski of Duke blew up, accusing them of spying, of trying to steal Duke's plays. When he said that, most of the State players began laughing. They knew they wouldn't have understood his complicated offense if they had been watching it on game films.

The wait for that opening-round game seemed interminable. After arriving on Wednesday afternoon and practicing for an hour Thursday afternoon, State was scheduled to play the fourth and final first-round game on Friday night. All afternoon that day, the players lounged around, watching the early games on TV. They were nervous, because Duke had beaten them the week before, and the Blue Devils were hot, playing well as a team.

Valvano's pep talk in the locker room before the game was lower-key than usual. He talked rather than yelled. He pontificated rather than castigated. He said, "This is *the* tournament. This tournament has a lot of prestige, and we are going into it with as good a chance to win it as anybody. It's anybody's ballgame."

The players were slouched in their seats, hearing but not paying much attention, and when he was finished, they went out to the arena, emerging from the tunnel onto the runway to watch the final minutes of Wake Forest vs. Clemson. The game went into overtime. The State players began rooting for Wake, the underdog, and as Wake pulled out the victory, the State players seemed to grow more and more excited about their own game and their chances against Duke.

State-Duke was a superior-quality game. Both sides played at the top of their ability. Quentin and Vinny again were outstanding, and Shack and Bennie led the team in scoring. On the bench, everyone was cheering, enjoying the competition. With the score tied, Duke had the last shot but missed. The game went into overtime, and State pulled away and won by 7 as Vinny hit nine foul shots at the end.

No one had figured N.C. State to win. It was a shock to everyone, especially the Duke fans. After the game, in a parody of the cheer, "That's all right, that's okay, we're going to beat them anyway," the Duke students chanted, "That's all right, that's okay, y'all are gonna work for us anyway."

44

A Wake for Forest

Kelsey Weems had been mistaken. He hadn't seen the last of Wake Forest's Muggsy Bogues. He and the rest of the State team had to face him in the semifinal round of the ACC tournament, and all game long, there was little Muggsy, running State ragged, dogging their guards, stealing the ball, and flying the length of the court for uncontested layups.

With Bogues leading the way, Wake led by 3 points with only twenty seconds left in the game.

State, in possession of the ball, called time out. At the bench, Valvano squatted down, pulled out his clipboard, and said, "All right, let's do this," and he started scribbling X's and O's with manic abandon, drawing lines and talking all the while. Coach McLean interrupted him. "No, Jim, do this." Valvano said, "I don't like that." Meanwhile, the players watched the two coaches arguing over which play to run. Simonds thought, "This is a circus. It's Laurel and his man Hardy."

Finally, Valvano wiped the slate clean. He said, "We'll do this," then he changed his mind again. "No, no, no, no, no," he said, as the players continued to eye each other, mystified. Vinny del Negro looked up at the clock to see how much time was left.

The horn sounded. Valvano finally said, "Fellas, we've got to stay in it. We've just got to." The public watching on TV had to be figuring that Valvano had come up with a super plan for a last shot, but he might as well have been scribbling his name on the blackboard for all the help it was worth.

The arena was packed to the ceiling, with most of the fans seemingly rooting for Wake. Behind the bench, one fan had singled out Valvano for abuse. At first, every time Valvano stood up, he called him, "you guinea," and then it became "you greasy guido." The first time the fan said "guido," Teviin thought he had said "burrito." "Burrito?" Teviin asked a teammate. "That sounds like what he said" was the reply. "Why's that dude calling him a Mexican food?" Teviin asked. It didn't make any sense, and they didn't figure it out until later.

With seconds remaining, Bennie Bolton took the ball out and hit Vinny with a perfect pass near halfcourt, just as he had against Wake the last time they had played. And again, Vinny took two dribbles and let fly from way out, and again he hit nothing but net, again sending the game into overtime with a dramatic 3-point shot.

In large part because of Valvano's insistence on using only six of his players in the key games, the State players were drained and exhausted. On the bench Valvano was pleading, "Fellas, you gotta suck it up. You gotta play for me just this one time. Just listen to what I'm saying: Play your dicks off."

Coach Stewart chimed in, "Fellas, you gotta play your tits off."

During overtime, neither team could score. Everyone was too exhausted, except Bogues, of course, but Kelsey Weems was again keeping him in check. The game went into a second overtime. On the bench, the players could barely get the water bottles to their mouths.

Valvano said, "Fellas, come on, you just got to suck it up. Fellas, this is it. This is what the tournament is all about."

State won it by 4 points. Shackleford finished the night with 17 points and 8 rebounds. Finally Shack was looking like the star everyone thought he would be. Chucky Brown, who got to play when Valvano put Bennie at shooting guard and benched Walker Lambiotte, overpowered Wake with 18 points and 10 rebounds.

In the locker room after the game, Valvano was ecstatic. He said, "Guys, I knew you could do it. I knew I could pull you through. I told you, 'If you just listen to me, we can win this thing,' and that's just what we did."

The players were slapping each other on the back, giving high fives and bubbling with excitement. Doormats in February, this was March, and they were going to the finals of the ACC tournament.

45

Dope, Hope, and Victory

Enthusiasm is not a substitute for reality. The final was scheduled for two P.M. on Sunday afternoon on national television, and for this game, even casual fans would be watching. By the morning of the final, nobody in the world thought State had a chance, and though they were looking forward to playing the game, none of the State players was looking forward to the result. Twice during the regular season State had gotten wiped out by North Carolina—both in blowouts. Carolina was rated number two in the country, they had won eleven straight, and the State players knew they didn't belong on the same court with the Tar Heels. So the players were thinking to themselves, "We ought to just pack our bags and go home. We're not going to win." Andrew Kennedy, the Virginia star, was visiting Teviin Binns in his room. (They had played together in junior college.) Kennedy said, "Man, you're going to get smashed. I hate to see you all against Carolina. You're going to get dogged."

Said Teviin, "I don't think we're going to have no way of winning."

The bus was scheduled to leave for the Capitol Center at eleven thirty. Around eleven, John Simonds was so full of nervous energy, so psyched with nothing to do, that he decided to visit the rooms of each of the players, making sure they were up and ready to go. He knocked on Shack and Teviin's door. They asked who it was. When Simonds identified himself, they said, "Come in." What he saw astounded him:

Said Simonds, "At first, I thought the lights had been turned off. Inside, the room was dense with smoke—pot smoke—so thick I could barely see them. Shack was reclining on his bed, holding a joint in each hand, contentedly puffing away.

"Teviin, who had been in the bathroom, came in and sat on his bed. They never said a word. I left.

"I then went to another room. I knocked, identified myself, and went inside. This room also smelled of pot. The player was in the bathroom with the fan on, toking up.

"There was the same smell in a third room I went into, too. When I entered, one of the players was lying on his bed, chilling out, while another sat two feet in front of the TV set watching Roadrunner cartoons. They smiled and slapped me a couple of high fives.

"I thought to myself, 'We have five guys who are going to play in the most important game of their lives who don't even know where they are.'

"When Shack and Teviin left their room to go to the bus, they had to come through the main hotel lobby, where a crush of fans and reporters were waiting for them. Shack walked very slowly, strutting through the mob, slapping high fives and smiling with a loopy look. Outside Shack and Tev started giggling and couldn't stop.

"When they got on the bus, they headed for the last row, plopped down, and sat still as statues the whole way, not saying a word, their grins pasted on their faces."

When the players arrived at the arena, there seemed to be a Carolina fan sitting in nearly every seat. It was like playing in the Dean Dome. State's small contingent was concentrated behind the team bench. Everyone else seemed to be waving Carolina Blue pom-poms. The Carolina fans were psyched about winning, because Carolina hadn't won a final in four years, and they were counting on breaking the skein on this day.

In the locker room before the game, Valvano gave a truly stirring speech. He said, "Fellas, there are times in your life when you are going to have to rise to the occasion. And this may only happen once or twice in your entire lives. You will be in a position where you'll go in as the underdog, and the people will be thinking you're going to lose, that you can't get the job done, and you will have to rise to the occasion."

Then he said, "Some people are born great, some achieve greatness, and some have greatness thrust upon them." He said, "Guys, several years ago I won the ACC championship for my dad. Today, we have a chance to win another ACC championship. My dad told me it would happen again. I'm just sorry he's not around to see it."

Nobody said anything, but this time, he had the players' attention. Everyone was solemn, serious. The coaches left the locker room, and Bennie Bolton gathered everyone around him and said, "Fellas, we've had a hard season. We lost Drum. We had fights. We've had grade problems. Everyone here hates V. After this season, many of us are going to leave here. Some are going to graduate, others will transfer. All of us here think that V has burned us."

He said, "Three weeks ago, the fans were dogging us everywhere we went, calling us losers and pussies. Fuck V. Fuck the fans. We need to win this game for us. V can give great speeches and all that kind of stuff, but we need to win this game not for him, but for us. Today we have to put aside all the differences between black and white, who's playing and who's not, and let's go out there and give it a shot—for us. Scrap everyone else—school pride and all that garbage. Let's just try to play one game one time for us, just like the old days prior to the start of the season when we used to go down to the gym and play for the fun of it."

Everyone chanted, "For us," and meant it. The players started making noise, butting heads, getting rowdy, and they went out onto the floor with their heads high and spirits even higher.

Valvano started Quentin and Vinny at guards, Shack in the middle, and Bennie and Chucky Brown at forwards, with Mike Giomi and Kelsey subbing off the bench. The starters played just about the entire game. Walker Lambiotte, instrumental in Friday night's opening ACC tournament victory against Duke, never even took off his sweats.

On the court, for really the first time all season long, N.C. State played like a team. The guards fed the ball inside, with Shack, Bennie, Chucky, and Giomi all scoring in double figures. Vinny was at the top of his game, driving for baskets, or driving in and passing off for easy layups, or driving in and stopping short and making jumps. He was, in short, a revelation.

Shack showed power and aggressiveness in the first half. In the second half, he wilted. But for the first twenty minutes, he was a dynamo, fighting J. R. Reid to a standstill and working with his teammates on defense to make Carolina struggle for baskets.

On the bench, Valvano was going crazy. With State up by 3 at the half, Valvano was all excited in the locker room. He said, "Guys, we just have to hang in there. Carolina is going to try to make one long run. Hold out for that one run, and we got 'em."

Carolina never did get the one long run. Every time the Tar Heels scored, State answered. With thirty seconds left in the game, State had a 1-point lead and the ball. A time-out was called.

Bennie Bolton waited out of bounds, ready to throw the ball in. It was a play he had made dozens of times throughout the season. It was such a simple play, he could have made it blindfolded. All he had to do was throw it over the head of the man guarding him to an open Vinny del Negro, and the ballgame was theirs.

Making it simpler was Vinny's adept way of getting himself open on the in-bounds play. The technique for getting free for the pass is to position the man guarding you between you and the player throwing out the ball, rush toward him, lean on his hip, push him with your arm, and then run in the opposite direction from the push. The ball comes in, and you catch it. Done right, it works every time.

Bennie slapped the ball over his head, Vinny got his man on his hip, pushed off, got free, and was breaking down the sideline fifteen feet away when Bennie let lose a bullet of a throw that went rocketing up through the air far over Vinny's head. Vinny, who can leap high enough to dunk, jumped as high as he could, and the ball still cleared his reach by a foot and a half! The other players couldn't believe it. Bennie had made that pass a thousand times. He had never thrown the ball away before.

Carolina recovered the ball, and Carolina's Kenny Smith ran the length of the court and scored easily, giving Carolina the 1-point lead. State was now down by 1 with fifteen seconds left.

* * *

When Bennie threw that ball away, the initial reaction of the other State players was a stunned silence. Valvano reacted first. He threw his towel in disgust. He screamed, "Bennie, what the fuck are you doing?" Andy Kennedy shouted, "Goddammmit!"

The mouths of the rest of the players on the bench hung open, nothing coming out, so absolutely stunned were they.

Bennie had been so good at throwing the ball out that Valvano had made it his job during the three years he started for State. Bennie had made that play hundreds of times and never once even made a teammate so much as jump for the ball.

Because his teammates knew how much Bennie disliked Valvano, a few of the State players wondered what was in Bennie's mind. Bennie's enmity reportedly had built since arriving at State four years earlier. As each year went by, it grew as he witnessed Valvano's callous disregard for his players—especially the black players.

Suggested a teammate, "Bennie had four years of contempt pent up within him, and this was as good a chance as any to wipe the slate clean."

But other teammates categorically insisted there was no way Bennie would have thrown that ball away on purpose.

Said another teammate, "This was our chance to win the ACC championship. Your name goes down in history, you win the ring, you go to the NCAA tournament. He wouldn't have given that up. But he sure did throw the ball away. It made me sick."

While the players on the bench were still shaking their heads, their team still down by 1 with fourteen seconds left in the game, N.C. State got the ball to Vinny del Negro, who was dribbling at the top of the key. Vinny head-faked, drove the baseline, beat his man, went up one side of the hoop, and shot through opposing blue-shirted arms trying to stop him. There was a slap, and the ball rolled off the rim and away, but the whistle blew and he was awarded two shots on the foul.

Seven seconds remained. Vinny del Negro, who had sat as a fixture on the State bench for almost two and a half years, the same Vinny del Negro who had turned from a frog into a prince, stood at the foul line with the possibility of an ACC championship in his hands. Not a single State player doubted he would make it, and both shots arched perfectly, kissing the back of the net each time.

Dean Smith called time for Carolina. Seven seconds was still plenty of time to make one shot. N.C. State led by 1 point. Valvano told his players, "Hang in there. Just don't foul anybody." What more could he say?

Carolina brought the ball down the court, seeking to pass it to Kenny Smith, the Tar Heels' scoring machine. Kelsey Weems, inserted into the game for the express purpose of keeping the Tar Heels from throwing Smith the ball, did his job beautifully. The ball went in to Joe Wolf, who took the shot. The ball hit the rim and bounced off to the side, and in the scramble, Ranzino Smith came up with the ball. He was wide open. The ball missed, bounding off the rim and coming down the other side of the basket. The seven seconds were taking forever. Underneath the basket, players from both teams were bashing each other with their elbows, climbing over the top, manhandling as hard as they could to retrieve that ball. The refs stood there, whistles in their mouths but not moving. The game was going to end whistleless.

Senior Mike Giomi, whose starting role had been reduced to that of marginal player, came up with the ball and fell on the floor. The whistle blew as the horn finally sounded. Was it "walking" or worse, a foul on State? The referees ran off the court, leaving everyone else to their own devices. N.C. State was the champion of the ACC tournament.

For the cameras, the State players rushed onto the court and participated in the usual piling on of bodies at center court. Valvano and the key players screamed with joy, so unexpected was the victory. There was also great satisfaction in watching the Tar Heel players sit sullenly on their bench and stare in disbelief. And when a cameraman went rushing up to Carolina coach Dean Smith to interview him, the usually unfazed Smith piquedly slapped the camera away, apparently so angry at losing to Valvano and N.C. State.

But for the majority of players—those who hadn't played much during the season—the victory seemed hollow. For them, the N.C. State fans had shown their true colors during the team's midseason losing streak. That was then, and this was now, but young kids never forget it once they've been booed by their own fans.

Said Andy Kennedy, for one, "I wasn't part of it. I didn't contribute at all. Who am I kidding? We won, and we all ran out, and everybody jumped on the floor, but we were just enjoying ourselves acting crazy, just to do it. I wasn't all electrified. I was just taking it all in, because the crowd was so into it. You couldn't help feel the enthusiasm. But it didn't mean hardly anything.

"All it meant was that everyone would be back sniffing our jocks, letting us into the clubs for free again, wanting to be near us. It wasn't about winning the ACC, like everybody thought it was. That was what the big joke was. It kept people off our backs, and we got a nice ring."

The State players went through the ritual of cutting the nets down and returned to the locker room. Valvano said, "Fellas, I'm so proud of you guys. You rose to the occasion. You came through all the trials and tribulations all season long. You are the 1987 ACC champs."

Quentin Jackson led the team in a prayer. He said, "Lord, thank you for this occasion. Thank you that we are all a team and that everybody played well and didn't get hurt. Amen."

The press came in for their interviews, and then everyone went back onto the floor of the Capitol to receive their individual plaques.

Valvano walked out of the Capitol Center with his assistant, John Simonds. The arena was empty now, except for a few camera crews packing up. Valvano and Simonds walked up a long ramp out into the sunlight. Valvano said, "John, we finally did it. We won the ACC championship. I've never been so proud in my life."

He then paused and said, "I wish my dad had been here to see it. But we got it, you got it, and you now know how that feels. This is what it feels like to win big." Valvano had tears streaming down his face. Simonds didn't know what to say, but at that moment—in spite of the broken promises of a scholarship and revised grades, and in spite of his dismay at how his teammates had been treated during the season—Simonds felt a burst of genuine affection for his coach.

After the flight back to Raleigh, the bus pulled into the gym parking lot, and waiting for the players were family, friends, and thousands of students.

While the players were proud of themselves, they were well aware that this was the same student body that had booed them off the court and had harassed them all during that long losing streak. The players didn't want to be rude, so they gave a couple of perfunctory waves to the throng before ducking away. Not a single player felt that the victory belonged to the fans. Said Simonds, "Our basic attitude was 'They can all go and get fucked.' "

They felt, too, that the win wasn't for the coaches either.

"It was for us."

46

Hmmmmmmm

The NCAA came up with a dramatic rival for N.C. State's opening round of the tournament: Valvano's predecessor, Norm Sloan, and his University of Florida Gators. Sloan had won the NCAA national championship in 1974 at N.C. State with such famed collegiates as David Thompson, Tommy Burleson, and Monte Towe, all of whom later went into the NBA.

Adding to the excitement was the fact that Florida was led by Vernon Maxwell, one of the few high school stars Valvano did not accept at N.C. State. Maxwell had desperately wanted to go to State, but he didn't get in because Slim Duncan, another star guard, committed to State first. So Maxwell went to Florida instead. Ironically, Duncan then decided to attend UNC-Charlotte.

Florida's center was a seven-foot white giant named Dwayne Schintzius. He was tall, but he wasn't anything Shack couldn't handle. After the players watched the game films, they were all convinced that Florida would be a walkover. Getting past Florida to the Final Thirty-two would be a cinch.

The game was scheduled for Friday at the Carrier Dome in Syracuse. On Tuesday everyone was in the locker room cutting up before practice.

"The guys were in the locker, goofing around, when Quentin shouted, 'We're going to kick Florida's butt.' When he heard what Quentin had said, Shackleford said, 'I don't want to win. I don't care about winning, because if we win, everybody's going to get drug tested after the game, and if we get tested, everybody in this room knows who's going to fail.'

The reaction in the room was a chorus of "Hmmm-mmmm."

47

The New NCAA Rule

Every basketball player, black or white, beginning when he is first old enough to throw a ball through a hoop, has his eye on the grand prize—the multi-year, multi-million-dollar pro contract. Nothing can be of greater importance—not teammates, not school spirit, not even winning the NCAA championships. And why should it be?

For many impoverished black youths in America, the ghetto has provided few escape routes. Education, the escape route of the past, is still the most widely taken route, but hundreds of thousands of black youths seem to have forsaken that path for the "I'm-going-to-be-the-next-Michael-Jordan" path of getting paid to play roundball. Never mind that there are 20,000 aspirants playing college basketball, each one convinced the NBA is just around the corner, and not more than about forty make it into the NBA each year. But how do you convince a kid with great high school and college talent that he's probably not going to be one of those forty new pros?

And so, for most of the college players who put in all those hours of practice in schoolyards, who have forsaken their education for the rush of competing in high school and college gyms, who have their four years of "illusory greatness," who among them does not believe in his heart that his destiny is the pro contract and the BIG MONEY? If the Final Four is the gold at the end of the rainbow for the college coach, then the players' pot of gold is the NBA. Which once again brings the world of college basketball back to one overriding concern: cash.

In February of 1987—in the middle of the basketball

season and without warning—the NCAA passed a new rule. The rule decreed that the five players with the most minutes of playing time and one substitute chosen at random would be drug tested from each team victorious in the opening round of the NCAA tournament.

"Anyone testing positive for any of 3,000 substances will be suspended immediately," the NCAA declared.

For college players whose coaches had been seriously monitoring drug use all season long, the new NCAA rule posed no problem at all. Players who knew drug use would be detected and punished by their school administration simply didn't indulge. To do so would be basketball hari-kari. As a result, players at the great majority of colleges strictly adhered to the drug ban. If a player had to take as mundane a drug as Comtrex or Nyquil, he faithfully followed procedures and reported the use to the team doctor, giving a copy of a prescription for his file, so that if evidence of the drug were detected in a test, the reason for taking such a drug would be documented.

At N.C. State, where the extracurricular activities of the players were less tightly monitored, pot smoking occurred. By itself, pot smoking is of little consequence. Surveys taken on college campuses around the country indicate that the majority of students smoke pot, some a little, others a lot. Recreational use of pot has become as common as recreational use of beer. If the occasional users of pot hadn't been basketball players, nobody would even have cared.

The first drug test conducted at N.C. State for the 1986–87 season came in late September prior to the start of official practice. One afternoon, while the players were lounging around the track, Coach McLean reported to the players that the drug-test results had come back. He said, "Good news, men, good news. Coach V told me to tell you that all of you passed."

"Several of the players started giggling. Quentin said to Shackleford, "Yeah, Shack, you're clean, aren't you?" Shack shot him a dirty look and laughed. Tev slapped Shack a high five.

"Mike Giomi, standing at the back of the group, said out loud, "That's a joke. There is no way this whole team is clean. No way."

Another time, when the team was flying from Raleigh

to Kansas City for the Kansas game, they had to switch planes in the Pittsburgh airport. With an hour and forty-five minutes to waste before departure, the players set off for adventure. As one group of players was walking from one terminal to another, they spotted policemen standing with two German Shepherds.

Teviin grabbed Kelsey who grabbed Shack. They stopped in their tracks. Teviin said, "I'll bet those are drug dogs." Kelsey swore. They turned around and started running in the other direction. Their teammates laughed at them as they motored off.

Said a teammate, "The reason pot use was so open was that no one considered it any worse than, say, drinking beer. There's a lot of pot being smoked in America. All you have to do is watch 'Miami Vice' every week. Plus, the guys knew no one was going to do anything about it. Look at Wash. He was on cocaine, and everybody knew it. And a guy like Bennie, who didn't believe in drugs, who hated drugs, was angry that no one took any interest to do anything about it."

At other colleges, one of the athletic director's tasks is to monitor the athletes to make sure they stay away from drugs. When Valvano was nominated for athletic director, one of the greatest fears of Dr. Roger Clark, one that he expressed to Chancellor Poulton and the entire Athletics Council, was that Valvano would abdicate his watchdog role.

Dr. Clark was not fooled by Valvano's tough public stance against drugs. In December of 1986, Valvano went before the Academic Council and not only called for mandatory drug testing of all N.C. State athletes, but set himself up as the Eliot Ness of college coaches. He stated, "If a youngster is shown positive, I want him off the squad."

He added, "I think we need to demand that they be drug-free. We can no longer think that we are going to talk sense into them or that they are going to become afraid because of something.

"Let's lead. Let's say that we don't want druggies here, and we're not going to accept it."

When the Athletic Counsel amended the N.C. State drug rules to allow a player first a warning, combined with drug treatment, then a suspension for a second offense, combined with drug treatment, and finally, for a third offense, expulsion and the withdrawal of financial aid—Valvano made it appear that the Athletics Counsel was composed of bleeding hearts and that he was a tough guy.

But educators such as Dr. Clark had heard Valvano's speeches about how athletes should also be students, and they were aware that few of his basketball players ever graduated, so there was much skepticism over just how much stock Valvano placed in the welfare of his players.

N.C. State's procedures for monitoring drug abuse actually worked as follows: The test results would be sent to the team doctor, who would inform the athletic director, Valvano, who then told the basketball coach, Valvano, who then arranged a conference with the player.

But one player described what happened whenever the test results came back positive.

"He calls you into his office and says, 'Is it a problem? Do you need help? Would you like to have counseling?' If the player says, 'No,' then that's it. There's nothing more said. If you say, 'I don't want help,' nothing is going to happen to you."

Nevertheless, according to one player, the players who smoked still tried to keep it a secret. Some of them reportedly took masking drugs before scheduled drug tests, the most popular being hydrochlorothiazide, a pink prescription drug effective for keeping marijuana use from showing up in a urine analysis. Once the players knew a drug test was coming, they would call their contact, the mysterious C.Lo, who then delivered them a supply. If taken two weeks before the test, hydrochlorothiazide would conceal the marijuana use entirely.

A capsule called Golden Seal was also taken. Golden Seal, which can be bought in any health food store, is also a blood and urine purifier. First used by American Indians to promote health, Golden Seal was popular with the basketball players because it was cheap and readily available.

If the knowledge of the upcoming drug test came too late for pills to be effective, there was another ploy: the old switcheroo. To take a drug test, the athlete got up early the morning of the test, went down to the trainer's room, and got a sterile bottle. An attendant went along with the player to the bathroom, but not into the stall.

The trick was to get some urine from a friend known not to do drugs, bring it to the test, and substitute his for the player's.

"They don't look at you," said a player. "Once you go into the booth, they are totally blinded from anything. You take the clean urine you've brought with you, pour it into the cup they give you, they put your number down, and they send it off."

Despite the precautions, there was little concern that they would be punished for smoking pot, hence Chris Washburn's levity when he squirted cologne into his urine sample before one blood test.

"It was hilarious," said a teammate who watched The Washer do it in the adjacent bathroom stall. "It was a joke. Because it didn't matter."

But now, with the passing of the new NCAA drug rule, it wasn't funny any more. The NCAA was doing the monitoring, not N.C. State. Anyone with pro aspirations who had smoked pot was between a rock and a hard place.

Before the ACC finals against Carolina, those who smoked did so because they didn't think there was a chance in the world of State beating the Tar Heels—they were figuring the Carolina game would be the final game of the season. Going to the NCAAs was the furthest thing from the minds of any of the players. But with that history-making upset, N.C. State was entitled to an automatic bid to the NCAAs as ACC champs. And an automatic drug test if the team won.

48

Florida

The day before the Florida game, the State team flew to Syracuse, New York, for the opening round of the NCAA tournament. The quality of the hotel accommodations depends upon the seeding of the team in the tourney. The number one seed stays at the finest hotel nearest the Carrier Dome. The number two team gets second choice, and so on. N.C. State was seeded number fifteen.

When the bus pulled up to its hotel, a two-story shabby-looking affair—looking, as one player put it, "like a Siesta Motor Court"—the players mumbled, "This must be a mistake. V'll do something about this."

But no, it was their place all right. All season long they had been staying at five-star luxury hotels, and they had gotten so used to it they hadn't appreciated the amenities provided them by Valvano. The joint was forty minutes from the city, near both the highway and the airport, and it had no wet bars, no telephones in every room, no amenities to speak of. They were actually embarrassed to be staying there.

Thursday afternoon the team practiced in the Carrier Dome. None of the players, except Mike Giomi, who had played there with Indiana, had played there before. When they walked in, it took their collective breaths away. Seating 80,000 for football, the Carrier Dome is so huge that the basketball court is put at one end and a huge curtain is erected behind it, so that only a third of the stadium is filled. From the field, the players could see row after row of chairs rising all the way up to the dome at the top.

Practice was uneventful. The players were loose. They

were enjoying the feeling of "the big Big Time." All the practice balls were brand-new, and there were reporters from national papers hanging around, asking questions, making them feel important. The only unsettling note hanging over the entire affair had been rung by Shack's announcement that he didn't want to win the game. Was he really going to play not to win just so he wouldn't have to take a drug test?

In the locker room, Valvano gave the players a talk. He said, "Gentlemen, the first two rounds are the toughest of the whole tournament, because you're far from home and you have no fan support—no one in the stands gives a damn who wins—so you really have to gut it out, because you're on your own."

After Valvano and the coaches left, the players finished getting dressed, and Shack repeated to a couple of his teammates what he had said before. This time he said, "Really, I don't want to win this game." He was adamant. One of the other guys said, "Come on, man. Don't let us down." Another told him, "Don't even think about that," meaning the possibility of a drug test.

Enough people had heard what the player said that word of it got out to the public. In the hotel before the game one of the alums who habitually rode with the team to all the away games, said to John Simonds, "John, what do you think he's going to do?"

He told him the truth. He said, "I really don't know."

The Carrier Dome was so huge and the fans so quiet that the players on the bench had to whisper to keep Valvano from hearing what they were saying. Just before the game was to begin, Teviin looked over at the far side of the court, and sitting with Norm Sloan and the Florida team he saw David Thompson, the star for N.C. State when Sloan won the national championship in 1974. Thompson had been a spectacular college player, but he had had a cocaine problem at State, and though he began his pro career spectacularly, it had suffered from drug use, and his reputation was tarnished when his drug addiction became public.

The players thought of Thompson as a curse, because

the year before in the NCAAs against Kansas, he'd showed up and they had lost.

"Oh shit, we're finished now," said Teviin. "Thompson's here. Talk about a bad omen." The other players said, "Where?" Teviin pointed him out. Kelsey said, "Shit, we might as well leave now." Teviin said, "God, get him out of here. That's the last thing we need."

State trailed Florida by 3 points at the end of the first half. Shackleford was playing solid basketball, and Bennie Bolton was leading the way with stellar shooting. For the eighth game in a row, Vinny del Negro would end up in double figures.

As the players filed into the locker room at the half, Avie Lester was ribbing Shackleford about getting a shot blocked by Florida center Dwayne Shintzius, the long-haired, big-bellied white boy. "How'd it taste, Shack?" Avie said.

Shackleford became infuriated and pushed Avie. Avie pushed back, and punches were thrown before the other players could break it up. Valvano didn't get upset about the fight. His mind was on beating Florida. He said, "We don't have time for this. I don't want to see that shit in here." And that was the end of it. That it happened when it did, however, was odd.

State returned to the floor and continued its stellar play. With twelve minutes and seventeen seconds left in the game, State led by 10 points, looking like a good bet. Valvano, meanwhile, was pacing up and down the sideline, remembering what had happened to his team against Kansas the year before, when the team blew a big lead late in the game.

Florida called time out. The starters ran over to the bench. Valvano said, "Gentlemen, we're up by ten points. We are eight minutes from the Final Thirty-two." It was the first time all season he had actually talked past the game he was playing.

The horn blew, and the players went back out onto the court, but for the rest of the game they were not the same players. After Valvano said, "We are eight minutes from the Final Thirty-two," it was clear something had happened. For the next few minutes, it was as if State was invisible. Florida began to press full court, and four times State lost the ball. Balls would hit State hands and bounce away into the hands of Florida players. Florida players were taking rebounds away. And without tough defense in the middle, Schintzius suddenly became a scoring threat, and Vernon Maxwell started looking like an all-pro.

Florida began scoring at will, and it seemed as if there was a lid on the basket whenever State shot the ball. And just like that, a 10-point lead became a 10-point deficit.

All game long Maxwell had been taunting the State players, and especially Valvano. Maxwell ran his mouth continually, yelling at the man guarding him, "You suck. You can't guard me." After he scored, he'd run by Valvano and, if Valvano was standing, shout at him, "Sit down, man," talking big, displaying his resentment at not getting accepted by N.C. State. Commented one of the State players, "He's nothing but a common street nigger."

With three minutes to go in the game and State out of it, one player still fighting hard was Kelsey Weems, who was guarding Maxwell with a fury, holding him, pushing him, trying to keep him from the basketball. Maxwell became so frustrated that he pushed Kelsey, who pushed him back. The referee blew the whistle, and Norm Sloan began berating Kelsey.

Sloan, his face contorted in rage, was heard to shout, "You mother-fucking, monkey-assed nigger, git off of my player." Kelsey stopped and looked at Sloan. He couldn't believe what he was hearing. Neither could the other State players.

The rest of the game was uneventful. Florida won by 12.

To the State players, Sloan's behavior was disillusioning, and so was their loss. The seniors, Teviin Binns, Bennie Bolton, and Mike Giomi were genuinely sad it was over. The Florida game marked the end of their college basketball careers.

Teviin choked back his frustration as tears streamed down his face. Valvano hadn't played him a single minute since the Brooklyn College game, and as a senior in his final game, a game that was lost with five minutes to go, he felt Valvano owed him the decency to put him in, if only for a minute.

When the clock ran down and the final buzzer sounded, Giomi stood looking at the clock. He had the look of a beaten soldier as he walked to the dressing room. His college eligibility was up. His career at an end. And it had ended poorly. He stoically said to a teammate, "It's over." The teammate nodded, feeling sorry for him.

Nobody was angry that they had lost. "Our players were not pissed off at all when it was over," said Andy Kennedy. "Nobody. It had been such an agonizing year, everyone on everyone else's nerves, the coach fucking us over. It was a bad year, and we just wanted it to be over. It was like a sigh of relief that it was over."

Nobody was angry about what had happened in the second half. Said a teammate who knew about it, "The only ones who could have said anything were the players on the court, but nobody had that feeling."

"They didn't care?" he was asked.

"Yeah."

When Shackleford was asked about the defeat, he said, "When everyone is good, we can beat anybody. When everybody's not playing together, any team can beat us."

The only one who was angry was Valvano. As soon as the team returned to the locker room, Valvano let the players have it. "Well, fellas, you lost it," he began. "I can't understand how you could have fallen apart that bad, how you could have made me look that bad. If you had only listened to what I was saying. But no, nobody listened to me. You guys were just goofing around, oblivious to everything. I kept telling you, 'The first two rounds are the toughest and after that, man, it's easy to play.'

"You just cost me a Final Thirty-two bid. I hope you're proud of yourselves. That's the end of the season. There isn't anything else. That's it. We're going to get back on the bus. We're going to fly back to Raleigh, hang the shoes up, and that's it." Valvano could not accept that State had lost a game it clearly was headed to win. He was incredulous.

For Valvano, the roller coaster ride had been steep—up and down. The team won early in the season, lost in the middle, and returned to form to win the ACC tournament. The press was saying, "The Old Pack Magic is back," and Valvano was a hero again, until this. He didn't know how he was going to explain away this one. He told the players, "I don't know what the hell I'm going to say when I get to the press room."

When the players began undressing, they opened their lockers to discover that someone with a key had snuck into the room and helped themselves to all their valuables. Their gold chains, Walkmans, and all their cash were gone.

On the bus waiting to ride to the hotel, the players' mood lightened. Teviin began yelling out the window at a couple of large girls walking by. "Hey, baby, why don't you swing that big booty over here?" The other players giggled. When the girls got closer, Teviin asked, "Why don't you come back to my hotel room?" One of the girls called him a "skinny goatee-wearing biscuithead." The players laughed uproariously at that. Teviin replied, "You fat black bitch. You know what? You not only have fat feet, you have fat shoes!"

Up in the front of the bus sat Valvano, fuming. He didn't say a word. There was no point. His season was over.

For the flight back to Raleigh, the team had to change planes and airlines at Newark Airport. They landed on Continental at the old North Terminal. They were scheduled to fly home from one of the three modern Space Age terminals. By airport bus, the trip would have taken five minutes. But Valvano didn't have the patience to wait for the bus and decided they'd walk. He asked directions, and he was told the route. What he didn't ask was the distance: two miles.

Valvano, trailed by his wife, his young daughter, and the players, went out the front door of the old terminal and walked across the parking lot in the snow. It was freezing outside, and in the distance, they could see their destination. Single-file, they began marching along the highway. In the lead, Valvano was still raging, walking at a brisk clip, his wife, Pamela, wearing high heels and a thin dress with a little fur collar, shivering but not complaining. The little girl was virtually running to keep up. Behind them, the players were cutting up, pushing and shoving each other, as cars whizzed past them at fifty miles an hour.

Valvano never let up for a second. Mrs. Valvano kept saying, "Jim, slow down," but he was so furious he probably didn't even hear her. The players began laughing at the scene in front of them. Thought one, "Here's a man making a fortune coaching, got a circus following him, marching along a highway to a terminal we can't find."

The trek seemed to take all afternoon. Everyone was frozen. When they finally arrived, the players were stage whispering, "Great directions, Coach." "Nice walk, Coach." "V's a regular Davy Crockett."

The plane flew into Raleigh, and the bus dropped the players off in front of Reynolds Coliseum. The luggage hadn't arrived, but nobody cared. Anything of value had been taken from them in Syracuse.

When the bus pulled into the parking lot, John Simonds turned to Teviin, whom he genuinely liked. Simonds was feeling nostalgic. Though the season had ended on a down note, he was going to miss the players during the off-season, and since Teviin was a senior, he knew he would probably never see him again. He said, "Well, Tev, I guess that's the end of the season."

Tev took on a deep, philosophical look. He said, "No, man. It's just like I told them at the end of last year. It's not the end of the season. It's just the beginning of the season."

Simonds said, "Tev, man, what are you talking about?"

Teviin grinned and said, "It's the beginning of the season—pot season, baby."

Teviin had come to N.C. State as an innocent. Inside of two years he had been corrupted.

Simonds thought, "My man, Tev. At least someone has something to look forward to."

The players took off, heading out of town to rest, to see their girls, to party. For most of them, basketball was over. The classes part could wait a couple weeks. The season was over. Pot season, baby.

49

Andy Flies the Coop

In the locker room after the Florida loss, one of the players said to Andy Kennedy, "We'll get them next year," and Andy replied, "Noooooooo. Not me. I'm leaving." Andy had been saying that since the middle of the season, so he wasn't taken seriously.

But Andy had made up his mind: He was transferring. His season had been one of shattered dreams. Valvano and his assistant, Tom Abatemarco, had promised him a chance to contribute significantly as a freshman. Abatemarco had told him, "Hey, man, we're going to hand you the ball the first day of practice." But Kennedy learned quickly that all the promises had just been ploys to get him to come. On the first day of practice he had been given a white jersey, and he didn't get to wear a red jersey once the entire season.

All he had wanted was some playing time. If he had played when it counted in the games, it wouldn't have mattered that he didn't start, but though he was averaging nine minutes a game, it was a scattered nine—two here, two there, three, and then two. He never once got into the flow of an important game.

Another thing that bothered him was that Valvano seemed to be trying to stereotype him as a player, labeling him a "three-point shooter." Whenever he drove to the basket, he would get yelled at, told he was playing out of control. Valvano was turning him into a one-dimensional player, and he was smart enough to get out before his game was hurt for good.

Most important for a guy like Andy Kennedy, a happy-go-lucky jock, was that basketball, the game he loved with a passion, had stopped being fun. He was the kind of player who always arrived at the gym an hour early to shoot and stayed an hour late to work on his game, trying to be better, dreaming his dream. Valvano had taken his dream away from him. Basketball wasn't what he thought it was.

Kennedy had learned a great deal in his freshman year, but what he learned sickened him. He learned that to play college ball you have to be mentally tough and that you have to develop a distant attitude toward teammates and not worry if the other guy was being hurt because you were taking all the shots. He learned you have to look out for number one and that college basketball has nothing to do with developing character and everything to do with making big bucks. He had turned cynical, and it appalled him.

Kennedy deeply regretted not having gone to Georgia Tech to play for Coach Bobby Cremins. Where Valvano overstocked his team, recruiting fourteen stars and playing only five of them, Kennedy knew Cremins to be the kind of coach who gave out ten scholarships and played everybody.

In his room at the College Inn after the season, Kennedy found himself so confused over how Valvano had used him that he had long, rambling confrontations with Coach V in his head.

"You bring me in from Mississippi, recruiting me from eleven hours away, Louisville, Mississippi, a small town. If you're not going to play me, why not just a local guy who everybody knows? I figured that since you came all that way to get me, you had something in your plans for me. I went up there, knowing no one, trusting you, and it's like you turned your back on me.

"Then you get down on me, and once I don't immediately become the superstar you thought I would be . . .

"I always wanted to ask you, 'Was I not the player you thought I was going to be?' What happened? Did I do something wrong?"

In high school, Kennedy had told himself, "One of two things is going to happen in college: Either I'm going to be a big success, or I will go straight to the coach and say, 'What do I have to do to be a star?' Either he will make it happen, or I will leave." Valvano was not the sort of coach to help a player become a star. Kennedy kept his promise to himself. He decided to leave.

Kenny Drummond was the one teammate who tried to talk him out of it. Drummond, the quintessential off-the-court team player to the end, told him, "I don't think you really want to leave." Drum felt that if someone talked to Kennedy, his mind could be changed. Drum said, "Stick it out, Andy." Andy said, "No way."

Kennedy went to see Valvano, who also tried to talk him out of it. Valvano said, "Andy, you're a freshman. Stay with us. Stick it out. Next year it'll be you and Walker as my scoring stars." Valvano's strong suit is his ability to get his way. If Kennedy hadn't been strong-willed and persistent, he would have stayed.

But when Kennedy talked to Brian Howard, who was also thinking of leaving, he reportedly discovered Valvano had told Howard, "Next year it will be you and Walker as my shooting stars," and when Valvano talked to Walker, he was reported to say it was going to be Walker and Brian as his shooting stars. Valvano never thought his players would put their heads together and compare notes.

Andy, Brian, and Walker were also well aware that freshman Rodney Monroe, Valvano's latest shooting star, would also be in the picture.

"He thought I was gullible to believe him," said Kennedy.

In order to transfer and get a scholarship your first year at a new school, a player must get from his coach a letter of transfer, which gives the coach's permission for the player to go. In most instances, the letter is signed freely, but not all the time.

Once Andy decided he was going to leave, he began calling around to other colleges, and it got back to the Raleigh press.

This was a big story: a top recruit, especially a white recruit, the second coming of Pete Maravich, leaving the hallowed basketball program after only one year. Andy was repeatedly asked why he was leaving.

Andy never gave a straight answer. He would say, "It's not playing time, and I love the school. It's just a lot of things that went on behind the scenes," but he wouldn't elaborate. All it did was raise more questions, making Valvano even angrier.

Valvano told Walker Lambiotte, who then told Andy what Valvano had said, "That goddamn Andy. I might not release him, that son of a bitch."

Walker regaled Andy with accounts of how much Valvano hated him for leaving and was threatening not to give him his release. Andy, however, wasn't worried. He knew that if Valvano didn't give him his release, he could go to the press and "bust his ass wide open."

As Kennedy suspected, it wasn't necessary. Kennedy walked into Valvano's office and told him, "I want my letter of transfer. I think I'm NBA material, and you're screwing up my chances." It was a Thursday in March, and while they were in his office, Valvano was distracted by some local reporters there waiting to ask him about his appearance the next day in New York on the David Letterman show. Valvano was holding a pair of Shack's size 19 shoes, which he was going to present to Letterman. Andy sensed that Valvano's mind was preoccupied with his upcoming match of wits with the host of NBC's "Late Night." Valvano perfunctorily signed a letter of transfer for Andy, they shook hands, and as Kennedy left, Valvano turned away to respond to the cameras and the TV reporters' questions about the Letterman show.

Kennedy was perplexed. He had been one of the top dozen high school prospects in the entire country, the MVP of the B/C Camp All Star Game. Valvano had been willing to offer him the moon to get him to come to N.C. State. One year later he was leaving, walking out of Valvano's life, and Kennedy thought it strange that Valvano didn't even seem to care.

50

Andy Causes Trouble

Andy Kennedy's phone rang. It was yet another reporter. But this time the reporter asked a different question. He wanted to know, "Is anyone else on the team thinking about leaving?" Andy said, "Walker Lambiotte, perhaps." As one player later said, "That was like a gasoline dump going off."

Walker Lambiotte was a Raleigh favorite—tall, handsome, a nice white kid who got good grades, was polite, acted like a Southern gentleman, and kept his nose clean. Kids loved him, old folks loved him, alums loved him, co-eds loved him. He was special, and no one wanted to see him leave.

At six-thirty on a Sunday morning, Walker's phone rang. It was the reporter. He said, "Walker, can you confirm what Andy Kennedy said about your thinking of transferring?"

Walker, unlike Andy, wasn't the type of person who could look you in the eye and give you a straight answer. He was shy around strangers, and having been warned by the coaches about the press, was terrified when questioned for print. He didn't want to give the reporter a straight answer, and he didn't want to lie.

Awakened from a deep sleep, Walker replied, "I don't know what you're talking about. I don't have any comment" —and then he added a lit match to the pyre—"*at this time.*"

If he had said, "No, sir, I am not transferring," Walker Lambiotte would still be at N.C. State today. But once he said, "I don't have any comment *at this time*," the local paper took what he said and made it into the headline: KENNEDY TO TRANSFER; LAMBIOTTE NEXT?

Sure, Walker had thought about leaving during the season. He hadn't been happy with his game or the way Valvano had used him. He didn't like being kept on the bench through most of the ACC tournament and the Florida games. Valvano had promised him he would be a star, but Coach V didn't use him like a star. One night he started and scored 18, and the next night he'd be riding the bench, playing five minutes and scoring 4 points. Or, as happened against Carolina in the ACC championship game, he wouldn't play at all. Nevertheless, Walker wasn't the type of guy who easily picked up stakes and moved on. It wasn't his nature. He wasn't very good at making momentous decisions—at pulling the trigger—and transferring was too big a move for him to make on his own.

After the first phone call from the reporter, Walker started panicking. Other reporters and TV camera crews began stalking him, and back in his room the phone never stopped. Walker stopped answering his phone, and whenever he saw reporters waiting for him in front of his classroom, he would turn around and skip the class.

What the commotion did was to bring the doubts he had about the N.C. State basketball program to the surface, prompting him to talk about all the things that were bothering him. He told a friend, "I'm not happy here, and my game sucks. V's not playing me. Maybe I should transfer." He began calling his parents every day to talk about it.

His ambivalence was overwhelming him. Intellectually, leaving to play for a less onerous and fickle program appealed to him, but his inertia plagued him. Moreover, Valvano had promised him, "Bennie is leaving, and next year as a junior you have the shooting forward position sewn up. You're a lock to start from the first game and play every game."

Lambiotte said to a friend, "That's a pretty good deal. Why should I leave now?"

The papers kept trying to keep the story alive, but the best they were able to come up with for the next couple of weeks was insipid headlines like "NOTHING NEW WITH WALKER."

Walker's parents were sufficiently concerned about how he was feeling to drive from their Poquoson, Virginia, home to Raleigh to meet with Valvano. Walker's mother, ordinarily a mild-mannered woman, had never liked the way Valvano treated her son. She told Valvano, "You've lied to me. I'm a mother, and this is my son, and you've jerked him around all season long." Usually Valvano controlled any given meeting. On this day it was Mrs. Lambiotte's turn. As he listened to his mother criticize his coach, Walker, who feared offending anyone for any reason, sat there shaking in his boots.

When she finished, things calmed down. Valvano did what he did best: He sold his program. He discussed his plans for Walker for the coming year.

He said, "I want to change the program next year, become more of a player's coach, hang with the boys more, so that if they have a problem they can come find me. I'm going to call the players' parents once a week on the phone, talk to them about their son's progress in school and in basketball, find out if the parents are getting feedback that I don't get from the player.

"Also, I want my players to graduate. I'm going to spend more time on that, because that's the purpose of their coming here."

Valvano promised the Lambiottes, "Walker has a lock on the three spot. Bennie Bolton's graduating, and Walker can step right in and play the next two years. He's served his time on the bench, and he is ready."

Walker liked the sound of that, but Mrs. Lambiotte was skeptical. She wasn't ready to forgive Valvano for the way he had treated her son. She said, "You didn't tell him anything all season long. When you put him on the bench, you never said a word. Where was the personal father-figure coach that you said you'd be when you first signed him?"

After Walker's parents left the meeting, Walker stayed behind to chat with Valvano. "Walker," Valvano asked, "are you going to stay or not?" It was a direct, yes-no question, because Valvano knew that was the only way he was going to get an answer out of him.

Walker said, "V, I'm staying. I've got problems with the way things are run, but I'm not as unhappy as my parents are, and I'm going to stay."

His parents returned home. The next day in the local paper Valvano announced that Lambiotte was staying at

N.C. State. He was quoted as saying, "I've talked to the Lambiottes and to Walker, and we've all come to the joint conclusion he's staying."

That didn't stop the reporters, who wanted to know why Walker had had a change of heart. But he had disappeared, and when the reporters couldn't find him, the story was allowed to fade.

Walker was hiding out—in the apartment of Valvano's anointed special assistant, John Simonds.

51

Simonds' Dilemma

Walker Lambiotte and John Simonds had first become friends during Coach McLean's conditioning program before practice had officially started. Walker ran woodenly, his arms shooting out like powerful pistons, and Simonds, the former high school track phenom, tried to get him to relax and use those arms to better advantage. Simonds also impressed Walker with his basketball skill during practices, and they became fast friends, sharing king crab in Alaska and enjoying competition as two expert video game players.

Like Walker, Simonds had been disillusioned by Valvano. To his knowledge, his failing fall grades hadn't been rectified, as Valvano promised, and he was facing the prospect of failing dismally again his spring semester. Moreover, the basketball scholarship, first offered in December, still had not materialized, though a couple weeks before the end of the season, Valvano had told him, "Hang with us through the summer, work our basketball camps, and you'll get a scholarship in the fall, for sure." It didn't do anything for his present financial mess, but he still had faith. He was figuring, "In the end, Coach V will take care of me."

More important, Valvano had discussed with him his dream of becoming a player on the team the next year, going so far as to ask Simonds what number uniform he wanted to wear. When Simonds told him "number 31," Valvano wanted to know why that number.

"That was the number my dad wore," he said.

"It's yours," Valvano said.

Like so many of his teammates, Simonds had given up a great deal just for the chance to wear the uniform. In high school he had been an honor roll student, he was generally admired by both headmaster and faculty, and his athletic prowess was admired by all the students. But it was his character that everyone admired most, prompting the headmaster to name him the boy who was most Christlike, the highest honor his small Christian Academy could bestow.

But once Simonds saw his chance to play basketball at State, his priorities changed. He decided he would do whatever he had to do to play for Valvano, even if it meant ignoring his studies to be available whenever Valvano needed him, even if it meant going out at eleven at night in the freezing cold of Alaska to get Coach Martin some BVDs, even if it meant making up a story to the manager of a hotel about why Shack and Tev stole bedspreads, even if it meant silently watching his friends on the team being taken advantage of by a system that rewarded the coach first, the college second, and a player or two third. Simonds was no different from any other college basketball player with aspirations. He was determined to do whatever he had to do in order to play basketball at N.C. State.

And that included leaving behind his job and friends at his dorm and ignoring his girl friend to spend most of his time with Walker and the other players. He and his girl had dated for two years, but as the weather was beginning to turn warm on campus, his girl was turning cool. And now it was Simonds' self-sworn duty to squirrel Walker away in his apartment, to keep him company and protect him from the press day after day, and he didn't know it, but he was losing his girl.

"You don't have time for me any more," she would tell him.

"I'm sorry," he would say, "but I have to do what I have to do."

"You've changed," she would say, "and I don't like the new you."

"I'm sorry."

Finally, one April evening, she visited his apartment with the news that they were through.

Here was the spot Simonds was in at season's end: His grades were 1.0 for the semester. He was set to lose an entire year of school if Valvano didn't do anything about it. His credit cards, which he had been living on, were at their maximums. His job at the YMCA was in jeopardy because he rarely came on time and often left early. He was drinking a lot. And his girl had left him.

"I am doomed," he told himself. "Doomed."

He didn't realize it then, but for John Simonds things would soon get worse, much worse.

Two days after his meeting with the Lambiottes, Valvano was whooping it up in the baseball office with a bunch of his cronies—his pals, a dozen of his buddies from the various sports—and they were having a bullshitting marathon. Valvano usually is king of these sessions—few men, even stand-up comics, are as quick on his feet as he is. As they were talking and boasting and acting catty, Valvano began regaling the other coaches with a replay of his meeting with Walker and the Lambiottes, and he began making fun of Walker's mother, deriding her words and manner.

Valvano's ego had gotten the best of him. He began making a big joke of the shrill way Mrs. Lambiotte had said, "You lied to me." Valvano told his coaches, "Who the fuck does she think she is anyway? Walker can't even play in the ACC, and she's yelling at me?" He said, "I don't deserve that. I'm above being treated like that." And he began making fun of her.

By revealing what had gone on at that meeting, Valvano went too far. He broke a cardinal rule. A coach is like a lawyer, a psychiatrist, or a priest. What a player says to a coach is expected to be respected and kept private. Players really have no one else they can confide in, because they can get burned so easily, by the press and anyone who might talk to the press, so the one person they expect to respect confidences is their coach, their final sanctuary.

Valvano, in revealing the substance of his meeting with the Lambiottes, breached important confidences, and one of the coaches at the meeting was so appalled that Valvano would break his trust and, worse, make fun of a player's mother, that he let John Simonds know what Valvano had said. He didn't call Walker directly, because he didn't think it was his place to do that, but he wanted

Walker to know. The coach said to Simonds, "If I were you, I'd pass along to him that V was joking about his parents." He said, "If V doesn't think Walker has the talent to play in the ACC, then Walk ought to think seriously about transferring."

It pained this coach to say that, because he liked Walker a great deal, was a die-hard State fan, and didn't want Walker to leave. But he'd noted that Valvano was dead serious, wasn't joking, when he denigrated Walker's game, and the other coach felt Walker had the right to know how Valvano really felt about his talents.

Without considering the consequences, Simonds, horrified as well, told his friend Walker, who immediately got on the telephone to his parents. They were apoplectic. Walker said, "I can't believe he would say that. V has stabbed me in the back for the last time. I'm leaving."

The next day Walker was supposed to eat lunch with Coach Stewart. Since the rumors of Walk's departure, Valvano had assigned Stewart the job of baby-sitting him, buying him lunch, sending his girl friend flowers. Valvano knew that if Walker left hard on the heels of Drummond and then Andy, people would wonder what was wrong with his program.

Walker stood Stewart up, causing panic among the coaching staff. They called his room, and his roommate said, "I haven't seen him." They found out he had been staying with Simonds to avoid the newspaper reporters, but when they called Simonds, John said, "I haven't seen him either." Walker was so angry he didn't want to see or speak to any of the coaches. Making things worse, the reporters were back on the trail of the story that Walker was thinking of leaving.

For three days Walker successfully ducked the coaches by staying at Simonds' apartment. Valvano, meanwhile, was in Hialeah, Florida, trying to recruit a high school guard by the name of Chris Corchiani.

Walker's disappearance was making Valvano crazy. He called Coach Stewart and told him, "I have to talk to Walker—tonight." Stewart promised that he would find him.

Stewart called Walker's girl friend. "Leslie Ann, where

is he?" She said, "I don't know." Stewart began to panic. Sternly, he said, "Leslie Ann, you have to stop pulling my leg. I know he's somewhere. I know you know where. Where is he? Coach V has to talk to him tonight. Leslie Ann, I'm begging you to tell me."

After five minutes of his relentless pleading, she said, "I think he's at John Simonds'."

52

Getting in Deeper

At two in the morning, the phone rang. Out of a deep sleep, John Simonds picked up the receiver. For a second, he worried that a member of his family might be ill. But it was Coach Valvano, calling from Florida.

"Goddammit, John, why are you hiding out one of my players?"

Simonds, half asleep, tried to bullshit the master. He said, "Coach, you know I'm always in your ball court."

Valvano said, "I don't know what to think. I can't find Walker, and then I find out you're hiding him. What's going on?" He said, "John, I think you're on the wrong side of this issue. I'm counting on you to pull through for me. I don't want you hiding my players. I want you to help me keep Walker at N.C. State. You're his best friend. You're the guy he talks to most. Now, John, you know you're a good man, and we're going to take care of you in this organization. You know we have big plans for you in our future. We need to work together."

Valvano made it clear that Simonds was either with him or against him. Simonds continued to hedge. He said, "Coach, I am Walker's best friend, and I want the best for him. I can't push him either way."

Valvano said, "Well, you need to want the best for me also—which is the best for him."

While Simonds was talking, Walker, who was sleeping in the guest bed, awoke, very nervous, because he knew he would have to explain to Valvano why he was so steadfastly avoiding Coach Stewart. Sure enough, after Valvano finished berating Simonds, he asked to speak to Walker. Simonds handed Walker the phone.

Valvano began, "Walker, why have you been ducking all the coaches? Why are you hiding?"

This time, and perhaps for the first time in his relationship with Valvano, Walker Lambiotte was not evasive but surprisingly tough. He said, "V, I'm hearing some bad things about you."

Now Valvano was on the defensive. He said, "Hey, Walk, people are always talking bad about me. What the hell are you hearing this time? You know you can't believe half of what people say about you."

Walker said, "I heard you told a bunch of your friends about the meeting you had with me and my parents."

Valvano was stunned. He paused. Then he lied, "Walker, that is totally untrue. I would never do anything like that. You know that anything we talk about is sacred between you and me and your parents. I love your parents. God bless them. They are fine people, salt of the earth. I would never do anything like that. Somebody is filling you with lies." He paused. "Who is it?"

Suddenly, Simonds, who could hear both sides of the conversation because Valvano was talking so loudly, began sweating profusely. He'd been the messenger. If Walker were to tell Valvano that he had conveyed the news, he would be finished at State. Simonds was feeling like the landed gentry during the French Revolution, waiting to step up to the guillotine.

Walker said, "I can't tell you that." Simonds exhaled in relief. Walker continued, "But I am telling you, it's true about what you said about my parents. I got it from a source who was there, and I know it's true."

Valvano then made up an entire scenario to prove his innocence. He said, "I wasn't even in that room with those guys. I know nothing about that, about a whole group of guys being there at that time. I was at the radio station taping a commercial. Walker, it's totally untrue that I did such a thing. And if anybody says anything different, let him come out and identify himself so I can see who it is, so I can face the person who is stabbing me in the back."

Walker replied, "V, I don't know what to think." There was grief in Walker's voice. Valvano, meanwhile, was beginning to get nervous. In the past he had always been able to smooth Walker down like icing on a cake.

This time Walker wasn't buying it. Walker said, "I think it's true."

Valvano tried putting Walker on the defensive. He bristled. "Are you calling me a liar?"

Walker, with as much diplomacy as an ambassador, replied, "Coach, I don't think you're a liar, but I have two different stories, and I don't know which side to take. All I'm saying is that I heard from a close source that you were joking about my folks and that you were making fun of my mom."

Valvano said, "Walker, I am telling you, I wouldn't do something like that to you. You're one of my prized players. You've got the three spot sewed up next year. You've already served your time on the bench. You already know the system. Everybody loves you. I love you. I think you're going to be a great player."

Valvano was really putting his arms to the pump. "Walker, I'm telling you, I would never say anything like that about your folks."

But Walker was still saying, "I don't know, Coach. I got this from a close source."

Telling Valvano 'no' was an extremely difficult thing to do. Valvano was used to getting his way, and he desperately wanted to know who it was that had spilled the beans to Walker, because that guy was sure to be unemployed by the end of the year.

Valvano finally said, "Walker, here's what I'm going to do. I'm flying home tomorrow. I had scheduled two more days for recruiting here in Florida, but I will cut my stay short, just to show you how much I care about you. I want you to meet with me tomorrow night at my house. Will you do it?"

Walker was tentative. "Well."

Valvano said, "Walker, I'm flying home tomorrow for the express purpose of seeing you. I'm leaving the rest of my family here. Will you meet me?"

Walker said he would.

Valvano flew home the next day as promised, and late that night Walker went to his home to meet with him. They ate spaghetti, as Valvano continued to give Walker the "I can't believe people would stab me in the back like this" line. Valvano kept telling him, "Walker, it's totally untrue. I really care about you. I flew all the way up here. We're going to take care of you next year."

Walker remained unsure.

All the while Walker was fencing with Valvano, he never came out and asked for his letter of transfer, because it wasn't in his personality to do so. Nevertheless, word had gotten out that Walker was thinking of leaving, so coaches from other colleges were calling his father, pitching his dad about their basketball programs. Coaches from Michigan, Richmond, Indiana, William and Mary, Ohio State, Providence, Virginia State, Furman, LSU, Pitt, Florida, UC at Berkeley, and Northwestern all called.

Every night Walker called his father to find out who was calling. And all the while Valvano and his staff were doing everything they could to convince Walker to stay at N.C. State.

Losing Andy had been a blow. To lose a second white kid, an academic All American, a McDonald's All Star Game MVP, that would be a crusher. Valvano somehow had to save the situation.

53

Shrink Relief

Shortly after Valvano flew back to Raleigh to meet with Walker Lambiotte, John Simonds got a call from Coach Stewart. "John, I need you to come up to the office," he said. "I got to talk to you about something."

When Simonds arrived, sitting with Stewart were the other assistant coaches, Ray Martin and Ed McLean. There was one topic during the one-hour meeting: Who told Walker that Valvano had made fun of his mother?

It was clear that Coach Stewart was taking the lead role in protecting his friend and boss. Stewart said, "John, we know you know. You're Walker's best friend. He talks to you. You're a good man. John, we've always liked you. We're going to take care of you. But I am telling you, we must root out this evil right now. Because Coach V is a great man. He looks after all of us, and we just can't have people like this spreading rumors and falsehoods about a great man. So, John, we need you to tell us."

Simonds wasn't about to tell Stewart anything. He said, "Coach, I honestly don't know. Walk is scared as a bunny rabbit. He's not talking to me."

Stewart said, "John, we've got to keep him at State. You've got to tell us. It's vital to everybody's future at N.C. State."

Simonds said, "Guys, I don't know who it was. I just don't know. I can't imagine who would tell him something like that. I can't imagine someone calling him up in this kind of state and telling him something like that." He was playing up to them.

Coach Stewart finally determined that Simonds either didn't know or wasn't about to tell him, and the meeting broke up. Stewart and Martin headed out the door and Coach McLean spoke just loud enough for Simonds to hear. "I know who it is," he said. Simonds' heart leaped, because if McLean said he knew, he knew, and if McLean knew who had said it, then he also knew that the culprit had passed it on to Simonds for Simonds to tell Lambiotte.

Fortunately for Simonds, Coach Mac must have figured that it would be in Lambiotte's best interest to leave. Coach McLean himself would soon leave to become the head basketball coach at Samford College in Birmingham, Alabama.

When Coach McLean said nothing, Simonds knew he was safe, that the secret would remain with the one coach he admired and loved.

But if Coach McLean had given John Simonds a reprieve, it was but temporary. Life's pressures were building.

Simonds' girl friend had left him, and even after a twenty-page, single-spaced letter of contrition, apology, and just plain begging, not only did she shoot him down, but he learned that she was dating someone else.

John's status in the program as man in the middle had really caught up to him. As Valvano's special assistant, he felt deep affection for his coach, but his heart had always been with the players, and his loyalty, too. Nevertheless, it pained him to have to evade Valvano, who hadn't let up on his crusade to get Simonds to lean on Walker to keep him at school.

Twice he got calls at his apartment from Valvano. Both times the tenor of the conversation was "John, we really need to keep Walker. Have you talked to him at all about staying? I really need you as a vital part of my staff next year. I've already promised you that you're going to play next year and wear number 31, and when our ACC championship rings come back, yours is going to have '31' on it. John, now don't let me down."

Valvano let Simonds know in no uncertain terms that he was banking on him to pull through for him. He was becoming their final hope. Walker had stopped talking to the coaches, had made himself scarce even to Valvano, so Simonds was their conduit. They were trying to make him think that he was an important piece in their chess game, but by this time Simonds knew better: He was merely a pawn.

The pressures on him were mounting. He didn't have anyone to talk to about his girl friend or Valvano, so he decided to go to the student counseling center on campus. He also had an ulterior motive: He was failing all his spring courses, and the way the wind was blowing, he suspected that either Valvano couldn't do what he had promised or, more likely, wouldn't do what he had promised. Simonds needed an escape hatch to keep from flunking out of college.

From having been a resident assistant in the dorms, he knew that if a student went to a psychiatric counselor and presented a strong-enough case for serious emotional disturbance, the counselors would try to lessen his anxiety by dropping some or, even better, all of his classes—get them dropped from the official record and allow him to start over fresh next fall.

Simonds went in and spoke to a counselor. He was genuinely aggrieved about the loss of his girl friend, but he was also putting on a show. Coach McLean had often told him, "Study V. Watch how he acts, and you'll learn a lot." Coach Valvano had taught him well, and in front of the psychiatric counselor, he displayed the skills Valvano taught him.

Simonds said, "My life is finished. She was everything to me." He discussed how he couldn't eat or sleep, which was true. But he knew that the counselor had heard every sob story going and that the one thing he really wanted to hear was that Simonds was considering suicide.

"Because when they hear that," said Simonds, "bells start going off. They jump up and shout, 'Praise God, I knew you were going to say it,' and then they go and get cheese and crackers and wine and call in the other psychiatrists, and they have a party."

He also knew that when a student admits to wanting to commit suicide, the first response is, "Do you want to quit school? If you do, we'll get your classes dropped, your record expunged. We'll do anything for you."

The counselor finally got around to the Big S. "Have you thought about suicide?" Simonds was asked.

Before he had been in the middle, torn between Valvano and Walker. Now again he was on the fence, caught between truth and expediency. His conscience did bother him. He didn't feel right answering "yes," because he knew it was a complete falsehood, and yet he didn't want to say 'no' either, because he desperately needed to get his grades dropped from his record. He pleaded guilty with an explanation. So that his answer would have an element of truth to it, he said, "Well, doctor, when I'm driving down the road, it's occurred to me recently that it would be life-threatening if I just pulled the wheel to the right and drove into a telephone pole." Which is something probably every driver thinks about at least one time or another. He said, "All I'd have to do is just pull the wheel over, and it would be ended, and all my problems would be solved."

As he had hoped, the answer was sufficient to set off the bells. The psychiatrist brought out the wine and cheese, and all the other psychiatrists came racing in and shook John's hand. And with this phalanx of white coats sitting around him, Simonds once more went through his explanation of what it would mean if he turned the wheel to the right just as he was coming up to a telephone pole.

The chief psychiatrist told him, "Don't go see your girl. Don't go back to class. Don't go back to school. We'll take care of your spring semester grades."

Simonds, thinking and calculating all the while, considered for a second pressing his luck and asking for his fall grades to be stricken as well, but decided to let that drop. He said, "Thanks, Doc. You have been a great help to me. I am very appreciative," while the doctors nodded at each other and told him, "Keep in touch."

As he left the office and walked the halls of the student counseling center, he kept his head down, appearing somber and sullen, but once he closed the entrance door behind him and got to the parking lot, he began jumping up and down, whooping and hollering, slapping fives with people he didn't even know.

When he went home and told Walker what he had done, Walker said, "No way you did that. You are such a con man. You're just like V."

54

Coach Stewart Kneeling

One evening Walker decided he wanted to go see Andy Kennedy to ask him about some of the colleges Andy had been talking to. Walker picked Simonds up and drove him to the College Inn. Had they been more alert, they might have suspected that the College Inn would be the first place staked out by the coaches. Valvano surely did not want Walker talking to Andy, and they didn't want any of the other players to get nervous about major defections in the program, so every night the assistant coaches dropped by to rap with the players, find out what they were thinking, and all the time sell N.C. State's program for the coming year.

Walker and Simonds pulled into the College Inn parking lot and headed for Andy's room. They saw Coach Stewart's car, but it didn't register. They entered Andy's room and shut the door without being noticed.

Andy's roommate needed to look up a word in a dictionary and asked if Simonds or Walker had one. Walker had one in his car, and Simonds volunteered to go out and get it. As he was walking back from his car, he ran into Coach Stewart.

Stewart said, "John, how are you doing? Good to see you."

"Great, Coach, how are you doing?" Simonds replied.

"Fine," Stewart said. "Have you seen Walker?"

Simonds was back on the spot. He knew that if he said 'no' and Walker came strolling out of Andy's room, he would be in trouble. If he said 'yes,' he was committing Walker to having to talk with Stewart.

Simonds said, "I've seen Walk."

"Where is he?"

"He's in talking with Andy. I was just going in to get him."

"Great, send him on out here."

Simonds went into Andy's room and told Lambiotte that Stewart was waiting for him outside. Lambiotte had Simonds tell Stewart he would be out as soon as he finished talking with Andy. They chatted for about an hour, and Walker suspected Stewart would still be out there waiting for him.

When Walker opened Andy's door to leave, Stewart was waiting, and as Walker headed back to the car with Simonds, Stewart tagged along. The three of them stood by the front of Walker's Toyota in the parking lot, with the thirty-degree temperatures biting them to the bone, while Stewart pitched Walker not to transfer.

Stewart said, "Walker, we really need you. People are filling your head with junk about Coach V. He's such an honest man. He's pulled me out of the pits. He's going to come through for you."

Walker wasn't listening.

At Walker's direction, Simonds got into the car, with Walker getting in behind the wheel. Stewart stood outside the driver's side of the car trying to continue his conversation with Walker. Stewart said, "Walk, please, talk to me, baby. Talk to me. Let's have lunch. Something, anything, but you have to talk to me. Walk, you just can't do this to me."

While Coach Stewart was talking, Coach Ray Martin pulled up in his car. Martin got out and as he was walking over to talk to Walker, Stewart began rolling his eyes, as if to say, "Oh no, not him." Martin began saying, "Walks, baby, Walks, what's goin' on? My knees are shaking. I'm hearing bad things, Walks. Walks, talk to me."

Stewart eyed Martin and gave him a withering glare, as if to say, "I'll handle the white players and you handle the black. You are ruining the situation. Get out of here."

Martin, perhaps realizing what the look meant, retreated. Stewart said, "Don't mind him, Walk." And then he returned to his agenda. "Walk, you can't do this to me." Then he said, "Walk, we've got to talk some more."

Simonds said, "Coach, I'll go back into the College Inn so that you and Walker can continue talking." Stewart said, "No, John, please stay. We're all family here. You're his best friend. I have nothing to hide from you. You're a good man."

But Walker had no intention of continuing the conversation. He turned on the ignition. Stewart shouted over the engine, "Walk, you just can't leave me like this." Then Stewart said, "Walker, I'll get down on my knees and beg you." And he did just that, a grown man in the freezing cold on his knees outside the car begging Walker Lambiotte to stay at N.C. State.

"Walk, I'm begging you. I'm on my knees. Please, stay. Walker, please stay."

Through the open car window Walker said, "Coach, I'm leaving," and he put the car in gear and started rolling forward.

"Walker, don't go," Stewart pleaded. "Please don't leave me like this. I'm on my knees begging you, Walker."

Stewart was holding onto the sill of the rolled-down window on Walker's side, and as the car rolled forward, Stewart, still on his knees, was trying to slide along with it. When Walker popped the clutch, the car surged forward, forcing Stewart to let go. As the car pulled out of the lot, in the side mirror Simonds could see Stewart still sitting on his knees. Simonds thought to himself, "The world has gone to hell in a handbasket."

Right after that, Simonds stopped going to the basketball office. He knew they wouldn't have anything more to discuss with him.

55

Bribery

Lambiotte and Simonds decided to get out of town for a few days. They headed for the coast to play some golf. After they returned, Simonds was working at the YMCA when a stranger wearing a business suit approached him.

He said, "Aren't you John Simonds?" Simonds said, "Yes, sir, I am." The man said, "Aren't you Walker Lambiotte's best friend?" Simonds hesitated, then said he was.

"I've seen you guys out at different places together," the stranger said. "Weren't you out playing golf a few days ago?" Simonds' head began whirling. Had this guy been following them? Simonds couldn't conceal his surprise and wonder over who the man was. "Let's just say that several of my friends and I are big supporters of N.C. State basketball," he said, "and we would like to see Walker stay and would go to any means to keep him here." He added, "If you know what I mean."

Simonds said, "Yes, sir, I think I do know what you mean." The man said, "Just pass that along to Walker." Simonds agreed.

After he left, Simonds was shaking. Someone he didn't know knew an awful lot about him.

The same man found Simonds at the YMCA two days later. He asked, "What did Walker say?" Simonds said, "He didn't say anything." The man said, "Do you guys like jewelry?" Simonds said, "Everybody likes jewelry." He then said, "I'm sure both of you could use a new set of Ping golf clubs." Ping makes a fine set of expensive clubs. Simonds said, "Yes, sir, we could both use some Pings, but I'll tell you, I wouldn't feel right taking them because I'm not going to push Walker either way whether to stay or go. It's up to him."

"I'm sure you feel that way, but Walker needs to stay," said the man. "Just think about my offer."

A week later he showed up for a third visit. Simonds was shooting baskets by himself at the Y. The man said, "John, I noticed that you're driving an old VW Rabbit. You know, if you could convince Walker to stay at N.C. State, me and my friends would be glad to supply both of you with new forms of transportation. I'm sure they aren't paying you much here at the Y, and we'd be glad to bankroll you for the rest of the time you're at school."

Simonds' eyes started bugging. He said, "Let me think about it. But I'll tell you, I'm his best friend, and I'm not going to push him either way."

"Think about it," he said.

Simonds was beginning to feel fear. First Valvano and the coaches had tried to bully him, and now the businessman-types were doing it.

A few days later Simonds got a package in the mail. It had no return address on it, just his name and address. He opened it, and inside was a gold diamond-cut rope necklace. In the box was a typewritten note that said: "Thinking of you and your buddy, Walk."

Simonds got in his car and drove to a local jewelry store, where he was informed that the necklace was indeed real and worth close to $650.

Simonds didn't feel right about keeping it, but there was no return address. He said to himself, "I don't *know* who sent it. I think I do, but maybe I'm wrong." He put it on. It felt luxurious.

Walker was incredulous when he saw the necklace: "I'm the one who's thinking about leaving, and you're the one getting the merchandise."

It was well into May when the stranger visited the Y for the fourth and final meeting. John was wearing the necklace. The man said, "Hi, John, just wanted to check in with you, see how you were doing. Has Walk made any firm decision yet?"

"No," John said. The man said, "Just tell him me and my pals are still thinking about him."

"I sure will," Simonds said. On his way out the door, the man turned around and said, "By the way, that's a nice necklace. Where did you get it?"

Simonds answered, "It was a gift."

"Take care, see you," the man said, and he left.

56

Walker Picks a College

Toward the end of May, Walker Lambiotte met with his parents and made a decision: He was going to leave N.C. State.

Walker told his father, "But wherever I go, I want the new coach to know that he also has to accept John. He's been through all this with me, he's going to get burned if he stays at State, and I need him, because I don't want to launch out into the unknown myself."

His father reportedly said, "I have the contacts. I'll start calling other coaches, and tomorrow, first thing, I'm going to call Valvano and tell him I want the letter of transfer, and I don't care what he says."

When Walker's father called, Valvano at first balked but finally said, "Okay, and if I can help out in any way, feel free to call me. I'll be glad to call any of my friends to get him set up."

Once Walker told Valvano he was leaving, things changed for Simonds. After missing a lot of work at the Y, the Y canned him. He was reduced to earning money by borrowing a friend's lawn mower and cutting lawns at five bucks a lawn. His summer plans changed as well. He knew it would not be a good idea to ask to work Coach Valvano's basketball camps.

Walker, meanwhile, was busy visiting college campuses. The first school he visited was the University of Richmond. His father had been an outstanding basketball player at Richmond. Walker was to spend two days there, and Simonds was to pick him up.

When John arrived, he went to the gym to find Walker, who was talking to a couple of assistant coaches. When they saw Simonds, they surprised him by addressing him by name. "Hi, John, how are you doing?" One of the coaches tossed him a basketball and told him, "Take a couple of shots. We hear you're not too bad." He hit a few long shots, and afterward one of the assistant coaches said to John, "If Walker would come here, we could use you."

Thought Simonds, "This is what I've been waiting for. This is my ticket out." The coach said, "Why don't you talk to him about it?" They felt, as Valvano had, that they could get to Lambiotte through Simonds.

Lambiotte, however, really didn't want to go to a college that played in a less prestigious conference than the ACC.

Lambiotte returned to Raleigh to get ready for the Five Star Basketball Camp in Pittsburgh. The last thing he told Simonds before he left for the summer was "I'm sorry for all the problems I've caused you. Don't forget, wherever I go, you're going to go with me. We will always be tight."

Simonds said, "Call me when you hear something," but after Walker turned down Richmond and their chance to play together, Simonds knew that, despite Walker's promises, he would not be a determining factor in Walker's final decision.

By July, Walker had narrowed his choice to between Northwestern University and the University of California at Berkeley. Berkeley said it would take Simonds if Walker joined up, but Walker was hesitant and scared about being 3,000 miles from home. Simonds' parents weren't too keen on it either. John's mother felt Berkeley to be too radical a school.

The other school, Northwestern University in Chicago, was coached by Bill Foster, who had given Valvano his first coaching job at Rutgers. Simonds, who knew how close Foster was to Valvano, told Walker, "When you go up there, you can talk to the coaches about bringing me, but, Walk, please make sure that it doesn't get back to N.C. State, because, Walker, as bad as things are with them losing Andy and you, there's a small chance I might be able to patch things up with V and get that scholarship he promised me. I'll go and kiss his ass if I have to, so please, Walk, whatever you do, don't close that door for me. I don't need them finding out."

When Walker returned from his visit to Northwestern, he told Simonds, "I talked to them about you, and they said they were going to start checking into it." Walker was excited. He said, "We are going to be together."

About a week later Coach Foster called Walker. He said, "I called Coach Stewart because I want things to be straight up between all the coaches. I told Coach Stewart about you and I told him about John."

Simonds counted on Northwestern coming through for him. To get a player of Walker's caliber, plenty of schools will take a best friend and give him a scholarship. Northwestern wasn't one of them.

Foster called Simonds and told him, "Northwestern will take you, but you're going to have to pay for your own education."

There was no way Simonds could afford to do that. And Walker apparently was not the type of person to say to Foster, "If you don't give John that scholarship, then I'm not going."

Simonds got himself a summer job working at an overnight camp on the North Carolina shore, and a couple days before Walker was to leave for Budapest, Hungary, to play in a tournament, he visited Simonds and gave a basketball clinic at the camp. Afterward, the counselors played a game, with Walker and Simonds guarding each other. As the game came down to its conclusion, the score was tied, and everyone began playing rough, because no one wanted to lose.

As Simonds tried to dribble in for the score, one of the counselors accidentally thumbed him in the eye. The game stopped. Simonds was on the ground screaming in pain. When his hands were pulled away from the eye, he couldn't see. He thought he was blind. As the doctors came running from the infirmary, Walker realized that Simonds' eyelid had been inverted, and he reached up and pulled it back to normal. The pain eased, but Simonds still couldn't see. The doctors put salve on the eye and patched it, running tape all the way around his head.

By the time the doctors had finished with him, the campers had all gone to bed. Walker had to leave. Neither had discussed the reality: Walker was going to Northwestern and Simonds wasn't.

Walker, in the end, despite his affection for Simonds, had followed the athlete's creed and put number one first, allowing Simonds to sink on his own. But Simonds never called Walker on it. Walker was his best friend. Simonds simply accepted his fate.

As the two stood by Walker's car, Simonds told him, "I have to figure out what I'm going to do. I'm probably going to have to go back to N.C. State and face the music."

Walker said, "I know. I feel so bad for you. I got you into this, and you stayed with me through thick and thin and lost everything you had for me. It's something for the storybooks."

He continued, "And I'm going to have to leave, and I know that you won't be able to go." He looked up and said, "But I want you to know that I love you." Walker was crying, and then Simonds began to cry. With a patch over his eye and the white tape around his head, Simonds said, "Yeah, and you know that I love you, too."

Walker gave him a fist and said, "Always tight."

"Always tight," responded Simonds.

And Walker got in his car and drove off.

With Lambiotte heading for Northwestern and the continuation of his basketball career, Simonds indeed was headed back to N.C. State, where he would be walking into the teeth of a hurricane.

57

V Tells Simonds Off

Before John Simonds returned to school for the fall semester, Walker told him that friends in the athletic department had warned, "Valvano is so pissed, John ought not to even show up."

John's first indication this was so occurred on drop/add day (the day students can drop a class and add a different class). He was standing upstairs in Reynolds Coliseum, waiting in one of the long, winding lines to get the classes he wanted, when he ran face to face into Coach Stewart. Valvano had assigned Stewart the job of keeping Walker Lambiotte at State, and Stewart had failed. Rather than accept the blame, he apparently turned to a scapegoat: John Simonds. Stewart, without saying a word, turned and walked away.

Coach Ray Martin, however, did speak to him. Martin told John, "I've heard that the V Man is pissed. He feels like you really stabbed him in the back. V took you under his wing, and look what you did. Walker left, and you tried to run off with him. You really screwed us, John."

Martin continued, "Most you can do is go talk to the V Man. What could he do, throw you out of his office?"

The first week of school Simonds went to find out. He arrived at nine-thirty in the morning outside Valvano's office, and he was very nervous. As he walked down the hall of the athletic department, running into people who had been friends the year before, it was as if he had leprosy, so studiously were they all avoiding him.

Simonds walked into Valvano's outer office feeling like a black Jew at a Ku Klux Klan rally. Valvano's secretary got out of her seat, went in and said, "John Simonds is here." Valvano said, "Oh yeah. John. I've been hearing a lot of bad things about him. Send him in." He was talking loud enough for Simonds to hear.

When Simonds entered Valvano's inner office, he found press and TV reporters and several members of the athletic department. Valvano was sitting behind his mammoth desk in his big red leather chair. He dismissed everyone else to spend an hour to talk to Simonds. He began, "John, Johnnie, John, oh, John, I've been hearing a lot of bad things about you."

"Coach, that's what I'm here to talk to you about," Simonds said.

Valvano got up, closed the door, and went back to his chair. Simonds pulled his chair close to Valvano's. Simonds said, "Coach, I've heard through a lot of people that you're really mad at me and the other coaches are all mad at me and that everyone thinks I've stabbed you in the back and screwed you. I've been walking around here ducking people, feeling I've done something wrong, and I don't think that's right. And I just wanted to come down here and see you today and tell you my side of the story, just so I don't have to feel I have to hide from you."

Simonds' opening monologue took about thirty seconds. For the next hour, Valvano let him have it with both barrels.

"John, I admire that," he began. "I'm glad that you came to see me. I hope all my guys will come down here to see me. But the fact is, you *did* screw me. You *did* stab me in the back." Simonds thought to himself, "Uh oh." Valvano continued, "You motherfucking did me wrong. I took you under my wing. I showed you everything. I trained you. I brought you up just like my own son, and you fucking stabbed me in the back. You don't even know what you got yourself into, do you? You thought you were in the big leagues, but really, you're just a small timer. You got yourself involved in a situation, and you cost me a blue-chip player. Not me. *You* did. You cost me a blue-chip player, and I'm still feeling the effects of that.

"You finagled yourself around so you could transfer with him, and when that didn't work out, now you're back here, and you're just trying to pull one over on me so that I don't think you're such a bad guy. But I don't believe that. You cost me Walker Lambiotte, and I'll tell you something, Mister Big Shot. I was glad you didn't get to go with Walker."

A lightbulb went off in Simonds' brain. If he didn't know it before, he knew it now. Valvano must have been responsible for his not getting a scholarship at Northwestern, he thought. How he did it or what Valvano had said to Coach Foster he didn't know. But down to his bones Simonds knew that Valvano had used his powers to stop him from going there. And here he was, gloating about it.

A red-faced Valvano leaned forward to talk to him. His veins were popping out, and spit was flying out of his mouth as Valvano called John foul names and berated him for letting Walker Lambiotte get away. John knew he wasn't going to get the chance to say another word of substance.

Valvano went on, "You want me to believe that you didn't have anything to do with Walk leaving and thinking about taking you. I don't believe that. I treated you so well, and then you turned around and openly fucked me. How am I supposed to feel about you? How would you feel about me if the shoe were on the other foot?"

Simonds said, "Well, Coach," but Valvano shouted, "I'm not finished yet. Let me tell you something about your friend Walker. He doesn't know what he wants out of life. Walker's leaving hurt me, but Walker's going to have the same problem anywhere, because, John, I'm a great coach. Look at my record. And Walker is leaving a great program to play for a school with a losing record. What does that say about him personally? And you call him your friend. What does that tell me about you?

"Andy Kennedy thinks he knows it all. All you guys do, but really, you don't. I know what's going on. I know what's best for each player. And you ought not to screw with me.

"Every one of you guys has a great thing going here. But you don't know it. No, you have to try something else. You can't believe me. It's like I've been telling the parents of the kids I'm recruiting. They keep saying, 'We hear that you're going to leave,' and I keep saying, 'I promise I'm staying at State.' But then my players leave. How the hell am I supposed to feel about that?"

Simonds thought, "That has to tell you something about the way you've been coaching," but Simonds now knew Valvano didn't see it that way. As always, the only thing he saw was the bottom line, the won-lost record. It didn't matter that very few graduated or that their dreams were being shattered or their fun taken away or that most of their pro career aspirations were ruined by him. All he saw was his own won-lost record.

Simonds said, "Coach, I thank you for taking your time out of a busy day to talk to me. I felt like I had to come and talk to you about this, just because it was bothering me. I know you don't want me back working for you, but if you change your mind, I'll be glad to talk to you about it."

Valvano looked at Simonds hard and said, "John, you fucked me. You really cost me more than you really know. I'll never change my mind about taking you back."

58

The Pariah

John Simonds was a pariah on campus the entire fall semester. Valvano and Stewart put the word out among their friends on campus that he had caused Walker Lambiotte to leave N.C. State, that he had betrayed Valvano, and that he was a traitor to the school.

People who knew him, former friends from his dorm, would come up to him and say, "I heard you had a rift with V because you made Walker leave." They'd say, "Why in hell did you do a thing like that?"

What could he say? If the questioner was genuinely interested, Simonds would take the time to explain what really happened. But usually the questioner was just trying to get a jab in, letting him know that everyone knew what he had "done." Classmates snubbed him on the way to class. It was as though he were wearing a neon scarlet letter and everyone could see it.

Though his teammates had not spoken to Simonds, they knew Valvano had excommunicated him. Simonds was working as a bartender at the ACC Tavern one night when Vinny del Negro came to check up on him. Vinny said, "John, let me do some asking around. Maybe I can smooth things out for you." Simonds thought, "Vinny, you have been hanging around V too long," but he said, "Thanks, Vinny, I appreciate that."

Another night Quentin, Brian Howard, Avie, and Shack came by to see him. Quentin, of course, did most of the talking, letting him know they had appreciated his standing up for them. Quentin said, "John, you got screwed, and it's wrong." But they also said there wasn't a thing they could do about it.

Quentin said, "Because you stood up for us and for Walker, you will always be a teammate."

For one shining moment they were one, and John was grateful.

On campus, Simonds' biggest problem came from faculty members. In the spring, before all the trouble started, he had signed up for a couple of courses with professors who eased up on the basketball players, figuring he was going to be a player himself in the fall. It hadn't occurred to him to switch out of their courses, but once classes started he knew he had made a mistake by remaining. He even suspected that Valvano or Stewart had called the professors and told them what he had "done." Those professors made their distaste for him public, and Simonds was stuck. Whenever he asked the professors for extra help, they refused it.

In his history class the first week, the professor was calling out the roll, came to Simonds name, and in front of the hundreds of students asked, "Weren't you part of the basketball program last year, Simonds?" John said he was. The professor said, "I've heard about you. Didn't you have something to do with Walker Lambiotte leaving?" It was like Groucho Marx's old line, "Do you still beat your wife?" There was no way to answer that question gracefully. Finally, he said, "Yeah, something like that."

Despite working harder in that class than any other, he barely passed the course.

Away from the classroom, things weren't any better. He couldn't go to the YMCA without someone glaring at him or asking him about his forcing Walker to leave. And some of these men were fathers of sons he had coached at the Y.

At times Simonds would return to his apartment at the end of the day and cry. One evening he went into Two Guys, a restaurant across the street from campus. He was by himself, and when it was his turn to be seated, the manager, a close friend of Valvano's, told him he would not be served. Rather than argue, he left. He thought, "I don't have the strength to fight it."

Valvano was doing his best to run him out of town,

and though he loved N.C. State, he realized that sooner or later he was going to get his wish. As much as it pained him, he had to transfer. He couldn't take the abuse any more.

59

A Parting Gift

Simonds left at Thanksgiving. When he transferred to Florida State, his new school, he was at peace. No one knew him, and tormenters were nowhere to be seen.

When he got to his new school, he was so traumatized he literally couldn't pick up a basketball. Once, he had spent four or five hours a day doing nothing else. He had loved the game so much he didn't want to do anything else. But after his experience at N.C. State, the sight of a basketball spooked him. He was literally afraid of becoming involved in the sport again.

The one time he did go to pick up a ball, he almost had a nervous breakdown. He was in a sports bar with some newfound friends, and one of the girls asked him to be her partner in a game at an arcade foul-shooting game. He agreed. The game is played with five cantaloupe-sized basketballs that are tossed into a tiny net. Each basket counts a point. The balls are very light. The game isn't easy.

At first Simonds didn't mind playing, until the betting started—a pitcher of beer, then two pitchers, and, unexpectedly, scoring baskets meant something more than playing for the fun of it. Simonds was wearing a T-shirt that said "Wolfpack Cheerleader" on it, and after he made six shots in a row, his new friends started teasing him, calling him a "ringer." As he stood there ready to shoot another shot, one of the spectators hollered out, "Come on, Jimmy V, shoot the ball."

In front of all those people, John Simonds began to fall apart. He wanted to run. He suddenly felt as if he were back at N.C. State again. He put the ball down, sat next to one of the girls, and told her, "I can't shoot it." There was pain in his eyes as well as tears.

The spectators began jeering. It was a big game, with two pitchers of beer at stake, and he was walking away. "Hey, what's going on?" Calmly, the girl friend told him, "Shoot it for me."

Simonds went back to the line, shot the ball, and won the game. He returned to his table, and the girl could see that he was trembling. She said, "Let's leave." And they did. Simonds understood that it was going to take many years to get over the trauma of N.C. State.

He didn't return to Raleigh until the following spring break. He went back to see a couple of old friends from State. Since he lived in Durham, it wasn't very far—as the crow flies.

It was a Friday night, and his friends decided they wanted to go to Amedeo's, a hangout on Western Boulevard owned by a friend of Valvano's. Inside the restaurant there is even a little booth reserved for Valvano called "AD's Corner." Simonds didn't really want to go to Amedeo's, because he feared running into someone who might remember him, but his friends said, "Come on, John, they make a good pizza pie," so he agreed.

Simonds had lived in North Carolina since he was six years old, and for the first time he felt like a stranger in his home territory. Worse, he was petrified the wrong people were going to recognize him.

After they ordered, Simonds got up to make a phone call. His arm was in a sling because two weeks earlier he had fallen off a bicycle and had sprained his shoulder. It wasn't serious, but the sling was a precaution. While he was talking on the phone, several of the N.C. State coaches came out of Valvano's special corner. One of the coaches walked up to him and with one hand grabbed Simonds' bad arm on the elbow from the back. He smiled and said, "Hi, John, how are you doing? What are you doing back in town?" Simonds said, "Visiting friends."

"We've heard that you've been thinking about doing some wrong things, and we don't want you to do anything wrong," the coach said.

Said Simonds, "This guy grabbed my left hand, pulled it up to my left shoulder, the one in the sling, and twisted it hard until my shoulder popped. He deliberately dislocated my shoulder."

This was Simonds' parting gift from the N.C. State coaching staff. When Simonds later considered a career in the Air Force, he had to take a battery of tests. He failed for one reason: his bad shoulder.

The other coaches, meanwhile, were kneeing Simonds in the legs, laughing, acting as if they were having a good time so no one would notice.

Simonds wanted to hit the coach, but though he wasn't concerned about getting the tar beaten out of him, he knew that Amedeo's was the wrong venue for a brawl. Fearing Valvano's influence with the Raleigh police, Simonds was concerned that the coaches would say that he had started it. Then the police would charge him, and he would probably end up in jail.

Simonds did nothing.

Holding his dislocated shoulder and enduring the pain as best he could, Simonds said, "Thanks, I really appreciate that." He stared at the perpetrator, who said, "It's good seeing you back in town. Don't stay too long."

And then the coach left, laughing.

60

The Next Generation

When Walker Lambiotte was chaperoning high school star Chris Corchiani around the campus, making him feel at home, promoting Valvano and the N.C. State basketball program, he told Simonds, "I feel like a fraud telling Corch all this stuff when I know in my heart it's not true and that State is the absolutely wrong school for this kid."

But Lambiotte feared that if he said, "Don't come here because you'll get burned," and Valvano found out, he would be playing basketball in Siberia, his career would be over. Finished. Kaput.

That fall, before he left N.C. State, John Simonds ran into Corchiani outside the gymnasium. Simonds had gone there to pick up his ACC championship ring. When he exited, he was grim-faced because, instead of the notation "31" that Valvano had promised would be inscribed on the ring, it said "Manager," and he was feeling demeaned.

As Simonds was walking down the steps, he saw Corchiani, also looking sad. They had become friends working out in the weight room. Corchiani had confided in Simonds, complaining how lost he felt, that he was getting picked on by the black players, who were forcing him to start fights. Corch wondered whether he hadn't made a mistake, but Simonds, despite his problems with Valvano, despite the names Valvano had called him—liar, cheat, traitor—despite the "motherfuckers" Valvano had attached to those names, still could not be disloyal to the program.

When they met outside the gym this time, the two hadn't seen each other for a while because Stewart had barred Simonds from using the weight room. Corchiani said, "John, I heard what happened to you. They really screwed you." John nodded.

Corchiani said, "You know, John, I signed my life away for the next four years to a guy who is nothing like the guy who came to see me when I was playing last year in high school."

"I can't even find V to talk to him," he said. "One of the promises he made was, 'All you have to do is just grab me. I'll put everything else down to talk you.' But he's on the road so much, I can never find him. And once I finally get to talk to him, I don't get to say anything. He does all the talking, and I leave more frustrated than when I went in there."

Simonds felt terrible for Corchiani. He genuinely liked Corch, a nice kid who had been sheltered in high school, coached by his father, taught the right values, and played for the love of the game.

Simonds thought, "Isn't there anyone to help the Corchianis, the Walker Lambiottes, the Andy Kennedys, the Kenny Drummonds, the Teviin Binnses, and the others who fall for the promises and lies, who are ruined because they expect coaching and guidance and instead are left to stagnate and fall by the wayside? What can they do to keep from falling into a trap from which there is no good exit? Who can the high school players ask?"

Simonds listened to Corchiani talk about how unhappy he was. Then Corchiani noticed that Simonds was wearing his ACC championship ring. His face lit up like a little kid. Like most of the basketball players, there was a lot of little kid in Corchiani.

"You must be really proud of that," Corch said, examining the ring. The statement was made with genuine honesty.

Simonds almost burst into tears. His eyes welling up, he said, "No, Corch, I'm not."

Corchiani looked at him and said, "I'm sorry." Simonds said, "Yeah, so am I," and walked away.

61

Epilog

In a program where the university makes millions of dollars and the coach makes a million a year himself from the talent of its basketball players, what can an athlete reasonably expect to receive from his four years at North Carolina State University? Only one of two things really: either an education, symbolized by a diploma; or the chance to have his skills honed and polished to enable him to play professional basketball and earn millions of dollars himself.

Of the fourteen basketball players on the 1986–87 N.C. State team, one, Vinny del Negro, has graduated, and perhaps one other will also graduate. Some critics of the present state of college basketball have suggested that the graduation rate for athletes at every college be made public. The NCAA only prints the *total* averages. It's clear why it won't do it by school: because schools like N.C. State will look bad. This is why Proposition 42 should be passed. The only way to keep a college coach from taking an atrocious high school student is to force the student to do enough work in high school to be eligible to play in college. Without such a law, nothing will ever change.

Below is a rundown of what the N.C. State players are doing on the basketball court. Two, Shack and Vinny, are pros, and Chucky Brown probably will be one. As for the rest, whether some of them will be scrapping for semi-pro paychecks and ultimately end up working the night shifts at 7-11, only time will tell.

Chucky Brown, who began developing into a star during the last part of the season, continues his progress and is expected to be drafted by the NBA when he leaves college.

Avie Lester, who played behind Shackleford, became the center for the Wolfpack in 1988–89.

Brian Howard, who had intended to transfer along with Andy Kennedy and Walker Lambiotte, correctly concluded that if they left, there would be room for him, and he has become an important member of the N.C. State team.

After Quentin Jackson arrived at N.C. State as a freshman, Valvano reportedly told him, "You have to sit your first two years, and you'll start as a junior." But in his junior year he continued to sit when Valvano brought Kenny Drummond from JUCO ball in California.

Only when Drummond quit did Jackson finally get the opportunity to play, and when he got that chance he helped lead N.C. State to the ACC championships. Based on his past performance, Quentin fully expected to start his senior year, but on day one Valvano handed the ball to freshman Chris Corchiani and made Corch floor leader.

"The Italian connection," said a teammate. "That was it for Q."

Quentin took a job with the Harlem Globetrotters and is presently playing around the world.

The other guard, Kelsey Weems, had also badly wanted to transfer, but a player needs a 2.0 average to leave, and Kelsey's grades didn't measure up. At the end of the 1987–88 season Kelsey left school for a semester "for personal reasons." He returned for the spring semester of the 1988–89 season and was the sixth man on the team. But he never did fulfill his potential as a basketball player.

Said a teammate, "Kelsey was as talented a player as anyone, fast, quick as a rabbit, a great player if put in the right program. At Georgetown, he would have been a star. But he's another guy who goes to State, no one hears from him for four years, and now he's back home without a degree and without basketball. What's he going to turn to?"

After senior Bennie Bolton finished his four years of basketball at State, he decided to remain in school and get his degree. After completing the fall semester, he was in his room at the College Inn one day and got a notice from the athletic department that he would have to pay rent for the time between the end of fall term and the beginning of his spring semester, about three weeks.

Reportedly, Bennie said to Valvano, "What's the deal with the three weeks rent?" Valvano said, "It's NCAA regulations." Bolton said, "Is this a new regulation?" Valvano said it was not.

But Bennie, as a player, had always stayed in his room during Christmas vacation, and he had never been charged for rent before. He reportedly asked, "Why do I have to pay now? Just because I'm not playing anymore?"

Valvano told him, "You have to find another place to stay. We need the room for an athlete."

A teammate said Bolton got so angry he quit school, forsaking his degree. Valvano begged him to return, but he wouldn't. A converted Muslim, Bennie had considered playing for the Harlem Globetrotters, but he knew he was unsuited temperamentally to be a Globetrotter. On last report, he was trying to get a professional contract overseas.

Mike Giomi, whose NBA future seemed assured when he was playing at Indiana, signed a contract to play professionally in France.

Of the three transfer students, Walker Lambiotte, Kenny Drummond, and Andy Kennedy, all had to sit out their 1987–88 seasons and all played well for their new schools in 1988–89. Walker seems happy at Northwestern, and Drummond, who transferred to High Point College, has not given up hope of playing pro ball, though he says that being accepted at High Point gives him a second chance for a college degree even more than another chance to play pro ball.

At the end of the 1986–87 season, Drum placed his name for consideration in the NBA draft but was not chosen. Drummond is convinced that it was Valvano's bad-mouthing him to the NBA scouts that kept him from being chosen.

Drummond says he will play college basketball one more year, and "if something happens, fine. If not, life goes on."

Andy Kennedy transferred to the University of Alabama at Birmingham. Gene Bartow, the coach, had recruited him out of high school, and as Kennedy wanted to get away from the lights and the hoopla, he went to UAB. "I just wanted a coach who would be honest with me," he said.

During the summer of 1987, while he was practicing on a schoolyard court, Kennedy went up for a dunk, and when he came down he ripped his right knee to shreds. After going under the knife, Kennedy spent the fall trying to build back his knee, hoping to be able to resume his college career where he left off.

"If I had hurt my knee at N.C. State, I'm not sure I would have still had a place to go to school," said Kennedy. "Once they had lost their use for me, I would have been gone from the team on a medical release. I don't see how the coaches live with themselves. How can they play with people's lives like that?"

Miraculously, Kennedy rehabilitated his knee to the point where he could play, and in 1988–89 he led UAB to the N.I.T., losing to St. John's.

Vinny del Negro, another player who didn't get to play at all until his junior year, went on to have an excellent 1987–88 season, and he was drafted in the second round by the Sacramento Kings.

Charles Shackleford in 1987–88 led N.C. State to an NCAA bid, but as occurred the year before, N.C. State lost in the opening round to a team it should have beaten one-handed, powerful Murray State. At the end of the year, Shackleford put his name up for selection for the NBA draft.

For those who watched him play in 1986–87, it came as a surprise when the New Jersey Nets selected him in the second round. Shackleford signed a two-year guaranteed $300,000 deal with the Nets.

Said a teammate, "I knew he was leaving. I knew as soon as Shack improved his game to where he was good enough to be a pro, he was gone. He was just looking to make money, and then he was gone. College was a steppingstone."

"Some guys, I don't know," said another teammate. "The good guys don't make it any more. That's what it seems to me."

Teviin Binns, who left State after two years without ever getting the opportunity to show his ability, had an NBA tryout, was cut, made the Palm Beach team in the United States Basketball League, was released and played one game for the Jersey Shore Bucks, coached by Henry Bibby. When Bibby was hired to coach the Oklahoma team in the Continental Basketball Association, Teviin was invited to be on the team. But he failed to make that team as well. He's home now, disillusioned. Coaches tell him that having languished on N.C. State's bench, he's two years behind in experience.

Of all the players, Teviin is the most bitter about his N.C. State experience. After the Florida game, Valvano asked Teviin to come and see him. When Teviin showed up, Valvano was out on the road. They never did have that meeting.

Teviin says, "Before I signed with State, my coach at home, Evander Ford, told me, 'Don't do it.' Another coach, told me, 'V just uses players like a meat rack. He just goes and gets them when he needs them.' I said, 'No, he ain't like that, man.' And when I go home, those coaches don't even want to talk to me. They get that look in their eye. Because they tried to tell me, and I didn't listen.

"Coach Ford told me, 'I told you not to go to N.C. State, because if you had gone anywhere else in the world, you'd be in the NBA right now. I told you how he treats his players.'

"But I was blind. I didn't know the other part of him. I only saw the fun and games. You see him on TV and you say, 'I'd love to play for him.' But when the camera lights go out, it's a whole different thing.

"Man, I never thought this was going to happen. Nobody who knew me coming out of junior college could have guessed this would happen.

"He's going to fall one day, 'cause bad things always keep going. One day V's going to fall. One by one he's destroying people. Last year he brought in Sean Green. He left, too. The team went to Hawaii, and he ain't played but two minutes out of the whole tournament, and he left and went to Iona. V lied to him, too, about playing time.

"And people don't say nothing about that. No one

ever says, 'Why do so many athletes leave your team, V?' They don't never ask him that. You know why? They don't care. It's Tobacco Road down here, boy. All they want is the hoopla and what's going around when basketball season rolls around. It's like a religion.

"But he is messing with people's lives. I know that. He changed mine. It's been rough, real rough."

The Fallout from *Personal Fouls*

As I write this, the 1990 NCAA basketball championships are underway, one year and two months after the initial controversy surrounding the *Personal Fouls* dust jacket. North Carolina State's Wolfpack wasn't eligible to play this year. The school was banned from the tournament because after the publication of the dust jacket, N.C. State coach Jim Valvano asked the NCAA to investigate his program in much the same way that Democratic presidential candidate Gary Hart asked the press to "follow me." When the NCAA caught some of the State players breaking some of its blatantly unfair rules, as part of its punishment N.C. State was ordered to stay home come tourney time.

At the time Valvano made his request for the NCAA to investigate his program, my Raleigh sources tell me he was boasting that my book, *Personal Fouls*, would never see print. He and his North Carolina allies certainly had reason to believe they had the clout to keep the book from being published. Once they successfully pressured Simon & Schuster, one of the most powerful publishers in the world, not to publish *Personal Fouls*, I doubt if anyone really thought the book would ever see print. As an attempt at censorship, well, even the Ayatollah Khomeini had waited until after *Satanic Verses* had been published to try to keep that book from being read. Every day I thank God for Kent Carroll and Herman Graf. Every day I thank God that I live in America.

Since the publication of *Personal Fouls* in late July of last year, the book and I have both been swept along by the competing tides of history, public opinion, myth, and outright distortion by Valvano, his attorney and agent,

Art Kaminsky, and by certain adherents of big-time basketball. In this final chapter I shall attempt to relate the saga of *Personal Fouls* as I lived it, but first I wish to make a couple of general comments about the institution of college basketball:

After researching *Personal Fouls*, doing media appearances, debating coaches, and hearing opposing viewpoints, I am of the opinion—more strongly than ever—that the collegiate athletic system for some money-making Division I schools as run by the NCAA can be an out-and-out con game perpetrated on gullible kids. Yeah, these youngsters get to play the game they love in front of thousands of people in flashy arenas, get seen on TV by their buddies and loved ones, and get to hobnob with rich alums, and yes, maybe they get a free stereo, a fancy new car, or make a few thousand bucks under the table. But as long as they don't end up with a diploma—and most of them don't—whatever crumbs they end up with turn out to be of little value compared with the booty they generate for the NCAA and its member colleges: fifty million dollars a year in net revenues. And what token cash they may be clever enough to scam—peddling their free Nikes, selling tickets to boosters, getting money for nonexistent jobs, extorting money from coaches unwilling to lose them to the pros—it is embarrassingly poor compensation compared to the five hundred thousand to one million dollars a year made by the nation's most successful coaches.

It's time for these young hoopsters to wise up and for the parents of these performers to wake up. The time has come to rise up against the people running this outrageous scam. The toil of thousands of talented, predominantly black kids is making a lot of very smart white guys very rich. If I remember my American history, it's precisely the system that financed the Southern plantations before the Civil War. The only difference is that the sharecroppers aren't picking cotton on national television.

The other major truth that struck me is that the sports media doesn't care whether these kids get an education any more than the coaches seem to. When the book's dust jacket came out, I wrote that not a single player on Valvano's team had graduated. Vinny del Negro howled. He said he had graduated and had a diploma to prove it.

Okay, one guy had graduated. Congratulations. The university spokespeople then threw in some doubletalk designed to cloud the truth further about State's abysmal graduation rate.

Where was the media outcry that *only* one player had graduated? There was none. Where was the perusal by the local media at any institution across America as to whether these kids are getting an education or just being used for their talent?

I dare the sports journalists to go back and find the players of five years before at just about any top-rated college basketball team, and see how many have graduated and what they are doing now. Does anyone care if a kid is working nights at a convenience store and is doomed to a life of hard toil, in large part because no one at his university cared about him enough to make sure he got his degree? Does anyone care if a kid ends up dealing dope because he doesn't have the education to do anything else? Do any of these writers care about anything but jump shots and foul-shooting statistics? Do any of the athletic directors wonder what happened to these young men who just happened to generate millions of dollars for their school's athletic department? Do any of the chancellors?

I understand why education doesn't interest the sports media. On newspapers there are beats. There are sportswriters. There are education writers. Few sportswriters care about education. Few education writers care about sports. So few write about it. And you can't cover an education the way you can cover a ballgame. An education is hard to see. The competition is in the mind and in the library. What makes the task more difficult is that most coaching staffs do everything they can to make sure journalists find out as little as possible about the kind of education their kids are getting.

An education doesn't have a point spread. You can't bet on a kid's education, though there might be money in it for the boys in Las Vegas if a betting line were established on whether a particular player graduated or not.

We should allow bets on whether, say, Kenny Anderson of Georgia Tech gets his degree. I can hear the expert making the line on Anderson. "In his favor: He goes to Georgia Tech, a good school. He's a bright kid.

Against him: It's ACC, he travels a great deal, and he's sure to make it in the pros, so maybe he'll let his studies slide. The line: 3 to 2 against." Maybe then alums and bettors will take a rooting interest in his education, as those who bet that he will graduate make sure he goes to classes and studies hard for tests and keep him on course.

The major event that convinced me that the basketball reporters didn't care about educational issues came from the resignation of N.C. State chancellor Bruce Poulton three weeks after *Personal Fouls* was published.

The first direct result of the book's publication was that Poulton was forced into resigning because it was eminently clear to everyone that what the administrators and professors said in *Personal Fouls* was true: Poulton had abrogated his duty to protect the educational integrity of North Carolina State University by allowing the athletic director and basketball coach Jim Valvano to operate without constraint.

As a result of Poulton's flagrant dereliction of duty, the coaching staff—not the admissions department—had admitted substandard candidates to play basketball, had license to doctor grades to keep them in, and generally had subverted the academic standards of the institution for the primary purpose of winning basketball games.

You would have thought the resignation of Poulton would have driven the sports media to campaign for academic integrity, to use the fall of Poulton as an important lesson for other colleges. Except in North Carolina, which covered every nuance of the Jim Valvano story, the story barely registered in the press nationally, despite the fact that Poulton was one of the six chancellors around the country last year who lost their jobs because of irregularities in athletic departments.

Why was there no press clamor to sound a clarion call to protect the rights of these student athletes from a basketball program that was, in effect, preventing them from getting the education to which they were entitled? Even if a writer didn't believe a single word I wrote, the issue still existed.

Go back to my introduction. The players I had interviewed had experienced the "why." It's because with few exceptions no one sincerely cares about these kids except to use them as a means to boost careers, athletically or journalistically. These kids are around for between two to four years and then, poof, they are gone, and the coaches and press get a whole new crew on campus. It's all so transitory—all that's lasting is the effect on the starry-eyed kids who finish college with their dreams shattered and end up with a lifetime of bitterness.

Coaches have said in the media that they are paid to coach basketball and are not responsible for their players ending up with an education. Poulton defined Valvano's role in those words. He believed in a separation of athletics and education. So did Valvano. It was a major reason why so few of their athletes ever graduated.

Sadly, they are not alone. Maybe we have to force chancellors, athletic directors, and coaches to do right by their players. Perhaps we should pay coaches according to how many players graduate in addition to how many games they win.

At N.C. State, coaches spent hours trying out ways to help their players *avoid* having to do the work. If they had spent that much time tutoring them and making them learn reading and writing and math skills, perhaps *Personal Fouls* would never have been written at all. In programs where coaches have no confidence that their players can do the school work, their players will never get the education they deserve.

If a coach takes a youngster into his program, he has an obligation to make sure he gets a reasonable shot at getting an education. When I appeared on talk shows, listeners continually would call up and say, "It's enough that these kids get to go to college at all. That's reward enough. If it weren't for basketball, they'd never go to college in the first place."

But what real value is college for a kid steered by a coaching staff into dead-end courses, guts, and courses taught by professors willing to give high grades just because the student is an athlete? What is that student athlete prepared to do after an educationless education?

I would argue that a kid who goes through several years of college without getting an education may be worse off than if had he not gone at all, because when he went in, his expectations were that college would be the key that would somehow open the magic door to success. When he finds out otherwise, bitterness dogs him the rest of his days. His spirit is crushed. I can say this firsthand. I have seen the tears and the pain and the sorrow over lost youth and missed opportunity.

If a university is unable to educate an athlete, it has two choices, it seems to me. The first choice is to admit he doesn't belong in college and kick him out. If the university does that, it is treating him like any other student.

But if the university decides to keep him on solely because he is a means of making a ton of dough for the athletic department, then it has to be honest enough to admit that the player is there solely to provide entertainment for alumni and fans. The university has admitted he is not getting an education in return for his services. The alternative then is to pay the athlete what he is worth, in the same way the Knicks and Lakers and Celtics pay their players.

If a university can't educate him, then it has to pay him. One or the other—school him or pay him. End the hypocrisy. Be honest. Admit to the world that college basketball has nothing to do with education but rather is an activity which has been set up to raise money for the university. If a university desires a booster club to raise ten million dollars, that's fine. But under the revised system, the players ought to get their fair share of the loot. Every kid who leaves a financially successful program should leave rich, just like the coaches. There's enough money to go around. If a team gets to the NCAA playoffs, the players should divvy up the swag, just like World Series winners. Why should a coach leave with $500,000 to go to another opportunity and the kids leave with but a bitter taste in their mouths?

Pay them or educate them. Perhaps if the colleges discover how expensive it will be to pay them, they will opt to set up special programs that will lead to these young men getting degrees. Senators Bill Bradley and Tom McMillan and other members of Congress who care about these kids must intensify the pressure on the seemingly uncaring NCAA.

As a result of political pressure, and perhaps because of the stink raised by *Personal Fouls*, the NCAA—kicking and screaming—passed a rule forcing each member college to divulge its graduation rates. This was after years of the NCAA dragging its feet on the issue. The NCAA also reduced the number of basketball games. It talked about a greater emphasis on educating its players. It talked, for the first time, about putting the student back in "student athlete."

That's fine, but the NCAA and school chancellors can do more. The NCAA rule book is a foot thick, and mostly it talks about prohibitions of players taking freebies. There should be a foot-tall chapter on dos and don'ts pertaining to the role of the institutions in the education of their athletes: No more shortcuts like doctored grades and sham courses. No more tutors writing papers for the athletes. No illiterate student athletes beyond freshman year.

The NCAA should force colleges to set up legitimate programs to teach your athletes how to read and write and learn. And if the NCAA won't, then someone must make them.

If coaches are really teachers, like many of them profess, then they should be prime movers in instructing the players in the value of an education, and they should be asked to teach them the values that go along with the sport—teamwork, sacrifice, fun, self-control, discipline. Tell the players of the self-defeating nature of a basketball-first attitude for most of our young men.

Why doesn't the NCAA do anything about the spate of felonies and misdemeanors committed on too many campuses by too many student athletes? Perhaps the NCAA should make coaches responsible for the actions of their players both on and off the court. After all, it's the coach who brought those players onto the campus in the first place.

Why shouldn't the NCAA outline a standard philosophy for coaches to pass on to their players? "Teach your players values. Teach them right from wrong. Teach them not to beat up women, not to steal, not to vandalize. Teach them the responsibility of being a role model for young kids in the community." Then when a kid busts up a fraternity, the coach can't say, "I have no responsibility for what the kid does off the court."

If a college program does its job and gives its players an education, the pressure for the athletes to make money on the side will ease, because the players will understand that they will make all the money they need later, whether or not they make the pros.

Often I am asked whether my experience surrounding the publication of *Personal Fouls* taught me anything. The most shocking lesson was that even if you write something you know to be true, there's no guarantee it will be published. Book critics always talk about how controversy sells and makes the writer so much money. They never talk about how difficult it is to get controversy published, or the psychic cost of the pounding you take during the fight to publish.

The concerns of lawyers have always been a big part of the world of publishing. Editors don't make final decisions. Lawyers do. And the bigger the publisher, the more lawyers it employs. The more lawyers, the less chance for publication.

One of the questions most often asked me has been "Why didn't Pocket Books publish *Personal Fouls*?" To this day I don't really know why. And I suspect the real answer will never be revealed. I know what the Pocket Books lawyers and editors told me. It's just that I never believed them.

I can say that what started the panic of the executives in the suits and the spiral toward demise was a series of threats in letters made by lawyers for North Carolina State University, Jim Valvano, and the Wolfpack Club, asking for millions of dollars in damages if *Personal Fouls* were published and found to be libelous.

In a letter sent to Richard Snyder, chairman and chief executive officer of Simon & Schuster and to Bender, vice president and general counsel of Simon & Schuster the office of the North Carolina attorney general wrote:

January 10, 1989

Gentlemen:

"We are counsel for North Carolina State University and are writing in connection with your plan to distribute *Personal Fouls* by Peter Golenbock on January 23, 1989. Our preliminary investigation leads us to believe that North Carolina State University can establish the following facts in connection with Mr. Golenbock's book:

1. Mr. Golenbock's "source" was an employee of NCSU who was dismissed for misconduct.

2. Mr. Golenbock did not have any conversations with Coach Valvano, any member of his staff, any other officer of NCSU, or any officer of the NCSU Wolfpack Club to determine the accuracy of the information provided by his source.

3. Mr. Golenbock did contact some former members of NCSU's basketball team. He, however, represented to those student athletes that he was writing a story for a national magazine about student athletes who had transferred from one institution to another. In the course of his conversations with these student athletes, Mr. Golenbock did not address the substance of the allegations about Coach Valvano, NCSU, and the Wolfpack Club apparently contained in *Personal Fouls.* On at least two occasions, Mr. Golenbock offered players money in exchange for "dirt" about the basketball program. The players had no knowledge of any "dirt" and declined Mr. Golenbock's unethical offer.

4. On one occasion, Mr. Golenbock pilfered the files of NCSU's student newspaper.

5. Representatives of Simon & Schuster have distributed a proof of the cover of *Personal Fouls* to bookstores. Statements contained in that proof are demonstrably false. Specifically:

a. Grades of players were not "fixed" by Coach Valvano or any member of his staff. They, in fact, have no control over the grading process for student athletes.

b. Other college officials and professors have not "fixed" grades for student athletes. Grades have been properly awarded to student athletes in accordance with the process that applies to all students.

c. The results of drug tests of student athletes have not been kept "secret so that players would not be suspended." We are sure that you are aware of the privacy issues associated with drug testing programs and appreciate the value of voluntary, confidential, nonpunitive drug testing programs. Further, drug testing results go directly to the team physician.

d. Wolfpack Club has not "secretly distributed" funds to the NCSU or Coach Valvano. Wolfpack Club funds are regularly audited by both the Wolfpack Club and NCSU to assure that those funds are properly expended.

e. Players have not received "drugs, cars, gold jewelry, even chemicals to mask the presence of drugs" through the actions or inactions of Coach Valvano or any other NCSU officer or employee. Coach Valvano, in fact, has in place procedures designed to assure compliance with NCAA regulations.

f. One member of NCSU's 1986–87 basketball team has graduated and several others are on track to graduate.

In our opinion, these facts form an adequate nucleus of facts to establish a libel claim against Mr. Golenbock, Pocket Books, and Simon & Schuster. In order to avoid any further damage to NCSU, we request Simon & Schuster (1) to provide NCSU with Mr. Golenbock's manuscript; (2) to defer distribution of *Personal Fouls* until such time as NCSU is provided a full and fair opportunity to demonstrate to you the falsity of Mr. Golenbock's statements; and (3) to announce publicly that the distribution of *Personal Fouls* has been deferred. We would appreciate your prompt response.

Very truly yours,
Lacy H. Thornburg
Attorney General

The letter was also signed by Andrew A. Venore, Jr., chief deputy attorney general and Edwin M. Speas, Jr., special deputy attorney general, and a copy sent to Chancellor Bruce R. Poulton

When the letter arrived at the Simon & Schuster offices, the lawyers rushed to caucus. To me the letter was so filled with lies and innuendos that it was ludicrous—except that because it came on the letterhead of the state attorney general, it was no laughing matter. The wording of the letter made it clear to me that Valvano had met personally with the authors of the letter. He and he alone could have been privy to information that led to some of the wording in the letter.

When I read the letter, I pondered the first four points one by one. Point one was talking about John Simonds, who not only had never been an NCSU employee, because Valvano had never carried through on any of his promises to give John the scholarship he deserved, and he had never been dismissed for misconduct. He had simply never been rehired the next year because Valvano was so angry John had aided Walker Lambiotte in his decision to leave the university.

As for points two and three, how the heck can you have a conversation with a man who has no intention of telling you anything except to say either "It never happened" or "I didn't know about it"? And once one of Valvano's coaches deliberately dislocated Simonds' shoulder, I decided I would get my information, even if I had to use a cover story and pay a few hundred bucks to sources who demanded it. As for offering players money for "dirt" about the basketball program, he made that up, as he did the charge of my pilfering files from the office of the student newspaper.

To this day no one has refuted a single charge made on the dust jacket. NCSU has had plenty of time to prove the "'falsity" of my charges. To date, neither they nor anyone else have done any such thing.

Nevertheless, S&S was taking the threat very seriously. I had to play for the lawyers the tapes of all my conversations so they could be certain what was on the tapes was matched by the transcripts. Still, everyone was confident the book would be published, but after Simonds went on TV, the book was put on hold. Five weeks later, S&S called me to a meeting to give me their final decision.

I suspect something more was at stake besides the fear of getting sued and having to pay out millions of dollars, because it's not easy to win a libel suit. Because Valvano is a public figure, he either would have had to prove that what I wrote was false, that I knew it was false and I published it anyway, or that I had a reckless disregard for whether or not it was false.

The university had even less chance of wining a libel suit since I was painting a scenario of a college chancellor who was subverting the system in order to win basketball games. I had plenty of information from administrators, professors, and players to document what was going on.

If I played the tapes of my conversations in court, I knew I'd win no matter who sued.

So why the hesitation on the part of the Pocket Book lawyers? I felt to my bones that something else was going on, that this whole to-do was bigger than one book about one basketball program

The smell of political infighting was in the air. Gulf & Western owns Simon & Schuster and Pocket Books. I knew that Gulf & Western executives were involved in whether Pocket Books would ultimately publish the book or not. I knew the Pocket Books officials were sending memo after memo to the public relations department of Gulf & Western. I even met the PR woman, so I knew G&W was involved, if only on that level.

There was gossip, a lot of it: Gulf & Western owns Madison Square Garden as well as Simon & Schuster, and it was rumored that G&W was worried that the publication of *Personal Fouls* might hurt its profits made from college basketball in the Garden. There was also talk that Al Bianchi, general manager of the New York Knicks, which is also owned by Gulf & Western, wanted Jim Valvano to coach the team, and that the publication of *Personal Fouls* would prevent his appointment. Everything reeked of politics. One rumor had Valvano and U.S. Senator Jesse Helms lined up together to fight the charges. Another rumor had North Carolina governor Jim Martin in Valvano's corner. There was also a rumor floating around the publishing world that Simon & Schuster head Dick Snyder was trying to stick it to Jack Romanos, the man who set *Personal Fouls* in motion, so that by killing the book he was punishing Romanos.

I shall never find out the real reason. All I know is that they refused to publish the book, and then when *Personal Fouls* was published by Carroll & Graf, not a single lawsuit was filed by anyone and shortly after publication, Poulton was forced to quit and Valvano forced to resign as athletic director because enough of the university officials believed what I had written.

How could Simon & Schuster not have published? I shall wonder until I die.

All I know is what the lawyers and editors told me:

that in the end they didn't trust me or my sources, so they pulled the plug. The beginning of the end at Pocket Books came when John Simonds, one of my main sources for the book, went on national television between halves of the North Carolina–North Carolina State basketball game to defend himself. Valvano had derided Simonds in the newspapers by calling him a "water boy" and "jock carrier," seeking to give the impression that he was a questionable source of information about his program. John, sensitive to the criticism, was trying to defend himself and he did so eloquently.

Unfortunately, when he did so, one of the top Pocket Books editors went berserk. He called me up late that evening, repeating over and over, "What are John Simonds' motives for doing this?" I stated why I believed he had done it. "This is very bad," he kept repeating. "I don't know why he did it."

That was the start of the pretext. From that day, all I kept hearing was that it was looking less and less likely Pocket would publish the book. They left me hanging for five weeks. It was clear to me that one editor, Jack Romanos, wanted the book published, but that the lawyers and others in the organization wanted it killed.

As the days went by, lawyers kept knocking out more and more incidents in the book, with reasons that were sillier and sillier. I kept hearing the theme from the "Twilight Zone" in my head.

Finally, my agent—who by my not naming him I shall treat far more fairly than he treated me—and my lawyer, Alan Neigher, and I had a meeting in a large conference room with Pocket Book editors and S&S's top lawyer, John Bender.

When I arrived with my lawyer, no one was smiling. Bender was sporting his usual arrogant air. One editor looked angry. Romanos seemed sad. I was on the verge of tears, only I refused to give them the satisfaction.

Bender smugly informed me that Pocket was not publishing the book because my research didn't stand up to legal scrutiny. Immediately I thought to myself: It certainly was good enough *before* the attorney general of the state of North Carolina threatened to sue the publisher. And it was good enough that the company set the entire book in print, preparing for a January 1989 publication. And it was good enough until the publication of the explosive dust jacket, which put Pocket Books in a bind, because editors admitted they could have published the book if it had toned it down a little, but feared taking that action because it had already made its claims public in the dust jacket.

Since I didn't write or publicize the dust jacket, where was my culpability? I wondered. And who was responsible for leaking its contents to the public? Pocket's dust jacket had "somehow" managed to wind up in a Raleigh bookstore and then appeared on the front page of the January 7 issue of the *Raleigh News & Observer* with a banner headline just above the death of Japanese emperor Hirohito. The whole country was reading the dust jacket that I didn't write, and Valvano and the state of North Carolina were blasting me and the book they hadn't yet read, and it was looking like no one would ever get the chance to read what I had written. Where was justice?

As S&S was talking about my deficiencies, what kept pounding in my brain was one thought, expressed in various ways: What they are saying doesn't make any sense. This is insane. This is crazy. This is unfair. This really sucks.

In that meeting I was feeling faint, and my head was spinning. My life was out of control. And never mind the financial considerations. There were a hundred thousand orders out there. I worried I would never write again. I would forever be known in the trade as the writer of one of the most famous books never to get published.

If Alan Neigher hadn't come with me, I am convinced that John Bender would have buried me for all time. Since Pocket wasn't publishing it, it was either my fault or their fault. They were intending to issue a press release. Alan stepped in to say that he wanted input into the statement. The issue was the language of S&S's statement about why they were not going to publish *Personal Fouls*. You have to understand that I was standing naked in public, about to get my nuts chopped off by the most powerful publisher in the free world.

After hours of negotiation—"If my client isn't happy with your statement, he's going to have to issue his own statement," Alan told them—Neigher got them to tone down their statement some, and they told the public that *Personal Fouls* didn't "meet our professional standards."

My public response was "I stand by my book, and I am confident it will be published in the future." I sincerely believed the former. I wasn't so certain about the latter.

As I left the meeting, I was in a state of shock. I was given but one glimmer of hope and yet another clue that politics may have been involved. As I was walking out of our final meeting, Jack Romanos, who had lovingly steered *Personal Fouls* to completion, put his arm around my shoulder and said quietly, "Don't worry. You'll sell it to another publisher."

But when I mentioned that to my agent, he scoffed. "The manuscript is radioactive," he said. "No one will publish it. Once Simon & Schuster turned it down, no one will take the chance."

"What do I do now?" I asked.

"Start by looking for a job," he said.

A few days later I learned that my agent—without telling me directly—was dropping me as a client.

I went to see a good friend, a book packager and agent, to see if he would represent me. I had done some research for him on a book, we had worked well together, and I had always had a high respect for his opinion.

He said he would represent me for any project but *Personal Fouls*. "It's dead," he told me. "Don't even bother. If you publish it, you'll be sued, and you'll lose, and you'll end up devoting too many years of your life in courts, paying lawyers, not being able to write because you won't have the time or the energy." When *Penthouse* magazine called to say they wanted to publish excerpts from the book, he told me to do it, take the five grand and move on.

I demurred. A dozen frightened administrators, professors, and ball players had put their trust in me to tell this sordid story. They were counting on me. To give up now would be to turn my back on them. I requested that my friend send an edited version of the manuscript to a half-dozen publishers. Alan Neigher advised me to omit the sections that the Pocket Books lawyers had used as their excuse not to publish *Personal Fouls*—a large chunk of some of the most interesting material. I felt that another publisher would possibly pick it up, but without the more than thirty pages the lawyers had objected to and with the specter of that dust jacket still lingering, I wasn't feeling optimistic.

Rather, I was feeling desperate. Several New York sports writers who routinely savage anything I write were having a good chuckle at my expense.

The publishers to whom I had submitted the book, a couple of whom I had been counting on to say yes, looked at the manuscript and were in agreement. Their verdict: "We love the book, but our lawyers have advised us to pass on it, and the decision is out of our hands." Radioactivity, my former agent had called it. My hopes were dwindling. Fast.

Life is funny. They say that for every action, there is a reaction. The trick is to be able to predict what that reaction will be. During this period of waiting during the latter part of April 1989, a time when I would spend the day lying in bed, trying to breathe, the covers over my head, my lawyer received a phone call from the owner of a small publishing house by the name of Kent Carroll.

Out of the blue, Kent had received a letter from the lawyer/agent for Jim Valvano, Arthur Kaminsky, who warned that if Carroll & Graf published *Personal Fouls*, that company would be subject to the same lawsuits that Simon & Schuster had faced. This is the text of that letter:

> Arthur C. Kaminsky, March 8, 1989
>
> Dear Mr. Carroll,
>
> As you may know from reading the newspapers, we represent Jim Valvano, coach of the North Carolina State basketball team. As you may further know (as it has been widely reported over the past two months) that Pocket Books, Inc., had contracted with one Peter Golenbock to write a book concerning the North Carolina State basketball program.
>
> A copy of the book (entitled *Personal Fouls*) jacket was distributed in January and caused an enormous furor as it contained a whole host of sensational allegations. Vigorous protests were lodged with Pocket

Books (and its parent, Simon & Schuster) by myself on behalf of Valvano, and the North Carolina state attorney general on behalf of the University. Presumably, in response to facts raised by us in this regard, Simon & Schuster announced last week that it would not publish *Personal Fouls.* We were gratified.

Now, however, Mr. Golenbock (and his main source, a Mr. John Simonds) have announced without equivocation their intention to seek a new publisher. Should they do so, we shall have no alternative than to pursue vigorously all available legal and equitable remedies. Further, I expect that the state attorney general's office would react similarly to protect the interests of the university.

Of course, I do hope that this communication is utterly unnecessary. Candidly, I cannot fathom why any reputable publisher would want to proceed with *Personal Fouls* given Simon & Schuster's determination that the manuscript failed to meet its standards for publication. Nonetheless, we must remain ever vigilant and fortunately, libel, slander, and defamation lie beyond the pale and are not above the Constitutional freedoms we prize and seek to protect.

Thank you very much.

Sincerely yours,
Arthur C. Kaminsky

cc: Mr. James Valvano, Becky French, Esq.

"Why is he writing to me?" Carroll wondered. His company, Carroll & Graf, primarily published reprints of novels. After making a few phone calls, Carroll had learned that apparently Kaminsky had sent that same letter to many publishers, major and minor, in America.

Kaminsky hadn't counted on two aspects of the ownership duo of Carroll & Graf. First, Herman Graf, who knew that there had been one hundred thousand advance orders for *Personal Fouls*, wasn't the type of man to let an order go unfilled. Second, Graf and Carroll had spent a large part of their careers at Grove Press, where a premium had been placed on fighting for First Amendment freedoms. Grove had published a number of famous books no other publisher dared to print, including Henry Miller's *Tropic of Cancer* and *Tropic of Capricorn.*

When Kent Carrol learned that the letter he received had been received by other editors in other publishing houses, he began to suspect the concerted attempt to keep *Personal Fouls* from being published was not because it was libelous but, on the contrary, because it told the truth.

Kent asked Alan Neigher if we could meet. My books had always been published by major publishers, so I was somewhat skeptical, but on the phone Carroll seemed sincere, and his outrage over Kaminsky's letter seemed genuine, so I agreed to meet with him in New York.

He made it clear that Carroll & Graf couldn't pay what the big publishers could pay. But he said, "If you publish with us, it's only Herman and me and our lawyers. And we have the ability to distribute the book as well as anyone."

At that point, considerations such as the advance money and whether it could become a best-seller were secondary. All I cared was that Carroll & Graf publish it and the sooner the better, regardless of the time of year. I said, "If you publish it the way I wrote it, unexpurgated, uncut, it's yours." He agreed to publish the book in late July or early August, subject to a thorough investigation of my sources by his lawyers. Kent assured me that both Dick Gallen and Martin Garbus were top-rated lawyers whose goal was to publish, not to censor.

Once we shook hands, my anxiety lifted. I wasn't worried about libel. And I was no longer worried about lawyers.

A week later a major publisher offered me $150,000 for the rights to *Personal Fouls*. I turned down the money.

The C & G lawyers, Gallen and Garbus, a nationally known expert on the First Amendment, listened to my tapes and read my transcripts just as Simon & Schuster had. They interviewed John Simonds, the one source willing to be named, just as Simon & Schuster had.

I had one serious problem. After I had submitted my manuscript to Simon & Schuster, it had been set in type, and subsequently a team of proofreaders and editors went over it with great care to correct my spelling and to make sure that every possible fact was checked. It was a month's work, and by the time the manuscript was ready for final printing, hundreds of corrections had been made.

When S&S and I had parted, I was bereft of a copy of that final version of the manuscript. All copies had been kept in a safe because everyone was so afraid Valvano's forces were trying to get a hold of one. I never imagined what ultimately transpired. I had foolishly not kept a copy for myself.

I had asked S&S to return that edited draft to me, so I wouldn't have to go through the effort of rechecking the spelling of every name again, but they refused. Their lawyers want to keep it, I was told. For the lawsuit. "It belongs to us, and we have no obligation to return it to you," they said.

I had the last version I had turned in to S&S, and that was the one I gave to Carroll & Graf. The Carroll & Graf lawyers poured over the manuscript, and they asked me to take out exactly one incident. Everything else they said they felt comfortable leaving in.

After Gallen vetted the manuscript, I asked him, "So why didn't Simon & Schuster publish the book?" He replied, "To be honest with you, I really don't know." Then he added, "But I'm glad they didn't."

Carroll & Graf announced in late April that they were going to publish *Personal Fouls*. In a letter dated May 16, 1989, Lacy H. Thornburg sent the publishing house the same letter it had sent to Simon & Schuster, adding:

"In conclusion, you should also be aware that NCSU is in the process of trying to raise $50 million for the institution. We will hold you and your company responsible for any inability to meet that $50 million goal which is attributable to your publication of libelous materials. We will appreciate your prompt response." It, too, was signed by Thornburg, Vanore, and Speas, with a cc to Bruce Poulton.

Carroll & Graf had a prompt response: "Take a hike." The publisher was risking its existence to publish this book. If they were wrong about me and my sources, and Valvano or N.C. State sued and won, they would be out of business. Sure, they stood to make some money if the book was a big hit, but any of the big publishers could have made the same money publishing a book for which

Simon & Schuster already had one hundred thousand orders.

Who would be willing to take the risk? That was the question. Kent Carroll and Herman Graf were willing. I can tell them now, and I have told them since: Few publishers in the history of the business have shown such courage for their convictions. Any success this book has had is owed to those two very brave and wonderful men.

Carroll & Graf's announcement that it would publish *Personal Fouls* sent shock waves in certain directions. Of the three Simon & Schuster attorneys, one had already left for another firm, and John Bender, the head mouthpiece, had left. Why? I don't know. Maybe the timing was coincidental. One day at lunch Dick Gallen ran into Bender in a restaurant. "Can we talk about *Personal Fouls*?" Gallen asked. "I'd rather not," muttered Bender. End of conversation.

And down in Raleigh, the university and Jim Valvano, smug in the knowledge that *Personal Fouls* would never see print, had been waiting to be cleared of any wrongdoing by investigations by the State Bureau of Investigation and the NCAA.

On January 9, 1989, two days after publication of the S&S dust jacket, Valvano had called for the NCAA to investigate the program. On January 14, the University of North Carolina System President C. D. Spengler announced that Dr. Poulton would conduct an internal investigation of allegations against the basketball program. The scenario was letter-perfect for Poulton and Valvano.

Though charges of wrongdoing from the dust jacket of *Personal Fouls* were heralded in the papers, the only faculty member with the guts to corroborate any of the charges was Richard Lauffer, who told the papers that he had witnessed Valvano change three of Chris Washburn's grades, had told Poulton about it, and was told to mind his own business. The next day Valvano, Poulton, and Washburn all tried to make it seem that Lauffer had made the whole thing up. No one else came forward with any information whatsoever. One former basketball player, Dinky Proctor, called me at Pocket Books to tell me how badly he had been treated at State, but he said he had been so afraid of being identified, at first he called using an alias. He told me he was working at the local 7-11 in Raleigh on the night shift. He said his life was ruined. He said Valvano had done it to him. He said he was sorry, but he didn't have the guts to come forward because he was afraid of what Valvano would do to him. I thanked him for his call.

With critics silent, all Valvano and the attorney general had to do was keep the book from being published, and there would be no basis for findings by either an NCAA or an internal investigation. My sources had indicated that only the coaches and the players had knowledge of most of what I had written. The coaches certainly wouldn't talk. And no player would dare risk his basketball career by talking. Moreover, the NCAA rarely goes after the coaches anyway. It's almost always the players.

As for the internal investigation into Poulton and Valvano's malfeasance, well, Poulton himself was in charge. He was the one who had abdicated his responsibility by handing Valvano absolute power over matters that rightfully should have been his to make. All along I felt Poulton more guilty than Valvano in the running of the basketball program. And here Poulton was conducting the investigation.

It sounds like something out of a dime-store novel, but to conduct this "investigation," who did they hire but the state attorney general, Lacy Thornburg, to find out the "truth" about basketball at N.C. State?

To get to the bottom of the matter, Thornburg's first order of business apparently was to threaten Gulf & Western with its libel lawsuit. I thought: Killing information is a funny way to get to the truth. I wondered for the first time whether I had underestimated the men about whom I had written. Later, when I heard the rumors that Governor Martin and Senator Jesse Helms had lined up on Valvano's side, I suspected this wasn't just about basketball.

Later, the attorney general's office would deny that the threatening letter had anything to do with attempting to keep the book from print. "We just wanted to make sure it was accurate," was the statement.

If that was so, they could have waited until after the book was published to sue.

Still later, I got a letter from Poulton's internal inquiry, called the Poole Commission, asking whether I would share with them any information I had. At first it seemed like a good idea. But then it occurred to me that the office asking for my information—the office of the attorney general of the state of North Carolina—was the same office that had threatened to sue me for libel. Life had become Kafkaesque. I didn't know who were the good guys and who were the bad. I demurred.

On July 18, 1989, C. D. Spengler announced that his investigation had come to an end. He delivered a three-hour oral report from a panel he had handpicked for the inquiry. The Poole Commission, named after Samuel H. Poole, the panel's chairman, announced, among other things, that there was absolutely no evidence of what he called "wrongful grade changing." Spengler said he would publish the full report after deleting the names of the students involved.

Asked if Jim Valvano had cooperated in the investigation, he said, "I can't comment on that."

The Poole Commission's investigators had talked to several of my sources. One told me that one of the State Bureau of Investigation officers had told him, "I admire what you're doing, but you know how it's going to come out." My source sadly agreed that he did. It was clear to me that though the Poole report might cite improprieties by a couple of players as a sop to the press, it was going to be a whitewash of both Poulton and Valvano.

When Spengler announced there would be no written report at all, I chuckled ruefully at their audacity. The *Raleigh News & Observer*—accused by both Poulton and Valvano as an enemy of N.C. State basketball—announced in an editorial: WHITEWASH IN THE *W*ORKS.

Said the editorial, "The absence of such a report would be a clear blow to NCSU's credibility. Further, it would deny NCSU the information it must have to take the remedial action that is necessary to see that all student athletes in basketball and football are students in good standing as well as athletes."

But neither Poulton nor Valvano seemingly were interested in either changing the system or making sure the athletes were in good standing. They seemed happy with the system just the way it was. And apparently they were doing everything within their considerable power to keep it that way, even if it meant stiffing the Poole Commission.

On July 20, 1989, Sam Poole revealed that Valvano had called his current players together and told them not to cooperate in the investigation. He also said Valvano had refused to open up the books of JTV Enterprises to the investigators.

I thought to myself, If this investigation had been legit, the university would have said: Either show us the books or you're fired. But I suspected that Poulton didn't want Valvano's books opened any more than Valvano did.

Asked if Poulton had cooperated, Poole refused to comment. Spengler said he would make his oral report to the board of governors on August 25. It did note that there "are many unanswered specifics" in part because of "the lack of access to information." I thought to myself, The only ones who know are the coaches and the players. If they don't talk, there is no evidence.

Asked Wilt Browning in the *Greensboro News & Record*, "Who's hiding what from whom?" Indeed.

Still others wondered why any investigation was being conducted at all. On July 20 Edward Weisinger, outgoing chairman of the NCSU Board of Trustees, criticized Spengler, charging the investigation was "unnecessary."

The NCAA investigation was just as much a sham. It, too, had begun in January just after the dust jacket appeared. The NCAA has a reputation for being the Gestapo of college sports. One time at the University of Bridgeport, star center Manute Bol was said to have taken a few plane rides and gotten a couple of pairs of pants on the sly, and the NCAA was all over that program like a dog in heat. But when it came to investigating Valvano's program, the NCAA apparently decided to confine its look to what the players were doing—not at what Valvano was doing.

There seems to be an overriding NCAA policy decision that underlies the reason for that. The NCAA's concern is first and foremost about money—making money for itself and its coaches and keeping money away from the players. The NCAA, like some of its coaches, has never seemed to care whether the players get an education or not. And so it seeks evidence of monetary wrongdoing, but doesn't concern itself with the education side of college life.

When Senators Bill Bradley and Tom McMillan, former college and pro basketball players, were pushing a bill to make colleges publish their graduation rates, the NCAA fought them hard, arguing that federal regulation had no place in the world of college sports. The NCAA kept hiding behind an athlete's right to privacy.

I've often thought that all college athletes should be forced to publish their courses and grades. I figure it might make them study harder. If the coaches who are concerned about the players' right to privacy were as concerned about their educational welfare, some of their players might even end up with a diploma.

When the NCAA report ultimately was issued, the sportswriters got a big chuckle over its disclosure that several players had made some money selling their basketball sneakers. Other findings were that the players had sold their tickets to make money and they had gotten some cut-rate jewelry in exchange for tickets.

But again, here was an investigation that found no wrongdoing on the part of the university or the coaching staff.

Later Valvano—and his allies in the media—would cite both these investigations as "proof" that what the players said about him in *Personal Fouls* was false. The scenario had an emperor's new clothes feel to it.

The truly frightening aspect of this whole story is that Poulton, Valvano, Thornburg et al almost got away clean. If that champion of truth and justice, Arthur Kaminsky, hadn't written to Kent Carroll and Herman Graf threatening to sue them, Poulton and Valvano might still be working hand-in-hand at N.C. State, wrecking kids' lives forever.

As it turned out, even with publication of the book, Valvano may still stay on as coach.

When *Personal Fouls* came out on July 28, 1989, the North Carolina papers raced to print the most sensational aspects of the book. Immediately the papers went to their sources to find out if what my sources had told me in *Personal Fouls* was true.

Neither Poulton nor Valvano had any comment. Poulton was said to be on vacation in Maine.

Albert Lanier Jr., vice chancellor for university affairs, gave his reaction: "A quick review . . . indicates the book is a work of fiction and has no relationship to the reality of the fine basketball program at NCSU. Therefore, the university does not find any reason to further address the book—point-by-point or in general." Since Lanier had had nothing to do with the 1986–87 basketball team, the subject of *Personal Fouls*, I was moved to wonder why Lanier had standing to even comment. And yet headlines across the country aped the "work of fiction" line.

Another ally of Valvano, former star player Terry Gannon, also commented on the book. Said Gannon, "From what I heard, this thing is the most talked-about comic book since Captain Marvel hit the stands, and probably much more expensive. It's been unbelievable the things that I heard."

He added, "This guy wrote a book based on research that, if I had done that at N.C. State in history with my papers . . . I'd be pushing a broom right now. I wouldn't have a degree. It's all on hearsay. The manuscript was written by a guy who was a manager, who went on national television, and said he was offered cars, an apartment, money.

"No offense to managers, but you can go in the stands and pull out any Joe and teach him to fold a towel, and you don't have to have any illegal inducements to do that. So the whole thing is kind of absurd to me. If it weren't so serious, it would be laughable."

Like Lanier, Gannon had had no connection to the '86–87 basketball team. Why would reporters go to him? I wondered.

In the same article NCSU player Bennie Bolton, someone who had played on the team I was writing about, said *Personal Fouls* was right on target. Nevertheless, to show balance, to give both sides of the story, Gannon, who had no knowledge of anything in the book, was given the same credibility as Bolton, who was there the whole year. I wondered why reporters didn't call Tim Stoddard or David Thompson or Tommy Burleson? They had as much right to comment as Gannon did.

It was clear early on that the battle of *Personal Fouls* was to be fought in the press, and it was going to be a drawn-out, ugly affair. My Achilles' heel was that because my athlete sources had been so afraid of retribution, they had insisted that their most serious charges be made anonymously in the form of "one player said," or "said a teammate." An easy and effective counter was "Golenbock didn't name him. Why should we believe either him or his anonymous source?"

Before publication, I knew full well that this would present a problem for me. But given the choice of writing it this way or not at all, I chose to do it this way, figuring that the story was important enough to write in the form in which I wrote it. Also, secretly I was hoping somebody out there would have enough guts to come forward and back me up. Even if no one did, I was figuring that the compelling nature of the book's entirety would be powerful enough to force the authorities at least to take a look at what my sources indicated was going on.

A mere three weeks after the publication of *Personal Fouls*, Chancellor Bruce Poulton resigned. *Personal Fouls* had shot his rowboat full of holes, but it was three of his professors who had sunk him. My sources told me that many more would have liked to, but that professors know they are at the mercy of an avenging chancellor. Poulton was used to getting his way, and they were aware that he regularly had used his power to still any opposition.

Fred Smetana, an engineering professor, confirmed some of the incidents on the day after the book first hit the Raleigh streets. I was surprised at Smetana's admissions. He had always been a staunch supporter of Valvano. But he was a guy who didn't see anything wrong with some of the things he and Valvano had done to strengthen the basketball program, and so he wasn't reluctant to talk.

I had written that "someone high in the college administration" had decided to let Charles Shackleford play in mid-term even though Poulton had ruled him ineligible for that term. That's the way my source described it to me, adding that he suspected it had been Poulton. Smetana came right out and identified that person as Poulton. He explained why the Athletics Council had killed a resolution that "athletes must go to class or they don't play."

Explained Smetana, "There were some committee people who felt that it was necessary for these people to play in order for them to have a desire to continue to attend school."

Smetana added, "There is certainly an incentive to win. Athletics are self-financing, and if they do not prove the entertainment value to the public, then the public won't support it. If you don't put on a competitive program, you lose money."

Smetana took issue with Personal Fouls' characterization of the Athletics Council as an apologist for Valvano. "The Athletics Council has no authority to order anything. It is an advisory body to the athletic director and the chancellor." He sure had that right.

If Smetana lit the kindling, Hugh Fuller, the director of NCSU's tutoring program, set the bonfire. I had known that Fuller knew where all the bodies were buried before the dust jacket excerpts had been released in January. I was told he had considered bringing forth his information at the time the dust jacket excerpts had been published, but wouldn't summon the nerve until the publication of the book. When Pocket Books didn't publish, Fuller held his counsel. Once the book was finally out, Fuller felt obliged to speak out.

Fuller's testimony was crucial, because the Poole Commission had already announced that there was absolutely no evidence of what it called "wrongful grade changes." Fuller's testimony indicated there may not have been proof of grade changes per se, but there certainly was proof of just about every other kind of abuse with respect to grades and that Valvano and his coaches were behind it.

Fuller told the *News & Observer* he had tried and failed to end the abuses of the educational system by Valvano's coaches and athletes for years, but had been thwarted at every turn by Poulton. Said Fuller, "I'm willing to be civilly disobedient on this thing. I've already told them at the highest levels. I've written reports to people telling them things are going on that we need to stop, and nobody does anything. The stuff keeps going on and on, and they keep putting the players back out on the gym floor. It's disillusioning."

Among Fuller's charges were:

- One Wolfpack star player was caught cheating on an English test, but still passed the class.
- A player received a final grade of B for a physical education class in bowling even after he had failed to attend any of the classes and was given a temporary "incomplete." Wrote Fuller, "Now, there is some kind of effort to bail him out so he can continue to play basketball."
- A player arrived in class with a paper already prepared and spent the class copying it word for word. When the teacher caught the player and asked him to name his tutor, he said he did not know the tutor's name.
- Players took advantage of the "withdrawal" system. If a player was failing a course, the coaches would arrange for the player to seek a psychological or medical withdrawal. That would allow the player to erase the course from his record. Wrote Fuller, "You have people whose parents and grandparents died several times while in college."
- University officials persuaded instructors to give basketball players who were in academic trouble an "incomplete" instead of a failing grade. The practice allowed an athlete to continue playing even when his grade-point average was lower than the university's rules allowed.

Said Fuller to the *News and Observer*, "There is a definite pattern, no two ways about it. The teachers . . . are duped into it. In most cases these guys [basketball players] don't have the initiative to pull the dupe off themselves. The coaches are behind it. They send them over there and tell them what to say."

In what Fuller described as his "most striking" story, he told of a star player who either showed up in study hall or not at all. One day he came carrying a television set. He didn't want to miss "The Cosby Show."

"We got upset and kicked him out," said Fuller. "A couple weeks later we got orders to reinstate him in study hall, which we reluctantly did." The player, said Fuller, then got suspended from school, but was allowed to return. "They needed him to win," said Fuller.

Fuller alleged that the assistant coaches were always

putting pressure on professors. He said basketball officials told players what classes to take. "One kid's entire schedule was changed to easy courses," he said. The dropped courses were Economics I, Elementary Spanish I, Composition and Reading, and the World in the 20th Century. The substituted courses were Interracial Communication, Foundations of Graphics, Principles and Practices in Industrial Cooperative Training, and General Ceramics.

Wrote Fuller in a memo to Valvano, "There are several important problems with this particular drop/add form. All four of the courses the student wanted to drop fit logically into his program of study and were approved during preregistration by his academic advisor and Dr. [Joe] Brown [head of the athletic tutoring branch of the Academic Skills program.]

"In contrast, the four courses he wanted to add, while they are good courses, do not make sense in the context of his program of study; in fact, it now looks like only one of the courses would count as a free elective, but the other three would not count towards his degree at all.

"Beyond this general concern, I must also point out that it is a university policy that ENG 111 and ENG 112 'must be scheduled in successive semesters until they are completely satisfactory.' Since [the student] has not yet satisfactorily completed ENG 112, he must be enrolled for that course this semester."

Fuller went on to inform Valvano that the course Principles and Practices in Industrial Cooperative Training had three prerequisites, none of which the player had taken.

Concluded Fuller in his letter to Valvano, "How his decision to take courses which will not count towards his degree will ultimately bear on his eligibility to play basketball is not presently clear. What is clear, however, is that he seems to want to disregard our best academic counsel; and that certainly violates the spirit of our effort to do all we can to ensure that our student athletes are making satisfactory progress toward their degrees."

Said Fuller to the *News & Observer*. "They don't care whether they graduate or not—it's a question of whether or not they can be out there on the floor."

As for the players, Fuller said, "These players are not

bad guys. They can do the work. All they need is for somebody to kick them in the ass and have them do the work. That's what is frustrating.

"I don't understand why people can't say, 'We're going to have a good program, we're going to win in the process, but we're going to have these guys doing the work and graduating. I know what a joy it is when it happens. But why can't that be our policy?"

Poulton, conspicuous by his still continued vacation in Maine, did not comment on Fuller's allegations. Neither did Valvano. Nash Winstead, the provost, told reporters, "We were doing anything we possibly could to enhance their ability to graduate." As provost Winstead should have been the one to be appalled. Why hadn't he protected his professors from the pressures put on them by the coaching staff?

Wrote the *News & Observer* in an editorial, "Most disturbing, Valvano and NCSU Chancellor Bruce Poulton have had little to say through all this turmoil. . . . Poulton, particularly, should demonstrate more concern about the integrity of the university."

An editorial in the *Fayetteville Observer* talked not about Valvano's derelictions but of Poulton's. "This is however the chancellor who advocated promotion of Valvano to the position of athletic director and basketball coach in 1986, when there was evidence that the popular coach was disqualified for the position by his lack of due respect for the university's overarching academic mission. That misjudgment and much that came before it with regard to NCSU basketball and what has followed disqualify Poulton for his post as chancellor of this state's leading technical and scientific university."

A cartoonist in the *Charlotte Observer* drew a picture of a hypothetical N.C. State player reading *Personal Fouls* and writing a letter that read: Deer Chancellor Poolton, I jist am riting to xpres my shok an outraje at the ackoozashuns bean made abowt N.C. State Baskitbal. The edjakashunal opertooniteez you an Coch Valvono giv me haz made me the uprite sitizin whut I am now. That Golenbock is a durty kreep an I'l say wurse abowt his book az soon az I find sumone to reed it to me."

The University Board of Governors could choose to

ignore what *Personal Fouls* had to say on that topic. But ignore Fuller? No way.

The pressure on Poulton to quit began to intensify. There also had been sentiment from the Faculty Senate that Valvano should step down as athletic director.

Some members of the University of North Carolina Board of Governors expressed outrage over Fuller's reports of the academic abuses and expressed their desire that Poulton and Valvano both be fired. The Poole Commission report was due to be made public in three weeks' time. Some members suggested that it should be released immediately. But Spengler acknowledged that the publication of *Personal Fouls* had fouled up the timing (and perhaps the content) of his report.

They didn't ask me when they could put the book out, and that's what has caused the resurgence of controversy," said Board Chairman Robert L. "Roddy" Jones.

Spengler, the author of the Poole Commission report, was unavailable for comment.

One unnamed board member called for an immediate release of the findings of the report. "[Spengler] needs to present the information soon, as openly as possible. Otherwise it will churn for three weeks. It will smell worse. When you have a bad problem, you deal with it directly.

"Who is minding the store? State is responsible for what State did, but the general administration is responsible for the way this thing has been handled. The way they're dealing with it is inappropriate."

On August 10, yet another State professor came forward to talk about what he had witnessed. His name is Dr. Frank Smallwood, and he had been chairman of the Faculty Senate during the year I had written about. Smallwood volunteered that even though he had chaired the Faculty Senate, he had not been interviewed by the Poole Commission. He said that during his tenure as chairman, the faculty expressed repeated concerns about Valvano, but that Poulton continually rebuffed them.

"To our knowledge, no action was taken. We'd make recommendations, and the recommendations were found to be unacceptable."

Among those recommendations was the elimination of athletic dormitories and a plan to prohibit students in academic difficulty from playing in extracurricular activities, including sports.

"We were all concerned that student athletes were actually bona fide, legitimate students making progress toward the primary reason they were here—getting an education," said Smallwood, a professor at NCSU's College of Veterinary Medicine. "Our feeling was that these students ought to be devoting attention to what was number one. And that is the basic problem. What is number one?"

And, according to Smallwood, it was Chancellor Poulton who was thwarting the will of a very frustrated faculty. He also said that Valvano had opposed the resolution at a meeting of the chancellor's liaison committee.

Smallwood said he was troubled by the perception that NCSU is dominated by its basketball program. "That perception is a misperception," he said, "and it has hurt this university."

As August 1989 dragged on, stories appeared in the Carolina press every day, with little comment from the usually ebullient Valvano. At a press conference to promote the second Diet Pepsi Tournament of Champions, to be played in the Charlotte Coliseum in December, Valvano told reporters, "I really prefer not to talk about basketball until a time in the future that would be appropriate." He said he thought he might have something to say after the Poole Commission report came out later in the month. When asked again to comment, he joked, "I allow myself four and a half minutes, and then I revert to 'no comments.' Incidentally, I can say no comment in seven languages."

On August 16, Spengler, the president of the University of North Carolina System, met privately with Valvano and others to "seek more information." Spengler would not comment on the meeting. He told reporters he had read *Personal Fouls* and found it to be a "sad" book. He declined to elaborate when asked to interpret the word "sad."

At this point I figured that both Poulton and Valvano, their backs against the wall, were going to mount a counteroffensive, with their lawyers crowing about the lawsuits they were going to win, telling reporters of the tales I had made up, that I had libeled them, that what I had said was in keeping with Terry Gannon's remark about the book being a "comic book."

But both Valvano and the state of North Carolina through the attorney general's office quickly announced there would be no lawsuits. Believe me, I certainly didn't want to face any lawsuits. Lawsuits are time-consuming and expensive, win or lose. But when the twin announcements were made public, my reaction was an odd one. Instead of being elated, I felt furious, because it brought home to me what I had suspected all along—that the threats of those lawsuits were really a naked attempt at censorship. And what made me even angrier, I had told the S&S lawyers that, and they had rebuked me for being naive and cavalier with their money.

As part of Valvano's announcement that he wasn't going to sue, his attorney, Art Kaminsky, opined that Valvano would remain as coach and weather the storm. "It's not even a storm," he said. "It's less than that, it's a mizzle. That's an English term for less than a drizzle." I thought, Kaminsky said it, but it certainly sounds like vintage V.

Kaminsky added, "The guy [Valvano] likes it here. He likes coaching, likes the university, and likes Raleigh. That's where he'll be until something unbelievable comes along that's incredibly attractive." This expression of Valvano's undying loyalty to N.C. State seemed both moving and powerful.

In announcing that the state would not sue, John D. Simmons III, a spokesman for Attorney General Lacy Thornburg, said that "no conclusion should be drawn about the book's contents from the attorney general's decision other than its opinion that nothing in its text meets the legal definition of libel toward N.C. State."

When asked about criticism of the book, unnamed sources and minor errors, Simmons said, "Bad writing isn't against the law." I thought to myself, "and neither is flagrant abuse of the power of the attorney general's office."

Said an editorial in the *Greensboro News & Record:* "Attorney General Lacy Thornburg said this week that after a careful reading of the controversial book *Personal Fouls*, he concluded that N.C. State has no grounds to sue the author for libel. He could have reached the same conclusion a lot quicker by reading the First Amendment."

On August 19, twelve professors, members of the N.C. State chapter of the American Association of University Professors, criticized "the university's leadership" in the wake of the allegations and called for the board of trustees to take immediate action to "correct these abuses and restore North Carolina State University to its proper position in the community and in the nation."

Once again Poulton and his spokesmen were unavailable for comment.

Two days later, on August 21, Poulton resigned, effective at the end of September. In a three-sentence statement, Poulton said, "This summer, in the tranquil embrace of the coast of Maine, my wife and I reflected on our personal situation and concluded in part that the time had come for us to 'step down' from the chancellorship of N.C. State University. Accordingly, I have given President Spengler my resignation.

"Betty and I have enjoyed the privilege of being part of the growth and development of N.C. State University, and we look forward to opportunities to make further contributions."

That night, when Poulton walked from his office on campus to his nearby home after meeting with North Carolina Governor Jim Martin, reporters were waiting. "I really don't have anything to add to what I've already said," he said.

I couldn't help notice how different it had been back in February right after Simon & Schuster announced they would not publish the book. The next day Poulton, in his Wolfpack-red blazer, smugly told reporters the decision by the publisher not to publish *Personal Fouls* was a vindication of N.C. State. This time Poulton didn't mention the book or the book's impact on his decision to quit.

But Robert L. "Roddy" Jones, chairman of the UNC Board of Governors, said that though C. D. Spengler had not asked for Poulton's resignation, the charges raised in *Personal Fouls* had merit. "A lot of what's been written is factual," Jones told the *Winston-Salem Journal*. "They are more than allegations. There are a lot of things that have not yet been written."

That night Governor Martin continued to defend the present NCSU administration. "I have great confidence in N.C. State University and great confidence in Bruce Poulton," he said. When asked, the governor also said he had "great confidence" in Valvano.

The next day, student leaders attempted to meet with Poulton. Brian Nixon, the student body president, said the students were upset that Poulton had not included them in the decision that led to his resignation. "We need to know the real impetus for his resignation," said Nixon. I suspect Nixon is still waiting for an answer.

Later, Poulton, rather than stand up and admit he had allowed Valvano the license to subvert the university's academic standards, instead blamed the *Raleigh News & Observer* for his resignation. "I feel like part of the problem is a personal attack that has been directed at me, and I frankly feel by taking myself out of the situation I might lesson the attack on the university. There are some very clear elements that suggest that at least the local newspaper would prefer that I not be here."

Poulton added that "there simply is no scandal at North Carolina State University, but there has been a tapestry of woven events." He added, "I'm concerned that there are a lot of people in North Carolina that are beginning to wonder if indeed there was a scandal at the university."

It was Poulton who predicted that Valvano would be asked to resign as athletic director. Again, though Valvano was on campus in his office, he declined to comment. Bruce Poulton had gambled his career on giving Valvano whatever he wanted to build a winning basketball team, he had lost, and now the coach had nothing to say.

Said the *Raleigh News & Observer* in an editorial:

> It is a foregone conclusion that Mr. Valvano must give up the athletic director's role, which he never should have held while coaching. But how can a search committee and Mr. Spengler recruit a top-flight administrator for the chancellorship if Mr. Valvano—whose disregard for academic integrity brought down Bruce R. Poulton—remains on campus even as basketball coach? . . .
>
> The coach should be asking himself if he would be

happy coaching under a new athletic director and chancellor who will hold him to a higher academic standard than he has ever known. The microscope will be on the basketball program henceforth. Mr. Valvano may be sure that no more will his players be playing while failing in the classroom, no more will tutors do their work for them, as has been alleged, no more will coaches ask teachers or tutors for favors, no more will students with little or no chance of graduation be admitted.

Would a free-wheeling coach be happy with the brakes on, with his public and private activities under continual scrutiny? Of course not. Mr. Valvano likes the spotlight, when it is flattering and lucrative. When it is not, he doesn't respond too well. He had exploited his position and N.C. State's reputation to enrich himself. Yet when the university asked for something back—namely, his cooperation and that of his team in the investigation by the university system—Mr. Valvano denied investigators access to his private business records and his players stonewalled the investigators.

The coach and his allies are mistaken in blaming their woes on *Personal Fouls*, the book that raised questions about the program. Many of the problems cited in the book—players selling their sneakers or hawking their tickets, for example—probably would not have provided reason enough to bring down a chancellor or an athletic director and coach.

But disregard for a university's academic mission—its very foundation—is reason aplenty, and in the last eight months that disregard has been reported and documented by the *News and Observer*. Memorandums from the files of the university's tutoring program have confirmed flagrant academic abuses by the basketball program. Those allegations have since been supported by faculty members. Now Chancellor Poulton has resigned.

It is an example Mr. Valvano should follow and thus relieve Mr. Spengler and the Board of Governors of the necessity to see that the coach does so.

On August 25th, C. D. Spengler issued his report to a closed session of the Poole Commission and made his recommendations. Among them was that no coach be allowed to remain as athletic director. Valvano, Jeff Mullins, basketball coach and athletic director of North Carolina-Charlotte, and Bighouse Gaines, basketball coach and athletic director of Winston-Salem State University, all were asked to resign one of the positions. Valvano had to quit as athletic director by December 31.

Spengler noted that "the rules have been manipulated in order to serve one overriding purpose: keep the players eligible." He asked that there be more effective drug testing, that booster club books be opened (If their books weren't closed, as I alleged, why would Spengler ask that they be opened?), and that there be a tighter adherence to academic rules.

One surprise recommendation was the return to making freshmen ineligible to play varsity basketball and football. Doing that would go a long way toward acclimating the young athletes into university life. But the entire ACC would have had to vote to make Spengler's recommendation a reality, and that wasn't likely to happen.

Valvano finally spoke in response to his being asked to resign as athletic director. Of that job he said, "I did not seek the job. If I were asked to step down, I would do so in the same spirit in which I took the job. But under my breath I'd tell you we've done a good job."

Seemingly unable or unwilling to comprehend what all the fuss was about, Valvano defended outgoing Chancellor Poulton. "No one deserved what happened and he certainly didn't. It's an absolute travesty of justice. He did nothing wrong. Just the opposite." Valvano said he and Poulton were victims of a news media vendetta.

Trustees and Poulton, in turn, generally supported Valvano and went out of their way to note that they saw little evidence that allegations of grade changing, lavish gifts to athletes, or drug abuse in *Personal Fouls* had occurred.

"I don't think they [trustees] have any serious doubts about him remaining as coach and I hope he does," said Chairman John Gregg.

"I don't see where it incriminates him," said another trustee, Alan Dickson.

Valvano told reporters, "If I was part of the problem,

one of the reasons I'm here today is because I want very much to be part of the solution."

Agreeing to step down as athletic director, he said, "Whether it's true or not, there can be an appearance of a conflict there. And in today's athletic world, you've got to remove that."

Poulton praised Valvano as athletic director and noted Valvano believes basketball players ought to be evaluated as basketball players alone and that he had manipulated rules to help athletes. He said there were "many cases where every opportunity to remain eligible has been pursued.

"I would not call that wrongdoing," Poulton said, which was a prima facie admission of his blind spot to the overriding issue of academic integrity versus professionalism in college sports.

And so Bruce Poulton bit the dust, riding out of town seemingly without a clear understanding that the scandal at N.C. State wasn't about the basketball program as much as it was his handling of it.

Credibility, more than anything, is what a chancellor has going for him. When a crisis arises, he is the one who must take action to control the situation. Only this time he was at the root of the problem. And no matter how hard his supporters tried to hide that fact, it was a conclusion that wouldn't go away. In the end, Poulton pulled a Joan of Arc. He was the victim, a martyr, skewered on the stake of public opinion.

What is hardest to fathom is that Poulton, even at the end, could have saved himself. All he had to say was "We were wrong. It won't happen ever again." But he couldn't bring himself to do that. He also couldn't bring himself to put the blame squarely on the shoulders of the one person who could have taken the heat from him. He was sticking to a course of action which dictated that Valvano and sports be the most important consideration at his university, and when Valvano was accused of coming up short, Poulton didn't have the stomach to ax him. Instead he grabbed his dagger and committed hari kiri—all for the love of winning basketball.

About a month after Spengler issued his report to the Board of Trustees, independent evidence surfaced that certain members of the Poole Commission may have been seeking a whitewash of Valvano.

On August 24, the night before Spengler was to present his report to the rest of the commission, two N.C. State student leaders said they had heard a recorded message left on Valvano's tape machine. According to student Senate President Brooks Raiford, the message, from Robert L. "Roddy" Jones, chairman of the UNC Board of Governors, was:

"Hello, Jimmy. This is Roddy Jones. I tried to catch you at the airport and at the office, but you weren't there. Don't worry about tomorrow."

Student body President Brian Nixon concurred. The two students said the message had concluded with a comment by Jones that began with either "I'll" or "We'll . . . take care of everything."

With regard to Valvano's culpability, the Poole Commission certainly did "take care of everything."

The next piece of funny business occurred when Bruce Poulton attempted to circumvent any change in the athletics program by attempting to name an interim athletic director before departing as chancellor.

At a meeting of the NCSU Board of Trustees on September 23, Trustee Troy Doby, an ally of Poulton's, introduced a motion authorizing Poulton to name the new athletic director. Poulton was intending to name Nora Lynn Finch, associate athletics director in charge of non-revenue sports, to the post. Critics said Valvano wanted Finch because he could control her, but the issue became moot when Trustee Dan Gunter thwarted the move by insisting that the resolution take effect October 1, a day after Poulton's scheduled departure.

The debate occurred despite the fact that the UNC Board of Governors had made it clear that the interim chancellor, not Poulton, make the appointment. Poulton nevertheless insisted the prerogative was his. "I am chancellor of the university until October 1, and will administer the university as I see fit," he said.

But Samuel Poole said that Poulton should not make any appointments. "I would see anything done by Chancellor Poulton at this point as being lame-duck action, and I would not think that would be very wise," said Poole. "Whoever comes in—and we know now that is

[Larry] Monteith—ought to come in with the full authority to do his own thing with the administration, including not only filling those vacancies but, if he sees fit, removing some people from administrative positions and filling them with other people."

Checkmate.

When the NCAA findings came out in early September, Poulton continued to defend his coach. His loyalty never wavered. He crowed that though violations by athletes had been found, he was pleased that many of the more serious violations in *Personal Fouls* had not been substantiated, despite evidence to the contrary.

Said Poulton, "There's nothing in what the NCAA has been able to uncover that led them to inquire . . . into changing of grades [had the NCAA interviewed Hugh Fuller or Dick Lauffer, it might have found something], millions of dollars of secret money [I never charged that. I said that Valvano had control over the millions from the Wolfpack Club to spend it any way he saw fit. I said that if he wanted to pay players, no one could stop him because no one was looking over his shoulder. Valvano, to make the statements seem foolish, chortled about the ridiculousness of his distributing millions of dollars to players], gifts of automobiles [where did they think Shack got his expensive car?], secret drug tests [my players didn't say they were secret, only that they were rigged], etc."

Poulton's defense after the NCAA findings was his last stand. At the end of September he departed the scene, still muttering about the vendetta by the press. He was replaced by interim Chancellor Larry Monteith, an educator who proclaimed his dedication to the ideal of academic integrity first, winning ballgames second. His interim athletic director, Harold Hopfenberg, was charged with watching all the athletic programs closely for violations and improprieties. When members of the varsity wrestling team beat up someone on campus, they were immediately suspended. The new administration thus made it clear that student athletes, for the first time in many years, were going to be held accountable for their actions.

Monteith made it clear that henceforth, N.C. State would stick to the rules. One of the by-products of sticking to the rules was that most of the incoming freshmen basketball candidates, some of whom couldn't have gotten in under the new regime, found themselves being declared ineligible to play under Proposition 48. Valvano's best recruit transferred to a junior college.

Without the network of friendly professors and without the ability to do those things needed to keep the kids eligible, there was no way any of these candidates could have played basketball and survived even the first semester at State. Under the Monteith regime, they didn't get to participate in the basketball program. For the first time in years, varsity athletes were being treated like all other students with respect to their academic expectations.

As a result of Monteith's public declaration of a policy of playing by the rules, when the NCAA handed down its punishment December 13, the penalties were relatively light.

"They have reorganized the athletic department, and the institution did a good job in its own investigation," said Charles Smart, an NCAA assistant director of enforcement. "We were encouraged . . . and believe they are on the right track."

The NCAA uncovered some of the misdeeds by the players that it had inquired about. Bennie Bolton, for one, had admitted publicly to having sold his sneakers and his tickets for money. Bennie had always resented Valvano's getting rich from his services, and once he had a public forum, he was quick to say that what was needed was a complete overhaul of the NCAA system. "Pay the players," Bennie said. "Why should everyone get rich except the guys on the court?"

Some journalists had some fun with the idea that the players made money by selling their sneakers. Edwin Pope of the *Miami Herald* wrote a column entitled, "HOW TO SHOE A WOLFPACK, by J. VALVANO."

Dan Moffett, the sports editor of the *Palm Beach Post*, wrote a column that began: "Economists are intrigued by one of the most surprising revelations to come out of the NCAA investigation of skullduggery at North Carolina State University.

"It seems that operating in Raleigh, N.C., was a system of exchange based not on the U.S. dollar, but rather on the basketball sneaker. . . .

"Drive up to an automatic teller at a Raleigh bank.

insert your card, punch in the secret code—clunk, clunk—sneakers fall as your withdrawal."

For the misdeeds uncovered, the NCAA placed N.C. State on two years' probation and barred it from playing in the 1990 NCAA Championship basketball tournament.

Valvano continued to defend himself staunchly. "There were no recruiting violations, nor were any coaches involved. . . . I was athletic director and coach, so I fully accept all responsibility. But you're talking about an area that is difficult to properly control," he said.

He was beginning to sound like what Richard Nixon might have said had he been a defendant at the Nurenburg trials.

In the *News & Observer*, Monteith announced no plans to fire anyone, including Valvano. "However, I will continue my evaluation of the men's basketball program." But he declined to give Valvano a vote of confidence. "Any discussion between the coach and myself would be private," he said.

In the article, university counsel Becky French gave her opinion that the violations were not sufficient to void a contract provision under which N.C. State would be obligated to pay Valvano $500,000 if he were fired.

I wondered why Becky French's legal opinion had appeared in the article. It was placed there deliberately. Was this a precursor for a battle between the university and Valvano? Now that, I thought, would be the ultimate irony. And which side, I wondered, would Attorney General Thornburg be on? And which side, I wondered, would Becky French be on?

As a piece of side business, Valvano's former chief recruiter, Tom Abatemarco, who had called *Personal Fouls* a figment of my imagination, was fired in February 1990 as the basketball coach of Drake University after the players staged a revolt. Investigators said that Abatemarco's conduct and language had been demeaning to the players. During an investigation of his program, it was revealed that one of his assistant coaches had written school papers for at least two players.

All was quiet at State until February 28, 1990, when articles began appearing in the Raleigh papers in anticipation of a televised report by ABC News that four former Wolfpack players had shaved points during the 1987–88 season.

I had been told by one source that Charles Shackleford had done some "funny stuff" in the year following the season I wrote about in *Personal Fouls*. When State lost to Murray State in the opening round of the NCAA playoffs in 1989, I wondered. Now, apparently, one of Shack's teammates was going to go on the air and charge him with shaving points. This latest piece of news didn't surprise me. That the teammate was willing to talk—that surprised me.

Before the ABC report, Shackleford volunteered in the papers that while a student at State he had received $65,000 from two agents, Larry Gillman and Robert Kramer, cash paid to him as an advance against future monies. Shack apologized for his indiscretions and said he had paid the money back to the agents. There was outrage on campus, however, because Shack's admission jeopardized about $400,000 that State had earned from playing in the 1987 and 1988 tournaments. Under NCAA rules, a player is not allowed to receive money from an agent until after he leaves school.

Valvano immediately sought the greatest distance between himself and his former players. Said Valvano about Shack's taking the money, "You're really talking about an area that I'm not sure any coach is not vulnerable to. A youngster who decides to do something without anyone's knowledge whatsoever. I'm not sure how you are able to counteract that."

Valvano told reporters he had gone before the state legislature to lobby for a measure that would regulate agents and their actions with the state's college teams. "I've gone to the State House. I've talked to our own players constantly. We've had a member of the SBI [talk to the team]. If you can tell me what more a coach could do if a youngster has a bent to do something which he knows is wrong and has been told is wrong, I'm not sure what else we can do."

In her continued defense of Valvano, Becky French said, "I have asked Jim about this. I'm convinced Coach Valvano had no prior knowledge about this. We just spent a year investigating these types of things and we did not uncover anything about this in our investigation."

I wondered: The Poole Commission report is sixteen hundred pages long, and Spengler has refused to make it public, even so far as defending a suit in court to keep it from the public. Perhaps knowledge of what Shack and the boys were up to was one reason he fought so hard to keep it covered up? Until the report is released, we'll never know.

On the night of February 28, 1990, ABC News reported that four N.C. State players, including Shackleford, conspired to hold down scores of four games for betting purposes during the 1987–88 season. An unnamed source said that Robert Kramer, through Shackleford, paid the players as much as $1,000 a game.

On television, an unidentified player explained how he felt about the school and the coach making millions of dollars and his not getting anything back for his efforts. He said his decision to shave points had been a purely economic decision.

"You're gonna throw the ball away and make sure they get a layup out of it. You do whatever is necessary at that particular moment." When asked if he would do it again, the player said he would.

Why should anyone have been surprised? What those players allegedly had done was the natural extension of playing in a program where the predominant theme and major emphasis was winning games to make tons of money. Coaches don't think their players become jaded when they see their big houses and fine cars while their players don't have enough money for gas or a good meal. But they do.

Despite Shackleford's denials, the press was closing in for the kill, calling for Coach V's head, even though Valvano had kept his nose clean since Monteith took over.

See, it's this way: Valvano's abusing the educational process didn't seem to concern too many of the basketball reporters. When Dick Lauffer back in January 1989 had said that Valvano had changed three of Chris Washburn's grades and had told Poulton, who had told him to mind his own business, the sports reporters merely recorded everyone's denials and let it drop. Not a single one said out loud, Why would a reputable former professor such as Lauffer be making something like that up?

In their defense, not a single faculty member rose to Lauffer's defense, either. It was only after the publication of the book that Hugh Fuller and Dr. Frank Smallwood came forward. But the question remained: Wasn't Lauffer's allegation enough to interest reporters to at least investigate the possibility that such an event took place? Wasn't it enough to send reporters scurrying to do a two-part series on how tough it is for athletes to get degrees?

As I said at the beginning of this chapter, jock reporters care about the game, not the players. In college the players come and go. The game marches on.

If players cheat on grades, that has nothing to do with the game. If a player is illiterate, that has nothing to do with the game. If a player commits armed robbery, that has nothing to do with the game, except how it affects the team's chances.

But point shaving, that goes to the very heart of the integrity of the game, and when the reporters heard Valvano's players might be involved in point shaving, across the country they sought Valvano's scalp.

For the first time reporters were saying things like, "Being a coach is more than finding players and pointing them toward the proper basket. Being a coach is caring enough to know what's going on."

And all of a sudden, over and over, after the allegations of point shaving came out, reporters were asking me, "Don't you feel vindicated?" No one had asked me that after Fuller or Smallwood came forward. No one had asked me that when Poulton quit.

Asking whether I felt vindicated seemed a fair enough question, considering that it was those same reporters who made it seem as though I somehow needed vindication. Because when *Personal Fouls* first came out, the sporting press did all they could to discredit the book. To most of them, the issue was spelling, not education or propriety.

My biggest supporters were Larry King and Howard Cosell, TV journalists, and academicians.

Because I tend to spell names wrong and because Simon & Schuster refused to give me back the edited manuscript, I had been forced to do in a week to my original manuscript what S&S had done in two months with a team of copy editors. I knew before publication that there was no way the Carroll & Graf copy editors were going to make all the corrections. S&S had made hundreds of them.

Carroll & Graf didn't have the time or the manpower of S&S. We all knew it, too, but we had no choice but to go forward. We feared the Poole Commission report would be a whitewash, and we wanted to get the book out before them.

And when the book came out, there were mistakes. Chucky Brown was Chuckie, and I spelled Abatemarco wrong, and I called Bob Staak "Bobby" (when he played for Darien High School he was Bobby), and I wrote Tarheels instead of Tar Heels, and I wrote WFTF instead of WPTF. And I spelled Krzyzewski wrong in the spot where I indicated it was a hard name to spell. I also had Muggsey Bogues dunking once, and I spelled other names wrong in places.

And so if the critics wished to ignore what the players, professors, and administrators were saying—that the entire collegiate system at worst was corrupt and needed a housecleaning—and concentrate on the spelling, it was a simple task to write articles with headlines like "Golenbock book has misspellings, errors."

Fortunately, the public was able to decide whether I had told the truth or not about N.C. State basketball in particular and the state of college basketball in general. My spelling mistakes notwithstanding, the old order seems to be changing.

When I wrote *Personal Fouls*, I wondered whether this book might be a catalyst toward change for the good for the college athlete, and though my detractors go out of their way to say that *Personal Fouls* has had nothing to do with the talk of reform in college basketball, some very reputable college administrators assure me that the ripples from *Personal Fouls* will continue to spread for years to come, pushing those who care to rework the system so that the college kids who play the game will have a better assurance that they will end up with a degree after their playing days.

The NCAA has already begun to do something to tip the balance back toward education and away from professional college sports. In January 1990 it voted to reduce the basketball schedules by three games and to cut spring football practice from twenty to fifteen days. "We must give these kids more time away from football and basketball," said Penn State football coach Joe Paterno.

Though some athletic directors complained about the loss of revenue from playing three fewer basketball games, Greg O'Brien, president of the University of New Orleans, responded, "It is a signal of great important beyond this room . . . that reforms are going forward."

It is most gratifying that people in power are beginning at least to talk about what is wrong.

Shortly after the publication of *Personal Fouls*, William Friday, former president of the sixteen-campus University of North Carolina system, told the *Charlotte Observer* that intercollegiate athletics "have gotten totally out of control." He said he expected a major national commission to be formed to combat the problems, a commission bringing together the NCAA, university presidents, the American Council on Education, and other prominent groups. He said it would have the financial backing of a major national foundation.

Said Friday, "Americans have turned sports into a religion. What we're getting pretty close to doing is turning our universities into entertainment centers. There are so many forces at work, the impact of television and the insatiable demand of more sports, more sports."

What Friday was admitting was something no one else had been willing to say to date, that some institutions don't have the integrity to say no to the win-at-all-cost philosophy. The lure of the money is just too great.

Said Friday, "It's time outside forces came to the aid of the individual institutions. The universities cannot carry the burden alone. There are incredible pressures. The pressures come from a variety of places, from money, TV, the fans, the public."

The commission Friday spoke about in August became a reality one month later. Rev. Theodore M. Hesburgh, former president of Notre Dame, and Bill Friday himself were named leaders of a commission financed by a $2 million grant over a two-year period by the Knight Foundation. It was announced that Dick Schultz, executive director of the NCAA, would also be named to the commission.

Commented Hesburgh about college athletics, "Greed has taken over."

Friday told reporters, "There is a place for a good intercollegiate athletics program at every college."

Hesburgh said he already had some proposals in mind. "All you have to do is control the money," he said.

As this edition of *Personal Fouls* goes to press, Jim Valvano is still basketball coach at N.C. State, but barely. He has been asked to step down, but apparently he won't leave unless he gets his $500,000. Wrote Scott Ostler in *The National*, "Valvano isn't the only coach heading up a Swiss-cheese college program. He *is* the only coach currently who is holding the school hostage." Wrote Mike Lupica, "The seventh March after Albuquerque, Jim Valvano plea bargains."

Finding itself boxed in by Valvano's unwillingness to leave without his payoff, the university announced it needed help in the negotiations and that it had hired Andrew Vanore, Jr., from the attorney general's office to help represent the university in its talks to get rid of Valvano. This was the same Andrew Vanore, Jr., who had threatened Simon & Schuster and me with the $50 million lawsuit for daring to write what I knew to be the truth about the university's scandalous basketball program.

With his money or without, Valvano probably will be gone from N.C. State. If he stays, that's fine, because no longer does he have the power to do the things he was doing in *Personal Fouls*. If he stays, he'll have to run a college program, not a professional one.

It will be interesting to see whether this experience chastens him or whether he will continue to act as though everything that happened was a result of malfeasance by everyone around him. After all, he could say, no one *proved* he did anything wrong. Perhaps he really does believe the legion of his accusers—administrators, professors, and former players—really were conspirators in a grand scheme to get him and he was an innocent victim.

Even if Valvano leaves N.C. State, one day he will go back to coaching college basketball, but not soon. After Monteith's arrival, Valvano's players continued their abysmal academic record. And once his own university began accusing him of a failure to see that his players performed in the classroom, he became a pariah to other colleges.

One of Valvano's options is to coach in the pros, where his concentration on winning and making money and his quick wit will endear him to a whole new community. He won't make his million and a half a year any more, but he will do just fine. He will bounce back. He always has. Whether his Wolfpack supporters, those students and alumni who fervently believed in him, will bounce back, that's another question, but I suspect in time they will, too. I am sure that chancellor Monteith wants a winning program as badly as the next guy, and with the right appointment as coach, State will win again soon, but this time more players will graduate than not. N.C. State University is too great an institution to be denied.

Valvano could also become a commentator on a network televising college basketball games. That also seems appropriate—the source of much of the corruption is the billion dollars that comes from TV. V can get the money right from the source.

There was so much noise about my unnamed sources and my spelling from certain writers who refused to hear what I was saying—even after Bruce Poulton resigned and Valvano was stripped of his athletic director job—that sometimes I doubted whether my message had been lost in the maelstrom.

But earlier this month in *The National*, I read Mike Lupica's discussion with Indiana coach Bobby Knight about the rightful place of athletics in college life, and I knew that there were others out there who believed as strongly in the athlete's inalienable right to an education as I did, and that as long as a dialogue continued, the future looked toward a day when both educators and athletic directors finally recognize the truth: These student-athletes deserve the help of the entire university to see that they get the education they are promised in exchange for their services on the basketball court.

Bobby Knight certainly has his faults, but not when it comes to education. He makes his players study, and they earn their degrees. And not only that, Knight does not play loose with the rules. And he still manages to win a national championship every few years.

Knight, in discussing Valvano, told Lupica, "A coach either gives a program direction or he doesn't. His program is a proper series of demands, or it isn't. I'm talking about being on time; I'm talking about appearance; I'm talking about schools and grades. I'm talking about conduct. A coach either pays attention to those things or he doesn't. And if he doesn't pay attention, then he is going to have every problem with his kids imaginable. I am talking about the overall quality of the program. I don't see how you can absolve yourself from the responsibility of that."

Then Knight asked Lupica, "Let me ask you a question: Do you really think [Valvano] had any other priority other than winning basketball games?"

"No," said Lupica.

"End of discussion," said Knight. "Now he sends in his agent. Education isn't done through an agent. It's you and me. Coach and school. As soon as a coach sends an agent in, he removes himself from being an educator."

Knight proposed a rule that would take away an athletic scholarship from a team for every athlete who went four or five years and didn't get his diploma. "That's the solution," said Knight. "You ever heard any school presidents outside of [Indiana] or athletic directors to back me up on it? Hell, no. It's like Vietnam. They don't *want* a solution. They don't have any graduation rates to speak of. Put in a rule like that and they wouldn't have a football program or a basketball program, and they all know it.

"Don't give me that kind of crap you can't do it right anymore. Don't we do it right here?"

Said Lupica, "Yes."

"Well," said Knight, "if we can do it right here, it can be done anywhere, if the school's willing. There's nothing different in the water in Indiana. We don't have access to kids everybody else doesn't have access to. We just have standards here."

Concluded Lupica, "Knight is a great coach. Valvano isn't so bad himself. Knight has won three national championships. Valvano has his one. The difference is that Bob Knight, like him or not, always had a program. Jimmy V., in the end, all he has is an act."

Postscript: On April 8, 1990, Jim Valvano left N.C. State as coach, walking away with approximately a half-million dollars from the school and the Wolfpack Club. He then signed a three-year, $300,000-a-year contract with ABC-TV to be a commentator for college basketball games. Soon he will write his autobiography. The rumor is that Simon and Schuster will publish it.

About the Author

Peter Golenbock has become one of this country's most respected and bestselling sports writers whose works have changed the way we view our sports heroes. His most famous book, *The Bronx Zoo*, written with Yankee pitcher Sparky Lyle, was on the *New York Times* bestseller list for six months and remains the top selling book on baseball. His other bestsellers include *Balls* (written with Graig Nettles), a further chronicle of the tumultuous life with the Yankees, *Dynasty*, the acclaimed history of the New York Yankees, *Bums: An Oral History of the Brooklyn Dodgers*, and *Number 1*, about the life of Yankee manager Billy Martin.

Peter Golenbock is a graduate of Dartmouth College and New York University School of Law. He lives with his family in Connecticut.